Violence against Women in Legally Plural Settings

This book addresses a growing area of concern for scholars and development practitioners: discriminatory gender norms in legally plural settings. Focusing specifically on indigenous women, this book analyses how they, often in alliance with supporters and allies, have sought to improve their access to justice. Development practitioners working in the field of access to justice have tended to conceive indigenous legal systems as either inherently incompatible with women's rights or, alternatively, they have emphasised customary law's advantageous features, such as its greater accessibility, familiarity and effectiveness. Against this background – and based on a comparison of six thus far underexplored initiatives of legal and institutional change in Ecuador, Peru and Bolivia – Anna Barrera Vivero provides a more nuanced, ethnographic understanding of how women navigate through context-specific constellations of interlegality in their search for justice. In so doing, moreover, her account of ongoing political debates and local struggles for gender justice grounds the elaboration of a comprehensive conceptual framework for understanding the legally plural dynamics involved in the contestation of discriminatory gender norms.

Anna Barrera Vivero is Programme Manager in Research and New Developments at the EU-LAC Foundation, Hamburg, Germany.

Law, Development and Globalization

Series editors: Julio Faundez, University of Warwick

Over the past few decades, a substantial transformation of law and legal institutions in developing countries has taken place. Whether prompted by market-based policies or the international human rights movement, by the relentless advance of the process of globalization or the successive waves of democratisation, no area of law has been left untouched. The aim of this series is to promote cross-disciplinary dialogue and cooperation among scholars and development practitioners interested in understanding the theoretical and practical implications of the momentous legal changes taking place in developing countries.

Titles in this series:

State Violence and Human Rights
State Officials in the South
Andrew M. Jefferson and Steffen Jensen (eds)

The Political Economy of Government Auditing
Financial Governance and the Rule of Law in Latin America and Beyond
Carlos Santiso

Global Perspectives on the Rule of Law
James J. Heckman, Robert L. Nelson and Lee Cabatingan (eds)

Marginalized Communities and Access to Justice
Yash Ghai and Jill Cottrell (eds)

Law in the Pursuit of Development
Principles into Practice?
Amanda Perry-Kessaris (ed.)

Governance Through Development
Poverty Reduction Strategies and the Disciplining of Third World States
Celine Tan

Lawyers and the Rule of Law in an Era of Globalization
Yves Dezalay and Bryant Garth (eds)

Policing and Human Rights
The Meaning of Violence and Justice in the Everyday Policing of Johannesburg
Julia Hornberger

Lawyers and the Construction of Transnational Justice
Yves Dezalay and Bryant Garth (eds)

Gender, Justice and Legal Pluralities
Latin American and African Perspectives
Rachel Sieder and John McNeish

Social Movements, Law and the Politics of Land Reform
George Meszaros

Land Law Reform in Eastern Africa
Traditional or Transformative?
Patrick McAuslan

Justice and Security Reform
Development Agencies and Informal Institutions in Sierra Leone
Lisa Denney

From the Global to the Local
How International Rights Reach Bangladesh's Children
Andrea Schapper

Governing Refugees
Justice, Order and Legal Pluralism
Kirsten McConnachie

Justice Reform and Development
Rethinking Donor Assistance to Developing and Transitional Countries
Linn Hammergren

Law and Society in Latin America
Cesar Rodriguez Garavito

Policing and the Politics of Order-Making
Peter Albrecht and Helene Maria Kyed (eds)

Violence against Women in Legally Plural Settings
Experiences and Lessons from the Andes
Anna Barrera Vivero

Forthcoming titles in the series:

Multinational Integration, Cultural Identity and Regional Self-Government
Roberto Toniatti and Jens Woelk (eds)

Violence against Women in Legally Plural Settings

Experiences and Lessons from the Andes

Anna Barrera Vivero

Routledge
Taylor & Francis Group
LONDON AND NEW YORK

First published 2016
by Routledge
2 Park Square, Milton Park, Abingdon, Oxfordshire OX14 4RN

and by Routledge
711 Third Avenue, New York, NY 10017

First issued in paperback 2017

Routledge is an imprint of the Taylor & Francis Group, an informa business

British Library Cataloguing in Publication Data
A catalogue record for this book is available from the British Library.

Library of Congress Cataloging-in-Publication Data
Barrera Vivero, Anna, 1980- author.
Violence against women in legally plural settings: experiences and lessons from the Andes / Anna Barrera Vivero.
pages cm
Based on author's thesis (doctoral – German Institute of Global and Area Studies and the University of Hamburg, 2014) under title: Promoting Change in Legally Plural Settings: Domestic Violence and Indigenous Women's Quest for Justice in the Andes.
Includes bibliographical references and index.
ISBN 978-1-138-93669-0 (hbk) — ISBN 978-1-315-67669-2 (ebk) 1. Family violence—Law and legislation—Andes Region. 2. Family violence—Andes Region. 3. Abused women—Legal status, laws, etc.—Andes Region. 4. Indian women—Legal status, laws, etc.—Andes Region. 5. Legal polycentricity—Andes Region. I. Title.
KG966.F36B37 2016
344.803'28292--dc23
2015025098

ISBN 13: 978-1-138-09281-5 (pbk)
ISBN 13: 978-1-138-93669-0 (hbk)

Typeset in Baskerville by
by FiSH Books Ltd, Enfield

Contents

Acknowledgements

I have many intellectual and institutional debts to acknowledge. I am deeply indebted to my thesis supervisors Detlef Nolte and Rachel Sieder who trusted in my capacities, provided constructive advice and critically accompanied the research project throughout all its stages. The study was funded by a doctoral scholarship from the Cusanuswerk, and the GIGA German Institute of Global and Area Studies in Hamburg and its staff provided a particularly stimulating environment for the work on this study. I owe special thanks to the members of the Andean communities, municipalities and local experts who allowed me to take part in their daily activities and generously invited me to their institutions and homes throughout my fieldwork. These persons contributed immensely to this study by agreeing to be interviewed and asking critical questions about my research. I would like to highlight the valuable advice from country experts in Ecuador (Bolívar Beltrán, Silverio Chisaguano, Fernando García, Agustín Grijalva, Raúl Llasag, Santago Ortiz, Judith Salgado, Floresmilo Simbaña, Jaime Vintimilla), in Peru (Mirva Aranda, Rocío Franco, Vladimir Pinto, Horst Schönbohm, Cecilia Serpa, Roxana Vergara, Raquel Yrigoyen) and Bolivia (Ricardo Calla, Irma Campos, Idón Chivi, María Eugenia Choque, Lucila Choque, Ivanna Fernández, Marcelo Fernández, Petronilo Flores, Paulino Guarachi, Monica Mendizabal, Marco Mendoza, Ramiro Molina, Filomena Nina, René Orellana, Enrique Rodríguez) – all of whom helped me to better understand the respective national contexts, to enter into contact with others and to carefully select the cases that are the focus of this book. Several NGOs offered institutional support to this project, particularly UNORCAC and Corcima in Ecuador, IDL and CODECC in Peru and Fundación Tierra and the Centro Juana Azurduy in Bolivia. I owe my friends Anne Ebert and Jana Höffken an enormous debt for their attentive reading and comments toward the end of the writing process. Not least, I wish to thank my family, and particularly Juan, for their patience and unconditional support throughout this challenging and inspiring period of my life.

In October 2014, I diffused my research results among the participating communities and municipalities by means of a short, Spanish-language booklet titled *Promoviendo la justicia propia, dejando atrás un trato indigno.*

Abbreviations

ACHR	American Convention on Human Rights
AIOC	Autonomía Indigena Originario Campesina (Autonomous Indigenous Territory)
AUCC	Asamblea de Unidad Cantonal de Cotacachi (Assembly of the Canton Unity of Cotacachi)
CEAMOS	Centro de Educación y Acción de Mujeres Otavaleñas (Centre for Education and Action of Otavaleña Women)
CEDAW	Convention on the Elimination of All Forms of Discrimination Against Women
CEM	Centro de Emergencia de la Mujer (Emergency Centre for Women)
CEPAL	Comisión Económica para América Latina y el Caribe (Economic Commission for Latin America and the Caribbean – ECLAC)
CIAWF	Centro de Atención Integral a la Mujer y la Familia (Centre of Integral Attention for Women and the Family)
CIDOB	Confederación de Pueblos Indígenas de Bolivia (Confederation of Indigenous Peoples of Bolivia)
CNMCIOB-BS	Confederación Nacional de Mujeres Campesinas Indígenas Originarias de Bolivia – Bartolina Sisa (National Confederation of Campesino Indigenous Originary Women of Bolivia – Bartolina Sisa)
CNTCB	Confederación Nacional de Trabajadores Campesinos de Bolivia (National Confederation of Peasant Workers of Bolivia)
CODECC	Coordinadora Departamental de Defensorías Comunitarias del Cusco (Departmental Coordination Group of Community Defence Offices of Cuzco)
COICE	Coordinadora de Organizaciones Indígenas de la Costa del Ecuador (Coordinator of the Indigenous Organizations of the Ecuadorian Coast)

CONAIE	Confederación de Nacionalidades Indígenas del Ecuador (Confederation of Indigenous Nationalities of Ecuador)
CONAIOC	Coordinadora Nacional de las Autonomías Indígena Originario Campesinas (National Coordinating Office of the Autonomous Indigenous Originary Campesino Territories)
CONAMAQ	Consejo Nacional de Ayllus y Markas del Qullasuyu (National Council of Ayllus and Markas of the Qullasuyu)
CONAMU	Consejo Nacional de Mujeres (National Women's Council)
CONEPIA	Comisión Nacional de Estadísticas para Pueblos Indígena, Afroecuatorianos y Montubios (National Statistics Commission for Indians, Afro-Ecuadorians, and Montubios)
CONFENIAE	Confederación de Nacionalidades Indígenas de la Amazonia Ecuatoriana (Confederation of Indigenous Nationalities of the Ecuadorian Amazon)
CORCIMA	Corporación de Comunidades Indígenas Maquipurashun (Corporation of Indigenous Communities Maquipurashun)
CSUTCB	Confederación Sindical Única de Trabajadores Campesinos de Bolivia Unitary Syndical (Confederation of Peasant Workers of Bolivia)
CWC	Comité Central de Mujeres de UNORCAC (Central Women's Committee of UNORCAC)
DEMUNA	Defensoría Municipal del Niño y del Adolescente (Municipal Defence Office for the Child and the Adolescent)
DNA	Defensoría de la Niñez y Adolescencia (Defence Office for Children and Adolescents)
ECMIA	Enlace Continental de Mujeres Indígenas de las Américas (Continental Network of Indigenous Women of the Americas)
ECUARUNARI	Ecuador Runacunapac Riccharimuy (Awakening of the Ecuadorian Indian)
FEINE	Consejo de Pueblos y Organizaciones Indígenas Evangélicos del Ecuador (Council of Indigenous Evangelical Peoples and Organisations of Ecuador)
FENOC-I	Federación Nacional de Organizaciones Campesinas e Indígenas (National Federation of Peasant and Indigenous Organizations)

FENOCIN	Federación Nacional de Organizaciones Campesinas, Indígenas y Negras (National Federation of Peasant, Indigenous, and Black Organisations)
FICI	Federación Indígena y Campesina de Imbabura (Indigenous and Peasant Federation of Imbabura)
FIMI	Foro Internacional de Mujeres Indígenas (International Indigenous Women's Forum)
FNMCB-BS	Federación Nacional de Mujeres Campesinas de Bolivia – Bartolina Sisa (National Federation of Campesino Women of Bolivia – Bartolina Sisa)
FPCC	Federación Provincial Campesina de Canas (Provincial Peasant Federation of Canas)
FUTPOCH	Federación Única de Trabajadores de Pueblos Originarios de Chuquisaca (Unified Federation of Workers of Originary Peoples of Chuquisaca)
GIZ	Deutsche Gesellschaft für Internationale Zusammenarbeit (German Society for International Cooperation)
ICCPR	International Covenant on Civil and Political and Rights
ICERD	International Convention on the Elimination of All Forms of Racial Discrimination
ICESCR	International Covenant on Economic, Social and Cultural Rights
IDL	Instituto de Defensa Legal (Legal Defence Institute)
ILO C 169	International Labour Organisation Convention No. 169 on Indigenous and Tribal Peoples
INE	Instituto Nacional de Estadística (National Institute of Statistics)
INEC	Instituto Nacional de Estadísticas y Censos (National Institute for Statistics and Censuses)
INEI	Instituto Nacional de Estadística e Informática (National Institute of Statistics and Informatics)
LJD	Ley de Deslinde Jurisdiscional (Law on Jurisdictional Delimitation)
LMAD	Ley Marco de Autonomías y Descentralización (General Law on Autonomy and Decentralization)
MAS	Movimiento al Socialismo (Movement toward Socialism)
MSM	Movimiento Sin Miedo (Movement without Fear)
MUPP-NP	Movimiento de Unidad Plurinacional Pachakutik – Nuevo País (Pachakutik United Plurinational Movement – New Country)
NGO	non-governmental organisation

ONAJUP	Oficina Nacional de Justicia de Paz y Justicia Indígena (National Office of Justice of the Peace and Indigenous Justice)
SLIM	Servicio Legal Integral Municipal (Municipal Office for Integral Legal Services)
SOMUC	Secretaria de la Mujer Campesina de Canas (Secretary of the Peasant Woman of Canas)
TCO	Tierra Comunitaria de Orígen (Indigenous Communal Land)
THOA	Taller de Historia Oral Andina (Andean Oral History Workshop)
UN	United Nations
UNDRIP	United Nations Declaration on the Rights of Indigenous Peoples
UNICEF	United Nations Fund for Children
UNIFEM	United Nations Development Fund for Women
UNORCAC	Unión de Organizaciones Campesinas e Indígenas de Cotacachi (Union of Peasant and Indigenous Organisations of Cotacachi)
UN WOMEN	United Nations Entity for Gender Equality and the Empowerment of Women
WHO	World Health Organization

Maps

The author has elaborated all maps submitted for publication. The maps are adapted from national and regional maps of *The World Factbook (2013–14)*. Washington, D.C.: Central Intelligence Agency. Online: www.cia.gov/library/publications/resources/the-world-factbook/index.html (last accessed 10.06.2015).

Tables

The author has designed all tables submitted for publication.

The respective sources for data included in the tables are indicated in the separate Table source lines.

Images

The author is the photographer of *all* photos submitted for publication. All individuals who can be seen in these photos gave the author their informed consent to take the photos and to use them for a later publication (orally, at the time of taking the photos).

Chapter 1

Introduction

Indigenous women's hindered access to justice in legally plural settings

Violence against women

Violence against women is endemic across the world. Rooted in persisting gender asymmetries between women and men, violence deprives women of their dignity, puts their health at risk and impedes their full participation in community-based, social, economic and political affairs (Beijing Declaration and Platform for Action 1995: para. 112–130; UN 2006; UNICEF *et al.* 2013: 19–20). Several risk factors were identified in cross-regional studies that help explain the occurrence of intimate partner violence, including women's low age (before and at marriage) and age differences between partners; a high number of children; women's low education level and educational differences between partners; women's assets, earnings and share of the household income; and prevailing social norms tolerating violence or supporting dominant male behaviour. The likelihood of becoming a victim or perpetrator of intimate partner violence as an adult tended to be higher among persons who suffered from abuse or experienced violence between parents as a child. Moreover, alcohol abuse was found to serve as a trigger for wife-beating in many places (Kishor and Johnson 2004: ch. 3; Morrison, Ellsberg and Bott 2007: 26–30). Women's exposure to violence had long been reinforced by non-protective legal frameworks. Over the past decades, the international community has mounted efforts so as to address discrimination against women and gender violence as a particularly concerning facet thereof. The 1979 Convention on the Elimination of All Forms of Discrimination Against Women (CEDAW) defined discrimination against women as

> any distinction, exclusion or restriction made on the basis of sex which has the effect or purpose of impairing or nullifying the recognition, enjoyment or exercise by women, irrespective of their marital status, on a basis of equality of men and women, of human rights and fundamental freedoms in the political, economic, social, cultural, civil or any other field.
>
> (ibid. art. 1)

The by now 188 signatory states[1] of this legally binding treaty committed themselves to take all appropriate measures to promote women's rights and equality between men and women and to regularly report on their progress to a specifically created CEDAW Committee. Subsequently, by asserting that violence against women has posed a substantial barrier to the achievement of gender equality, development and peace, the UN General Assembly established the right of women to live free from violence in the 1993 UN Declaration on the Elimination of Violence against Women. Violence against women was herein defined as

> any act of gender-based violence that results in, or is likely to result in, physical, sexual or psychological harm or suffering to women, including threats of such acts, coercion or arbitrary deprivations of liberty, whether occurring in public or private life.
>
> (ibid. art. 1)

This process, accompanied by relentless lobbying from the international women's movement, entailed the adoption of a considerable number of UN programmes, regional treaties (such as the 1994 Inter-American Convention on the Prevention, Punishment and Eradication of Violence against Women – Belém do Pará Convention) and national action plans – all of which are aimed at the prevention and reduction of violence against women (UN 2006: ch. 1).

Despite progress on all these grounds – at least 139 national Constitutions guarantee the equality between women and men (UN WOMEN 2011: 8) and more than 60 countries enacted laws against domestic violence (World Bank 2011: 83) – these measures have far too seldom translated into a difference in women's lives. Many people continue viewing wife-beating as acceptable under specific circumstances (World Bank 2011: 83), and the numbers of battered women both in armed conflicts and in non-conflict regions remain alarmingly high: according to a report of the World Health Organization (WHO), one in every three women (35 per cent) worldwide has experienced physical and/or sexual intimate partner violence, or non-partner sexual violence, in her lifetime, with violence perpetrated by (ex-)partners accounting for the overwhelming majority of such acts (WHO 2013: 2). The 2010 Global Burden Disease Study singled Central Sub-Saharan Africa out as the region with the highest prevalence of intimate partner violence (65.64 per cent), followed by Western Sub-Saharan Africa (41.75 per cent) and South Asia (41.73 per cent), whereas the lowest rate was reported for East Asia with 16.30 per cent. With 21.05 per cent, women in Central Sub-Saharan Africa were also among those most affected by non-partner sexual violence, followed by 17.41 per cent women in Southern Sub-Saharan Africa and 16.46 per cent women in Australasia; the lowest estimate in non-partner sexual violence

Table 1.1 Prevalence of intimate partner and non-partner violence by region

Region	*Physical and sexual intimate partner violence among ever-partnered women (in %)*	*Non-partner sexual violence (in %)*
Asia Pacific, high income	28.45	12.20
Asia, Central	22.89	6.45
Asia, East	16.30	5.87
Asia, South	41.73	3.35
Asia, South East	27.99	5.28
Australasia	28.29	16.46
Caribbean	27.09	10.32
Europe, Central	27.85	10.76
Europe, Eastern	26.13	6.97
Europe, Western	19.30	11.50
Latin America, Andean	40.63	15.33
Latin America, Central	29.51	11.88
Latin America, Southern	23.68	5.86
Latin America, Tropical	27.43	7.68
North Africa/Middle East	35.38	4.53
North America, high income	21.32	13.01
Oceania	35.27	14.86
Sub-Saharan Africa, Central	65.64	21.05
Sub-Saharan Africa, East	38.83	11.46
Sub-Saharan Africa, Southern	29.67	17.41
Sub-Saharan Africa, West	41.75	9.15

Source: Global Burden of Disease Study 2010, cited in and adapted from WHO 2013: 47–48.

was reported for South Asia (3.35 per cent; see Table 1 and WHO 2013: 47–48).

Within Latin America, the Andes (referring in this survey to Bolivia, Ecuador and Peru – the three countries this book focuses on) stood out as the sub-region with the highest prevalence rates in physical and sexual intimate partner violence (40.63 per cent) and sexual non-partner violence (15.33 per cent).

Indigenous women, violence and intersectionality

Given this book's specific concern with indigenous women, the search for reliable data on violence differentiating between distinct identity groups proves challenging: first, despite increased efforts worldwide to gather systematic information on the issue of gender violence (e.g., Camarasa i

Casals 2009; García-Moreno *et al.* 2005; Johnson, Ollus and Nevala 2008; Kishor and Johnson 2004), most surveys lack harmonised definitions, indicators and data-collection methodologies, thereby rendering the comparability among surveys extremely difficult (Bott *et al.* 2012: 5–18; WHO 2013: 10–15). Second, many studies fall short of disaggregating data according to identity groups, by which indigenous women's particular situation tends to be invisibilised (CEPAL 2013: 73; FIMI 2006: 46–47; UNICEF *et al.* 2013: 4, 14). Third, where statistics differentiate between ethnic groups, the disproportional affectedness of indigenous women by violence vis-à-vis non-indigenous women comes to the fore. The probability to be affected by violence in Canada, for instance, was three times higher for aboriginal women compared with non-aboriginal women. A disproportionally high number of aboriginal women were registered as long-term missing, and their homicide rate was seven times higher than the one of non-aboriginal women (Amnesty International 2014: 2). Similarly, around 39.0 per cent of American Indian and Alaska Native women suffered from intimate partner violence, an experience shared by 29.2 per cent African American women, 26.8 per cent white women, 20.5 per cent Hispanic women and 9.7 per cent Asian women living in the United States (Centers for Disease Control and Prevention 2008).[2] Available data from the Andean Region tend to confirm this pattern. In Ecuador, for instance, 59.3 per cent indigenous women were affected by violence practised by (ex-)partners compared with 47.5 per cent mestiza women (INEC 2011a; see the country chapters for more details).

While such data unequivocally point to the need to address gender violence, they do not tell us much about the particular circumstances in which indigenous women endure violence. In this respect, indigenous women have repeatedly emphasised that interpersonal violence needs to be analysed from an intersectional perspective (e.g., Crenshaw 1991), i.e., in relation to other dimensions of their identities and taking into account other and mutually reinforcing dimensions of inequality which affect these women's lives and prospects (Beijing Declaration of Indigenous Women 1995; ECMIA and Chirapaq 2013; FIMI 2006). Sure enough, identities and living conditions of indigenous women in Latin America vary considerably, but there are experiences that many of these women share:[3]

- Monolingualism and illiteracy are more prevalent among indigenous women compared with indigenous men and the non-indigenous population – a problem closely related to indigenous women's shorter school enrolment periods and lower school-leaving qualifications. This imbalance can be explained in part by local gender roles that tend to prioritise the longer education of boys while assigning girls tasks in the household and the care of their younger siblings from a very young age. At the same time, States have also fallen short of providing rural areas resided by indigenous populations with high-quality, culturally appropriate and sufficiently equipped education institutions.

- Indigenous people inhabiting rural areas often lack access to culturally appropriate and high-quality reproductive and basic health services, they are disproportionally affected by infant and maternal mortality and child malnutrition and their life expectancy is shorter compared with non-indigenous populations.
- Indigenous women's access to land titles and credits for income-generating agricultural activities is limited compared with their male counterparts. Women tend to be disadvantaged when it comes to the distribution of a family's heritage, they confront information gaps and access barriers when seeking to sell their products in regional and national markets, and banks are reluctant to extend financial support to indigenous women.
- Indigenous women have great difficulty in accessing formal and qualified forms of employment in urban centres and rural areas. In the context of the monetarisation of local economies and the enhanced dependency from goods and services produced outside of the community, indigenous women's unpaid reproductive and productive activities in the household and the agriculture have become devalued in comparison to the (often unqualified and temporary, but still income-generating) labour performed by indigenous men outside of their communities.
- While some progress in the political representation of indigenous women has been achieved in recently (e.g., by the introduction of women's quota in national elections), they still do not participate in community affairs on an equal footing with male community members. Indigenous women are under-represented in leadership positions at all levels of indigenous organisations and state institutions. Sometimes, their participation remains confined to a symbolic level or the positions they occupy imply only a small scope of responsibility. In other situations, female leaders are silenced, inhibited from attending important meetings due to time overlaps with their domestic duties, or face acts of political harassment.
- Indigenous populations disproportionally endure poverty and extreme poverty. Despite advances in the reduction of the overall poverty rates in Latin America throughout the past two decades, the proportion of indigenous peoples living in poverty has not been altered accordingly.
- More generally, the dignity of indigenous women and men continues to be impaired by the persistent marginalisation and racist attitudes present in many Latin American societies.

Thus, even if the present study focuses on one specific manifestation of violence (domestic violence, here defined as 'emotional, physical or sexual acts perpetrated by intimate – married or unmarried – partners or other relatives against an adolescent or adult woman without her consent'[4]), this aspect cannot be separated from other forms of aggression, oppression or colonisation perpetrated by public and private agents against the bodies, dignity and habitat of indigenous women and men, such as assaults, displacements, land dispossessions or human trafficking perpetrated by armed forces or organised crime; the non-consented exploitation and contamination of natural resources on their lands; the criminalisation of their protests for collective rights; the carrying out of development projects and the formulation of policies without taking into account indigenous people's values, knowledge and capacities; humiliating and culturally inappropriate treatment in public institutions; or misleading representations of indigenous people in the media (ECMIA and Chirapaq 2013; FIMI 2006; Huarcacho 2011: 78–82; UNICEF *et al.* 2013).

Legal pluralism and obstacles in women's access to state and indigenous justice

In order to confront domestic violence, the access to a legal forum at which women can denounce aggressions and claim justice for the harm caused to them seems of utmost importance. However in many countries the state judicial systems have failed indigenous women in this regard. Despite States' commitments to protect women's mental and bodily integrity by international treaties and domestic legislation, the enforcement of the legal frameworks has remained ineffective along the entire chain of justice operators, starting from the police and the prosecutors through to the courts and the institutions guaranteeing the implementation of a court's ruling (UN WOMEN 2011: ch. 2). In Latin America, legal systems have been often negatively associated, with

> political, economic and social elites behave[ing] as if they were above the law, [and] the majority of the people regard[ing] law as an instrument of oppression, rather than of empowerment or protection.
>
> (Faundez 2010: 751)

The justice systems in this region are among the least effective worldwide, and corruption, procedural delays and impunity are widespread (The World Justice Project 2014: 38). While the overall low confidence in the formal legal system among Latin American citizens thus comes as no surprise,[5] an intersectional perspective is again necessary to comprehend the specific access barriers to justice that indigenous women living in rural areas confront: as the presence of state judicial institutions in the countryside is typically scant, geographic distance from a women's home village to the nearest police station or a court constitutes a first mayor problem for battered indigenous women. The lengthy duration of state legal procedures, combined with the requirement to repeatedly return to these institutions so as to give their testimony or appear before a responsible officer, often enter into conflict with indigenous women's various tasks in the household, child-rearing and their work in agriculture or with livestock. Moreover, approaching the official legal system also involves high costs for women who have to pay for the transport, accommodation, food, legal certificates or photocopies of relevant documents. Women's unfamiliarity with state laws often goes hand in hand with a lack of culturally appropriate procedures and linguistic barriers, given that legal proceedings are usually conducted in the official, but not native languages. State legal operators are often not free from racial, class and gender stereotypes, which diminishes the credibility of these women in the eyes of those adjudicating their cases. If such procedures lead to convictions at all, then the solutions offered for domestic violence by state laws such as a temporary sentence in jail are usually not helpful for resolving underlying conflicts between the couple. Municipal police forces often lack the capacities to offer protective measures for battered indigenous women in their communities, thereby leaving them with continuous fear of retaliation by the perpetrator. The fact that denouncing one's own husband before the state judiciary often elicits repudiation on the part of a women's family or community likewise inhibits them from taking legal action against violence before the official justice system (Ardito and La Rosa 2004: 64; Coordinadora de la Mujer 2011: 53; Franco and González 2009; Lang and Kucia 2009; Pequeño 2009a; Sieder and Sierra 2010; Uriona 2010; Zabala 2011).

Indigenous women from other world regions have also articulated obstacles to access state judiciaries of a very similar kind.[6] What is more, in post-colonial, multiethnic and religiously diverse countries there is typically more than one legal order in place – a constellation commonly referred to as *legal pluralism* (e.g., Griffiths 1986; Hooker 1975; Merry 1988), with each normative order originating in distinct and potentially contradictive values, conceptions of justice and sources of legitimacy, and guided by its own rules, procedures and authorities (Kuppe 2009). Such legal forums include traditional, customary, indigenous, clan- or kin-based legal councils that co-existed and evolved in response to, or were established and transformed through encounters with colonial and state legal orders over time; religious judges and tribunals (e.g., rabbinical, shari'a or jirga courts); and alternative centres for dispute resolution of more recent date (e.g., neighbourhood committees, vigilante groups, mediation centres), which are often established due to the lack of available and affordable alternatives.[7] Some of these forums claim competence for specific legal matters; others adjudicate all sorts of disputes. As emphasised by Boaventura de Sousa Santos, such multiple legal orders cannot be conceived of as impermeable and separate entities, but rather as 'different legal spaces superimposed, interpenetrated, and mixed in our minds as much as in our actions' (1987:

297–298), thereby creating complex and often uneasy configurations of *interlegality*. The concrete quality of the relationship between co-existing legal orders is temporally and spatially variable and may take complementary, subsidiary, competitive or even oppressive forms (Eckert 2009). Whereas some non-state legal orders have been officially accommodated or recognised by the State in which they operate, others have remained outside its purview (Yilmaz 2005). But independent from a State's willingness to recognise legally plural landscapes within its territory, cross-regional evidence suggests that the overwhelming majority of women and men prefer turning to non-state justice systems instead of state courts in order to settle their disputes (Wojkowska 2006: 5, 12).

In addition to aspects such as accessibility, short duration, cultural closeness and low costs, indigenous peoples in Latin America have also ascribed a higher degree of legitimacy to their own legal institutions (Brandt and Franco 2007: 146–153; Cóndor 2009: 234), which, among other things, is a reflection of the historically asymmetrical relationship between indigenous legal practices and the dominant 'official' legal orders throughout the past five centuries (Sierra 1997: 134; Stavenhagen 1990: 33–34). As a matter of principle, the shape of this relationship varied and was contingent on the geographic proximity between a power centre and an indigenous group, the rulers' interests with regard to a specific region or pre-colonial society and the governors' effectiveness in dominating them.[8] For the colonial period, Raquel Yrigoyen (2006) identified three modes of relationship: (1) the colonisation of indigenous peoples (especially in areas previously incorporated into the Inca empire, but also the Maya and Aztec territories); (2) the signing of agreements with indigenous peoples who resisted their colonisation (many of whom reside in what is today Chile and Argentina); and (3) the sending of missionaries to the Amazon region, a path that was initiated later than the former ones. Regarding the first model (under which the region of the present book can be subsumed), a two-tier system comprising the *Republic of the Spanish* and the *Republic of the Indians* reorganised and fractionalised pre-existing forms of indigenous organisation (such as *ayllus*[9]) into new administrative entities (such as *reducciones*) and provided these with specific regulations and new political and judicial authorities (e.g., *corregidores, caciques, etc.*). Being excluded from the real sphere of power (which resided with the Spanish rulers) and levied with tributes and forced labour, indigenous peoples still retained a certain degree of autonomy, for even though the competences of their legal authorities were reduced,[10] indigenous peoples maintained the right to govern themselves according to their own law (Fernández 2000: 13–23; Hurtado and du Puit 2006: 214–217; Rivera [1993] 2010: 54–55; Simon 2012: 62; Yrigoyen 2006: 540). This system was dissolved in the republican era which began in the early nineteenth century, when the newly independent Latin American republics enacted constitutions in which indigenous peoples and their institutions became invisibilised behind the concept of allegedly 'free and equal citizens', the ideal of a homogeneous nation, a unified state law, one religion and a sole cultural and linguistic identity (Clavero 2000: 27–28; Fernández 2000: 23–25; Hurtado and du Puit 2006: 221–225; Yrigoyen 2002: 173). The increased appropriation of lands by the criollo-mestizo elites and the expulsion of indigenous peoples from their lands went hand in hand with acts of resistance and the emergence of movements which sometimes even called for the reconstitution of the entitlements conferred to indigenous peoples under colonial rule (Choque and Mamani 2001; Rivera [1993] 2010: 56; THOA [1984] 1988). To the extent that racialised hierarchies and patterns of internal colonialism, joined by assimilationist and protectionist policies, continued to characterise the political regimes and societies of the region, this asymmetrical relationship between dominant state law and subordinated indigenous jurisdictions persisted until the late twentieth century (Amry 2007: 83–91; Fernández 2000; Rivera [1993] 2010; Stavenhagen 1990: 33–36; Yrigoyen 2002: 172).

Importantly, while indigenous groups were partly able to uphold their norms and institutions, changes in the local context and the centuries-long interplay between 'official' and indigenous normative orders resulted in modifications of indigenous law. Indigenous legal authorities had to respond to exigencies posed by state law, and recently also by international law (e.g., laws obliging communities to adopt a specific internal organisation, to comply with land tenure rules or to meet human right standards). But given the scant presence and law enforcement capacities of many States, such external exigencies provoked reactions ranging from the partial adaptation of colonial, republican and contemporary elements of law, to the revitalising of pre-existing norms, to resistance against external impositions, all of which combined to safeguard the coherence and survival of indigenous peoples (Brandt and Franco 2007: 45–48; Kuppe 2009: 43–43; Orellana 2005: 125–135; Sierra 1997: 133–136; Stavenhagen 1990: 33–36). It is here where the non-statist and adaptive nature of indigenous law comes to the fore, prompting anthropologists to direct our attention to the misleading but widely held notion of indigenous law as immutable and stable across long periods of time – a view which is often conveyed by concepts such as 'traditional' or 'customary' law.[11]

Despite the differentiated relationship between community-based and state legal systems, as well as the fact that indigenous law varies from one place to the other, some features can be found across a wide range of instances of indigenous law. Broadly speaking, indigenous law does not constitute a separate or autonomous sphere of social organisation, but instead forms an integral part of a community's social and cultural life (Kuppe 2009: 41; Sánchez and Jaramillo 2009: 154; Stavenhagen 1990: 29). Community members commonly know norms, but they are typically not codified. Nevertheless, throughout the twentieth century, communities (especially in the Andes) had to adopt community statutes in order to be officially recognised by the State. Some also started to write protocols (*actas*) of their legal processes, affirming thereby the legality of their jurisdiction and utilising the protocols as a means to claim their competence over a given case before state legal operators.[12] Instead of trained professionals, it is group members themselves who participate in legal disputes and exert positions of jurisdictional authority. Depending on the type, severity and recurrence of a problem or conflict, distinct instances of authority may exert judicial functions, including family members, elected councils, community assemblies or higher-level organisations. Procedures are dialogue-based and place much weight on the analysis of the underlying causes of a conflict. In addition, the administration of indigenous justice often involves a spiritual dimension, which is reflected in the performance of accompanying rites or the presence of spiritual authorities in juridical processes. In the Andes, this aspect also comes to the fore in symbolic, reconciliatory and purifying elements of a legal process such as the confession of guilt (or the pledging of innocence), the demonstration of repentance, the asking for forgiveness or in corporal sanctions with medical plants meant to purging the transgressor and offering him or her the possibility to reintegrate into the community (Brandt and Franco 2007; Cóndor 2009; Fernández 2000; Kuppe 2009).[13] More generally, sanctions may be at the same time moral, exemplary, compensatory, reconciliatory, rehabilitative or punitive in nature and typically aim at the prevention of further harm and the restoration of social relations and communal peace (Brandt and Franco 2007: 90–96; Inksater 2010: 115; Stavenhagen 1990: 41). Sometimes, people also forward their problems to state legal operators, be it as a form of sanction emitted by indigenous authorities (Assies 2001: 87), as a way to maintain the communal peace by shifting conflictive issues to external forums or because a legal transgression exceeds local problem-solving capacities (Brandt and Franco 2007: 154–157; Cóndor 2009: 234), or as a strategy to exert pressure on local authorities or to obtain solutions that cannot be provided locally (Chenaut 2004; Sierra 1997: 137). Today, indigenous legal practices are still widespread in rural and semi-rural settings of the Andes. In peripheral or marginalised urban neighbourhoods, by contrast, the absence of both state and indigenous legal authorities means that popular forms of justice such as vigilante or self-help groups strive to fill the vacuum of order, although admittedly it is not always easy to draw clear distinctions between indigenous and popular jurisdictions (Goldstein 2005; 2012; Van Cott 2006).

Meanwhile, international criticism has arisen especially because of such legal systems' presumed incompatibility with human rights standards. With respect to women, community-based legal forums tend to reflect prevailing gendered hierarchies, for example by excluding women from judicial authority positions and decision-making, by failing to recognise rape or domestic violence as crimes, and by providing biased outcomes that tend to perpetuate gender inequalities in legal matters such as marriage, divorce, custody, inheritance, property and land tenure.[14] The issues Andean indigenous women confront when trying to denounce acts of domestic violence before indigenous legal institutions can be summarised as follows:[15] In Andean highland communities, the family (godparents of marriage, parents or elder siblings) acts a first instance of conflict mediation. Kin intervention is based on dialogue, the offering of advice and reconciliation, but its effectiveness varies and depends, among other things, on the integrity of family ties and the authority kin members exert over the aggressor. If violence prevails despite kin intervention, the victim or her family may intend to turn to the legal authority of the community. However, indigenous legal authorities often decline their competence by declaring the matter of violence as a family matter – as opposed to issues such as commoners' non-compliance with their community duties, robbery, cattle theft, crop damages, land tenure or intercommunal conflicts, which are regarded as matters appropriate for community mediation. Where legal authorities are willing to deal with cases of violence, women are often confronted with predominantly male legal authorities who preside over the process and steer deliberations. This, in turn, has implications for legal proceedings and rulings: male authorities sometimes downplay the problem; only consider severe, life-threatening or repeated acts of violence as worthy of real concern; allude to external causes such as gossip or poverty as the main drivers behind conjugal violence; or assume that the woman provoked the aggressions. The same is true for cases of conjugal infidelity that – albeit regarded as a justiciable act in many indigenous communities – is treated with more tolerance and milder sanctions when the accused is a man. Legal procedures tend to focus on dialogue among the couple or among extended families, guidance and reconciliation. The option of separation of married couples is usually not considered by community authorities, particularly because the unity of the family and the wellbeing of children are commonly ascribed a higher value compared with the wellbeing of the individual parties in conflict. Well aware of the risk of becoming exposed to social ostracism if they abandon their families, and considering their economic dependency on their husbands, many indigenous women themselves also prefer solutions targeting in the first place the ending of violence and a return to a more peaceful living together. Thus, when a case is presented for the first time before an indigenous legal authority, it is likely that it ends with the signing of an agreement in which the aggressor acknowledges his wrongdoings and pledges to change his conduct – often independently of the severity of the harm caused. Unfortunately, community interventions of this kind are not exemplary enough to break the cycle of violence. Sanctions are more often resorted to in cases of recidivism, when earlier agreements are not complied with, or if violence takes on an alarming scale, and may include public shaming, community services, fines, economic transactions or corporal 'corrections'.[16] Sometimes, the threat to forward the case to state authorities is used to provide an authority's ruling with more weight; in other cases (e.g., rape of girls), indigenous authorities may decide to immediately pass the case to state operators. None of this, however, seems sufficient to guarantee that continuous conjugal violence will not result in absolute impunity, as exemplified in the case of an influential political leader from an Ecuadorian highland community, whose social position prevented him from being condemned by state and indigenous justice systems alike (Picq 2012).

Accommodation of legal pluralism and indigenous women's struggle for collective and individual rights

Within academia, such intra-group inequalities have formed part of a highly controversial normative debate revolving around the accommodation of multiculturalism in democratic states, the weighing of individual rights and liberties against the right to cultural difference and autonomy of ethnic and religious minorities, and the universality of human rights more broadly (Cook 1994; Kymlicka 1995; Okin 1999; Taylor *et al.* 1994; Young 1990). Universalists advocated for the global application of human rights as the only means to guarantee the protection of the dignity of all human beings, whereas cultural relativists – arguing that norms could only be regarded as valid and legitimate in the society they emerged – remained highly sceptical that legal standards originating in Western liberal thought could travel globally. While some scholars stressed States' responsibility to engender reforms of non-state legal systems and to enact policies balancing group rights with gender equality (Deveaux 2000; Shachar 2001), others viewed such interventions as unduly impinging on a group's autonomy (Spinner-Halev 1994). Abdullahi Ahmed An-Na'im (1990; 1992) is an exponent of a middle-ground position in this debate. He argued that in post-colonial contexts the down-the-line implementation of international human rights could be easily repudiated as an act of cultural imperialism unless these norms acquired legitimacy on its own in a targeted society. Later on, anthropologists interested in the ways people make use of and navigate through plural legal repertories found that legal concepts travelling from external places would typically have to undergo processes of *vernacularisation* and dock on local realities, understandings and identities so as to gain relevance and become appropriated by locals (Merry 2006a; 2006b). Furthermore, scholars also cautioned against overtly essentialist, non-historical and static views of the concepts 'culture' and 'rights' and highlighted the dynamic nature of cultural practices and norms that evolved over time in response to changing social, political, economic and cultural contexts (Benda-Beckmann and Benda-Beckmann 2006; Cowan, Dembour and Wilson 2001; Merry 2001; Phillips 2001; Stavenhagen 1990). Monolithic views on culture convey potentially flawed associations such as the existence of internal consensus and overlook that cultural values can be subject to contestations from within – a statement that is clearly confirmed by the case studies presented in this book.

The subject of legal pluralism and women's difficulties to access adequate forums of justice has also raised the interest of international institutions (World Bank, UN bodies, development cooperation agencies and non-governmental organisations (NGOs) over the last decade.[17] Until recently, international reform efforts in the areas of justice, rule of law and security in (post-)conflict and developing countries focused mainly on (re-)building or strengthening the capacities of formal state institutions. However, by realising the many limitations of state-centred 'top-down technocratic initiatives' (Wojkowska 2006: 12) that were informed by models of consolidated democracies and insensitive of the specific contexts in which they were carried out, and acknowledging that a great share of disputes were actually adjudicated in non-state legal systems, international institutions started to commission studies and to design strategies that took account of the legally plural landscapes in their areas of intervention (Chopra and Isser 2011: 23; Harper 2011: 33–36; Kyed 2011: 3–5; Ubink and McInerney 2011: 7–9). In light of donors' anchorage in the international human rights framework, most of them have been willing to engage with non-state justice systems to the extent that they not contradict rule of law and human rights standards. They have recognised that non-state legal forums may be beneficial for women in some contexts and oppressive in others, and that legally plural settings may enhance women's choices, or else leave women without any option to seek justice (UN WOMEN 2011: 68–78; World Bank 2011: 164–165). For this reason, their approaches have oscillated between those targeting the enhancement of the capacities of state legal systems so as to gradually eliminate the access barriers of women and increase their use of the official system, and others promoting the transformation of harmful practices and the gradual alignment of informal legal systems with human rights while retaining their positive attributes (Chopra and Isser 2012; Harper 2011: 33–38).

In Latin America, many countries have recognised the multiethnic character of their citizenry and enacted multicultural constitutional reforms from the mid 1980s onwards. This regional trend was the result of several concomitant developments, most notably (1) indigenous peoples' active mobilisation at the national and international level for recognition of their right to self-determination (Iturralde 1990); (2) the need for Latin American states to construct more inclusive and legitimate democracies by expanding citizenship rights to disenfranchised sectors amidst profound political crises (Van Cott 2000a; 2006); (3) pressures from multilateral and bilateral development agencies to reform the often inefficient justice systems (Domingo and Sieder 2001); and (4) the advancement of international legal instruments delineating the fundamental human rights of indigenous peoples (Assies, van der Haar and Hoekma 2000; Sieder 2002), namely the International Labour Organization Convention No. 169 on Indigenous and Tribal Peoples (ILO C 169; adopted in 1989 and in force since 1991) and the 2007 United Nations Declaration on the Rights of Indigenous Peoples (UNDRIP).

Based on the principle of non-discrimination, ILO C 169 recognises indigenous peoples' distinct identities and guarantees a set of collective cultural, social, economic and political rights to them, among them the right to decide on priorities of their development, to collectively own their lands, territories and natural resources, to use their languages, to maintain their values, practices and institutions, to access adequate educational and health services, to enjoy indiscriminate labour rights, and to be consulted on policies affecting their lives and habitats. The Convention has been ratified by 15 Latin American states to date and is legally binding for its signatory parties.[18] The contents of the rights enshrined in this Convention significantly influenced constitutional reforms in Latin America throughout the late 1980s and 1990s (Van Cott 2000a; 2006; Yrigoyen 2011). UNDRIP, in turn, was adopted by the UN General Assembly in September 2007, with most Latin American states voting in favour of the Declaration.[19] In this (legally non-binding) Declaration, the rights enshrined in ILO C 169 were essentially affirmed and simultaneously subsumed under the fundamental right to self-determination, from which all other group rights of indigenous peoples can be inferred. Given that the final negotiations on this Declaration paralleled the work of constituent assemblies in Bolivia and Ecuador, UNDRIP influenced the elaboration of the most recent Constitutions of Ecuador (2008) and Bolivia (2009). Moreover, immediately after its adoption, UNDRIP obtained the status of national law in Bolivia (Law No. 3760, 7 November 2007; see Schilling-Vacaflor and Kuppe 2012). Importantly, both international instruments explicitly include indigenous peoples' right to maintain and strengthen their legal institutions:

> In applying national laws and regulations to the peoples concerned, due regard shall be had to their customs or customary laws.
>
> (art. 8.1. ILO C 169)

> Indigenous peoples have the right to maintain and strengthen their distinct political, legal, economic, social and cultural institutions, while retaining their right to participate fully, if they so choose, in the political, economic, social and cultural life of the State.
>
> (art. 5 UNDRIP)

Interestingly, both ILO C 169 and UNDRIP allow for the exercise of indigenous law on the condition that it conforms to international human rights standards:

> These peoples shall have the right to retain their own customs and institutions, where these are not incompatible with fundamental rights defined by the national legal system and with internationally recognised human rights. Procedures shall be established, whenever necessary, to resolve conflicts which may arise in the application of this principle.
>
> (art. 8.2. ILO C 169)

> Indigenous peoples have the right to promote, develop and maintain their institutional structures and their distinctive customs, spirituality, traditions, procedures, practices and, in the cases where they exist, juridical systems or customs, in accordance with international human rights standards.
>
> (art. 34 UNDRIP)

By means of recent constitutional reforms, Bolivia, Ecuador and Peru have affirmed, in one way or the other, the right of indigenous legal authorities' to dispense justice according to their own customs and procedures, while simultaneously providing for similar or even more restrictive limiting clauses with respect to human rights issues. All constitutional passages have left much room for interpretation and pointed to later statutory legislation in which these were to be concretised and mechanisms of coordination and cooperation between state and indigenous jurisdictions delineated. However, the reforms were accompanied by growing controversies in Latin America about rule of law issues and doubts about indigenous legal systems' capacity to uphold individual human rights. Despite various efforts to elaborate such draft laws, most Andean states have thus far not enacted such legislation (with the exception of the highly controversial Bolivian Law on Jurisdictional Delimitation 2010).[20] In the absence of more concise and generally accepted definitions about the extent and limits of indigenous jurisdiction, in some contexts acts of lynching have been conflated with indigenous justice (Albó 2012a: 233, 248; Barrera 2012; Bazurco and Exeni 2012: 119–120), sanctions adopted by indigenous authorities have been qualified as 'barbaric' (El Vistazo 26.05.2010; Santos 2012: 15, 21–22; Simon 2012: 72–74), state legal operators have denied indigenous authorities' legal competences and criminally prosecuted indigenous authorities for adjudicating legal matters (García 2005; Llasag 2012a; Poveda 2009: 475; Simon 2013; Yrigoyen 2002: 171–172), and state courts have reserved the right to supervise indigenous jurisdiction without providing for participation of indigenous legal authorities on equitable grounds in such supervisory mechanisms (Schilling-Vacaflor and Kuppe 2012: 352; Yrigoyen 2011: 148–149). Needless to mention, these developments were far from helpful for addressing the obstacles many indigenous women encounter when seeking justice before indigenous and state legal systems.

The inconclusive and highly contested way legal pluralism was dealt with has been mirrored by a general lack of enforcement of the constitutionally enshrined rights of indigenous peoples in the Andes and Latin America more generally (Stavenhagen 2006). If taken seriously, many of these rights would presuppose comprehensive reforms in the cultural, health, educational, economic and political realms, which have thus far been blocked by political and economic elites who have disqualified indigenous demands as divisive and 'backward' and thus inimical to 'development' or 'progress' (García 2011: 45–46; Hernández 2002: 95; 2008: 87–88; Santos 2010). In addition, and related to the first aspect, indigenous peoples' livelihoods have been negatively affected by the expansion of neoliberal economic policies based on the removal of corporativist programs (Yashar 2005) and the promotion of large infrastructure projects (e.g., hydroelectric dams, highways) and extractive economies (logging, mining, gas and oil exploration), which have mostly been carried out in violation of indigenous peoples' right to consultation (Anaya 2005; Bebbington 2009; Rodríguez 2010; Schilling-Vacaflor 2013). In some countries, the insufficient protection of human and women's rights in indigenous legal systems was also invoked to condemn indigenous cultures as anti-democratic – this despite the often highly deficient human rights record of national state judiciaries (Blackwell *et al.* 2009: 25; Hernández 2002: 90, 96). Amidst such a hostile environment in which their entitlements were ignored or delegitimised, some male indigenous leaders in Latin America have tended to essentialise their cultures as 'millenarian' sets of shared values and traditions and to highlight their positive features while dismissing internal debates on specific cultural practices as harmful for the collective struggle. In response to this, indigenous women emphasised instead the fundamentally dynamic quality of indigenous law and governance systems more broadly, underscoring thereby these systems' openness for change (Hernández 2002; FIMI 2006). Furthermore, far from accepting the role of mere victims of rights violations, indigenous women came to view themselves as active political subjects with agency and voice. Throughout the past two decades, a growing number of them seized the opportunity to meet in newly created spaces of rights awareness, training, deliberation and representation (workshops, leadership schools, women's organisations, summits and conferences at local, national, continental and international level)[21] and to reflect upon aspects of culture and rights from their own standpoints. The numerous enunciations emerging from such forums bear testimony to indigenous women's self-understanding as bearers of both collective *and* individual rights (e.g., Beijing Declaration of Indigenous Women 1995; ECMIA and Chirapaq 2013; FIMI 2006; Lang and Kucia 2009; Sánchez 2005). But against a homogenising interpretation of universal human rights that remains detached from their lived realities, many indigenous women have opted for the appropriation and resignification of these rights discourses in order to bring them more in line with their own cultural frames of reference. In response to non-indigenous sectors who regard the right to cultural difference as a threat to indigenous women and to those indigenous movement sectors who fend off internal contestation as inimical to the collective struggle, indigenous women have positioned themselves alongside their male counterparts to defend their rights as indigenous peoples and to denounce racist and discriminatory attitudes they encounter within their countries. Simultaneously, they have problematised the unequal and disrespectful treatment they experience as women within their families, communities and organisations. Indigenous women have not sought to disown or reject their cultural identities, but to the contrary have striven to strengthen them by confronting internal oppressions and insisting on more balanced relationships within the cultural spaces which they strongly endorse (Blackwell *et al.* 2009; ECMIA and Chirapaq 2013; Hernández 2002; 2008; Hernández and Canessa 2012; FIMI 2006; Santos 2010: 100, 106; Sieder and Sierra 2010). The concrete strategies women have developed in this context have varied and responded to local circumstances and needs. As for the realm of access to justice, indigenous women's engagement has targeted the establishment of culturally appropriate state justice services, reforms of community-based legal institutions, reinterpretations of prevailing norms and the creation of new institutions aiming to close existing legal vacuums. It is precisely this site of activism and contestation that constitutes the focus of the present book.

Research questions, research design and methodological approach

Against the background of the increased global circulation of human rights discourses (Benda-Beckmann, Benda-Beckmann and Griffiths 2005; 2009; Goodale and Merry 2007) and the reactions this circulation has evoked in local settings, a growing number of scholars have accompanied women's grassroots groups in Latin America and other world regions. They have started to critically reflect upon local legal practices, which circumscribed their entitlements, positions and relationships to others within their respective societies, and who, based on such reflections, have developed strategies and actions aimed at changing those legal norms and practices, which they believe have a harmful impact on their personal and the collective wellbeing (e.g., Blackwell *et al.* 2009; Hernández and Canessa 2012; Merry 2006; Richards 2005; Sieder and McNeish 2013; Speed,

Map 1.1 Andean region and localities studied

Hernández and Stephen 2006; Tschalaer 2010; Yüksel 2010). This study aims to contribute to this field of inquiry by focusing on thus far underexplored local initiatives carried out throughout the past decade in six Andean highland localities in Ecuador, Peru and Bolivia, targeting legal norms and institutions dealing with domestic violence. As for Ecuador, this research involves the Kichwa communities La Calera and San Francisco de la Rinconada (Imbabura Province), where the change initiatives started off in 2004 and 2003, respectively. In Peru, the Quechua communities Chacabamba and Tungasuca (Cuzco Department) are analysed, with change initiatives beginning in 2002, and 2001, respectively. In Bolivia, the Quechua municipalities of Mojocoya and Tarabuco (Chuquisaca Department) are included in the study, both of which initiated in 2009.

Given that the effectiveness of the change initiatives explored here varied from place to place towards the end of the research period (2012), the present study addresses the following main research question:

> Why have some indigenous communities and municipalities in the Andean Region more effectively than others initiated reforms of their legal norms and institutions in order to improve women's legal standing in the realm of domestic violence?

The concept 'norm' in this study refers to 'a [single] standard of appropriate behaviour for actors with a given identity' (Finnemore and Sikkink

1998: 891), which may imply a sanction in the case of non-compliance (Popitz [1980] 2006: 86), whereas an 'institution' constitutes an aggregation of interrelated norms and rules for appropriate behaviour (Finnemore and Sikkink 1998: 891). Both concepts refer, in the first place, to indigenous legal systems operating at the site of interest, but they may also include new rules for cooperation with the state judicial system in cases of violence against indigenous women. 'Reforms' may imply the modification of pre-existing of legal norms or institutions or the creation of new ones. Legal change efforts are considered as 'more effective' when a targeted norm or institution related to domestic violence was indeed changed or created towards the end of the investigation period and if the local population showed a propensity to invoke these altered norms and institutions, and authorities to apply them. Alternatively, the prospects were very high that a location was about to implement such measures in the near future. Conversely, change efforts are conceived of as 'less effective' if no or only minor measures have been adopted so as to alter the legal treatment of cases of domestic violence. If such minor measures were in place, the local population displayed a low propensity to invoke them and authorities to apply them by the end of the investigation period. Alternatively, the prospects were low that such measures would be implemented in the near future.

Some comments on the term 'law' are also in order at this stage. While there have been many attempts to define 'law' among legal anthropologists,[22] the conceptualisation of 'law' as an 'authoritatively asserted cognitive and normative framework for conduct and social interaction claiming validity for a social group' seems appropriate for the purpose of the present study.[23] Legal concepts such as rules, principles, norms, procedures, regulations or rulings define judicial facts, ascribe artefacts and individuals a certain legal status, determine mutual obligations between persons, validate the form and admissibility of activities and transactions, provide means and authorities to settle legal disputes and establish consequences for impermissible behaviour (sanctions). In contrast to moral or ethical principles, law is authoritatively enforced, typically by legal institutions (courts, authorities, law-enforcement agencies, etc.) that dispense and apply legal rules; in case of non-compliance with prevailing norms, these authorities are entitled to enact sanctions (Benda-Beckmann and Benda-Beckmann 2006: 12–13; Kuppe 2009: 39; Popitz [1980] 2006: 86).

Importantly, law is of human design. It is created, interpreted, affirmed, reconstituted or questioned through social practices (Benda-Beckmann, Benda-Beckmann and Griffiths 2009: 1; Cowan, Dembour and Wilson 2001: 12). In light of the preeminent role of human agency, law is not an impartial mode of regulating social interaction. The current shape or dominant interpretation of law often tends to reflect the outcome of pre-existing conflicts of interest among groups (Starr and Collier 1987: 368).

In this sense, law and the control over its application and interpretation constitute important sources of legitimacy and the exercise of power. With law, more and less influential positions, roles and resources are distributed among groups and individuals, and the continued application of given norms perpetuates a certain legal, social, political or economic status quo. Given the inequalities and inherent processes of inclusion and exclusion that law tends to generate, legal provisions often constitute the very locus of conflicts within and among social groups (Benda-Beckmann, Benda-Beckmann and Griffiths 2009: 1; Starr and Collier 1989: 6–9). Indeed, this is precisely what has occurred in the cases explored in this book, where women's claims on the inadequate legal treatment of domestic violence by local legal authorities have impinged on long-established gender privileges and practices in their families and communities, which is why we should expect from the outset that these efforts would neither be welcomed by all community members nor yield quick results.

In order to better understand the forces that positively or negatively affected the contentious change efforts throughout their evolution, the six observed processes were divided into four stages: (1) phase preceding the change initiative in which change claims emerged; (2) the moment in which change agents decided to initiate change efforts; (3) the subsequent phase in which change agents engaged in legal mobilisation and carried out activities related to their change initiative; (4) the status quo at the end of the research period (2012). Every phase was headed by a respective research question, which guided the analysis in each case:

1 Why did claims for legal change emerge at the site of interest?
2 Which factors facilitated or obstructed the change initiative at its initial point?
3 Which factors have affected the change efforts throughout the subsequent stages of their evolution?
4 Which were the results of the legal change efforts at the end of the research period?

As for the theoretical approach, this study aims to build bridges between three different research strands in the social sciences – legal anthropology, social movement theory and new institutionalism, all of which have analysed processes of legal change. By synthesising and grouping variables derived from these three approaches according to a specific phase of a change process, and by adapting them to the context of indigenous communities, a comprehensive conceptual framework is proposed within which the research questions raised in the present study can be addressed. The purpose of this approach is twofold. On the one hand, the study aims to assess whether the variables and related assumptions posited by the three reviewed bodies of literature are appropriate for exploring legal change processes related to domestic violence in Andean indigenous contexts. On the other hand, by providing the aforementioned innovative framework, this study aims to contribute to the cumulative construction of theoretical and empirical knowledge in the field of legal pluralism and indigenous women's access to justice.

Methodologically, the author's concern is that most of the literature on legal and institutional change reviewed is based on single case studies that tend to focus on 'salient' cases in which some kind of 'change' – however defined – indeed occurred. But if such 'interesting' cases are not compared against others where change efforts were not observed or where these efforts came to face insurmountable challenges at some stage of the process, readers are left with doubts as to the validity and relevance of the variables identified by the literature, given that some of the dynamics assumed to be essential for facilitating change may have also been present in cases where change efforts remained rather ineffective.[24] Moreover, sometimes we may learn more about the concrete effect of specific variables or come across new or thus far unconsidered factors when we compare cases against each other. To tackle this issue, the present study proceeds by means of a structured–focused comparison between a small number of cases in which three change initiatives that have yielded 'more effective' results at the end of the research period are systematically compared with three other cases carried out in communities or municipalities where same-minded change efforts turned out to be 'less effective' in this regard. Such a small-N comparison allows for the analysis of differences and similarities across cases (Ragin 1987: 6) and offers criteria to both hypotheses testing and theory building (Collier 1991: 7; Sartori 1991: 244). Furthermore, this study is guided by a most-similar cases design, which is associated with the comparison of relatively homogeneous cases that share many background properties (i.e., geographic, historical, economic, social and cultural aspects) but vary ideally in respect of one aspect (in our case, a higher or lower degree of legal change; see George and Bennett 2005: ch. 8; Lijphard 1971; 1975; Przeworski and Teune 1970; Sartori 1991). The idea behind this design is to facilitate the identification of independent and intervening variables that are causally linked with an outcome of interest while assuming that all relatively common contextual features of the cases can be excluded from the explanation (Sartori 1991: 250). Given that social reality hardly ever provides phenomena that are as identical as proposed by the scientific model (George and Bennett 2005: 151–152), scholars tend to understand notions of 'similarity' and 'difference' as essentially relative ones that depend on the perspective from which a scholar explores a set of cases (Collier 1991: 17). For the present study, a 'case' shall refer to consciously promoted legal change efforts in the realm of institutions and norms dealing with domestic violence in indigenous localities (or briefly: *change initiative*).

In order to provide a comprehensive explanation of the outcomes of interest (more and less effective change of indigenous legal norms and institutions in local settings), the reliance on one or a few explanatory factors and the expectation that such a pattern will invariably hold true in countless settings, seemed highly unlikely from the outset. Instead this research departed from the premise that 'causation' in this thematic field would involve the interaction of several independent and intervening variables that would be more or less relevant at distinct phases of the process, and that the concrete causal paths leading to an outcome would differ from one another. The strategy chosen to compare the processes of interest is therefore case-orientated, analysing each case in an in-depth manner by means of process-tracing and paying particular attention to similarities and differences across all cases (Collier 2011; Ragin 2000: 22). The comparison among the individual cases is 'structured', i.e. guided by the same research questions and standardised data collection, and 'focused', i.e. addressing only selected aspects of the cases at hand (George and Bennett 2005: 67, 206; George and McKeown 1985: 35). While the studied change initiatives started off at distinct moments in time, the systematic comparison of these processes according to distinct phases facilitated the identification of factors and patterns that have shaped the direction and the effectiveness of all the processes reviewed, allowing thereby for the generation of arguments that go beyond the scope of individual cases.

The decision to select cases from Ecuador, Peru and Bolivia, in turn, can be explained by the relative similarity of these three states in geographic, historical, social, cultural and political terms. These states share a pre-Columbian past (with many highland indigenous groups temporarily incorporated into the Incan Empire that stretched across these three countries); a colonial period under the rule of the Spanish Crown and its administrative centres installed across the highlands; and an ethnically diverse and numerically significant indigenous population inhabiting both the Andean corridors and the Amazon lowlands that cut across all three neighbouring countries (Barié 2003: 484). Unless their members have opted to migrate to urban spaces, indigenous groups continue living in partly traditional, partly state-regulated entities of social organisation (e.g., *ayllu, comunidad campesina, comuna*) where – depending on their degree of interrelation with the white and mestizo population and their capacity to maintain their internal cohesion – a certain degree of self-rule and the practice of indigenous forms of law can be observed (Cóndor 2009: 233–234; Gonzales de Olarte 1994: 175–195). From the 1990s onwards, these three countries adopted relatively similar legislation on the issue of domestic violence, but these measures suffered from serious shortcomings in terms of addressing the particular situation of indigenous women living outside of urban centres. In the same vein, all three states have recently recognised indigenous peoples' right to administer their own legal systems, even though the actual scope of recognition has varied. In order to ensure greater internal coherence of the focus population and their socio-political organisation, I decided to concentrate on one ethno-linguistic group – the Quechua (in Ecuador Quichua/Kichwa) who, with an estimated eight to twelve million members residing in the Andean corridor stretching from Colombia to Chile, are considered one of the largest surviving language groups in South America (Clark and Becker 2007: 10). In cooperation with national experts on indigenous affairs, one local setting was first identified where substantial advances in regard to the protection of women against domestic violence by local legal institutions had been observed; in a second step, another location was sought that was situated in the same geographic area and that shared many contextual aspects with the first site, but where similar efforts were thwarted or had thus far yielded only minor results. This selection process also involved a consideration of the time frame. The initiation of the change processes should not date too far back in time for two reasons: first, we could hardly expect such a sensitive matter as domestic violence to be raised among indigenous groups *before* the emergence of a more generalised awareness on this subject in the broader society, something that has been only gradually and unevenly achieved by first legal measures and public campaigns adopted by the national governments from the mid 1990s onwards. Second, as this study would heavily rely on the testimonies of local community members and experts – few other sources existed about the processes of interest at the beginning of this research project – we should be mindful of the fact that human memory may become imprecise the further back in time we go (Tansey 2009: 487). As a result, La Calera and San Francisco de la Rinconada in Ecuador, Chacabamba and Tungasuca in Peru and Mojocoya and Tarabuco in Bolivia were chosen for the present study. All cases have been linked to some more extended regional, cantonal or municipal projects,[25] and as the Peruvian and Ecuadorian *change initiatives* had relatively more time to be carried out in local communities, a comprehensive analysis of these processes was viable at the community level. Due to the differing context (conversion into indigenous autonomous territories), the two Bolivian cases started off at the municipal level, and due to only three years of evolution until the cut-off year at which data collection was concluded, an assessment of the impact of these *initiatives* at the community level was not yet viable. Thus, these two cases refer to the municipal level, composed of several dozen indigenous communities and larger in size and population compared with the four other cases.

Data for this research was collected during an extended fieldwork (October 2011–May 2012) involving shorter stays in the political centres of the three countries (Quito, Lima, La Paz) and conversations with country experts about potential cases as well as about national developments with regard to gender violence and legal pluralism, and longer stays in the selected locations and the nearest towns to these settings. Informants were purposively selected[26] among local experts (i.e., representatives of governmental or non-governmental institutions who disposed of a privileged access to information on the topic of interest),[27] and, most importantly, individuals who were directly or indirectly involved in the change processes: male and female elected authorities, leaders from organisations or community-based groups, active participants of a *change initiative* and 'ordinary' community members. Throughout fieldwork most of the methods pertaining to political ethnography as delineated by Charles Tilly (2006a: 419) were applied: (semi-structured) in-depth interviews; conversations; participant observation; passive observation of interaction; and unobtrusive observation concerning residues and consequences of interaction.[28] I took field notes, wrote 'in-process memos' (Emerson, Fretz and Shaw 2011: 123) and started to transcribe my first interviews right away, so as to gain first ideas on the key agents, events and processes, and to become aware of aspects in which my data coverage was still weak or inconclusive. This procedure allowed for identifying additional relevant interview partners and for asking more informed and specific questions in the subsequent interviews. I fully agree with Emerson, Fretz and Shaw (2011: ch. 1, 5) in that the 'data' I was looking for did not simply consist of 'objective' facts waiting 'out there' to be 'discovered'. Much rather, the information extended to me can neither be separated from local people's understandings of their social reality, the circumstances of the dialogue and their personal reasons for sharing experiences and views with me at a certain place and moment of time, nor from my own 'lenses' while observing, listening, transcribing and interpreting the information. Thus, bearing in mind the many limitations of this 'data *construction*' process, I chose various strategies to check apparently relevant bits of information as to its comprehensibility, plausibility and consistency while conducting, transcribing and analysing the interviews (Emerson, Fretz and Shaw 2011: 163–165; George and Bennett 2005: 99–100; Tansey 2009: 487–488). I also sought to clarify some matters and discuss my preliminary impressions and findings personally, by phone and via e-mail during and after the fieldwork with some interviewees and observers of the processes of interest. These cross-checks and awareness of subjectivity involved in this inquiry notwithstanding, I assume the full responsibility for all contents and potential misunderstandings that might have slipped in throughout this process.

Organisation of the book

Departing from this introduction, the book continues with a theoretical chapter reviewing three bodies of literature (legal anthropology, social movement theory and new institutionalism) as to their ways to conceptualise processes of intended legal or institutional change. Based on a critical assessment of the propositions and variables elaborated by scholars working within these theory strands, an innovative interdisciplinary framework that combines elements from the three approaches is presented. This framework provides the fundament for the six in-depth studies, which stand in the centre of chapters 3, 4 and 5. Each chapter relates to a distinct country (Ecuador, Peru and Bolivia) and briefly introduces to the degree to which indigenous legal jurisdiction has been recognised and sketches this State's legislation addressing violence against women respectively. Each chapter then shifts to in-depth analyses of two sub-national cases, which are guided by the four above-mentioned research questions. It starts off with the case in which change efforts have yielded more substantial results and then turns to the second case, situated in the same geographical region and sharing many background conditions with the first case, but where results of similar change efforts have remained more limited when data collection ended. In the following chapter a comparison of all six cases is provided which allows for the identification of variables that have secured more effective outcomes in the three 'more effective' cases as well as those accounting for the more limited results encountered in the three 'less effective' cases. In a 'nutshell', this study finds that instances of intended legal change targeting the issue of domestic violence in Andean indigenous contexts can be best conceived of as dynamic and highly contingent processes characterised by the advancing of institutional innovations, but also phases of intense debates, negotiations, contestations and setbacks. The variation in the effectiveness of legal change efforts can be explained by the interplay of several factors that exert a major impact on such change processes throughout distinct phases of their evolution. These include: the diffusion of new legal ideas or concepts into a site that capture local interest by pointing to the core of prevailing grievances; change agents' ability to construct a meaningful frame for action resonating with wider sectors of the local population, as well as to delineate realistic goals, strategies and change-orientated activities; the openness of local authorities and influential actors to the legal reform efforts; and the availability of human, material and immaterial resources, community-based organisations and supportive external allies. Based on this argument, chapter 7 closes with a discussion of this study's implications for further research, policy and development practice in Latin America and beyond.

Notes

1 See the United Nations Treaty Collection website: https://treaties.un.org/Pages/ViewDetails.aspx?src=TREATY&mtdsg_no=IV-8&chapter=4&lang=en (last access 10.06.2015).

2 On the situation of indigenous women in Australia, see Cox, Young and Bairnsfather-Scott 2009.

3 The here presented information on the situation of indigenous women reviews findings from the following sources: CEPAL 2007; 2013; Deere and León 2002; ECMIA and Chirapaq 2013; FIMI 2006; Hall and Patrinos 2006; Radcliffe 2014; Sieder and Sierra 2010; UN DESA 2009; UN Office of the Special Adviser on Gender Issues and Advancement of Women and the Secretariat of the United Nations Permanent Forum on Indigenous Issues 2010.

4 This definition stands in line with UN Secretary General's in-depth study on all forms of violence against women (UN 2006) and the legislation on domestic violence in the three countries studied here (Bolivia, Ecuador, Peru) that prevailed until the end of the research period of this study (2012).

5 More than 50 per cent of Latin American women and men surveyed regularly between 2004 and 2012 said to have no confidence in their country's judiciary; see LAPOP 2012: 193–194.

6 See, for instance, the special double issue about The Socio-Legal Position of Women in Changing Society in the *Journal of Legal Pluralism and Unofficial Law* No. 30–31 (1990–1991) and the special issue Human Rights and Legal Pluralism in the *Journal of Legal Pluralism and Unofficial Law* No. 60 (2010). Online: http://commission-on-legal-pluralism.com/nl/journal_of_legal_pluralism (last access 10.06.2015); Cook 1994; IDLO 2013; Sieder and McNeish 2013; UN WOMEN 2011.

7 See, for instance, An-Na'im 2002; Benda-Beckmann and Benda-Beckmann 1985; Chanock 1985; Comaroff and Roberts 1981; Fitzpatrick 1984; Santos 1987; Santos and Rodriguez Garavito 2005; Sartori and Shahar 2012; Stavenhagen and Iturralde 1990; Yilmaz 2005.

8 Guillermo O'Donnell (1999) raised our attention to the many regions of Latin America that have long been characterised by a weak or inexistent state presence.

9 An *ayllu* refers to a basic form of socio-political organisation that was prevalent among pre-colonial Andean societies and constituted by kinship groups bound by complex ties of reciprocity and collective land; see Choque and Mamani 2001.

10 Indigenous legal authorities were competent to rule on conflicts among indigenous individuals and only on minor offences. Indigenous norms could neither contradict norms of the Catholic Church nor laws introduced by the Spanish colonial administration; see Simon 2012: 62; Yrigoyen 2006: 540. Indigenous authorities were also supposed to adopt some new rules (e.g., the prohibition of polygamy) and to modify some sanctions; see Amry 2007: 76; Fernández 2000: 22.

11 See Blackwell *et al.* 2009: 25; Brandt and Franco 2006: 6; Sierra 1997: 133; Speed 2008: 123. Sally Engle Merry (1991) provides an insightful review of studies disclosing the complex relationship between law and colonialism in distinct world regions, many of which clearly revoke the idea of an immutable 'customary law' while giving evidence of how 'customs' were created and modified throughout the colonial period; see also Fitzpatrick 1984; Starr and Collier 1989.

12 See Brandt and Franco 2007: 43–44; Cóndor 2009; Fernández 2000: 37; Hueber 2009; Orellana 2005: 139–148. On attempts to codify indigenous law by distinct indigenous peoples in Panama, lowland peoples from Peru and Bolivia, and the Mixe in Mexico, see Assies 2001: 89–92.

13 The Constitutional Court of Colombia has forged a jurisprudence on the issue of physical sanctions according to which indigenous legal authorities

were entitled to apply such measures as long as these would not violate the right to life; amount to torture, slavery, cruel, inhumane, or degrading treatment; and be transparent and predictable for community members; see Sánchez and Jaramillo 2009: 168–169.

14 See, for instance, the special double issue about The Socio-Legal Position of Women in Changing Society in the *Journal of Legal Pluralism and Unofficial Law* No. 30–31 (1990–1991) and the special issue Human Rights and Legal Pluralism in the *Journal of Legal Pluralism and Unofficial Law* No. 60 (2010). Online: http://commission-on-legal-pluralism.com/nl/journal_of_legal_pluralism (last access 10.06.2015); the special edition of Third World Legal Studies Vol. 13 (1994); Faundez 2003; ICHRP 2009; Khadiagala 2001; Nyamu-Musembi 2003; Sierra 2004; Speed, Hernández and Stephen 2006; Whitehead and Tsikata 2003.

15 The here presented information on access barriers of women to indigenous justice resumes findings from the following sources: Barragán *et al.* 2005; Decoster and Rivera 2009; Estremadoyro 2001: ch. 5; Franco and González 2009; Lang and Kucia 2009; Nostas and Sanabria 2009; Pequeño 2009a; 2009b; Salgado 2012; Sieder and Sierra 2010; Van Vleet 2002.

16 Corporal sanctions in the Andes may include, among others, a determined amount of lashings or a bath in cold water or with stinging nettles. Such 'corrections' are associated not as much with the infliction of physical pain or humiliation as with the spiritual, moral, and social rehabilitation and purification of the person who confessed his or her wrongdoings. On the debate about the compatibility of such practices with human rights, see Ariza 2010: ch. 3; Inksater 2010; Sánchez 2004; see also Fn 13.

17 See the 'Justice for the Poor Project' of the World Bank (website: http://go.worldbank.org/SMIKY7M6O0; last access 10.06.2015); DANIDA 2010; GIZ 2014; OECD 2007; UK Department for International Development 2004; UNDP, UN WOMEN and UNICEF 2012; UN Security Council 2004: Item 36; UN WOMEN 2011: ch. 3; USAID 2005; 2007; Wojkowska 2006.

18 The Latin American countries that signed ILO C 169 were Mexico (1990), Bolivia (1991), Colombia (1991), Costa Rica (1993), Paraguay (1993), Peru (1994), Honduras (1995), Guatemala (1996), Ecuador (1998), Argentina (2000), Brazil (2002), Dominica (2002), Venezuela (2002), Chile (2008), Nicaragua (2010); see: www.ilo.org/dyn/normlex/en/f?p=1000:11300:0::NO:11300:P11300_INSTRUMENT_ID:312314 (last access 10.06.2015).

19 After more than 20 years of negotiations between states and indigenous peoples, a majority of 144 states voted in favour of the Declaration on 13 September 2007. Eleven countries signalled their abstentions (among them Colombia) and four voted against UNDRIP; see Charters and Stavenhagen 2010. All four countries that had voted against (Australia, Canada, New Zealand, USA) later reversed their positions.

20 See the chapters on Bolivia, Ecuador, and Peru, and Aranda 2011; Cóndor 2009; García 2005; Grijalva and Exeni 2012; Poveda 2009; Salgado 2002; Vintimilla 2012; Yrigoyen 2006.

21 The International Indigenous Women's Forum (Spanish: *Foro Internacional de Mujeres Indígenas*, FIMI, website: www.fimi-iiwf.org; last access 10.06.2015) and the Continental Network of Indigenous Women of the Americas (Spanish: *Enlace Continental de Mujeres Indígenas de las Américas*, ECMIA; website: www.ecmia.org; last access 10.06.2015) have evolved into important spaces of supra-national activism and representation for indigenous women.

22 For an insightful review on the debate about the concept of 'law' among legal anthropologists, see Benda-Beckmann 2002.

23 This definition is adapted from Benda-Beckmann and Benda-Beckmann 2006: 12.

24 This methodological objection not only refers to legal anthropology where single case studies are the most frequently used research design. The procedure is also common in social movement research where the focus lies on existing (or historical) movements and not on their absence. Awareness of this issue can also be found among institutionalists (e.g., Capoccia and Kelemen 2007: 352; Pierson 2004: 140). More generally, this concern is echoed by the methodological literature in political science, which tends to recommend scholars to adopt a comparative perspective and to consider cases in which the variables of interest show some degree of variation, see George and Bennett 2005: 250; King, Keohane and Verba 1994: 129.

25 Administrative divisions and denominations are not uniform in Bolivia, Ecuador, and Peru.

26 On the importance of a strategic, purposive sampling procedure for a process-tracing-based data collection, see Tansey 2009.

27 On the definition of 'experts' in the realm of social science research, see Meuser and Nagel 2009: 467–468.

28 Semi-structured interviews constituted the most extensively used tool for gathering information for this study. The questions asked during an audio recorded interview focused on aspects related to the theoretical framework used and were adapted to an interviewee's role in the process in focus. Some interviews were very short; some stretched over several hours or were continued on the following day. Some interviews were carried out with one person, some jointly with two or more persons. In case I should later use aspects articulated during the interview for the present study, I committed myself to referring to the respondents in an anonymous form. Interviewees gave their informed consent to the interviews and were free to decide whether they wished to respond to the questions raised and to interrupt or finish the interview at any time.

Chapter 2

Theoretical approaches to legal and institutional change

The present study aims to identify the main forces that have the potential to either facilitate or obstruct processes of consciously promoted modifications of local norms and institutions targeting gender violence in indigenous communities. In this chapter, three research strands – legal anthropology, social movement theory, and new institutionalism – are enquired as to their respective propositions on the variables held to create the conditions for and to affect the direction and results of processes of legal and institutional change. This review proceeds by dividing change processes into four stages: (1) an initial phase in which change claims emerge; (2) the moment in which change agents decide to initiate change efforts; (3) the phase in which change agents carry out activities related to their *change initiative*; and (4) the potential results of change efforts. Based on this review, the variables identified by the literature according to these four phases of a change process are synthesised and adapted to the context of Andean indigenous highland communities in a comprehensive conceptual framework, the same of which will be used to analyse and compare the six case studies in focus of this book.

Legal anthropological analysis of legal and institutional change

Legal anthropology is particularly relevant for the present study given its long-held interest in normative orders of autochthonous societies in colonial and post-colonial contexts[1] and its concern with legal pluralism (Griffiths 1986; Hooker 1975; Merry 1988). The so-called Gluckman-Bohannan debate of the 1950s and 1960s on the question of whether the phenomena anthropologists studied could be interpreted and compared by recurrence to categories of Western legal science (Gluckmann 1955; 1965) or whether legal concepts were unique to a culture and should be better derived from the prevailing juridical reasoning of a studied group (Bohannan 1957), was later (at least partly) accommodated by the understanding that description, analysis, and comparison of legal concepts across societies would rely on inter-subjectively shared categories such as 'law' (Benda-Beckmann and Benda-Beckmann 2006: 15–16; Merry 2006b: 41–42).[2] The focus of legal anthropologists expanded from the study of normative orders of particular groups, to analyses of legal dispute processes, to legal phenomena and sub-cultures in industrialised countries. Since the 1980s the State and legal developments at regional, national, transnational, and international levels were increasingly taken into consideration (Benda-Beckmann and Benda-Beckmann 2006; Merry 1992; Moore 2001; Starr and Collier 1987). Given the rising transnational and global circulation of legal norms and concepts (such as human rights, good governance or sustainable environment) and the multiplication of governmental and non-governmental agents promoting them, anthropologists became interested in the inter-connectedness of global and local sites and the ways local legal processes related and responded to these developments.[3]

In order to study people's understanding and use of law, anthropologists tend to analytically separate law from the social processes through which it is generated, reproduced, and changed (Spiertz 1991: 195). Many studies inquiring into processes of change rest upon Giddens' concept of 'structuration' (1979), which emphasises a dynamic and mutually constitutive relationship between social structures and human agency. Structures (legal rules, regulations, rulings, etc.) place constraints upon human agency. But as these legal limitations are neither conceived of as all-embracing nor naturally given but instead socially constructed, law also facilitates agents with venues to adjust its forms and contents to new circumstances. Legal structures thus limit and enable human agency, they are reinforced and modified in processes of social interaction, and their altered contours become the context for further interactions (Benda-Beckmann and Benda-Beckmann 2006; Spiertz 1991; Starr and Collier 1989).

Why do claims for legal change emerge in given sites of interest?

Current anthropological research on legal change in post-colonial settings is often conducted against the background of historically specific configurations of interrelated plural legal orders at given sites of interest ('interlegality'; see Santos 1987). The concrete ways in which legal orders become related depends on agents moving in-between these orders, their perceptions, interests, and actions: state and non-state actors (e.g., institutions, aid donors, NGOs) may intervene in a given locality so as to promote or impose new legal ideas and models originating in external legal orders. They may incentivise deliberations on these legal ideas in reunions, workshops or development projects, or seek for the implementation of policies at the local level. In the same vein, local groups or organisations that are connected to external spaces of dialogue (associations, federations, movements, international forums, etc.) can carry new ideas or debates on values or norms into local spaces. Also, the enhanced exchange with other locations or urban zones (through trade, education, temporary work migration, etc.) may bring individual community members in contact with distinct legal concepts, which they can diffuse in their communities of origin (Benda-Beckmann and Benda-Beckmann 2006; Corradi 2010; Cotula and Cissé 2006; Hernández 2002; Kent 2007; Ströbele-Gregor 2004; Tschalaer 2010).

In legally plural constellations, there may be legal domains over which jurisdiction is claimed by several legal orders at the same time, each proposing specific but contradicting normative standards. Such contradictions may confront agents with dilemmas, considering that the compliance with the normative standards of one legal order may imply the violation of rules of another legal system (Benda-Beckmann and Benda-Beckmann 2006: 7). Moreover, the self-evidence of any single system may be challenged and '[c]hoices between legal systems are thinkable' (Benda-Beckmann 2002: 69). Even if particular local norms or practices were already, but yet vaguely perceived as inappropriate, it is typically the familiarisation with alternative norms that serves as a catalyst to concretise these feelings in form of a heightened sense of injustice. In this way, hitherto prevalent understandings and interests with regard to the existing regulatory context may be altered (Ströbele-Gregor 2004). Thus, the emergence of alternative legal concepts provides a fertile ground for disputes over the legitimacy of norms and institutions attributable to a legal order and opens up a plural legal repertoire to which social agents may resort in order to claim change (Assies 2001: 84, Fn 3; Benda-Beckmann and Benda-Beckmann 2006: 19, 24; Sierra 2008: 18).

A second source for the emergence of change claims is seen by anthropologists in the alteration of power relationships between or among social groups (Benda-Beckmann and Benda-Beckmann 2006: 31; Starr and Collier 1989: 8). At the heart of such a view lies the assumption that legal orders distribute privileges and disadvantages among dominant and weaker societal groups. By perpetuating unequal social relations, legal orders shape peoples' interests and their understandings and uses of law (such as efforts to consolidate, modify or circumvent law). But power relations can become altered across time – either because of more general social, political, economic developments (e.g., change of a political regime) or due to changes in law (e.g., constitutional reforms).[4] In such a context, formerly disadvantaged groups may be empowered and thus be prompted to engage in the modification of those legal norms or institutions, which had a discriminatory effect or excluded these groups from the participation in public affairs (Starr and Collier 1989: 6–14).

Which factors facilitate or obstruct legal change efforts at the starting point of a change initiative?

Anthropologists emphasise that the diffusion of new legal ideas into a given site of interest, or the empowerment of previously marginalised people, do not automatically translate into the mobilisation for legal change. Taking the broader context of a given location into account, and mindful of Sally Falk Moore's conceptualisation of local legal orders as 'semi-autonomous social fields' (Moore 1973), scholars argue that any new legal concept travelling from outside into the community must typically make its way through a web of existing institutions, practices, relations, and perceptions. Due to these various filters, the probability that a legal idea raises the interest of the local population and becomes adapted may actually be as high as the chance that it will be rejected, manipulated or result in unintended consequences (Benda-Beckmann and Benda-Beckmann 2006: 6–7; Levitt and Merry 2009). One of the decisive factors, therefore, is the question of how a proposal to change existing norms and institutions affects local power relationships (Benda-Beckmann and Benda-Beckmann 2006: 7). The diffusion or imposition of legal alternatives may challenge long-held privileges or practices of local authorities, which will render efforts of legal change particularly difficult. In the Andean highlands, decisions affecting entire groups are typically taken in collective spaces of deliberation, such as community assemblies, which are constituted mainly by men (Brandt and Franco 2006). To convince such forums of reforms in the realm of gender injustices will thus be an enormously challenging task.

In moments in which local agents decide whether to engage or not in legal change efforts, anthropologists pay attention to the question of who is the one promoting change (e.g., state bureaucrats, donors, religious authorities, local groups), bearing in mind that agents may differ in their standing and voice before a local community (Benda-Beckmann and Benda-Beckmann 2006; Levitt and Merry 2009). In addition, they analyse how the need to alter local norms is justified. Explanations bearing the potential to mobilise wider sectors of the local population and to acquire a minimum degree of legitimacy may have better prospects of eliciting a positive response in local decision-making processes (Benda-Beckmann 2002: 69). In order for new external ideas to gain legitimacy within a given society, scholars found that such concepts must relate to people's pre-existing experiences and understandings and connect to their own needs or grievances. To the degree that new legal concepts help local people to advance their own interests, strengthen ongoing local initiatives or provide alternatives to unjust local norms or practices, these bear the potential to be selectively appropriated (Eckert 2009: 205–206; Sieder and Macleod 2009: 60, 63; Tschalaer 2010: 64) and 'vernacularised' in a locally situated language (Levitt and Merry 2009; Merry 2006a; 2006b).

Which factors influence legal change processes throughout their evolution?

Anthropological studies reveal that, more often than not, legal change efforts are shaped by prolonged conflictive and dynamic interactions between groups promoting legal reform and others defending the status quo, even more so if they address concerns, such as gender ideologies, which have remained unchallenged over long periods of time (Benda-Beckmann and Benda-Beckmann 2006; Sierra 2008; 2013; Tschalaer 2010; Yüksel 2010). A frequently used strategy with which change proponents aim to raise public awareness about identified problems and to stress the need for reforms is legal mobilisation, the same of which can take various forms: change agents can write down their key demands and make them accessible to a broader public (such as the *Women's Revolutionary Law* of Zapatista women in Chiapas; see Speed, Hernández and Stephen 2006). Agents may also produce radio programmes (Sieder and Macleod 2009; Sieder 2013) or use theatre, storytelling or songs in order to capture the attention of broader audiences (Corradi 2010). Legal mobilisation may be carried out through the monitoring of courts' decision-making, as exemplified by members of the *House of the Indigenous Woman* in Cuetzalan, Mexico (Sierra 2008; 2013; Villa 2012). For many women, their involvement in such legal mobilisation campaigns may imply the spelling out of hitherto silenced or unspoken grievances. By denouncing inequalities, abuse or violence to wider audiences, women gain a public voice and, in the event that their legal mobilisation strategy proves successful, their demands cannot be as easily erased from the local agenda as they might be in the more intimate spheres in which many acts of abuse and violence occur.

To be sure, opponents defending the legal status quo will not remain inactive throughout ongoing change efforts. They may participate with their own arguments in the debates, intend to obstruct reforms or set out to disqualify proposals as illegitimate transplants from external places which go against local cultures and values (Hellum 2013; Richards 2005; Sieder and Macleod 2009; Sierra 2008). Therefore, factors such as the legitimacy of a proposed legal alternative and the justification of the reform by means of a locally understood and accepted language will remain decisive factors throughout the evolution of the change process. Moreover, change promoters may seek to build coalitions with like-minded groups or obtain the support of influential actors who enjoy a less-contested standing before reform opponents. Such external allies can help local agents to persist amidst adverse contexts or offer specific know-how and means deemed necessary to surmount existing difficulties (Hellum 2013; Sieder 2013; Yüksel 2010). In order to expand their bases of support, change agents will need to act in 'multivocal' ways, that is, articulating their claims and proposals in different arenas, including neighbourhoods, legal authorities, community assemblies, NGOs or amongst external supporters, and drawing on distinct 'legal idioms' in order to rationalise and legitimate their efforts and convince the respective audience of their cause (Benda-Beckmann and Benda-Beckmann 2006; Galanter 1981; Merry 2006a; 2006b). Moreover, change agents will need to develop capacities to negotiate and reach agreements with those opposing the reforms (Salgado 2012: 273–274; Sierra 2013: 64; Tschalaer 2010: 52–54). Depending on the viability to turn to agents other than their own (indigenous) legal authorities in a given site of interest, actors may consciously seek redress before such alternative forums (e.g., state courts, religious authorities, mediation centres), be it to obtain more effective resolutions or to put their own communal authorities under pressure to alter their legal practice ('forum shopping'; see Benda-Beckmann 1981; Chenaut 2004; 2007; Corradi 2010; Hellum 2013).

Which results do legal change processes yield?

Anthropologists argue that the outcomes of intentional legal and institutional change efforts at the local level are often complex, contradictory, uneven, and not least limited. Setbacks cannot be ruled out. The repertoire of available legal institutions and norms might become more plural or, to the contrary, tend towards homogenisation. New judicial bodies may become institutionalised; existing bodies may be partly reformed or be assigned new labels; parallel, hybrid or contradictory legal concepts or interpretative schools may be established (Benda-Beckmann and Benda-Beckmann 2006; Cotula and Cissé 2006; Eckert 2009; Tschalaer 2010). Accounts of women's struggles for more gender-balanced community norms and institutions show that such efforts may result in the increased inclusion of women within indigenous legal processes (Hernández and Canessa 2012; Speed *et al.* 2009); the establishment of more culturally appropriate methodologies for existing judicial bodies to attend to indigenous victims of violence (Sieder and Macleod 2009); women's enhanced capacity to use their constitutionally enshrined rights (Hellum 2013; Hellum *et al.* 2013); the appropriation and modification of state-imposed local institutions (Sierra 2008; 2013; Villa 2012); or the creation of new or alternative legal forums (Bourdon 2013; Hellum 2013; Tschalaer 2010).

In addition, legal anthropologists also take a close look at what actors actually 'do' with the new legal provisions or forums so as to assess their degree of acceptance. Thus, they explore whether and how authorities apply new rules, whether people invoke new norms or if there are groups resisting change, for instance by evading new rules and instead opting for non-legal means in order to pursue their interests (Benda-Beckmann and

Benda-Beckmann 2006; Merry 1997; 2003). Scholars are also interested in the consequences of change initiatives for the very agents who actively participated in these efforts. In some places, indigenous women questioning gendered norms and promoting change in their communities have been reported to suffer from unverified but yet harmful rumours, ostracism, and conflicts within their families and neighbourhood as well as physical threats or even sexual harassment. Resistance may also stem from other women of the community who do not share the views of the change-orientated group (Blackwell 2006; Hernández and Canessa 2012; Speed 2008). At the same time, the participation in joint reflections about discriminatory experiences and the articulation of claims in the public sphere may also have an empowering effect on women who assume new roles and responsibility for the development of their community and increase their skills to face up to ongoing and future challenges (Sieder and Macleod 2009; Stephen 2006; Tschalaer 2010). Especially in the realm of gender injustices, authors also caution against judging the 'success' of such local initiatives by parameters provided by universal human rights standards. The outcome of legal change efforts in a society at any given moment of time will much rather reflect the extent to which change agents have thus far been able to bargain reforms with other, more conservative forces advocating for the maintenance of the status quo (Tschalaer 2010; Yüksel 2010).

Social movement theory and the analysis of legal and institutional change

Attempts to change legal institutions and norms in indigenous communities in the Andean highlands, staged by local groups and their allies, can also be looked at through the lens of social movement theory, considering that social movements are commonly understood as an avenue by which social groups give voice to their and others' grievances and strive to change (or defend) political, social, economic, cultural or religious authorities, institutions, policies or practices by engaging in distinct forms of collective action, thereby bearing on the interests of others (Snow, Soule and Kriesi [2004] 2007: 3; Tilly and Tarrow 2007: 4–7). In the case of indigenous women in the rural Andes standing in the focus of the present book, their discontent is directed at local, indigenous authorities who, from the women's perspective, have not addressed the subject of family violence in an appropriate manner, as well as national governments that, despite having committed themselves by means of international conventions and national laws to combat violence, have still not found adequate mechanisms to reach out to this particular sector of their society. Simultaneously, as institutions and norms of indigenous groups reflect unequal gender relations more generally, women's demands transcend the political–legal sphere and impinge upon the normative system guiding social relations, practices, and roles within their respective group.

Theory development in the field of social movements was for a long time nurtured by US and West European examples of large-scale social movements targeting domestic, transnational or international issues (e.g., US civil rights movement; labour movements; anti-nuclear power movements). Even so, scholars admit that small-scale or local movements – often passing unnoticed by the broader society, media, and academics – actually occur much more frequently than the former (Snow, Soule and Kriesi [2004] 2007: 4–5; Tarrow 2005: 23–24). As to the transferability of the concepts and underlying assumptions of social movement theory to Latin America, regional experts recommend we be particularly mindful of the specific historical, socio-political, cultural context and the time in which social movements emerge; the quality of democracy; often unfulfilled citizenship rights and social inequality; the particular constituencies, internal logics, and articulations of movements; and the linkages between particular movements and the State and other relevant actors (Burchardt 2012a; 2012b; Foweraker 1995).

Academic interest in social movements throughout the last third of the twentieth century crystallised into three major theoretical strands: resource mobilisation theory highlighted the organisational capacities, resource availability, and collective coordination of social movements (Gamson 1975; McCarthy and Zald 1973; 1977). Political process theory focused on the critical role of the political setting and actor configurations at a given moment in time (political opportunities), which structured and facilitated or discouraged collective action. This approach also enhanced our knowledge about dynamic and strategic interactions between challengers, their addressees, and third parties, as well as the currently known and available repertoires of contention (or array of means to stage claims) of particular actors that they could draw upon or cultivate throughout phases of social protest (McAdam 1982; Tarrow 1998; Tilly 1978; Tilly and Tarrow 2007). A third strand, in turn, has been dedicated to inquire into the cultural aspects of social movements. This line of enquiry became associated with research on the so-called 'new social movements' concerned with cultural, moral, symbolic, and identity-based targets rather than material or class-based demands (e.g., Castells 1977; Habermas 1981; Melucci 1985; Offe 1985; Touraine 1977).[5] More generally, this strand reflected the adoption of social-constructivist perspectives in the social sciences and paid attention to topics such as agency, discourse, meaning, and emotions. Particularly prominent became the study of 'collective action frames' in which grievances, rationales for action, and solutions were presented in order to attract publicity and motivate adherents (Benford 1987; 1997; Benford and Snow 2000; Jasper 1997; Snow and Benford 1988; Williams and Benford

2000). Given that all three approaches made relevant contributions to the social movement research agenda, there were fruitful attempts over the two past decades to integrate insights into a synthetic approach to social movement theory in which the importance of resources, opportunity, and framing all play a role (McAdam, McCarthy and Zald 1996).

Why do claims for legal change emerge in given sites of interest?

The emergence of social movements and other forms of political conflict were explained by early accounts with reference to structural constraints and the relative deprivation of groups that were disadvantaged within a given polity as well as the resulting breakdown of social control (Davies 1962; Geschwender 1968; Gurr 1970; Smelser 1962).[6] For several decades, these approaches were tightly coupled with the sub-field of collective behaviour in the discipline of sociology, which qualified movements, protests, riots, and other instances of political contention as essentially spontaneous, irrational, and disruptive elements of social life (Blumer 1951). These assumptions became challenged by a new generation of scholars (McAdam 1982; McCarthy and Zald 1973; Skolnick 1969; Tilly 1978) who stressed the need to differentiate between distinct types of collective action (e.g., a social movement as compared with a riot). These authors argued that existing research underestimated the political nature of many instances of collective action and posited that many participants in such joint action would neither act impulsively nor be incapable of strategically devising their actions. Not least, grievances alone could not explain the emergence of movements, as the empirical world was full of examples in which aggrieved groups did not resort to collective action.

Based on these reflections, scholars began to differentiate more carefully between shifts in the broader socio-political and cultural context, which altered or deepened existing cleavage lines, and thus rendered the mobilisation of specific groups more or less likely (thereby responding to the first research question of the present study), and factors that were considered as decisive elements for a successful initiation of mobilisation (thus addressing the second research question of the present study examined in the next sub-section). With regard to the first question, Ruud Koopmanns ([2004] 2007: 22–23) recommended to think of polities as relational fields made up of institutionally and informally sustained hierarchies, cleavage lines, and networks among actors and groups. Accordingly, in times of 'conventional' politics, such relational fields remain relatively stable. There could well be dissidents testing the boundaries of the regime, but these incidences often do not seriously challenge the institutions as such. What may render such sites more vulnerable to change, however, are alterations of the broader social, political, economic or cultural environment, which reduce power disparities among powerful and aggrieved groups (e.g., demographic shifts, economic crises, changes of long-standing and consequential policies). With the cultural context, the author refers to a cultural climate and the consciousness, values, identities, and interests of individuals and groups that are likewise dynamic and may parallel socio-political or economic shifts.

Which factors facilitate or obstruct legal change efforts at the starting point of a change initiative?

While a look at such social, political, economic and cultural shifts helps scholars to identify those groups whose grievances may become particularly salient and who are most likely to raise demands, three sets of factors are considered crucial for translating these grievances into effective social mobilisation. Representatives of Resource Mobilization Theory (Gamson 1975; McCarthy and Zald 1973; 1977) highlighted the role of tangible and intangible resources (time, labour, skills, solidarity, legitimacy, knowledge, status, contacts, technical assistance, facilities, technology, money, etc.)[7] as well as mobilising vehicles through which collective action is organised and coordinated and which may provide access to other resources. Such vehicles may range from formal organisations spearheaded by paid professionals (or movement entrepreneurs) who skilfully devise strategies to speak on behalf of larger aggrieved groups, up to informal groups and social networks, such as religious community groups, friendship ties, neighbourhoods, grassroots groups, with more flexible leadership structures and divisions of labour (Jenkins 1983; McCarthy 1996; Zald and McCarthy 1987). These groups facilitate the entering into contact with others and the provision of information among individuals that would otherwise be unavailable to them (Wiktorowicz 2004: 12–13). Precisely this latter attribution helps explain why organisation matters: according to what social psychologist Lee Ross (1977) called the 'fundamental attribution error', many people tend to attribute their (troublesome) situation to individual characteristics and deficiencies, even if there are sufficient grounds to believe that the actual reasons for the situation reside in external circumstances. This tendency is much more likely to occur if the individuals concerned are isolated and do not belong to some form of social network where perspectives, ideas, and information are exchanged (McAdam, McCarthy and Zald 1996: 9). Some organisations may exist beforehand and evolve into a platform where issues are debated and out of which mobilisation arises. Other organisations may be the result of constraint or of strategic choice (Jenkins 1983). The general assumption is that the disposability of an organisational vehicle and a certain degree of resources enhances the likelihood that collective action will be successfully initiated. Moreover, the amount and range of resources accessible to an emerging movement will also have implications for the pace and scope of mobilisation. Choices made about the organisational form and the goals and types of collective action (which will require the investment and deployment of specific resources) at an initial stage of a movement will imply consequences for the entire mobilisation process (Edwards and McCarthy [2004] 2007; Zald and McCarthy 1987).

Bob Edwards and John McCarthy ([2004] 2007) emphasised that many kinds of resources, such as money, expert knowledge or access to technology, are highly unevenly distributed among 'centres' and 'peripheries' of world regions and within single polities, as well as among and within social groups. Governmental and non-governmental institutions, private corporations or individual supporters may help redirect required resources to enhance the chances of less-privileged or grassroots groups to engage in collective action. The motives behind this engagement vary and may be nurtured by the interest to co-opt or control groups, self-interest, political, religious or ideological commitment, or altruism. Overall, these authors differentiate between five ways by which social movements may acquire resources: resource aggregation (whereby individuals' resources are pooled into collective ones); resource co-optation (permitted borrowing of resources assembled by other movements or groups); resource appropriation (exploiting resources of others without permission); self-production (producing new resources or adding value to existing resources that had been provided, aggregated or co-opted beforehand); or financial patronage (external agents bestow a movement with resources and retain some control over their usage). Social movements regularly draw resources from various sources simultaneously, and the question as to which extent they depend on certain sources and how deeply their emergence and work is constrained by external donors needs to be evaluated empirically.

A second set of variables mediating between grievances and the emergence of mobilisation has been commonly referred to as 'political opportunity structure'. This term was originally coined by Peter Eisinger (1973) who argued that the relationship between political opportunities and collective claim-making would have a curvilinear shape: in a tolerant regime that provided its constituents with ample avenues to take part in official decision-making processes, few citizens would need to shift their claim-making to the streets or other unconventional forms of protest; conversely, in an authoritative regime, no viable means for its constituency to influence political decisions – neither via official avenues nor by protests – were available. Accordingly, protest was most likely to occur in relatively open regimes where citizens were not entitled to channel their demands through officially sanctioned spaces of decision-making, but where they still maintained the ability to articulate their claims by unconventional means (see also Meyer 2004: 128). Broadly defined, 'political opportunities' can be understood as

> consistent – but not necessarily formal or permanent – dimensions of the political struggle that encourage people to engage in contentious politics.
>
> (Tarrow 1998: 19–20)

The concept is typically associated with the organisation of a regime or a single policy domain and includes not only formal institutions and rules regulating decision-making processes and access to the political sphere of interest, but also the positioning of actors within this realm (Kriesi [2004] 2007; Tarrow 1996). Much to the regret of various scholars,[8] movement theorists have not operationalised this concept in a consistent way. The present study cannot pretend to remedy this issue, but it is orientated by those variables on which many theorists agree, not least because these aspects seem to be transferable to local governance systems of Andean indigenous groups. These are:

- the relative openness (or closedness) of a regime for new agents;
- the (in)stability of current political alignments;
- the (un)availability of influential allies or supporters for challengers; and
- the extent to which the regime represses or facilitates collective claim-making.

Shifts in one or several of these aspects of the opportunity structure, such as a realignment of agents, the incoming or loss of an influential ally or the opening of elites towards demands of an aggrieved group, may provide potential challengers with new opportunities or threats and thus facilitate or discourage mobilisation (McAdam 1996; Tarrow 1996; Tilly 2006b). In addition, this opportunity structure is also held to render some strategies for specific challengers more feasible and potentially efficacious than others (Tilly 1978).

To a certain degree, activists also have the capacity to push existing opportunity structures towards greater openness by adding a novel quality to their means of claims-making. Such novelty can consist, for instance, of a redefinition of a collective identity, new actors, tactics organisational forms, demands or interpretive frames (Koopmanns [2004] 2007). Innovations may result out of rapid political and technological change (such as the globalised access to the internet or the television) or be the product of day-to-day experiences of challengers and their tinkering with pre-existing repertoires of contention (Tilly and Tarrow 2007). Thus, next to entirely new schemes created at a given site, many innovations are also diffused through communication channels by which a place or group becomes connected to other national, transnational or international spheres. As Koopmanns ([2004] 2007: 24–27) explained, local actors are not simply passive receivers of such external innovations. Instead, they evaluate their applicability for their own purposes and make their choices based on the perceived similarity of the context as well as the potential success of an innovation, even though such aspects may not always be as easy to determine.

Importantly, opportunities and threats for staging claims are not simply 'out there', but must be perceived and interpreted as such by potential challengers (Gamson and Meyer 1996). Therefore, researchers examine framing processes by which activists bestow relevant events with meaning and provide rationales for action so as to mobilise others to join their collective struggles and to gain support from bystanders or potential allies. According to Robert Benford and David Snow, such 'collective action frames' need to fulfil three core tasks: First, frames should involve a diagnostic dimension that identifies a problem and attributes responsibility for this problem to specific actors or targets. Second, frames have to be prognostic, i.e. offering solutions to the identified problem, including strategies that might help ameliorate injustice. Third, frames require a motivational aspect in order to provide adherents and bystanders with rationales for supporting and engaging in collective action (Benford and Snow 2000; Snow and Benford 1988). Similarly, William Gamson (1992) argued that a frame must include the dimensions of injustice, agency, and identity so as to motivate individuals to take action. Of equal importance is the aspect of resonance: in order for collective action frames to be effective, they need to resonate with potential participants and wider publics. Depending on the degree and type of change proposed by a movement, a frame may remain within the scope of what is considered as legitimate by a society or come close to its boundaries, rendering this latter frame much more difficult to become acceptable to broader audiences. Resonance is a function, among other things, of the intelligibility of the frame, its credibility, and its congruence with peoples' daily experiences and cultural understandings. The group presenting the frame, including its reputation and expertise, will likewise be a decisive factor for a frame's resonance in the targeted public (Benford and Snow 2000; Williams [2004] 2007). Just as is the case with contentious performances, collective action frames can become diffused across social and cultural settings, either via 'strategic selection' (intentional cross-cultural borrowing by the transmitter or the adopter of a frame, which was elaborated elsewhere) or via 'strategic fitting' (intentional tailoring of a frame to a host culture by a transmitter; see Benford and Snow 2000: 627).

Overall, many movement scholars concur that these three sets of variables – resources and mobilising vehicles, political opportunities, and collective action frames – all play a role and are interdependent when it comes to analysing the context that facilitates or curbs collective action. A given opportunity is thus unlikely to be seized unless actors have some form or organisation and resources at their disposal, and unless they are convinced that action is urgently needed and that the proposed action will be potentially efficacious. In the same vein, it is difficult to imagine how collective action frames can emerge and become diffused targeted publics without some organisation where a given situation is collectively discussed and from which a message urging people to join collective action is spread (Koopmanns 1999; McAdam, McCarthy and Zald 1996).

Which factors influence legal change processes throughout their evolution?

Movement scholars maintain that contentious phases of intended transformation (or struggles to maintain a given status quo) unfold amid higher levels of uncertainty compared with more stable periods. Such processes are contingent on dynamic interaction between involved agents and precipitating events (Koopmanns [2004] 2007; Kriesi [2004] 2007). In principle, all previously mentioned aspects – resources, opportunities, collective action frames – will continue playing a relevant role in the interaction among challengers, opponents, and third parties (Benford and Snow 2000; McAdam, McCarthy and Zald 1996). As for mobilising structures, it will no longer be the availability of some form of organisation but much more the organisers' concrete goals, strategies, and tactics that will evoke reactions from the environment and thus shape the transformative process. Quantitative studies comparing various examples of social protest groups in the USA have found, among other things, that movements targeting the outright displacement of an opponent or policy were usually less successful than those with more reform-orientated goals. Of significance was also whether a movement organisation tended towards factionalism or not, as more united groups typically had much better prospects to effectively stage claims than those that were internally divided (Frey, Dietz and Kalof 1992; Gamson 1990). Movement scholars also pay attention to the evolution of the organisational profile alongside intensive periods of mobilisation. Initially less-formalised associations may expand due to successful mobilisation of adherents or professionalise as a result of training and accumulation of experiences; certain organisational structures may facilitate the adoption of new forms of claim-making while discouraging others; and changes in the environment may prompt activists to rethink their organisational practices or their techniques of resource acquisition. In the same vein, scholars are interested in the ways how agents pool and deploy resources for specific strategies and tactics and how they manage to gain new resources (such as new members, expertise, money) or to diversify their resource pool – all of which aspects that will affect the pace and efficacy of collective action (Edwards and McCarthy [2004] 2007; Jenkins 1983).

Shifts in the political opportunity structure remain of equal importance for tracing contentious processes. In this phase, political opportunities will be determined by the ways the movement interacts with its environment, especially with the targeted authorities, emerging countermovements or allies (McAdam, McCarthy and Zald 1996; Tarrow 1996). Activists may be more or less successful in persuading important institutional actors of their cause. Debates on the issues problematised by a movement may generate divisions among ruling elites. A regime's responsiveness may be improved though elections and a new ruling coalition that is more open-minded towards the demands the challengers (Kriesi [2004] 2007; Tarrow 1996). While many scholars turn to classical political analysis in order to shed light in these dynamic processes, others prefer to work on the basis of mechanisms, or 'a delimited class of events that change relations among specified sets of elements in identical or closely similar ways over a variety of situations' (Tilly 2001: 25–26), in order to make such sequences more comparable across a wider spectrum of forms of political contention (revolutions, protest waves, etc.) and to provide causal explanations at the level of sequences of interaction. Combinations of mechanisms typically alter the configuration of actors and thereby affect the further level, form, and consequences of contention. While the present study does not adopt this mechanism-based approach, the identification of a broad range of mechanisms by these authors is highly indicative as to the potential processes we might observe when studying instances of contentious collective action: processes of 'diffusion', for instance, are essential for spreading information from one setting to another. An effective 'brokerage' occurs when previously unconnected sites become linked. 'Coordinated action' is present when two or more separate actors decide to articulate their claims on the same target simultaneously. 'Certification', in turn, refers to the signalling by an external authority of its willingness to recognise the existence of a mobilising group and to support its demands, thereby enhancing the salience of the proffered frame and the credibility of the group. Actors may also withdraw from joint action ('defection'), become incorporated into a centre of authority from which they were previously excluded ('co-optation') or be exposed to 'repression' by authorities (McAdam, Tarrow and Tilly 2001; Tilly and Tarrow 2007).

By the same token, movement scholars want to know what happens to a collective action frame after the successful initiation of mobilisation. Once a frame becomes diffused, a movement can often not control for the ways in which it will be understood by distinct audiences, given that codes, symbols, and concepts may evoke differentiated associations (Williams [2004] 2007: 103). As contention evolves, challengers may feel prompted to modify their frame, for instance, in order to react to specific events, shifts in opportunities, strategies, and contentious performances, to enlarge the resource base or to gain acceptance and raise the interest of specific audiences. Benford and Snow identified four types of modification: 'Frame bridging', with which formerly unconnected frames addressing a particular issue become connected; 'frame amplification', by which existing beliefs are idealised, clarified or invigorated; 'frame extension', whereby a movements' frame is presented as going beyond its genuine interests; and 'frame transformation', by which former interpretations are revised or new meanings are generated (2000: 624–625). The construction of reality is by all measures a conflictive issue, and disagreements may emerge from within a challengers' group (Benford 1993) or from opponents and authorities seeking to undermine a movement's frame ('counterframing', see Benford 1987: 75), eventually leading to 'frame contests' waged in distinct arenas. In case a movement becomes particularly salient, mass media may likewise play a considerable role both in spreading and validating a movement's frame across wider audiences and framing the ongoing political contention by their own analyses and interpretations (Gamson [2004] 2007; Gamson and Wolfsfeld 1993).

Which results do legal change processes yield?

Efforts of collective claim-making can potentially have consequences for many realms of political, economic, social, and cultural life. An early attempt to assess a movement's 'success' or 'failure' was made by Gamson (1975), who offered a typology that focused on two types of outcomes: the recognition of a challenging group as a legitimate actor for the promotion of a particular set of interests, and the gain of new advantages by the group's beneficiaries throughout or after a period of mobilisation. By combining these two dimensions, four possible outcomes were conceivable: full response (in both aspects), pre-emption (opening with respect to the groups' demands), co-optation (of the challenging group), and collapse (failure in both aspects). Subsequent authors attempted to refine this typology, whereas others stressed the methodological problems related to this procedure, for instance, with respect to the difficulty of causal attribution in complex settings with many stakeholders and co-occurring outside influences; the potentially different outcomes as seen from a short-, medium- or long-term perspective; the assumption that mobilising groups are homogenous and that all their constituents pursue the same goal; the fact that movements may alter their goals and promote their agenda over considerable stretches of time; and the problems of contradicting or unintended consequences (Guigni 1998).

Also, movement scholars have evaluated the extent to which challengers were able to achieve their explicitly stated goals or programmes (such as concrete changes in legislation and its implementation). Such results are typically not straightforward, but assessed against a more or less favourable political (sub-national, national, transnational or international) context in which they had been achieved (Amenta and Caren [2004] 2007; Guigni 1998; Tarrow 1998). Partly because it is far more challenging to assess cultural changes compared with policy-based outcomes, and due to distinct conceptualisations of 'culture', much less scholarly attention has been dedicated so far to this field of inquiry. Jennifer Earl's ([2004] 2007) review of studies evaluating the cultural consequences of social movements informs us that authors were interested in such distinct aspects as shifts in public opinion, consciousness, and values; artistic performances and practices; language and discourse; collective identities; or the emergence of sub-cultures. Another understudied topic is the question of how the involvement in a social movement can affect the personal life course and identity of individuals (Benford and Snow 2000; Guigni [2004] 2007). Not least, some scholars have inquired into the consequences of distinct social movements on one another, or else the results of their combined efforts (Tarrow 1998; Whittier [2004] 2007).

New institutionalism and analysis of legal and institutional change

A third body of literature – new institutionalism – can likewise provide some answers to the research questions of this study. Institutionalists tend to define institutions as formal and informal 'rules and procedures that structure social interaction by constraining and enabling actors' behaviour' (Helmke and Levitsky 2006: 5). Institutions are held to reduce uncertainty by creating shared expectations concerning the conduct of others and thus facilitating interaction, cooperation, and the solution of collective action problems (North 1990; 1991), as well as providing social, economic, and political life with elements or order (March and Olsen 1984; Olsen 2009). With regard to the question where the line between formal and informal institutions should be drawn, Gretchen Helmke and Steven Levitsky conceptualise formal institutions as

> rules and procedures that are created, communicated and enforced through channels which are widely accepted as official', and informal institutions as 'socially shared rules, usually unwritten, that are created, communicated and enforced outside officially sanctioned channels.[9]
>
> (2006: 5)

The authors' categorisation of indigenous law in Latin America as an informal – because 'unofficial' – institution,[10] however, seems problematic, particularly if studied as something of the same quality as clientelism, corruption, extrajudicial practices of the police or other sorts of unwritten but commonly followed arrangements within the legislative, executive or judicial branches of the State, the public administration, the electoral system or political parties. As indicated in the introduction of this book, Latin American indigenous peoples had formed their polities and governed themselves according to their own rules and procedures before the foundation of colonial states – a fact that is well documented in rulings of the Spanish Crown and chronicles of that time (Fernández 2000; Yrigoyen 2006). Just as in other societies or polities, indigenous law has adapted to both internal and external developments and exigencies. Where indigenous law survived or was revitalised, it has indeed preserved much of its uncodified character. Although it was assigned an 'unofficial', if not unlawful status by subsequent ruling elites, this has not prevented indigenous peoples from regarding their own legal systems as a legitimate form of self-regulation, not only because of the scant presence and dysfunctional nature of state legal institutions, but also because they considered their own law as a key component to safeguard internal coherence and a scope of autonomy. Lastly, the 'unofficial' quality of indigenous law was put into question by Latin American states themselves, considering the recent tendency to recognise the right of indigenous peoples to practise their own law in various national constitutions. Albeit subject to specified limitations, indigenous law has thereby been converted into something 'legal' from the perspective of the State. Thus, whether indigenous law is qualified as formal–official or informal–unofficial is historically contingent and depends on the perspective from that it is looked at. This critical comment notwithstanding, less doubt should exist about the fact that indigenous law meets the requisites of the abovementioned definition of 'institutions', which, in turn, allows us to review this strand of literature as to its propositions on institutional change.

New institutionalism is not a unified body of research. There are various approaches that, while unanimously ascribing institutions an important role in shaping the political, economic, and social world, cultivate distinctive understandings of institutional development and the nature of human beings who create institutions and whose behaviour is simultaneously constrained by institutional settings.[11] While the 'old institutionalism' in political science is more closely associated with early stages of a rather atheoretical and descriptive analysis of formal government structures, procedures, and rules, 'new institutionalism' emerged in part as a reaction to behaviouralism in which institutions seemed to have lost any relevance to explaining individual or collective action (Lowndes 2002; March and Olsen 1984). From among the distinct new institutionalist approaches, historical institutionalism and sociological institutionalism have the greatest potential to contribute insights to the present inquiry, first, because these approaches' views of the nature of human beings are more compatible with those of legal anthropologists and social movement scholars compared with the picture drawn by rational choice institutionalists, in particular;[12] second, because in recent times these two strands were particularly active in theory development in the realm of institutional change processes; and third, in doing so, these approaches' ideas on how institutions change partly overlap with those elaborated by legal anthropologists and social movement theorists, thus providing a fruitful ground for interdisciplinary dialogue.[13]

Historical institutionalists tend to define institutions as the formal and informal rules, procedures, conventions, and norms that shape human behaviour (Mahoney and Thelen 2010; Steinmo, Thelen and Longstreth 1992). Scholars working in this sub-field depart from a bounded rationality and knowledge of actors (Hay and Wincott 1998; Immergut 1998). In principle, human preferences can oscillate between self-interest and rationality on the one hand and altruism or orientation on collective habits or routines on the other hand. Drawing from empirical evidence and even modern evolutionary theory, some historical institutionalists have come to claim that

> human preferences are not neatly structured and consistent. They are, in fact, complex, multilayered, overlapping, and sometimes competing. For example, individuals face dilemmas, change their minds, and behave inconsistently because they are concerned about both individual and group-oriented utility.
>
> (Lewis and Steinmo 2012: 330; see also Blyth *et al.* 2011)

Historical institutionalism not only posits that agents' interests, ideas, choices, and actions are influenced by the institutional settings in which they are embedded – much more articulately than other schools of thought – it also inquires on how institutions shape relationships between agents, thereby generating power imbalances and consequential distributional effects (Mahoney and Thelen 2010; Thelen 1999). Authors related to this school are often interested in comparing a limited range of units of analysis situated at the national level, such as political regimes, national health care policies, tax systems or unionisation, and explaining why such institutions, starting from their origins, have acquired distinct characteristics or developed according to different patterns over time. Such analyses imply going back in time and tracing institutional development over long periods covering decades or even centuries (Erdmann, Elischer and Stroh 2011; Pierson 2004) – which should make us particularly cautious when assessing the transferability of concepts elaborated by this school to the processes that the present study focuses on. At the same time, the particular orientation of scholars on empirically grounded cases renders their analysis highly sensitive to context and timing. Instead of identifying single independent variables that invariably lead to a certain outcome across a wide array of cases, scholars show how sets of interdependent variables engender certain consequences in a particular place and time (Immergut 1998; Steinmo 2008; Thelen 1999).

Sociological institutionalism, in turn, is rooted in the study of organisations and organisational fields.[14] As early representatives of this approach such as John Meyer and Brian Rowan (1977) argued, many institutional forms and practices, including government agencies and their policies, or firms and their production techniques, were less efficacious than suggested by traditional theories of organisational decision-making; instead, many organisations have assimilated cultural models highly valued or considered as legitimate by their organisational environment. Therefore, this strand has adopted a more extended concept of institutions that includes not only formal norms, rules or practices, but also normative and cognitive frameworks – templates, conventions, scripts – in which formal institutions are embedded. Accordingly, institutions are not only helpful to organise social interaction, but essentially they are also constitutive of actors' ideas and interpretations of themselves, their roles, activities, and the world around them (Clemens and Cook 1999; DiMaggio and Powell 1991; March and Olsen 1989; Scott, Meyer and Boli 1994; Scott 2001). Human beings are conceived of as rule-followers who see and express themselves in socially appropriate ways:

> Behavior is governed by standardized and accepted codes of behavior, prescriptions based on a logic of appropriateness, and a sense of obligations and rights derived from an identity, role, or membership in a political community and the ethos and practices of its institutions.
> (Olsen 2009: 9)

Here, as well, scholars tend to focus on relatively large phenomena, such as corporations, nation-states, international organisations, on horizontal or vertical linkages across organisations at the sub-national, national, transnational, and international level, on convergences and differences between features of organisations (production models, staffing, etc.) or sector policies – for example, educational or pension systems – and often resort to comparative and longitudinal analyses to observe institutional developments over longer periods of time (Schneiberg and Clemens 2006).

Why do claims for legal change emerge in given sites of interest?

Until recently, new institutionalism was criticised for not providing plausible explanations of institutional change, particularly because the very object of study – institutions – was commonly associated with rather stable, isomorphic, and enduring patterns of social life, and because scholars had focused too heavily on the constraining dimension of institutions (Fligstein 2001; Peters 1999). Researchers from the historicist tradition, for instance, have long invoked a 'punctuated equilibrium' model in order to conceptualise institutional development: sudden, brief, and contingent moments of crisis ('critical junctures'), caused by some exogenous 'shock' (war, revolution, economic crisis, etc.) that prompted agents to redesign or change institutions, were followed by relatively stable and lasting periods of a path-dependent institutional development, in which early events and decisions significantly affected its later trajectory (e.g., Collier and Collier 1991; Fligstein 1990; Krasner 1984; Steinmo, Thelen and Longstreth 1992). Such path-dependent patterns, in turn, were sustained by a 'positive feedback' mechanism through which actors gained 'increasing returns' for adapting to and behaving in ways facilitated by an institution (Pierson 2000). To deviate from such a path-dependent logic was regarded as difficult, among other reasons, because agents invested time and other resources to become familiarised with new rules. Once they learned to navigate in a new institutional context, actors would typically hesitate to change it soon again in order to avoid new investments. Change was also difficult to achieve in case institutions yielded continuous benefits for relevant societal sectors or political agents. Not least, there were institutions deliberately designed in a way to principally rule out frequent changes by potential political rivals (Pierson 2000). With time passing, institutions would also affect peoples' preferences and acquire a taken-for-granted quality for those covered by it. Thus, to the degree that an institution became habitual, routine or self-understanding, people would tend to resist any attempt to alter it (Jepperson 1991).

More recently, institutionalists have come to understand the relationship between institutions, agents, and their environment as a more dynamic one, and institutional change is now regarded as a much more common feature of institutional development than assumed earlier, particularly if we take into account small, incremental instances of change during more stable periods of political, economic, social life. Next to shifts in the environment of an institutional setting, authors sought for alternative sources of change and found them in the properties of institutions as well as ideas and perceptions of agents (e.g., Bell 2011; Blyth 2002; Blyth *et al.* 2011; Campbell 2004; Carstensen 2011a; 2011b; Clemens and Cook 1999; Crouch 2007; Lieberman 2002; Mahoney and Thelen 2010; Streek and Thelen 2005). Historical institutionalists continue viewing institutions as political legacies of historical struggles and bargaining processes (Mahoney and Thelen 2010: 6). Furthermore, some sociological institutionalists point to the unequal distributional effects implied by many institutions (e.g., Campbell 2004; 2010; Clemens 1993; Olsen 2009). Both schools of thought emphasise that social cleavages may arise and deepen over time precisely because rules and procedures tend to place some agents in a more advantageous position vis-à-vis others. Those who benefit from and thus have an interest in maintaining existing institutions will need to dispose of enough strength and support by the population covered by this arrangement in order to secure their reproduction. But changing conditions in the environment,[15] as well as effects of the very same institutions in which agents are embedded, may alter power asymmetries and interests of agents within a given polity. Hence, one source that may unsettle the reinforcement of an institutional arrangement is seen in shifts in the balance of power at a given site of interest, leading to the emergence and organisation of new agents who have been marginalised by prevailing rules, or to divided elites where at least one sector alters its preferences towards institutional reform (Mahoney 2000; Mahoney and Thelen 2010; Olsen 2009; Schneiberg and Clemens 2006; Thelen 2003). Time is of utmost importance to historical institutionalists, as preference shifts and the mobilisation of agents require time to mature before becoming salient (Streek and Thelen 2005; Streek 2009).

On the cognitive side of the process, sociological institutionalists stress that existing institutions require a constant reproduction, revalidation, and reaffirmation by the collective in which they are embedded in order to remain a legitimate feature of the general order. But generalised trust in institutions may erode, for instance, because of the emergence of a group promoting critical reflection and scepticism to existing knowledge and demanding change on the basis of new insights that become available to them (Olsen 2009). Such new impulses may originate in the external environment and arrive at a site of interest by means of diffusion. Agents who move between distinct fields (educational, scientific, organisational, etc.) and transpose alternative options to resolve collective problems into a new setting often perform this process (Schneiberg and Clemens 2006). Diffusion may grow out of normative concerns of agents, this is, when agents become convinced of the appropriateness of an external model, or out of a mimetic dynamic, in which agents first observe the performance of a model elsewhere and then decide to take over some key features so as to improve the performance of own institutions. But diffusion may also underlie a coercive logic, for instance, in cases in which external rules are imposed upon a given site by powerful agents (DiMaggio and Powell 1983). Moreover, agents may also push toward the adoption of foreign models in order to prevail in the competition with other sites. In some cases, several of these diffusion mechanisms may operate simultaneously (Campbell 2010). On a broader level, intersubjective exchange of ideas is possible through the capacities of human beings to communicate and learn and to consciously and strategically copy and replicate innovations from other spheres (Lewis and Steinmo 2012).

Another source of change that has been explored by both historical and sociological institutionalists refers to the frictions that may emerge over time within single institutions or between distinct, but connected, institutional patterns (Clemens and Cook 1999; Lieberman 2002). Against an often prevailing picture of internally coherent, complementary, and mutually reinforcing rules and practices that compose and maintain a political or social order, scholars contend that most institutions have been created and adapted in distinct moments of time. Often, rules are implemented with diverse purposes and goals in mind. While some rules are regularly reformulated in order to address new circumstances, others may go unchanged for considerable periods of time and become dysfunctional (Lieberman 2002). In addition, the replication of rules or procedures constitutes an imperfect process with much variation down its historical trajectory, as well, given that the meanings ascribed to an institution may change or be interpreted distinctly, and that the concrete enactment and compliance with rules may vary (Lewis and Steinmo 2012; Mahoney and Thelen 2010). As a result, institutions may show evidence of contradictions, ambiguities or considerable scope of indeterminacy. Agents may experience these features of institutions in moments in which they are exposed to vague or contradictory imperatives for action, or, to the contrary, in circumstances in which the standard operating procedures prove unsatisfactory to resolve existing or emerging problems (Campbell 2010; Olsen 2009; Schneiberg and Clemens 2006). In principle, such tensions may lead to a variety of consequences, such as an enhanced uncertainty and the reduced or instable reproduction of rules, or the emergence of some type of mediating or coping strategy such as the evasion of institutions (Clemens and Cook 1999; Rueschemeyer 2009: ch. XII). But to the degree that such inconsistencies or performance failures also shape agents' convictions about the inappropriateness of rules, these may also lead to claims for change in order to remedy problems and render institutional sets more compatible again. The existence of alternative proposals, including historical local elements or insights on how similar problems were addressed elsewhere, in turn, can facilitate the development of potential solutions (Clemens and Cook 1999; Olsen 2009).

Which factors facilitate or obstruct legal change efforts at the starting point of a change initiative?

The emergence of strong impulses for institutional change does not necessarily imply that such change will indeed take place. Institutionalists point to two interrelated aspects that render the initiation of change processes more or less difficult, and which may also point to the potential scope of change: first, scholars highlight the institutional capacities of change agents, i.e., the degree to which existing institutional arrangements facilitate or place limits on agents' ability to promote change in a given site of interest (Cortell and Peterson 2002). Given that institutional capacities are often unevenly distributed in a political or social field, agents occupying influential positions will have more political weight and possibilities to defend a status quo or to push for reforms than those who remain outside of the institutionalised spheres of decision-making (Carstensen

2011a: 159). Of relevance will also be the question of whether there are external agents who can exert pressure on local rulers, and to which degree local agents are able to forge coalitions with others – defenders or opponents of the status quo (Mahoney and Thelen 2010; Olsen 2009; Rueschemeyer 2009). Where change-orientated actors are confronted with powerful opponents vested with institutional 'veto capabilities' to block change efforts, strategies directed towards a straightforward displacement of rules are likely to have little chance to succeed. Instead, strategies orientated towards a more subtle transformation that leaves the existing rules intact may prove as more promising options (Mahoney and Thelen 2010; Pierson 2004: ch. 5).

Second, even if ideas on how to overcome existing problems are available, change-orientated agents need to dispose of interpretive capacities so as to convince a critical mass of persons of the necessity and appropriateness of this solution for the local context. For Sven Steinmo, ideas constitute

> creative solutions to collective action problems (…) [and] institutional change comes about when powerful actors have the will and ability to change institutions in favour of new ideas. A group or collective may agree that a particular idea is a 'good idea' if they agree that there is a problem that needs solving, and they agree that this idea might actually solve the problem.
>
> (2008: 131)

Sociological institutionalists have likewise moved towards this direction by positing that institutions do not only have a taken-for-granted dimension that limits agents' ability to imagine alternative paths, but that agents also strategically use available institutional elements to pursue their interests (such as promoting change; see Campbell 2004; Clemens and Cook 1999; DiMaggio 1997; Swidler 1986). This proposition is based, among other things, on research conducted within the discipline of psychology where two distinct forms of human cognition were identified: 'automatic cognition' rests upon implicit, unverbalised, and routinised patterns with which much of everyday behaviour can be explained, whereas 'deliberative cognition', based upon explicit, verbalised, and deliberate patterns, enables individuals to step out of their everyday routines and think more critically and reflexively. Importantly, people are more likely to change to this second mode of thought in circumstances in which their attention is deliberately being shifted towards a specific problem; moments in which their dissatisfaction with a status quo is raised or an issue becomes particularly salient; or in cases in which they realise that existing ways to deal with an issue fails to understanding new circumstances (DiMaggio 1997). Based on such findings, scholars started to think of the role of 'institutional entrepreneurs' who dispose of particular skills and resources (know-how, interpersonal networks, etc.) in order to raise awareness on particular problems and place them on the agenda, who exchange and debate their views and ideas with others, who seek for potential solutions of identified problems by revising and discussing available repertories, who push for experimentation with alternatives, and who advocate for change or reform by demonstrating to their addressees the costs of sticking to the status quo while comparing them to the potential benefits of the proposed alternative (Campbell 2004: ch. 3; 2010; Clemens and Cook 1999).[16] In this context, the use of a culturally accepted language and, thus, translation become relevant, as institutional entrepreneurs have to explain emerging issues in a way that corresponds to local experience and at the same time mobilises distinct audiences ('multivocality'), and because new ideas are most likely to be embraced if they are aligned with existing arrangements (Blyth 2002; Campbell 2010; Carstensen 2011a; 2011b; Clemens and Cook 1999):

> When political entrepreneurs seek to transform the overarching institutions of political life, they face particularly high demands to embed calls for change within accepted models. Consequently 'no institution is created de novo' (Riker 1995: 121), and the most ambitious innovators may well cloak their efforts for change in appeals to restore tradition (...). Alternatively, political challengers may mobilize by deploying familiar models of social organization in unfamiliar ways
>
> (Clemens and Cook 1999: 459)

or by casting fairly distinct concepts as more coherent than they actually are (Carstensen 2011a: 156).

Which factors influence legal change processes throughout their evolution?

The institutional literature suggests that deliberately promoted change efforts are often highly contingent and contested. Such processes may involve the emergence of mobilising groups and opponents and be played out within established institutions where agents will try to take advantage of their positions and competencies, but also through extra-institutional channels; sometimes, the distinction between these spheres may become blurred (Schneiberg and Lounsbury 2008). The scope and direction of change will depend on the strategies and choices of the challengers and the reactions or contestation they engender. Overall, transformative processes may involve struggles, the deployment of resources, brokering, and attempts to arrange for some deal or compromise (Bell 2011; Campbell 2010).

Next to the outright displacement of older forms with new arrangements, scholars identified a variety of modes of change: 'layering' refers to the attachment of new rules on top of or alongside existing ones. This may occur, for instance, in circumstances in which change agents either lack the power or the interest to entirely remove older arrangements (Schickler 2001; Streek and Thelen 2005; Thelen 2003). 'Conversion', in turn, describes situations in which rules, while remaining formally untouched, take on new ends or purposes, for instance, because newly incorporated groups in a polity push existing rules towards new directions. 'Drift' is present when a rule's impact changes as a result of shifts in the broader environment (Streek and Thelen 2005; Thelen 2003). But the impact of an existing rule may also change due to a fresh interpretation:

> thoughtful and imaginative reasoning about current and historical experience and the meaning of behavioral codes, causal and normative beliefs, and situations can also generate change – even a re-interpretation of an institution's mission and role in society.
>
> (Olsen 2009: 14)

Change can also be pursued by 'bricolage' – a creative rearrangement of elements that are already at hand, combined with the blending in of new schemes that have diffused from elsewhere (Campbell 1998; 2004; 2005; Carstensen 2011a). Not least, if actors find formal institutions too constraining, they may also develop 'informal coping strategies' that, if they become widespread and enduring, may encourage or leave political decision-makers with no other option than to ultimately reform the formal structures (Tsai 2006). Thus, while some strategies such as bricolage may be deliberately designed to alter existing norms within a foreseeable period of time, thereby reflecting what historical institutionalists continue conceptualising as 'critical junctures',[17] other change patterns such as drift or informal coping strategies may be of incremental nature and hence effectuate outcomes as a cumulative effect of various small steps, decisions or events evolving over longer periods of time (Mahoney and Thelen 2010; Tsai 2006).

Which results do legal change processes yield?

Institutional change efforts are, as institutionalists argue, highly contingent. So are the potential outcomes of such efforts. Given that reforms are often subject to power struggles and negotiations, new rules will not necessarily represent the most effective solution for the underlying problem; quite to the contrary, they may exhibit deficiencies, engender new problems or new and older models may co-exist for extended periods (Campbell 2010; Schneiberg 2005). Such 'imperfections' and 'unintended consequences' of institutional design thus often stand in focus of institutionalists' inquiries: Paul Pierson (2004: 118–122) points to the multiple interests and motivations present in often heterogeneous institutional design coalitions, which may become reflected in the outcome of joint change efforts. Of relevance may also be the fact that the planning horizon of designers is incongruent with the time required to make an innovation fully practicable. We might observe a generational turnover of responsible actors, all of whom with potentially distinct interests in mind. Furthermore, actors will typically have a limited foresight of potential effects of institutional innovations. Thus, after first experiences and lessons learned with the performance of an innovation, people may correct or eliminate those elements that have proven unnecessary or dysfunctional. Other institutionalists emphasise that even if models developed elsewhere become adopted in a new setting, their concrete shape, implementation, and performance is likely to vary from the original model, among other reasons, because people will develop their own preferences and understandings about the new rules and because these will have to be incorporated in and interact with other, pre-existing institutions and practices (Lewis and Steinmo 2012). Equally important, institutional development may be adversely affected by factors stemming from the broader social environment. Scholars also suggest that changes be evaluated against the broader institutional setting, given that some innovations may ultimately turn out to be 'cosmetic' if other, more fundamental features remain unchallenged (Shepsle 2001). Other scholars remain attentive to the ways how new institutions reconfigure the fundaments for social cleavages or lines of conflict. Institutional transformation may lead to the emergence of opponents, or people adversely affected by the new rules, who will form alliances or engage in strategies designed to subvert or evade new rules. Alternatively, the accommodation of opposed interests or the co-optation of potential critics may become a major source of institutional stability (Rueschemeyer 2009).

Many sociological institutionalists, therefore, are concerned with the degree to which new institutional forms become accepted and considered as legitimate over time. In this regard, scholars propose to assess, for instance, the degree to which there exists clarity and agreement about the functioning and contents of new rules, the degree to which people come to share explanations and justifications about the new rules, and the degree to which people agree on the way how authority and resources related to the new rules should be allocated (Olsen 2009). Others concentrate on whether new institutions engender public criticism, controversies, and acts of resistance or norm deviation – which would rather point to a low degree of public acceptance of reforms – whereas the cessation of debates and rule-conform behaviour would rather foreshadow a high level of acceptance and, over the longer term, the institutionalisation of a changed institution (Schneiberg and Clemens 2006).

Table 2.1 Overview of three approaches and their conceptualisations of legal change processes

Research question	*Legal anthropology*	*Social movement theory*	*New institutionalism (historical and sociological variants)*
Why do claims for legal change emerge?	Diffusion of legal alternatives by agents linking distinct normative orders Legal contradictions and alternatives may challenge the exclusiveness of prevailing norms and catalyse reflections on local injustices Changes in power relations may prepare the ground for legal and institutional reforms	Shifts in the socio-economic and cultural environment alter or deepen existing cleavage lines or grievances of specific groups Alteration of power disparities between powerful and aggrieved groups	Changes in power relations Trust in existing institutions erodes because: • new ideas or models to resolve collective problems diffuse into a site of interest • contradictions within or between institutions arise • existing institutions seem ill-prepared to address pressing problems
Which factors facilitate/ obstruct legal change processes at the beginning?	Change proposals may affect local power relationships and privileges Standing of the promoters of change in the targeted group Perceived legitimacy of a proposed change, which depends on its linkage to local understandings, interests and needs Capacity of change promoters to appropriate and vernacularise external concepts	Existence of organisational vehicle(s) and availability of tangible and intangible resources More or less facilitative political opportunities Capacity of change promoters to construct a collective action frame that resonates with potential adherents and wider publics	Institutional capacities of change agents, constraining their room for manoeuvre or providing certain avenues for action Option of alliance-building with others Interpretive capacities of institutional entrepreneurs (translation, multivocality)

Table 2.1 Continued.

Research question	*Legal anthropology*	*Social movement theory*	*New institutionalism (historical and sociological variants)*
Which factors affect change processes throughout their evolution?	Dynamic, lengthy, contested interactions between change promoters and others defending the status quo Strategies of change agents: • legal mobilisation • gain public voice • defending or adjusting vernacularised ideas • coalition building • gain support from influential allies • multivocality • involvement, bargaining, agreements with opponents • forum shopping	Dynamic and highly contingent interaction between challengers, addressees of claims, opponents and third parties Strategic use of resources and mobilising vehicle(s) in order to meet a movement's goals, strategies and tactics; evolution of the organisational vehicle and resource base Shifts in political opportunities Eventual modification of initial collective action frames; change agents capacity to deal with contested interpretation of frames, the emergence of counterframes or frame contests	Contingent nature of reform efforts, pursued within or outside established institutional channels, often involving contestation, deployment of resources, brokering, arrangements or compromises between involved agents Modes of change: • displacement • layering • conversion • drift • re-interpretation • bricolage • informal coping strategies
Which results can legal change processes yield?	Uneven, contradictory, limited results; setbacks Homogenisation versus pluralisation of local legal repertoires Degree to which locals apply changed norms or institutions Effects on change agents' lives	Degree to which goals targeted by a movement were achieved Impacts on culture Personal and identity-based consequences Consequences of social movements for one another	Imperfect, ineffective, deficient outcomes Unintended consequences of institutional design Degree of acceptance and legitimacy of new rules; contestation versus accommodation of critics

Source: Own elaboration.

Towards an interdisciplinary conceptual approach to legal change

How should we deal with the results of this literature review? One option would be to exclusively concentrate on the legal anthropologist literature, particularly because of its closeness to the dynamics of interest for this book, i.e., locally situated processes of change within indigenous groups in the context of settings marked by legal pluralism. In contrast to legal anthropological accounts, studies about social movements, and even more so institutionalist inquiries, are typically concerned with larger phenomena at the national, transnational and international level, which occur throughout extended periods of time. An alternative option, however, would be to take advantage of the striking similarities regarding various variables and patterns highlighted by the three revised strands (see Table 2.1) and to elaborate an interdisciplinary framework on normative and institutional change, which is potentially more comprehensive than a single theory strand. Indeed, there are many aspects of change processes on which the three approaches converge:

With regard to the *first research question* (on aspects engendering claims for change), all three theory strands point to shifts in power relations between more and less powerful groups as one potential source for the emergence of claims for change. By the same token, legal anthropologists and institutionalists share a concern for the diffusion of new ideas from elsewhere by which peoples' awareness of problematic norms and institutional designs may be raised and where these may lose their taken-for-grantedness or legitimacy.

As for the *second research question* (inquiring about factors facilitating or obstructing change initiatives at their starting point), all three approaches put emphasis on processes of translation of external ideas into a locally appropriate and resonant vocabulary and the 'persuasion work' done by purposeful change agents so as to convince wider sectors of the urgency and legitimacy of their claims. All strands inquire into the degree to which change agents face obstacles or avenues posed by current power-holders and institutionalised ways of decision-making. Social movement scholars tend to include the aspect of coalition-building or the forging of alliances with influential agents within their concept of 'political opportunities', whereas institutionalists and legal anthropologists treat this aspect either as an important additional variable next to the 'institutional capacities' of change agents, or as a strategy to promote change, respectively. Researchers from all approaches remain attentive to the dynamic nature of such political opportunities throughout all stages of an observed process.

As concerns the *third research question* (exploring variables influencing the further course of reform efforts), all three bodies of literature agree in that change processes evolve in highly contingent ways. Given that claims for change often impinge on the interests or privileges of others, change processes will typically involve instances of contestation and resistance, the experimentation with distinct strategies and tactics, and episodes of bargaining or compromise. Throughout such processes, change agents will often have to move between various institutional levels or spaces and present their demands and proposals in differing 'idioms' in order to attract the interest or support from different audiences or potential allies.

With respect to the fourth *research question* (addressing the potential results legal and institutional change efforts), all research perspectives stress the broad spectrum of potential outcomes, which change efforts may yield. Next to evaluating the degree to which the targeted change has actually been achieved, legal anthropologists' interest in whether and how new rules are applied by authorities and ordinary people parallels the inquiry of institutionalists as to the degree to which changed rules become accepted or remain contested over time.

Where one approach offers insights not considered by the other perspectives, in turn, it may provide important complements or correctives that should be taken into account in the study of legal change:

- In addition to the diffusion of external ideas, institutionalists have identified other sources for an increased erosion of trust in existing institutions, namely tensions emerging within or among distinct but interrelated institutional sets and the ill-preparedness of rules to solve emerging problems.
- The concept of 'resources' elaborated by movement scholars entails not only aspects such as discursive skills, know-how, and network ties held by challengers, but also pays attention to the existence of an organisational platform and other material and financial resources, which can play a decisive role for the design of strategies and tactics as well as the actual scope, efficacy, and sustainability of change efforts.
- Because legal anthropologists are typically more familiarised with lived realities of indigenous peoples, they can provide us with fundamental insights to processes of appropriation or contestation of ideas travelling from elsewhere to local sites, to prevailing power asymmetries and the role of women within indigenous systems of governance, and the specific difficulties these women encounter in their attempts to gain public voice and to develop such a purposeful institutional 'entrepreneurship' as suggested by the other theory strands.
- Institutionalists highlight the various ways in which institutional change may crystallise, including bricolage, re-interpretation, layering, and other forms. The usefulness of these schemes to exploring concrete patterns of change in indigenous legal systems cannot be rejected from the outset and may prove helpful to compare them against the modes of change found to be at play in indigenous communities.

- The institutionalist literature also makes us aware of the unintended consequences of institutional change efforts and points to the many variables of a local setting and the broader environment that may interfere between a purposefully designed reform or change of rules and the actual outcomes of such efforts.

Given the plausibility of the propositions and the similarities between some variables regarded as relevant by all three perspectives, and considering that some scholars have themselves already engaged in a selective borrowing of concepts from the other research traditions (e.g., Campbell 2005; Davis *et al.* 2005; Schneiberg and Lounsbury 2008), the conceptual approach of the present study to explore change processes in indigenous communities and municipalities in the Andes should likewise be informed by all three here examined theory strands, while adjusting the variables and indicators to the context of Andean indigenous localities and the area of domestic violence.

Table 2.2 Research question 1: Why do claims for legal change emerge in a given site of interest?

Variables	*Indicators*
Shifts in local power relations	• Reduction of power disparities between groups advantaged and disadvantaged by the existing institutional setting • Divisions among authorities and/or influential community groups
Diffusion of new legal ideas or models	• New state legislation requires or enables the reform of existing institutions or the implementation of new institutions at the local level • External agents introduce new legal concepts to the community • Community members bring new ideas in from external settings
Inappropriateness of existing norms or institutions to resolve cases of domestic violence	• No rules, procedures, sanctions to deal with domestic violence exist • Existing rules, procedures, sanctions are perceived as inappropriate to resolve cases of domestic violence
Incompatibility between norms or institution addressing domestic violence and other institutions	• Perceived contradictions between community rules/institutions dealing with domestic violence and national or international rights • Perceived tensions between community rules/institutions dealing with domestic violence and other community rules/institutions

Source: Own elaboration.

Table 2.3 Research question 2: Which factors initially facilitate or obstruct legal change efforts?

Variables	*Indicators*
Political opportunities	• Relative openness or intolerance for change-orientated collective action by local authorities and decision-making forums • (In)stability of political alignments among authorities and influential groups from which change agents benefit • (Un)availability of allies or supporters of change-orientated group
Frame for collective action	• Change agents' capacity to construct a shared understanding of the targeted problem • Change agents' capacity to develop a potential solution addressing the targeted problem • Assessment of potential benefits and risks of change-orientated action by change-orientated agents • Degree of resonance of the targeted problem, the solution addressing the problem and benefits of proposed solution among targeted population
Mobilising vehicle and other resources	• (Un)availability of mobilising vehicle(s) (e.g., organisation) • (Un)availability of immaterial resources (e.g., skills, experience, time) • (Un)availability of material resources (e.g., facilities, money)

Source: Own elaboration.

In terms of the first research question, the underlying assumption is that claims for change of indigenous community norms and institutions dealing with domestic violence will be more likely to emerge if:

- shifts occur in local power relations from which change-minded groups benefit; and
- if local institutions lose their taken-for-grantedness (a) because new legal models or ideas diffuse into the community, (b) because pressing problems cannot be satisfactorily addressed by existing community norms, or (c) because community norms dealing with domestic violence enter into conflict with other community institutions or national or international norms.

With regard to the second research question, the underlying assumption is that change-minded agents will be more likely to engage in efforts to change community norms related to domestic violence if:

- shifts in political opportunities open avenues for change-orientated actors to promote their claims in the public sphere;

Table 2.4 Research question 3: Which factors affect legal change efforts throughout their evolution?

Variables	*Indicators*
Target of change, strategies, tactics	• Concrete object of change (norm; institution) and eventual changes of thereof throughout the process • General approach chosen to achieve the targeted change and eventual changes thereof throughout the process • Use of known and innovative forms of collective action directed towards the achievement of the targeted change • Eventual adjustments of initial frame for action
Shifts in political opportunities	• Changes in openness or intolerance of communal decision-making forums for change-orientated collective action • Changes in (in)stability of political alignments among authorities and influential groups • Changes in (un)availability of allies or supporters of change-orientated group
Shifts in the availability and deployment of mobilising vehicle and other resources	• Changes in (un)availability and deployment of mobilising vehicle(s) • Changes in (un)availability and deployment of immaterial resources • Changes in (un)availability and deployment of material resources

Source: Own elaboration.

- change agents establish a shared and resonating interpretive frame for the targeted change that includes a concise solution for the problem and which presents the benefits of this solution as more salient than the potential risks; and
- if change agents have an organisational platform and a minimum of material and non-material resources at their disposal, which enable them to initiate activities for change.

With regard to the third research question, the underlying assumption is that collective efforts towards institutional change will evolve in dynamic and highly contingent ways. The concrete direction, scope, and efficacy of the change initiative will be influenced by:

- actors' goals, strategies, and tactics and later adjustments thereof;
- shifts in political opportunities; and
- change in agents' disposability and use of material and immaterial resources.

Table 2.5 Research question 4: Which results can legal change efforts yield within a short time frame?

Variables	*Indicators*
Achievement of targeted change	• Existence of a changed norm and/or institution • Character of the changed norm and/or institution • (Co-)existence of former or alternative institutions regulating the same realm • Unintended consequences
Enforcement of changed norm or institution	• Degree to which local authorities apply the changed norm/institution • Degree to which the local population invokes the changed norm/institution • Degree to which alternative norms, institutions or strategies are applied by authorities and the local population
Sustainability of changed norm or institution	• Aspects of the broader environment increasing the likelihood that the changed norm/institution will be maintained or strengthened over the medium term • Aspects of the broader environment increasing the likelihood that the changed norm/institution will be abandoned or weakened over the medium term

Source: Own elaboration.

The reviewed literature suggests that intended legal and institutional changes typically take a considerable time to become palpable, and that highly contradictory results, serious setbacks or strong resistance may be just as likely to occur as some kind of 'success'. Considering the relatively short time frames within which the *initiatives* of the present study have evolved, and the equally short period within which fieldwork in the selected locations was carried out, the assessment of the consequences of the *change initiatives* shall remain limited to the most visible and direct achievements as observable towards the end of the research period (2012). If reformed norms or institutions were in place, I was interested in the degree to which these were actually enforced and applied. In addition, indicators in the broader environment that pointed to a more or less sustainable development of the reforms were likewise taken into consideration.

Notes

1 For a brief review of legal anthropological studies of the twentieth century, see Starr and Collier 1987.

2 One opponent of this view is Simon Roberts 1979; 1998.

3 To name but a few examples of this strand of literature, see Benda-Beckmann, Benda-Beckmann and Griffiths 2005; 2009; Cowan, Dembour and Wilson 2001; Goodale 2002; Merry 2006a; Wilson and Mitchell 2003; Woodman, Wanitzek and Sippel 2004.

4 Recent examples for a changing state courts' interpretation of Muslim family law in India and South Africa were analysed by Subramanian 2008 and Reutenbach 2010, respectively.

5 For an overview of the new social movement literature see Steven Buechler 1995. Many contemporary social movements of Latin America, however, were found to transcend the dichotomy of political and identity-based claims; see Alvarez, Dagnino, and Escobar 1998; Escobar and Alvarez 1992; Jelin 1990; Motta 2009.

6 This paragraph summarises the comprehensive review of breakdown and strain theories of Steven Buechler [2004] 2007.

7 Social movement theorists have offered distinct classifications of resources. Cress and Snow 1996, for instance, developed a four-fold typology of moral, material, informational, and human resources. Edwards and McCarthy [2004] 2007, in turn, distinguish between moral, cultural, social-organisational, human, and material resources. On earlier attempts to classify resources, see Jenkins 1983.

8 See Gamson and Meyer 1996; Goodwin and Jasper 1999; Kriesi 2007 [2004]; McAdam 1996; Meyer 2004. Ruud Koopmanns 1999, by contrast, contends that due to the variety of political regimes, social movements, and their interrelations, a uniform conceptualisation of political opportunities would be rather unrewarding. She therefore advocates for a more flexible and context-sensitive use of this concept.

9 Helmke and Levitsky (2006: 5) identify at least three ways of conceptualising informal institutions in the existing literature: informal institutions are (1) treated broadly as culture; (2) understood as norms and organisations constituting civil society, as opposed to formal, state-controlled rules; or (3) conceived of as self-reinforcing patterns vis-à-vis formal rules which are enforced by a third party.

10 See also Lauth's (2000: 40–43) discussion of 'custom law'.

11 Hall and Taylor (1996) identify three institutionalist approaches: rational choice, historical, and sociological institutionalism. Peters (1999) and Lowndes (2002) speak of seven strains of new institutionalism, among them normative, rational choice, historical, empirical, international, sociological, and network institutionalism. Because representatives of distinct institutionalist approaches have ever more engaged with the search for endogenous sources for change and focused on the role of ideas, Schmidt (2008; 2010) has posited the emergence of a new discursive institutionalism.

12 Rational choice institutionalism in political science draws heavily on institutional economics where human beings are conceptualised as rational and strategic individualists whose interests are relatively static and exogenously given and who follow rules because, in so doing, they can maximise their personal gains. According to this school, the creation of institutions occurs on the basis of voluntary agreements among relatively equal agents who dispose of all information required to correctly foresee the effects of the institutions they create. Institutions, in this view, constitute coordinating mechanisms that sustain equilibria from which no agent has an incentive to depart. Correctives or changes are most likely to occur though mechanisms such as competition and learning; see, for example, Shepsle 1989; Williamson 1993. Hall and

Taylor (1996: 950–952) qualified this approaches' assumptions as simplistic, as these miss the fact that motives for action are more multifaceted, ambiguous, and also endogenously determined. A more realistic picture of the world would include human fallibility and a higher sensitivity to power imbalances among actors. Some representatives of this approach have distanced themselves from overtly narrow assumptions on human preferences and resorted to emotionally, culturally, normatively, ideologically filtered perceptions and ideas in order to shed light on the constrains that affect human ability to design functional, optimal, or effective institutional outcomes; see, for example, Elster 1998; 2000; Garret and Weingast 1993; North 2005; Weingast 2005.

13 With regard to the new discursive institutionalism, the first distinguishable conceptual contours have been developed by Vivien Schmidt (2008; 2010). The main factors held to explain institutional continuity or change are seen in agents' 'foreground discursive abilities' (enabling agents to deliberate about rules and persuade others to maintain or reform them) and 'background discursive abilities' (allowing agents to make sense of their institutional setting; Schmidt 2008: 314). Given that such an approach would miss much of the material constraints and the unequal positioning of Andean indigenous women vis-à-vis their male counterparts in social, economic, and political life, which arguably have a severe impact on their ability to 'speak' and to gain 'voice' in the public sphere, approaches that adopt a more comprehensive view by integrating both structure *and* agency (including discursive action based on ideas) into their analyses of change – as historical and sociological institutionalism have strived to do in recent times – seem more promising for the present study than the discursive institutionalist account.

14 Organisational fields are made up of groups of organisations engaged in common activities. Some authors such as John Campbell (2004) therefore opt to term this approach 'organisational sociology'.

15 Changes in the environment do not necessarily imply those far-reaching 'shocks' envisioned by earlier institutionalist accounts, but may well refer to non-crisis events or processes such as demographic shifts, changes in the labour market, elections, the adoption of a new legislation, etc.; see Cortell and Peterson 2002; Harty 2005.

16 Constructivist theories within the field of International Relations make a parallel argument on 'norm entrepreneurs' who, based on some kind of organisational platforms, skilfully advocate for the adoption of socially appropriate norms at the domestic and international level. Shifts in ideas and normative conventions of agents are seen as a key factor for normative transformation in the realm of international politics; see, for instance, Finnemore and Sikkink 1998.

17 Capoccia and Kelemen (2007) refine historical conceptualisations of critical junctures (e.g., Krasner 1984) by defining them as 'relatively *short periods of time during which there is a* substantially *heightened probability that agents' choices will affect the outcome of interest*' (ibid. 348). They ask scholars to remain cautious as to their concrete unit of analysis, given that what might constitute a critical juncture for a single institution does not necessarily constitute a critical juncture for entire institutional systems and the other way round. They clarify that during critical junctures agents act more freely and that the impact of choices taken during critical junctures is typically larger compared with 'normal times'. In comparison to gradual modes of change where small and cumulative causes ultimately lead to a threshold at which a considerable institutional change is particularly likely to occur, critical junctures are rather

preceded by short-term causes. Lastly, they also summon us to not presuppose that critical junctures will necessarily lead to change: '*Tempting as it may be to equate critical junctures and change, this view is not commensurable with the emphasis on structural fluidity and heightened contingency that are the defining traits of critical junctures*' (ibid. 352).

Chapter 3

'Many women hadn't even thought about what it means to be a woman'

La Calera and La Rinconada, Ecuador

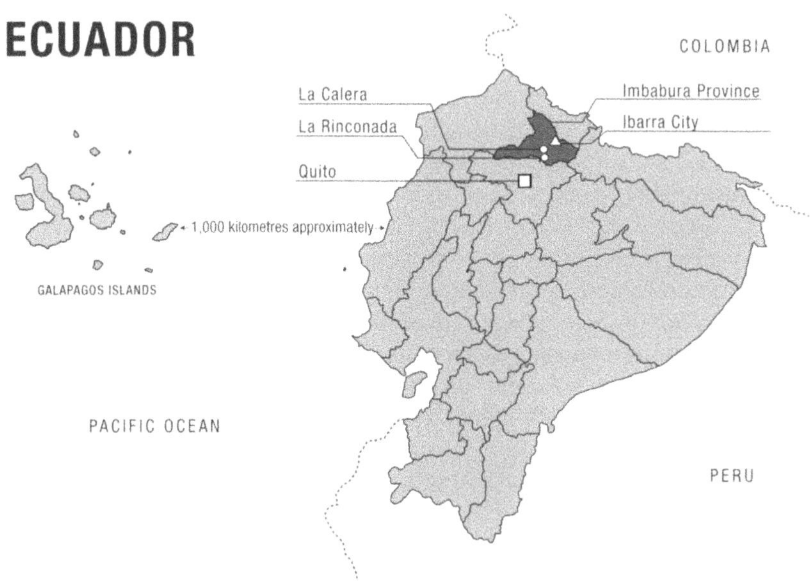

Map 3.1 Ecuador

Around 14,483,499 persons lived in Ecuador in 2010.[1] This country is smaller, and at the same time more densely populated than Peru and Bolivia,[2] especially with regard to the Pacific Coast (which accounted for 52 per cent of the Ecuadorian population in 2010) and the Andean highlands (resided by 43 per cent of Ecuadorians). The Amazon constitutes the largest part of the Ecuadorian territory, but only 5.1 per cent of the overall population resided there in 2010. According to the National Census of 2010, 7 per cent or 1,018,176 people self-identified as indigenous[3] (vis-à-vis a mestizo majority of 71.9 per cent or 10,417,299 people, 7.2 per cent or 1,041,559 Afro-Ecuadorians, 7.4 per cent or 1,070,728 Montubios[4] and 6.1

per cent or 882,383 whites).[5] While this Census confirmed the trend of the previous 2001 Census (which estimated that 6.8 per cent of Ecuadorians were indigenous), the results stood in contrast to other estimations such as 25–35 per cent (Barié 2003: 306; Van Cott 2005: 101). Such discrepancies can be partly explained by the way questions are asked during the censuses, the continued stigmatisation of indigenous people by the dominant mestizo culture and the increased migration of indigenous people from rural communities to urban centres where some of them have tended to adapt to lifestyles commonly associated with mestizos.[6] Representing about 70 per cent of Ecuador's indigenous population, the Kichwa, who pertain to the ethno-linguistic Quechua population, which stretches all over the Latin American Andes (Clark and Becker 2007: 10), were the largest of the 13 officially recognised indigenous 'nationalities'.[7] Organised in sub-groups (*pueblos*) with strong local identities, the Kichwa resided across all provinces of the Ecuadorian Sierra and also constituted the largest indigenous group of the Amazon.[8] Of the 398,244 residents of Imbabura, the region in which the two communities studied in this chapter were located, 25.8 per cent self-identified as indigenous in the 2010 Census.[9]

A considerable proportion of today's indigenous population residing in the rural areas of the Ecuadorian highlands lives in small administrative units called *comuna*. The conversion of previous autochthonous communities into these standardised units was facilitated by the 1937 Law of Organization and Regime of Comunas (*Ley de Organización y Régimen de Comunas*) and later promoted through incentives such as the improved access to land titles, schools, credits and two agrarian reforms (1964, 1973; see Llasag 2012b: 104–112; Van Cott 2005: 103; Yashar 2005: 90-95).[10] *Comunas* regulate themselves on the basis of written statutes and a community council (*cabildo*) consisting of five individuals (and substitutes) elected once a year by all adult commoners; issues of major importance are commonly dealt with by a community assembly. Formally, the Ecuadorian Ministry of Agriculture has the oversight of the *comunas*: it administers the registration process, approves the *comunas*' internal statutes, and maintains the option to veto *cabildo* elections. Administratively, the *comunas* are grouped within rural and urban parishes. Given the traditionally scant presence of the State in rural areas, *comunas* have offered a legally sanctioned space to maintain a degree of autonomy and self-determined development, which includes the administration of justice (Llasag 2012b: 104; Yashar 2005: 89–90).

Recognition of legal pluralism

Against the background of a regional wave of multicultural constitutionalism (Assies, van der Haar and Hoekma 2000; Sieder 2002a; Van Cott 2000a), the increased mobilisation capacity of Ecuadorian indigenous organisations such as CONAIE (*Confederación de Nacionalidades Indígenas del Ecuador*;

Confederation of Indigenous Nationalities of Ecuador), with the *National Indigenous Uprising* (May-June 1990) representing a powerful national wake-up call in this regard,[11] and amidst a general political–economic crisis, a new Ecuadorian Constitution was adopted in 1998, wherein indigenous representatives had been able to inscribe many of their demands: For the first time in the national history, the *pluricultural* and *multiethnic* nature of the State (art. 1) as well as collective rights of indigenous peoples (and Afro-Ecuadorians) referring, among others, to their identity, lands, forms of organisation, bilingual education, health, ancestral knowledge and intellectual property were recognised (art. 83–85). The Magna Carta guaranteed indigenous authorities the right to exercise legal functions, the same of which should be 'harmonised' with the state jurisdiction (art. 191). In the same year, Ecuador's government also signed ILO C 169 within which indigenous peoples' rights to administer justice was equally stipulated.[12]

While the implementation of these norms would have presupposed the development of statutory laws and constitutional jurisprudence, the lack of political will and expertise within all branches of the State (Grijalva 2011: 97–98), disunity on key issues within the indigenous movement (Van Cott 2002: 61–67) and a prolonged governability crisis that led to the irregular removal of four of nine presidents between 1997 and 2005 (Clark and Becker 2007: 1), were among the reasons why no palpable progress was achieved in this regard.[13] Consequently, legal uncertainty, conflicts over competences between indigenous and state legal operators leading to the violation of the principle *ne bis in idem* and the usurpation of indigenous legal competences by non-authorised agents, characterised the legal landscape after the adoption of the new constitution (Grijalva 2011: 98; Poveda 2009; Simon 2009; 2012).

With President Rafael Correa's taking of office in 2006, a new constituent assembly (2007–2008) set out to reformulate the State's foundations. Even though indigenous peoples' representation in this assembly was relatively low, their collective rights were reaffirmed and even extended (García 2011: 47–48; Grijalva 2011: 101–105; Schilling-Vacaflor and Kuppe 2012: 355–356): The 2008 Ecuadorian Constitution, approved by a 63.93 per cent majority in a referendum in September 2008, stipulated the *plurinational* and *intercultural* nature of the State (art. 1), declared the promotion of a sustainable and redistributive development to achieve the *Sumak Kawsay* (Good Living) as one of the State's obligations (art. 3 no 5), and introduced constitutional innovations such as the rights of nature (art. 71–74). An ample range of rights of indigenous peoples, Afro-Ecuadorians and Montubios was enshrined in art. 56–60; as for indigenous justice, the Constitution ruled the following:

> Indigenous comunas, communities, peoples and nationalities have the right [...] to create, develop, apply and practice their own or

> consuetudinary law, which cannot violate constitutional rights, in particular those of women, boys, girls and adolescents.
>
> (art. 57 no 10)

> The authorities of indigenous communities, peoples and nationalities exert jurisdictional functions on the basis of their ancestral traditions and their own law within their territories, guaranteeing women's participation and decision-making. The authorities apply their own norms and procedures in order to resolve their internal conflicts; these should neither be contrary to the Constitution nor human rights recognised in international instruments. The State guarantees that decisions emanating from an indigenous jurisdiction be respected by public institutions and authorities. These decisions shall be subject to control of constitutionality. A law will establish mechanisms of coordination and cooperation between indigenous and ordinary jurisdictions.
>
> (art. 171)

> Nobody shall be judged more than one time for the same cause or material issue. Cases resolved by the indigenous jurisdiction shall be considered in this respect.
>
> (art. 76 no 7 i; author's translation)

While these constitutional norms doubtlessly strengthened the rights of women and their participation in indigenous legal processes,[14] the fact that indigenous law was deemed applicable to 'internal conflicts' raised concerns, as it remained unclear to which kind of conflicts and addressees the term referred. In the same vein, a clear delimitation of indigenous 'territories' proved particularly complicated given that many areas were inhabited by ethnically mixed populations, and considering the pending task of creating indigenous territorial circumscriptions (a figure incorporated in art. 60 and 275 of this constitution; see Barrera 2012: 375–376; Grijalva 2011: 105–107; Simon 2012).

After its adoption, several efforts were made to concretise some norms of the 2008 Constitution: First, the new Law on the Judicial Branch (2009)[15] established a set of principles defining intercultural justice in cases where indigenous individuals were involved in state judicial processes. The Law on Jurisdictional Guarantees and Constitutional Control (2009)[16], in turn, introduced the 'extraordinary action of protection' by which individuals or groups could appeal against rulings emanating from indigenous legal authorities if they believed that their constitutional rights had been violated. Despite its shortcomings (limited time frame for taking action, potentially long distance to the appellative body – the Constitutional Court situated in the capital Quito), this instrument still provided significant progress in terms of the justiciability of constitutionally guaranteed rights (Barrera 2012: 379–382; García 2011: 48). Second, with the participation of former indigenous judge Nina Pacari, the Constitutional Court made initial steps towards an innovative intercultural interpretation on several issues brought forward by indigenous claimants (García 2011: 48–49; Santos 2010: 86). However, a later resolution ruling that crimes affecting the lives of indigenous community members would not fall into indigenous authorities' jurisdiction, has raised the criticism of indigenous leaders (El Universo 01.08.2014). Third, new drafts of a coordination and cooperation law between indigenous and state justice systems were developed by distinct agents and submitted to the National Assembly in 2010 and 2011, but no further advances have been achieved in this regard thus far (Vintimilla 2012), thereby reflecting a worsening relationship between the indigenous movement and President Correa (re-elected in 2009 and 2013), whose *Citizens' Revolution*, combining an economic model based on extractive industries with redistributive programmes,[17] was carried out without due consideration of indigenous peoples' rights.[18]

Legislation on violence against indigenous women

Ecuador ratified the international pacts on civil, political, economic, social and cultural human rights, which enshrine the principles of equality and non-discrimination.[19] The country also ratified the CEDAW (in 1981) and the Convention of Belém do Pará (in 1995). As a consequence, the right to freedom from violence was protected in the 1998 Constitution (esp. art. 23 no 2) and the recent 2008 Constitution (esp. art. 66 no 3 a, b). Its most visible legal instrument to prevent, reduce and sanction violence against women was Law 103 on Violence against Women and the Family (*Ley 103 Contra la Violencia a la Mujer y la Familia*; in force since 11.12.1995).[20] This law defined psychological, physical and sexual violence, determined the scope of potential aggressors (family members until the second degree of kinship, (ex)spouses, (ex)partners, others who lived in the home of the victims) and shifted jurisdictional competence for domestic violence to the *Comisarías de la Mujer y la Familia* (Women's and Family Offices) and family courts for minor offences (or police stations and political lieutenants in case the former were not available), and penal courts for more severe cases of violence. During the juridical process, the integrity of victims could be secured by a restricting order banning the aggressor from coming into contact with the victim or approaching their home, or similar protective measures. Depending on the type of violence committed and the concrete number of days for which the victim remained unable to work (evaluated by a doctor), the sanctions envisioned by this law involved monetary or material compensations (or community works in case the aggressor had insufficient economic resources)or a certain amount of days of imprisonment. The generally ascertained weaknesses of Law 103 included the insufficient human and financial resources provided for the *Comisarias* and other legal operators, lacking knowledge about relevant international and national norms among legal operators, the heavy workload of courts and their ineffectiveness in investigating and sentencing violence,[21] the concentration of legal institutions in urban centres and the insensitivity of existing instruments to the economic, social and cultural contexts of women (Ernst 2007; Franco and González 2009: 39–40; Salgado 2000).

More recent measures addressing gender violence included the Plan of Equal Opportunities 2005–2009 (CONAMU 2005) and the National Plan to Eradicate Gender Violence 2007 (Presidente Constitucional de la República 2007), the latter of which focused, among other things, on a public campaign addressing gender stereotypes, a better articulation among all institutions attending victims of violence (in form of centres of integral attention of violence) and an improved registration of cases of violence. But despite some advances in the implementation of this Plan, including the fact it was better funded than any previous measure addressing gender violence in this country,[22] the prevalence of violence remained high: according to the 2011 National Survey of Family Relations and Gender Violence Against Women, 48.7 per cent Ecuadorian women above the age of 15 have suffered from psychological, physical, sexual or patrimonial[23] violence exerted by current or former intimate partners throughout their life course. With 59.3 per cent, indigenous women were disproportionally affected by any of the abovementioned forms of violence practised by (ex-)partners compared with 55.3 per cent Afro-Ecuadorian, 48 per cent Montubio, 47.5 per cent mestiza and 43.2 per cent white women. The most frequent form of violence exerted by (ex-)partners against women in Ecuador was psychological in nature (43.4 per cent), followed by 35.0 per cent physical, 14.5 per cent sexual and 10.7 per cent patrimonial forms of violence (INEC 2011a).

With regard to violence in the Imbabura Province, where two communities analysed in this chapter were located, the overall rate of

Table 3.1 Violence against women in Ecuador (2011)*

	Psychological violence by (ex-)intimate partner (in %)	*Physical violence by (ex-) intimate partner (in %)*	*Sexual violence by (ex-) intimate partner (in %)*
Nationwide	43.4	35.0	14.5
Imbabura	45.1	37.1	13.1

Source: Adapted from Encuesta de Violencia de Género; see INEC 2011a, 2011b.

* This survey was conducted in 18,800 households; in each household, one randomly selected woman above the age of 15 participated in the study.

(psychological, physical, sexual and patrimonial) violence experienced by women on part of their current or former intimate partners was 51 per cent. Here, 45.1 per cent women were affected by psychological, 37.1 per cent by physical, 13.1 per cent by sexual and 11.4 per cent by patrimonial forms of violence exerted by former and current intimate partners. Unfortunately, ethnically disaggregated data for the province level was not provided in this survey (INEC 2011b).

La Calera – Cotacachi Canton (2004–2012)

La Calera is a small Andean community pertaining to the canton Cotacachi in the Imbabura Province. The canton is located in the northern part of the Ecuadorian Sierra; about 120 km or a 2.5 hour bus drive along the Pan-American Highway separate this place from the capital Quito. The canton is divided into three parts – the town of Cotacachi with a predominantly white–mestizo population and some indigenous residents; the Andean zone surrounding the scenic Cotacachi Volcano where the majority of the indigenous population lives in over 43 communities (or *comunas*), including La Calera; and the subtropical Intag zone at the western foothills of the *Cordillera de los Andes* inhabited by mestizos and a smaller group of Afro-Ecuadorians. The altitudes of the canton vary accordingly between 4,939 m.a.s.l. (Cotacachi Volcano) and 1,600 m.a.s.l. in the Intag zone, which joins

Image 3.1 Volcano scenery between the Cotacachi and the Otavalo cantons

into the northern coastal area of Ecuador. Combined with the non-delimited zone of Las Golondrinas at the western extreme of the canton, the territorial extension of Cotacachi amounts to 1,800 km^2 approximately (Gobierno Municipal de Santa Ana de Cotacachi 2011: 2, 29, 38; UNORCAC 2006: 8). According to the 2010 Census, the canton was resided by 40,036 inhabitants, 53.5 per cent of whom self-identified as mestizos, 40.6 per cent as indigenous (mostly Kichwas), 2.8 per cent as Afro-descendents, 2.5 per cent as whites and 0.5 per cent as Montubios.[24] Administratively, the canton was divided into ten parishes, eight of which were registered as rural and two others as urban. La Calera represented the most populated highland community of the urban parish San Francisco and was situated a few kilometres from the urban centre of Cotacachi.[25] An unpaved, north-bound road connected this community with the town, and its residents either walked by foot (about 45 minutes), took the school bus, or a taxi in order to reach the centre of Cotacachi. By 2006, La Calera had around 1,174 inhabitants and 223 families (*hogares*), from which we could conclude that a family unit was typically made up of five persons. Of these families, 86.6 per cent self-identified as indigenous and 13.4 per cent as mestizos. Around 18 per cent of female and 13 per cent of male residents were illiterate, whereas the overall illiteracy rate in the highland communities stood on average at 25.5 per cent for women and at 17.6 per cent for men. Among the reasons for the lower literacy rates in La Calera was the relative proximity of various educational institutions based in Cotacachi town (in addition to a community-based elementary school) and the fact that a considerable number of adults – men and women – had attended primary school (277 men and 281 women), and a lower number of them also secondary school (66 men and 55 women; see UNORCAC 2006: 15–22, 48). Extreme poverty (as measured by two or more unsatisfied basic needs in terms of safe housing, economic dependency, education and health) was reduced from 68.5 per cent (2001) to 48.9 per cent (2010) among the entire rural population of the canton; still these rates stood in stark contrast to the town of Cotacachi, where only 14.6 per cent in 2001 and 6.5 per cent in 2010 found themselves in a similar situation.[26] Therefore, in addition to cultivating their small land parcels in the community (with products such as corn, potato, wheat, barley, beans and quinoa), many male residents complemented the family income by accepting work in large agricultural farms or as masons in cities such as Otavalo, Ibarra or Quito; some men engaged in commerce. Many of such jobs implied the temporary migration of male residents during labour days and their returning to the community on a daily or weekly basis. Women in La Calera were involved in agriculture and took care of the animals. Some of them earned money as domestic workers or in the service sector of restaurants and hostels in the centre of Cotacachi. A handful of women obtained jobs in public institutions such as the local office of National Institute for the Child and the Family (INNFA) where they took care of pre-school children. Finally, a small group of women was engaged in the production of handicrafts and textiles.[27] Most of these sources of income were neither easily accessible, nor permanent, nor well-paid, which explains why 70 per cent of indigenous residents of the canton were beneficiaries of the cash transfer programme *Bono de Desarrollo*, and 10.1 per cent of the *Bono de Vivienda* at the end of the 2000s.[28] People in La Calera had access to a hospital and university-trained doctors, as well as a traditional health service centre situated in Cotacachi town (Gobierno Municipal de Cotacachi 2011: 14–16; UNORCAC 2008: 88–91). Child mortality in the canton accounted for 35 per 1,000 children born alive (UNORCAC 2008: 87), and significant progress was made in terms of the provision of the indigenous population with water piped directly into houses (60.8 per cent in 2009 compared against 21.9 per cent in 2001) and permanent electricity (95.4 per cent in 2009 compared against 74.8 per cent in 2001; see Ortiz 2011: 221).

Cotacachi gained prominence not only because some of its inhabitants eventually came to occupy important positions in national organisations or public institutions, with many of them gathering their first experience in leadership positions of the Union of Peasant and Indigenous Organisations of Cotacachi (*Unión de Organizaciones Campesinas e Indígenas de Cotacachi*, UNORCAC), which was founded in the late 1970s and which is an affiliate

Image 3.2 Two former indigenous promoters of the Centre of Integral Attention for Women and the Family

of the left-wing National Federation of Peasant, Indigenous and Black Organizations (FENOCIN; see Cameron 2010; Lalander 2010; Ortiz 2011; UNORCAC 2008; Van Cott 2008). Internationally, this place has also become known for its innovative model of local participatory democracy, introduced by Cotacachi's first indigenous mayor Auki Tituaña in 1996 (Cameron 2010; Lalander 2010; Van Cott 2008). At the heart of this model stood the annual Assembly of the Canton Unity of Cotacachi (*Asamblea de Unidad Cantonal de Cotacachi*, AUCC), a citizens' forum to discuss local development issues and propose resolutions to guide the upcoming municipal policies. The Assembly was complemented by a permanent Council of Development and Management overseeing five committees, which met throughout the year to monitor the implementation of the decisions taken in the Assembly. Indeed, the *change initiative* that stands at the centre of this chapter has constituted a direct, albeit little explored consequence of the opening of spaces for citizen's participation.

Why did claims for legal change emerge in La Calera?

Shifts in local power relations

Beginning in the 1980s, women from La Calera gradually achieved an alteration of existing power asymmetries between women and men through their enhanced participation in community and cantonal affairs. With regard to the community, an annually elected council (*cabildo*; comprising a president, a vice-president, a syndic – assisting the president with legal issues, a treasurer – and a secretary) was responsible for the administration and external representation of the community. Traditionally, public affairs were understood as male realm, which is why a woman was hardly ever elected for a position of the *cabildo* in the general assembly, which was convened towards the end of each year. However, with a growing number of men accepting jobs outside of the community, these became ever less able to fulfil the tasks implied by authority positions. In La Calera, community authorities did not meet at a regular date; instead, they were expected to be available at any time in order to immediately respond to the commoners' requests and resolve conflicts at the very moment of their occurrence. Thus, women who used to stay in the community to take care of the children, the household, the fields and the animals, came to understand that they themselves would have to take on more responsibility in community affairs. Consequently, they became ever more present in collective works (*mingas*), and some of them accepted positions as treasurers and secretaries of the community council. Once these women gained confidence and experience in these positions, they also became eligible for more responsible positions such as the syndic and vice-president throughout the 1990s. Lastly, La Calera was the first highland community in Cotacachi to elect a female community president by the end of the 1990s, the same of whom was re-elected several times.[29]

These women also gained confidence in their capacities because of their parallel engagement in the activities of UNORCAC. The more this organisation succeeded in raising funds for local projects in realms such as health, education and agricultural development, the more women became involved in these projects, not least because they had considerable knowledge of these issues. Still, compared with women, male UNORCAC members much more self-assuredly raised their voices in debates and decision-making processes of the organisation. Therefore, beyond the creation of a women's secretariat in the1980s (which was held in the beginning by a woman from La Calera), women sought to gain an autonomous space within the organisation that would allow them exchange views and experiences and collectively search for proposals and strategies to improve their political, economic and social situation. The result of these efforts was the establishment of the Central Women's Committee of UNORCAC (*Comité Central de Mujeres de UNORCAC*, CWC) in the first half of the 1990s, headed by an executive committee elected for three years, and constituted by women's groups at the community level. The executive committee met regularly with the presidents of the community groups to plan and evaluate activities. Meanwhile, these group presidents reported and discussed issues dealt with during the CWC meetings with their respective local groups and also channelled concerns from the local towards the executive level. Initially, women used this organisational space to work on their self-esteem that they felt posed a huge obstacle to stepping outside of their socially accepted scope of activities and becoming engaged in community affairs. Later on, women more willingly accepted active roles in the planning and realisation of development projects (under the umbrella of UNORCAC) and encouraged other women from their communities to becoming engaged, as well. At the time of the author's fieldwork in Ecuador (October-December 2011), the CWC comprised 29 community-based groups, each of which including 15-25 women.[30]

The CWC was strengthened by the participatory municipal governance model introduced by Cotacachi's mayor Auki Tituaña in 1996, whom would also win two subsequent elections in 2000 and 2004, respectively.[31] The incipient participation of several representatives of the CWC from La Calera and other communities in the AUCC became much more numerous after one female leader from La Calera was elected in 2000 as the first female indigenous municipal councillor for the Pachakutik Plurinational Unity Movement – New Country (MUPP-NP), which was also the mayor's political vehicle. She was able to establish a strategic alliance with other female councillors and organised the first female panel at the 5th Annual Assembly of the AUCC (October 2000). The impulses emanating from this canton-wide and mixed women's panel, which became institutionalised throughout the following decade, added to the empowerment of indigenous women and, thus, to the exceptional success of the here-reviewed case:[32] At this platform, female councillors sat together with representatives from the CWC, women from the urban centre of Cotacachi (grouped since 2001 in the Coordinating Group of Urban Women, *Coordinadora de Mujeres Urbanas*) and women from Intag and Manduriacos[33], who later would likewise form their respective coordinating vehicles. Considering the diverse realities, views and experiences of indigenous, mestizo and Afro-Ecuadorian women, it was not easy to find points in common and consent on issues to be converted into concrete proposals in order to submit them for approval by the Assembly.[34] Among the subjects discussed and agreed upon during the first annual meetings was the lack of female leadership and political participation. From the view of urban and mestizo women, too few women showed an interest in public affairs and made use of their right to participate in the political sphere. Indigenous women's weakness resided not so much in their lacking engagement in public affairs, but rather in their limited political, legal and administrative know-how and, partly, in their illiteracy, all of which prevented them from effectively assuming leadership roles in the *cabildos*, the CWC, UNORCAC and the AUCC.[35] These discussions resulted in the securing of a minimum of three seats for female representatives within the Council of Development and Management of the AUCC (Van Cott 2008: 140) and the contracting of an indigenous permanent staff member charged with strengthening the organisational capacities of women in the canton. From 2004 onwards, this person organised leadership schools for women:

> In these trainings, we have worked a lot on the conceptualisation of being a woman. Three dimensions were touched upon: being a woman as a person, as I myself; a woman in the community, in the neighbourhood; and a woman as a political person. (…) You touch upon topics such as patriarchalism, capitalism and some development models. (…) We worked on these issues and gave them some instruments with which they eventually could step out of this—. There are many women who just started–, I mean, they hadn't even thought about what it means to be a woman. So we are working with them so that they step out into their community and from the community to the political sphere, the public sphere. (…) We ask how they can become politically active from their very homes, their own spaces, towards the public space. And we try to achieve that the compañeras don't simply participate in the trainings, but that they also take action – even though this is very complicated.
> (Interview 04.11.2011)[36]

Indigenous women participating in these spaces became familiarised with women's rights and began to 'translate' selected pieces of national legislation to their own context. For instance, becoming aware of the Ecuadorian Quota Law designed to guarantee determined percentages for female participation in political elections,[37] these women analysed their representation in the *cabildos* and the executive committee of UNORCAC, which claimed to represent *all* members of highland communities of the canton. While half of community members were female, many authority positions in the councils and the UNORCAC executive committee had thus far been occupied by men, prompting these women to demand a quota for female representation in these bodies. This was met with success: UNORCAC's executive committee gradually opened for more female representatives in positions reserved for delegates from the highland parishes and positions related to health and nutrition, woman and family, as well as children and adolescents;[38] also, a growing number of women came to be elected in the community councils, until reaching an impressive 48 per cent of participation in 2008.[39]

A last point of concern for the female panel throughout the first half of the 2000s was domestic violence. All panel members had either experienced violence themselves or knew of victims of violence in their immediate environment. Connecting to the global campaign against gender violence, they organised local awareness-raising activities on violence from 25 November (International Day for the Elimination of Violence against Women) to 10 December (International Human Rights Day) in 2002 and replicated this campaign throughout the following years. Moreover, they invited experts on this issue in order to inform themselves about Law 103 on Violence against Women and the Family and the respective state mechanism to sanction violence (*Comisaría de la Mujer y la Familia*), one of which had been established in the relatively nearby town of Otavalo in 1998. While agreeing on the need to establish a similar instance in Cotacachi, indigenous women held that its purpose would have to be extended from the denouncing and sanctioning of violent acts to a more integral accompaniment of entire families, and that the proceeding of such an institution would have to be sensitive for the needs of indigenous women and take into account the presence of the community-based indigenous legal authorities – a proposal which was met with approval by the other women of the panel. The Coordinating Group of Urban Women elaborated a proposal and solicited financial and infrastructural support from the CONAMU (National Women's Council) and the municipal government so as to establish a Centre of Integral Attention for Women and the Family (CIAWF; *Centro de Atención Integral a la Mujer y la Familia*) in Cotacachi. Due to a positive work relationship between the panel and mayor Tituaña, these efforts proved fruitful and the Centre opened its doors in December 2004. Meanwhile, members of the CWC, including some women from La Calera, helped to design an intercultural work methodology for this Centre, and some CWC members would regularly engage as interns in the institution after its inauguration. In addition to three mestizo professionals (a coordinator, a lawyer and a psychologist), two indigenous women (one of them the former female president from La Calera), were hired as promoters to establish close ties with victims of violence and legal authorities from the canton's indigenous communities. As this Centre would soon convert into a major site from which change claims would be staged, the year 2004 can be regarded as the starting point of the here analysed *change initiative*.[40]

Incompatibilities among institutional sets relevant for women's lives

Even though this empowerment process of women from La Calera (and other indigenous communities) might seem straightforward at first sight, it must be stressed that women faced considerable resistance while gradually expanding their scope for action. It is precisely these frictions between realms in which women made some progress, on the one hand, and spheres in which seemingly no change has occurred on the other hand, that made women even more aware of the importance of their demands with respect to an improved legal treatment of gender violence. Over the past decades women's school attendance improved considerably compared with the schooling of the generation of their mothers. Out of pure necessity, many women have also looked for their own sources of income so as to contribute to the maintenance of their families. Due to increased male labour migration, women have also taken on more responsibility in community affairs and *mingas* so as to safeguard the local order and social coherence. They gained organisational spaces and participated in projects designed to improve their living conditions. In the associational spaces at canton level, they became familiar with constitutional rights such as freedom from violence and recent national legislation on women's political participation. However, they simultaneously found that at home and in their neighbourhood, this increased engagement in areas which previously had not pertained to their realm of responsibilities was not necessarily appreciated, and at times resisted. First, there were still a considerable number of women in La Calera who did not follow their example and did not engage in community affairs or participate in any of the three local women's groups in La Calera affiliated with the CWC, either because these felt that women should limit their interests to the wellbeing of their family and agricultural production, or because they did not feel strong enough to face the resistance of their partners or families.[41] Second, partners of active women were highly suspicious of their growing participation in public spaces. Not only did they regularly reproach their wives about their neglect of the household, they also accused women of seeking to contact other men while participating in their organisation's meetings. Despite being elected as CWC president and even for municipal councillor, one woman still had to hide most of her activities from her husband:

> I wanted to participate, but my husband would not let me. Therefore I had to do things behind his back. Based on this I said: "This has to change. It shouldn't be like this". (...) And when I engaged in this [position], again my husband did not allow me. He said: "Why are you going there? What are you able to do at all? If you go there you will just sit there with your mouth open". Or when I tried to leave, he said: "Take your animals with you! Just walk there with your pigs! And you should take the hens with you, too!"(...) We continued in this struggle. But all of us engaged women, we always encountered this problem with our spouses: "Why? Are you meeting with your lover?" I have always faced these kinds of accusations.
>
> (Interview 1–27.10.2011)

Third, many women were still expected to accomplish all their traditionally assigned roles in the household, and if they did not meet these expectations, then they would face severe psychological pressure and physical violence:

> Unfortunately, within the community, a woman from her very childhood, from her mother's belly, was taught by her mother that she belongs to the house. We had to remain in the house. We had to become mothers and spouses and serve the husband; we had to work at the field, in the house, but not go outside, much less work and earn money outside. With the passing of time some things have changed, some more liberal ideas entered into the society because of studies, education, migration – some things have recently become different for women. But when I was growing up, they told us that a woman has to be in the house. If she would go out, smile, say 'hello' - immediately they would think you had a lover. Thus you either married or at least accepted this person as your boyfriend. (...) When I came to participate in the *cabildo* in 1999, 2000, I opened my mind a little bit. But then I married, and although I was able to express myself, to talk, it was difficult with my husband. I was there only to serve him; independent of the fact that I was working, I could not find the means to defend myself from him. I was always afraid - more than anything else. It was the husband who decided how things should be. So I had to respect whatever he told me, even though I was working and wished to be more independent, I had to obey him and do what he told me. (...) What I lived through with my husband was much worse than [what I experienced] at my parents' house. Because if I would not clean up the entire house with the brush, he would hit me, kick me, give me a clout. "Why don't you obey?" If he went to work and returned home, and I hadn't finished doing something, he would say: "Why isn't this finished? What have you done all the time, you slug? You went out with your lover! You went out just because you felt like it, slug! It's me who

> is earning our income. So what have you done?" In this sense, looking at all this from today, it was psychologically very difficult. He had a girlfriend, then another girlfriend, he walked alone, leaving me and my son alone. And I returned from work to serve him, washing clothes, preparing the meal.
>
> (Interview 26./27.10.2011)

These contradictions were felt more intensively once women from La Calera engaged in the newly created CIAWF, given that here they were supposed to accompany and give advice to other battered women. They tried to gradually reduce these internal contradictions by introducing small changes within their families, be it by extended and regular dialogue with their husbands in which they tried to explain their standpoints, by communicating what they did when they were working in order to reduce their spouses' suspicions, and by signalling their strong will to continue with the projects designed to improve the communal wellbeing. Women also tried to avoid reproducing traditional gender roles whilst educating their children, for instance by asking their sons to accomplish some 'typically female' tasks in the household. Needless to say, in these attempts women also suffered serious setbacks and encountered resistance within their own and their husband's families.[42]

Inappropriate resolution of cases of domestic violence by existing institutions

In order to seek redress for domestic violence, a first instance to which women could turn to were the witnesses to a marriage (*padrinos de matrimonio, compadres*) and other close kin members, such as the parents or the siblings. This kin intervention was based on intimate conversations between the persons involved and the giving of advice. The effectiveness of this conflict resolution was highly dependent upon the attitudes and skills of the consulting persons, but also on the authority they had with the aggressor.[43]

While being elected authorities of the community council, women also became familiarised with the community statute and written regulations of La Calera. These documents had been formulated several decades ago and had never been formally updated, among other reasons, because this would have implied a lengthy and bureaucratic process at the Ministry of Agriculture in Quito. According to this statute, the *cabildo*, or in more severe cases the general assembly, could legally process cases such as animal theft or territorial disputes among neighbours, but it remained silent as to cases of family violence. Therefore, council members' reactions to women soliciting their intervention in cases of domestic violence depended very much on their own attitudes and relations to the affected parties to the case. Some council members tolerated minor acts of violence or argued that they would have no means of intervening in such conflicts precisely because they lacked a written justification that would allow them to act. In such cases, battered women were sent back home without receiving any sort of support or protective measure. Other council members did intervene, but had difficulties in remaining neutral because of their close relationship as friends, neighbours or kin members either to the victim or to the perpetrator of violent acts. Others, in turn, would invite the couple to a conversation to jointly seek for the underlying problems that had ultimately resulted in violence. They tried to achieve agreements that usually included the aggressor's apology and his pledge to refrain from violence in the future. The first violent act thus remained unsanctioned, but aggressors were warned that recidivism would no longer remain unpunished. Recurrent cases could, for example, be punished by a physical sanction or the forwarding of the case to the police. When one female leader from La Calera, together with another woman from a neighbouring community, were hired as promoters by the CIAWF in 2005, they found that the indigenous authorities from other highland communities – with which they were supposed to coordinate cases of violence occurring within their jurisdiction – neither disposed of more effective means nor the willingness to really support the resolution of such cases.[44]

Indigenous women's access to the state justice system, in turn, was complicated, as well: Many women were not familiarised with Law 103, and even though the indigenous promoters of the CIAWF were able to explain to indigenous victims the contents of this legislation and the legal process that would follow a formal accusation in their native language, these women did not understand why the processes were so lengthy and why they would have to repeatedly give their testimonies before numerous authorities, including lawyers, police, hospital, attorney and court. For them, the walk to the CIAWF in the town of Cotacachi – often amidst a very critical situation, and sometimes with clear markers of physical violence visible for the public – had already cost them all their willpower and courage. Indigenous women also felt that the mechanisms proposed by Law 103 were one-sidedly focused on denouncing and sanctioning perpetrators, without duly taking into account the background and underlying problems of the family. In addition, the sole response of the state justice to severe cases of violence was the sending of the perpetrator to prison for a given number of days or weeks. As provision of food, clean clothes, soap and other items to inmates in the prisons of the region was essentially non-existent, battered women themselves had to spend money to travel and to look after their spouses. Imprisonment also implied the temporary loss of an income, which meant that the family would actually enter into uncertain financial straits. Besides, having a husband in prison was often punished by ostracism from the own family and community. And after a man's release from prison, women feared acts of vengeance or the continuation of violence against them, as no protective measures or family assistance were made available by Law 103.[45]

Diffusion of new legal concepts

After CIAWF's operation in Cotacachi for over a year, its staff organised a meeting in January 2006 and invited local politicians, legal operators, health and educative staff of the canton, the donors of the project and representatives of other women's rights institutions based in Quito, in order to report about the first results and impact of the Centre's work, but also to discuss the obstacles of indigenous women to access justice. In 2005 the CIAWF attended more than 352 people (98 from the parish San Francisco, including 19 from La Calera), with more than half of them self-identifying as indigenous.[46] The staff explained to the audience the specific difficulties indigenous women encountered when seeking justice before their own and the state judicial systems, and added that even if an indigenous woman decided to denounce a violent act before the state justice system, she would most probably withdraw her accusation soon afterwards. As a consequence, female indigenous leaders regarded Law 103 as an urban-mestizo law with no practical relevance for indigenous women's lives. While listening to this account, a representative of UNIFEM (United Nations Development Fund for Women) invited to the meeting was reminded of very similar problems which women from the Chiapas Region in Mexico had encountered. She had worked for a period in Chiapas and briefly mentioned in the discussion in Cotacachi the *Revolutionary Law of Women*, which had been elaborated by women in Chiapas more than ten years ago.[47] The indigenous promoters from the Centre became curious to learn more about this experience and invited this representative for a second visit in which she presented this *initiative* in more detail. The promoters were fascinated by the fact that indigenous women in a remote country were facing very comparable problems in terms of the failure of their own authorities to deal with domestic violence. They felt frustrated by the mechanisms provided by the State, and just like women in Chiapas, they held that more effective means to combat violence had to be sought primarily within their own legal systems. They invited the representative of UNIFEM to a third meeting, this time jointly with the CWC as the representative body for all highland women. During these talks, the idea of elaborating a 'law' on domestic violence in a participative process amongst women from indigenous communities and afterwards promoting its implementation in the communities and before the UNORCAC took shape. They agreed that the Centre's staff would take on the task of formulating a concrete proposal and searching for funds to realise the *change initiative*, whereas the CWC wished to be informed on the advances of these efforts and promised to support the elaboration of this document.[48]

Which factors facilitated or obstructed the initiation of legal change efforts in La Calera?

Interpretive frame providing justification for change-orientated action

Given the change agents' decision to elaborate the draft law among indigenous women from the highland communities (before advocating for its implementation before other audiences), it were first and foremost the CWC members who had to be convinced of the urgency and adequacy of the proposed *change initiative*. In meetings between the CIAWF, the CWC and also the AUCC member responsible for women's empowerment, in the first half of 2006, the participants realised that consensus existed as to the interpretation of the concrete problem they wished to address: indigenous women's hampered access to community and state legal systems when facing violence. Less unity, in turn, existed with respect to the concrete process of elaborating the draft law: The solution proposed by the CIAWF staff was to select five representative pilot communities in the Andean zone[49] where workshops with indigenous women would be held in order to encourage them to unveil and share their experiences about family violence. In a second step, the same groups of women would be asked to reflect upon legal procedures and sanctions to be taken by community-based legal authorities that would have the potential to re-establish the victims' dignity and provide a just solution vis-à-vis the harm caused. These proposals would afterwards be systematised in a document named *Law for good living together* (*Reglamento para la Buena Convivencia*, Kichwa: *Sumak Kawsaipa Katikamachik*) and presented for its discussion and approval at the directives of the CWC and UNORCAC. Once the document was endorsed by these two instances, change agents would advocate for the adoption of this Law at the community level.[50] One objection raised against this procedure was that even though many aspects of indigenous justice practised at community level seemed comparable, a considerable diversity of norms, rules, procedures and sanctions still existed among the communities. If the draft law was overtly specific about procedures, the risk existed that not all community authorities would identify with and be willing to follow all these elements. Some argued that instead of conducting the *initiative* in five pilot communities, it might be more appropriate for each community to draft its own document, thereby guaranteeing greater acceptance of the law by authorities and commoners. Besides, some reckoned that the name 'law' was commonly associated with lengthy paragraphs and regulations, whereas indigenous authorities would typically not read through long texts while resolving cases.[51] The proponents of the *initiative* responded that it was not viable to carry out such a process in all 43 highland communities considering the time required and the scarce human and financial resources they had at their disposal. In addition, they feared the *initiative* might lose strength if local female groups had to struggle separately from one another in order to implement their respective laws in their communities. They agreed in that this law should be written in a comprehensive manner. In their view, the document was intended to provide legal authorities with some guiding elements they could use in case they were approached by victims of domestic violence. But if authorities felt that other measures would better fit into their administration of justice, they would be free to adapt this document to their own practices. The main message this law should convey was that domestic violence was no longer tolerated and that it deserved thorough consideration by indigenous authorities. Lastly, despite the articulated problems with the proposed Law, and particularly considering the ineffectiveness of existing mechanisms to combat violence, CWC members came to the conclusion that the *initiative* was worth trying.[52]

Political opportunities at the starting point of the legal change efforts

The promoters of the CIAWF presented the *initiative* in assemblies held with the *cabildos* and community members in the five pre-selected communities. In one of these, Topo Grande, authorities were opposed to the *initiative* and would not even let the promoters explain their request in detail, thus prompting the *initiative's* organisers to look for another community in the same parish which was more receptive to their idea (Yambaburo). In La Calera and the other pilot communities, by contrast, community authorities responded positively to their requests. Given women's relative organisational strength and effective participation in community affairs in La Calera over the past two decades, and considering that one of the *initiative's* promoters was a former community president, it was not difficult to seek for the approval of current authorities to conduct activities related to the *change initiative* in this community. Many women from La Calera likewise signalled their interest in the workshops that would be held in the community. Some elder women, however, continued to view violence as natural within marital relations. Others wondered whether the authorities would really be willing to implement the law once it was actually written. Male villagers, in turn, generally showed little interest in the *initiative* at that time.[53]

In addition to the very sites at which the *initiative* was to be started, the CIAWF staff also maintained the female panel of the AUCC, as well as its main supporters of that time, CONAMU, female municipal councillors and mayor Tituaña, informed of their activities in indigenous communities, all of whom were supportive of this *initiative*. One space which the organisers decided not to involve from the beginning was UNORCAC, following thereby the model from Chiapas, where women had decided to organise meetings and consented on the final draft of the *Revolutionary Law of Women* exclusively among women, before advocating for its implementation among the community authorities and the male population in general. The *initiative's* organisers in Cotacachi wished to provide women with a space where they felt secure and where nobody would challenge their ideas or override their voices – a situation that often occurred in mixed spaces of dialogue and decision-making. They also thought that the proposal would carry more weight once a consensus among all participants of the *initiative* and CWC was guaranteed, as UNORCAC could not easily ignore a proposal endorsed by a considerable part of the female highland population.[54]

Availability of resources at the starting point of the initiative

The CIAWF soon evolved into the single and most visible institution to combat violence in the canton, and its mestizo and indigenous staff pooled both professional skills (legal expertise, project-management, fundraising, communication) as well as high credibility by victims of violence. Therefore, it became the natural site from which all activities related to the *change initiative* were coordinated. In La Calera, the indigenous promoter of the CIAWF held close ties to the local women's groups. She encouraged these women to participate in the planned workshops and made use of these groups' extended circles of contacts in order to invite other, non-organised women to join the activities. In line with the other four pilot communities, the community authorities of La Calera allowed the *initiative* organisers to use the communal hall for the workshops.[55]

The CIAWF staff understood that frequent visits to the communities and the organisation of workshops would also involve the spending of money, and it successfully applied for a small fund from a German foundation (*Stiftung Umverteilen*) in 2006 that allowed it to elaborate the methodology of the *initiative* and to seek for its authorisation by the authorities of the pilot communities. Considering that CONAMU planned to reduce its funding for the Centre in order to encourage the municipality of Cotacachi to take on more responsibility for this institution, the CIAWF also lobbied before the municipal council for a more stable institutional status and financing from the municipal budget. Given the strong presence of five supportive female councillors in the legislative period (2004-2008) and an equally positive stance of the mayor towards the Centre' work, a municipal ordinance approved in November 2006 converted the Centre into a municipal department and thereby secured the infrastructure and the wages of its staff for the legislative period.[56] In addition, the UNIFEM representative who had familiarised the CIAWF with the example of Chiapas signalled her willingness to accompany the *initiative* with her technical know-how. She also encouraged the CIAWF to apply for UNIFEM funds that would become available for indigenous women's projects from 2007 onwards – advice that the CIAWF readily followed. Taken together, this outlook made the organisers confident that the *initiative* would secure sufficient backing and feasibility.[57]

Which factors have influenced the *change initiative* throughout the subsequent stages of its evolution?

Target of change, strategy and tactics

The goal of the *change initiative* was to create a binding mechanism through which acts of violence could be processed and sanctioned by indigenous legal authorities in the highland communities of Cotacachi. The strategy to achieve this goal was the participative elaboration of a *Law for good living together* among women from indigenous communities, the seeking of its approval by the main representative bodies of the highland population – the CWC and UNORCAC – and the promotion of its implementation among the community councils. Several lines of action were planned to implement this strategy: First, between 2006 and 2007, women in five communities were invited to participate in a series of workshops in order to share their experiences about domestic violence. As for the community La Calera, some women had been prevented from participating in these workshops by their husbands, but around 20 others did regularly attend. Initially, many women felt shame and found it difficult to articulate the sufferings they had experienced throughout their lives. Thus, the indigenous promoters of the CIAWF themselves started to share their experiences with violence with the groups. Gradually, an atmosphere of trust was built among the participants and more and more of them felt able to speak about their histories of violence, which often started with their growing up as small girls and ended with continuous suffering during their marital relation. They talked about the consequences of injuries caused to their bodies and souls, and they also self-critically reflected on their own roles and practices as mothers, spouses and mothers-in-law, by which they themselves sometimes reproduced certain types of conduct and caused harm to others. They also clearly found that not only women, but men as well sometimes suffered from violence, for example, when a son hit his father to demand his inheritance. In a second phase of these workshops, women were asked about the types of violence that should be incorporated into and become justiciable under the new Law. Women also considered the legal procedures, agents to be involved and potential sanctions to be enacted, all of which should ideally be in line with justice practices in their community. Having received these inputs from women in La Calera and the other four participating communities, the *initiative* organisers systematised the results of the workshops in a single text and sought for its approval by the participating women.[58]

The final draft law, finished by mid 2007,[59] condemned distinct categories of violence – psychological, physical, sexual and economic violence, but also forced marriage, infidelity and gossip. Gossip (for instance about a married woman who allegedly was seen by someone smiling at another man on the street) often sufficed for a husband to exert violence against his wife. The document also established the right of children, adolescents and women to participate in communal life and decision-making. For each case, the Law proposed a specific procedure and sanction by local authorities, except sexual violence which should be directly forwarded to state judicial instances. The sanctions were symbolic or moral in nature, but also involved corporal punishments or, as a last option, the forwarding of the case to state legal operators. In cases of recidivism, sanctions would be toughened. Physical violence, for instance, defined by this law as mistreatment by clouting, booting, the pulling of hair, pushing, causing harm with artefacts, cuffing, burning or scratching, was to be sanctioned by the perpetrator carrying a heavy stone and walking through the community to the godfathers' or the in-laws' house. Along the way, the perpetrator would be accompanied and given guidance by the *cabildo* and other community members. If alcohol was involved in the violent acts, the community authorities could extend a prohibition on the perpetrator buying alcohol in local shops and drinking alcoholic beverages for a determined amount of time. In case of recurrence the case would be discussed by a community assembly where the aggressor would have to publicly recognise his wrongdoing and submit himself to a purification bath (which typically implied ice-cold water and medicinal plants). The assembly could also impose certain communal works such as garbage disposal or the painting of communal infrastructure. Lastly, a third recidivism would imply the *cabildo's* forwarding of the case to state authorities and the prevention of the perpetrator from escaping until the police arrived.

The *initiative's* participants from La Calera strongly endorsed the final draft law, and some of them accompanied the CIAWF staff to a meeting with the CWC where the text was presented and discussed. While CWC members reiterated the concerns they had already expressed at earlier meetings (see above), but nevertheless approved the text and urged the organisers to seek its approval at the next UNORCAC general assembly scheduled for the end of 2007.[60] At this assembly, the two indigenous promoters approached the UNORCAC directive headed by a new president and solicited a space in the assembly agenda to present their proposal to combat of violence in indigenous communities. The women were offered only a few minutes of time, which they used to explain to the representatives of all highland communities the process of elaborating the *Law for good living together* that counted with the approval of the CWC and now required the consent of the UNORCAC so as to promote the adoption of the law in the communities. As there were no questions or reactions to their brief presentation, the two promoters finished their intervention and (erroneously!) presumed that their *initiative* now counted with the approval of UNORCAC.[61]

Throughout 2008, the change promoters arranged meetings with authorities and organised groups in most of the 43 highland communities. They familiarised these commoners with the content of the Law, explained the ideas behind the document and lobbied for the authorities' to incorporate it into the community statutes. The organisers used creative methods such as socio-dramas in which they simulated different types of violent situations and then presented possible means by which the authorities might act upon such cases. This process encountered diverse reactions, ranging from very positive ones such as in La Calera, where authorities were open to the *initiative*, to mixed feelings in other communities where authorities complained of not having been involved in the elaboration process. Some authorities also expressed fears of acts of vengeance by kin members of perpetrators of violence if they proceeded according to the Law. Still, 37 communities signed an agreement with the CIAWF in which they committed themselves to incorporating the Law into their community statutes.[62]

Another line of action pursued throughout 2008 was the training of male and female promoters of the Law. These were delegates from those communities who had agreed to adopt the Law; La Calera selected four people as future promoters who attended workshops where different thematic issues ranging from constitutional rights, violence and mechanisms to combat violence in Cotacachi were touched upon, before being familiarised with the contents of the *Law for good living together*. The idea to train community-based promoters was that these people could accompany victims to the community authorities in order to denounce violent acts and to offer advice on how elements of the Law might be applied in the case at hand. As opposed to the fluctuation of *cabildos* who were elected every year, promoters of the Law were thought to provide a more stable service for all those seeking information on the Law, including newly elected authorities who were not yet familiarised with the document.[63]

In addition, with the technical support of the AUCC, the change agents prepared several radio spots in Kichwa in which they promoted the implementation of the Law. These spots were broadcasted by a local radio station that covered the entire highland zone of the canton between the end of 2008 and the beginning of 2009.[64]

Political opportunities

Up to the first half of 2009, several developments overshadowed the process. First, even though the CWC had initially pledged support for the workshops and visits to the communities, these activities frequently clashed with other commitments of CWC members, thus leaving the CIAWF staff alone with a substantial part of work.[65] Further, from the perspective of the CWC, the indigenous promoters of the CIAWF had not informed the CWC on a regular basis on the advances of the project and had taken important decisions without prior consultation.[66] Second, it was not until early 2009 that the UNORCAC president actually obtained a printed version of the *Law for good living together*. In a meeting with the *initiative* organisers, CWC members and an AUCC member, he expressed his incomprehension with respect to the fact in that in an introductory paragraph it was claimed that the Law was approved at the UNORCAC assembly in 2007. He showed the women the protocol of this assembly (which he himself had edited) to prove that at no time a formal vote on the approval of the *initiative* (as signalled by the raising of hands of the participants) had taken place at the assembly.[67] Even though the organisers explained the steps followed and their reasoning, and showed him the agreements signed by the *cabildos*, he rejected the *initiative* in the way it was elaborated and promoted. From his perspective, the law's formulation was not sufficiently participative and rather responded to the logic of a development project than the way local processes were conducted. He insisted that each community should maintain its freedom to elaborate its own legal proceeding in cases of violence or selectively incorporate elements from the Law into its statute. The president's stance represented as a strong setback for the change promoters, particularly considering that his voice was very influential among many community presidents. Moreover, the fact that in this meeting, CWC members neither helped clarifying some misunderstandings nor unanimously defended the *initiative* was interpreted as a sign of a lack of support from this organisation.[68]

Third, in a context of major political changes at the level of the municipality at the end of 2008 and first half of 2009, the *initiative* was deprived of its main protagonists, and thus came to a halt for almost two years. The underlying reasons for these shifts include growing discontent on the part of UNORCAC with the participatory governance model of mayor Tituaña, which had resulted in a gradual weakening of UNORCAC's role as the exclusive representative of the indigenous communities (Cameron 2010: 120–123; Lalander 2010: 72). Not only had the mayor strengthened municipal relations with communities by the direct provision of infrastructure and basic services to these localities, thereby circumventing UNORCAC, which had hitherto acted as an intermediary administering such projects for its member communities. The governance model also attracted the interest and funds of aid agencies and in this way threatened to diminish the financial basis of UNORCAC. Moreover, even though UNORCAC was guaranteed a voice in the decision-making processes of the AUCC, many others now enjoyed the same right (Cameron 2010: 120–123; Lalander 2010: 71–76). The mayors' negative stance towards the new Ecuadorian Constitution (2008), which stood in stark contrast to its popularity amongst a considerable part of the canton's population,[69] was used as pretext by UNORCAC to withdraw its support for Tituaña and instead nominated its own candidate for the next municipal elections: Alberto Anrango, who was one of the founders of UNORCAC, the first indigenous municipal councillor of Cotacachi in 1979, and, besides, the father of current UNORCAC president Rumiñahui Anrango. Indeed, with 27.89 per cent of the votes, Tituaña lost the election by a wide margin to Alberto Anrango (45.95 per cent), who ran as candidate for the official government party Alianza País (Lalander 2010: 117).

What did these developments mean for the *change initiative*? During the electoral campaign, the *initiative* organisers were asked to interrupt their promotion of the Law in the communities, as it was alleged some people might confuse their visits with a sort of indirect political campaigning for the municipal elections. After Tituaña's defeat, the new mayor restructured the municipal institutions and replaced municipal staff assumed to belong to the followers of the former mayor with his own supporters. Given Tituaña's supportive stance towards the work of the CIAWF, its staff was believed to belong to his supporters, too, which is why all of these were dismissed in mid 2009. The new team neither took up the intercultural work methodology that was considered a key aspect for providing adequate attention for indigenous women, nor did it display any interest of continuing the coordination of the *initiative*, which is why this process lost its 'motor'.[70] Despite the changed political context, several women wished to conclude the process as originally agreed by the organisers and its main financial supporter at that time (UNIFEM). Therefore, they conducted community workshops from September to November 2009 and planned to symbolically hand out a rod of authority (*bastón de mando*) to all those *cabildos* who had agreed to incorporate the Law into their statutes. This event should take place during a ceremony of all newly or re-elected *cabildos* in December 2009, organised by UNORCAC, and with the presence of the new mayor. However, their presentation by which the women intended to remind the *cabildos* about their commitments with respect to the Law was not particularly welcomed by several leaders who reiterated that they should have been included in the elaboration process of the Law. Among the audience were also many newly elected community presidents who ignored the agreements signed by their predecessors. Thus, with exception of a handful of communities, among them La Calera, many other authorities have not attached much value to the women's concern.[71]

Most participants of the *change initiative* felt exhausted after their frustrated struggles at the canton level. However, in 2010 they were approached by women who complained about the reduced quality of the attention of the CIAWF, prompting some of them to seek the means to retake the *initiative*. After intense lobbying from various spaces such as the cantonal Network against Intra-Family Violence,[72] the intervention of the municipal Human Rights Office, and the fact that the municipality eventually became interested in replicating in Cotacachi the model of an integrated 'Equity and Justice Centre', which had yielded first positive results in cities like Quito,[73] the municipal government decided to reconsider its policies on the issue of gender violence. As a result, several former members of the CIAWF were re-employed in the first half of 2011. The municipality also signed a one-year agreement with UN WOMEN (previously UNIFEM) for the reestablishment of the former intercultural methodology of the Centre and the realisation of a participatory process involving all 43 communities by which the contents of the draft law could be re-evaluated, and reformulated in a consented text, the same of which would form the basis for a municipal ordinance to be approved by the municipal council and the mayor in 2012.[74]

Availability and deployment of resources

Financially, the *initiative* received assistance from UNIFEM through two consecutive one-year agreements (2007–2008; 2008–2009). This support enabled the *initiative* organisers to cover the costs for their community visits, the print of the draft Law, the trainings of community-based promoters of the Law and the production of the radio spots. After the interruption of the process, the same agency (now with a distinct representative in charge and renamed in UN WOMEN) showed interest in recommencing the process and extended its technical and financial assistance for one additional year (2011–2012). As a result of 'lessons learned' from the previous period, the cooperation agreement was this time signed directly with the municipality of Cotacachi. Because the renewed support of the municipality to the CIAWF in 2011 did not cover all the wages of the re-established team, additional support was solicited from the Rosa Luxemburg Foundation based in Quito, which also helped strengthen the Network against Intra-Familiar Justice in Cotacachi.[75]

As far as immaterial resources are concerned, the *initiative* participants from La Calera and elsewhere enhanced their expertise in the realm of violence and community justice. Through the intermediation of UNIFEM, they extended ties to indigenous leaders from other regions such as the Kichwa Women's Network of Chimborazo and participated in the formulation of demands about women's equal access to indigenous justice systems, which were successfully forwarded to the Constituent Assembly in 2008.[76] They also exchanged their experiences with indigenous representatives from other countries at an international congress on women and indigenous justice in Quito in October 2008 (Lang and Kucia 2009). Not least, the two CIAWF promoters became protagonists of a documentary film on women's role in indigenous justice systems (*Justicia Nuestra*), which was produced in La Calera (with some of its residents) and other regions.[77] These incidences increased the self-esteem of these women and were met by a growing respect of their families, communities and authorities. All the more frustrating for the women, therefore, turned out to be the at times ambiguous positioning of the CWC and UNORCAC towards their *initiative*.[78]

What results has the legal change process yielded in La Calera by the end of the research period?

Normative and institutional change

Due to the direct involvement of a group of women from La Calera in the planning, deliberations on and realisation of the *change initiative*, the *Law for good living together* enjoyed a relatively strong backing by subsequent community authorities in this community. Still, particularly because of the unsupportive position of the UNORCAC towards the law, community authorities felt insecure as to whether their acting upon cases of violence was actually sanctioned by their superior organisation and whether it would withstand a revision by the state legal operators in Cotacachi if someone complained about their intervention.[79] Therefore, the fact that all highland communities were able to participate in a revision of the Law throughout 2011 and 2012 and that their ideas became reflected in a corresponding draft for a municipal ordinance, which substituted and at the same time endorsed the objectives of the previous draft law (Ordenanza Sustitutiva para el Sumak Ally Kawsay 2012), reduced the local authorities' uncertainty and made them more self-assured in their administration of justice.

The draft text for the ordinance, submitted by the AUCC to the municipal council in 2012, defined physical, sexual, psychological, economic and patrimonial, social and political forms of violence as well as femicide and ruled that no violent act should remain in impunity. Indigenous legal authorities were deemed responsible for cases of violence occurring within their jurisdictions, for which they could seek support by the CIAWF. Responding to earlier criticism on the first draft, a detailed description of procedures and sanctions was omitted, so as to leave it to the discretion of indigenous authorities to define a procedure most consistent with existing local practices; still, the former draft was regarded as a reference for this purpose. The competence on cases of sexual violence, rape and feminicide, in turn, should reside in the state legal operators of the canton, the same of which were supposed to adjust their services to the ethnic and gender identities of the users and to adopt an intercultural jurisprudence. The commitments of the municipality included the provision of regular financial resources for policies and activities targeting violence; the creation of a specific municipal office for women, the family and priority groups in charge of carrying out the municipal policies on violence; the continued support for the work of the CIAWF; and the extension of the annual campaign against violence between the 25 November and 10 December. Simultaneously, the ordinance fully recognised the collective rights of indigenous communities, including their right to administer justice according their own norms. The ordinance determined that there should be funds earmarked for the strengthening of indigenous legal systems, for example through the promotion of intra- and intercommunity dialogue processes on legal procedures, the intercultural interpretation of human rights, gender violence and the rights of women. In addition, the municipality committed itself to support indigenous communities in the updating of their territorial boundaries by means of geographic information systems so as to gain more clarity on their respective jurisdictions.

Despite the much more participatory elaboration for the draft ordinance and the fact that the ordinance addressed several long-standing demands of *cabildos*, the municipal government, dominated in this legislative period by representatives of Alianza País, only approved the ordinance in a first debate in December 2013 (Gobierno Municipal de Santa Ana de Cotacachi 2013: 40). Due to a lapse in funding from Spanish aid agencies (caused by the recent domestic financial crisis), UN WOMEN was forced to close its programme for Andean indigenous women in 2012, meaning that an important source for financial and technical support dried up. With a new mayor taking office in 2014 (Jomar Cevallos), the final approval of the ordinance continued in a stage of limbo until the time of writing.

Enforcement of reformed norms and institutions

Regardless of the pending adoption of the ordinance at municipal level, in La Calera, the prospects for the Law's enforcement looked relatively positive towards the end of the investigation period: First, if compared to the starting point of the *change initiative* in the mid 2000s, more women were willing to denounce acts of violence by their partners before the *cabildo* in La Calera or before the CIAWF.[80] Second, a higher number of women participated as authorities in the administration of justice as compared with previous years.[81] Third, when processing cases of violence, the community authorities applied some elements of the printed version of the *Law for good living together*. In some occasions, the *cabildo* requested the assistance of women who were familiarised with the Law so as to consent about the possible procedural steps to take. If confronted with resistant attitudes, women tended to argue with the respective passages of the National Constitution of 2008 that protected both the right to freedom from violence and required indigenous justice systems to respect their rights as women, which demonstrates how national norms may play a supportive role for women's local struggles for more gender justice.[82] In addition, women from La Calera were sometimes approached by *cabildos* from other communities in order to help them with their case resolutions.[83]

Among the challenges associated with the enforcement of the Law in La Calera was the fact that sanctions involving *public* exhibition and punishment of perpetrators came to be greatly feared by transgressors, their families and even some authorities themselves.[84] In minor cases of violence, indigenous authorities often preferred to limit their intervention to a

–confidential conversation among the couple instead of immediately turning to more visible forms of conflict resolution. They insisted that the mere mentioning that recidivism would imply a more severe and public punishment, would often suffice to make aggressors reconsider their conduct. Also, *cabildo* members complained that not all commoners were willing to accept their authority as an instance of conflict resolution (which applied to all kinds of conflicts occurring within the community). Thus, sometimes, their acting upon cases was thwarted either because commoners directly turned to state authorities, or because a party to a conflict proposed the forwarding of the case to state legal operators in the middle of a community-based process.[85]

Sustainability of reformed norms and institutions

In order to render the *change initiative* more sustainable, female leaders from La Calera stressed the need for a more continuous sensitisation of the population about violence and the instruments that existed at the community and canton level in order to prevent violent conduct. A considerable amount of villagers had not actively participated in the *initiative* and hence were unaware of the draft law. Special concern was expressed with regards to the youth who spent much more time in urban spaces for educational reasons and for whom a distinct approach of consciousness-building would have to be designed. The fluctuation of community authorities posed another challenge to the *initiative*, as some *cabildo* members failed to pass all relevant information to their successors. Last, the willingness to support victims of violence by those individuals who were trained to become promoters of the *initiative* have not been taken advantage of.[86] Only in cases where the municipality could eventually facilitate more permanent processes of dialogue on indigenous justice and gender violence in the communities (as envisioned in the draft ordinance), and provided that the CWC and UNORCAC leadership would more willingly than before embrace the *initiative* as one which actually reflects their interests, could some of the here-mentioned shortcomings might be ameliorated in the medium term.

San Francisco de la Rinconada – Otavalo Canton (2003–2012)

San Francisco de la Rinconada, about 110 km (or a two-hour bus drive) north from the capital Quito, is a community situated in the canton of Otavalo (Imbabura Province). With an impressive view at the Imbabura Volcano and the San Pablo Lake at its foothills, this canton was smaller in its territorial extension (579 km^2) and, according to the 2010 Census, more densely populated (104,874 residents) than the Cotacachi canton.[87]

Image 3.3 San Francisco de la Rinconada

Administratively, it is composed of the town (Otavalo) with a mixed population of mestizo and indigenous residents; two urban parishes (El Jordán and San Luis) made up of urban mestizo neighbourhoods and 14 indigenous *comunas* in its rural zones (such is the case of La Rinconada, which pertains to San Luis); and nine rural parishes (Municipio de Otavalo 2002: 18). With the exception of the sub-tropical Selva Alegre with its mixed population, the rural parishes are inhabited predominantly by indigenous residents organised in 71 *comunas* (Ortiz 2011: 103). The Otavalo canton stretches over altitudes ranging from 4,650 m.a.s.l. (Imbabura Volcano) and 1,500 m.a.s.l. in the west-bound Selva Alegre parish (Municipio de Otavalo 2002: 19-20). With 57.2 per cent (or 60,023 persons), the indigenous population (mainly Kichwa) constituted the majority of the canton's population, followed by 40.3 per cent (42,260) mestizos, 1.1 per cent whites, 1.0 per cent Afro-Ecuadorians and 0.2 per cent Montubios.[88] Comparing data on the indigenous population of the Otavalo canton from the 2001 Census and the Survey on Citizenship and Rights 2009, Ortiz (2011: 221) found an increased literacy rate (69.8 per cent in 2001; 85.2 per cent in 2009), an improved primary school completion (36.9 per cent in 2001; 66.9 per cent in 2009), a rise in secondary school completion (18 per cent in 2001; 25.7 per cent in 2009) and the involvement in advanced training at a technical school or university (for at least one year) by 3.7 per cent in 2001 and even 10.9 per cent in 2009. The provision of permanent electricity had

Image 3.4 Woman from La Rinconada

reached 95.9 per cent of indigenous families, and 68.5 per cent were connected with a water supply line in 2009. Still, the opportunity to access basic infrastructure, services, education and employment, were much lower for the rural (mainly indigenous) population compared with the (mestizo and indigenous) residents of Otavalo town (Van Cott 2008: 146–147; Ortiz 2011: 139–140, 225–230). Around 41.6 per cent of Otavaleños were beneficiaries of the cash transfer *Bono de Desarrollo*, and 3.8 per cent of the *Bono de Vivienda* (Ortiz 2011: 221). Child mortality (below the age of one) affected 66 of 1,000 children in the canton (Municipio de Otavalo 2002: 24).

The community La Rinconada was situated a few kilometres away from the town of Otavalo and could be reached at its entry point (*Cuatro Esquinas*) by a public bus. Although it was inhabited almost exclusively by indigenous people[89] (approximately 225 families), a considerable share of cultivable lands belonged to mestizo landowners who neither lived in the community nor complied with the communal duties. Their selling or bequeathing of lands to others without involving the community posed a particular challenge for local authorities. These landowners used to contract local residents to grow agricultural products at their lands and, in exchange for their work, these were paid with half of the harvest they brought in. On other occasions, commoners tried to convince landowners to lease shares of their unused land to them, or simply occupied it when these lands were left unattended for prolonged periods of time. One of several haciendas still existed in the community, and due to constant conflicts over commoners' access to irrigation water, the community became involved in legal processes at state courts against the hacienda-owner throughout the 2000s.[90] Indigenous commoners usually did not own more than minimal land parcels (*minifundios*) on which they grew corn, potatoes, some vegetables and held a handful of animals. Considering that – until recently – families in La Rinconada could include up to seven children, agriculture alone could not secure the survival of most families. A considerable part of the male population migrated on a monthly, weekly, or daily basis to towns like Otavalo, Ibarra, Quito, the coast or the Amazon lowlands, in order to work as masons or in the construction sector. Young and unmarried women worked as domestic employees, in restaurants or textile manufactures in Otavalo town; some sold vegetables at the market. Married women were expected to stay at home and take care of the children, the household and the fields, but extreme poverty would sometimes force them to look for alternative sources of income. Such attempts were not only complicated by the lack of jobs, but also because an increasing amount of employers in Otavalo sought personnel who at least had a bachelor's degree (even for relatively unskilled jobs) – a requirement most adults of the community could not meet.[91] There was a primary school in the community, but for higher level education adolescents drove to the town of Otavalo. No health services were available in La Rinconada, thus commoners either turned to the sparsely occupied health station in a neighbouring community or went directly to the hospital in the town of Otavalo.[92]

Otavalo is known for its weaving tradition that dates back to pre-Inca times and which has been maintained, refined and opened for international commerce up to the present.[93] The market in the *Plaza de Ponchos* in the town centre attracted an estimated annual number of 145,000 tourists in the 2000s (Meisch 1998; Van Cott 2008: 146). Ever since the 1970s, the increased resistance of the indigenous population against discriminatory and abusive treatment by the white–mestizo urban elites, commerce intermediaries, municipal employees, police officers and Catholic priests, found its expressions, among other things, in the foundation of the Indigenous and Peasant Federation of Imbabura (*Federación Indígena y Campesina de Imbabura*, FICI; see Ortiz 2011: 133–151), which affiliated with ECUARUNARI (*Ecuador Runacunapac Riccharimuy*; Awakening of the Ecuadorian Indian; highland organisation affiliated with CONAIE) and struggled for the recognition of cultural diversity and equal rights of the indigenous population. FICI gradually expanded its presence to neighbouring cantons and became a key agent of indigenous mobilisation in the northern Sierra throughout the 1980s and 1990s.[94] As in Cotacachi, municipal governance in Otavalo took a new shape with the taking of office of the first indigenous major elected in 2000 (Mario Conejo). His administration became known for the opening of participative spaces for the citizenry; the shifting of decision-making competences to urban neighbourhoods and parish juntas; the principle of financial co-responsibility of *barrios* and *comunas* in the conduct of development projects; and an innovative system of transparency in government activities and public contracting. He was confirmed in office for two consecutive terms (Lalander 2010; Municipio de Otavalo 2002; Ortiz 2011; Van Cott 2008).[95]

Why did claims for legal change emerge in La Rinconada?

Shifts in local power relations

In comparison to La Calera, the asymmetries in terms of participation in communal affairs and decision-making capabilities between women and men were more accentuated in La Rinconada until the late 1990s. The access of young girls to school was extremely limited. While parents tended to send their male children for a minimum of three years to elementary school so that they could cope with the challenges they might encounter in their future engagement with community affairs and the job market, girls typically attended school for even fewer years, if at all, as their future tasks were typically expected to remain confined to the household, the raising of children and agriculture. As a consequence, many women were illiterate and suffered from low self-esteem because they felt that they lacked the basis for contributing monetarily to the family income, and because they were unable to assist their children with their homework.[96]

By the same token, women from La Rinconada were neither associated with each other in a local group where they could share some common activity or discuss relevant issues, nor were they involved with organisational spaces provided by FICI in the canton. There were single outstanding women, such as midwives, who were associated with a canton-wide network of midwives who were trained and assisted by NGOs and the Health Ministry of Imbabura throughout the 1900s. However, as for Rinconada, such leadership of women was extremely rare. Thus, the spaces where women talked to one another remained limited to casual conversations on the streets, in *mingas* (collective works)or local celebrations. But here, it was not as easy to touch upon more profound concerns, to discover shared grievances and to think about potential ways to overcome them.[97]

Furthermore, the role of women in communal spaces of decision-making in La Rinconada was severely limited until the end of the 1990s. The community was divided into five sectors and each sector was to be represented in the community council (*cabildo*), made up of a president, a vice-president, a syndic, a treasurer and a secretary and several deputies. Elections for the *cabildo* and other communal groups (such as the water junta) usually took place in November each year. The community assembly that elected these authorities and which also met in case of emergencies or severe conflicts, typically was made up of all 'heads of families' (*cabezas de familia*), referring to all-male, married commoners who possessed a land parcel. Women only participated in these assemblies in substitution of their spouses; in situations where they did, their voices would not carry much weight, especially amongst elder male commoners. Only single women – those who could read and write – had ever been elected to a position (mostly secretary or treasurer) in the *cabildo*. Their participation in the weekly *cabildo* sessions was also complicated due to their symbolically 'male' timing and location: The sessions invariably took place at Monday evenings (around 6 p.m.), and, depending on the amount and nature of problems treated, they sometimes ended late at night. The *cabildo* met in the community hall situated at the entry to the community (*Cuatro Esquinas*) and thus favoured male commoners who just arrived by bus from their external workplaces. After the sessions, *cabildo* members had to pass in the dark on non-illuminated paths towards their (sometimes far off) homes. At this time of the day, women were expected to be at home, to prepare the dinner and to put children to bed.[98]

Incompatibilities among institutional sets relevant for women's lives

Domestic violence was prevalent in many families of La Rinconada, and interviewees provided many reasons for its occurrence. Some of them referred to the asymmetries and conflicts in marital relations, which had been increased by men's more frequent engagement with the world outside of the community, by prolonged migration periods of male commoners, and, more generally, the increased relevance of money in family life:

Q: What are the reasons for the prevalence of family violence?
A: I think that some aspects of our life have been changed by external influences. And there are other aspects that were already present inside. This is complemented by economic aspects – the lack of employment. And former spaces of dialogue have been lost. When the majority still disposed of enough space to work on their lands, they used to work together – man and woman. They even shared some reproductive activities; the taking care of children was shared – not entirely, but in some aspects. More recently, by contrast, these [activities] pertain exclusively to the realm of a woman. A man is more present in external spaces. And while he is outside, he experiences social frictions with other people, with other life styles – and the woman stays alone. Also in migration contexts, it's the man who leaves, and sometimes other types of situations occur: he finds another partner, and his wife waits for him. Or it's the woman

> who finds another partner. Thus problems may arise on both sides. (…) [O]ur reality is monetarised. The one who has more money, or who gains more money, believes to have more power, as well. And the man, as he is leaving, as he works outside, has access to money. And the woman, as there is no one who pays her, is devalued in some situations, especially with respect to her activities at home.
>
> (Interview 1–23.11.2011)

Within this broader context, there were also situational, but recurring circumstances that provoked violence, such as excessive alcohol consumption during community or family celebrations. Violence was also practised when women did not meet their roles as spouses or mothers, or conversely, when men felt they had to control the conduct of their wives. Often, social pressure exerted by parents, parents-in-law, kin members, neighbours and friends – all of whom were close observers of the conduct of the couple – played a considerable role in this regard. In this sense, women suffered from violence when they did not complete all their tasks in the household upon their husbands' arrival; when their husbands became aware of (unverified) rumours about their wives' infidelity during their time of absence; or even if women did not become pregnant with a desired child for a prolonged time – which was perceived as a refusal to constitute or enlarge the family and which could also put into question a man's fertility.[99]

To become aware of the incompatibility of the violent conduct against women with other norms or institutions would have implied women being familiarised with other sets of norms that would disapprove this type of behaviour and provide alternative forms of living together. However, until the late 1990s, the overwhelming majority of women in La Rinconada had never learned about the existence of such alternative norms, as there were no agents in the community who could have held conversations on the issue of violence, and as women themselves did not share a space where they could have articulated their grievances and jointly sought non-violent alternatives. In the same vein, there were no other realms of life in which most women's lives in La Rinconada had undergone shifts, such as improved access to education, increased political participation or more economic autonomy, by which incompatibilities between the violent behaviour of their partners vis-à-vis progress in other realms would have made themselves felt more easily. Instead, many patterns of their lives continued to follow clearly differentiated gender roles, while violence constituted a socially tolerated conduct.[100]

Inappropriate resolution of cases of domestic violence by existing institutions

As domestic violence was still regarded as a 'normal' element of family life, many women endured such conduct without communicating their suffering to the external world, much less denouncing violent acts. Out of lack of self-esteem, but also fear of the consequences for their life and their relationship with their husbands, women often even tried to deny observable markers of violence. If they told anyone, women would turn to their closest family members (such as parents, godparents, brothers or sisters, uncles or aunts) and ask for their advice or intervention.[101]

Q: What did they do whilst trying to resolve conflicts within the family? Is this an effective forum of intervention where a lot of trust prevails?
A: Yes, there is a very strong atmosphere of trust. (…) [T]hey usually don't look for a culprit. They also don't try to protect the man or the woman with respect to the mistakes they've made. What they attempt to do is – as such cases often occur among young couples (which does not mean that it does not exist among elder persons, because this does exist as well, but it is more common among young couples) – thus, one says that they've just recently started to live together, and if they don't rectify [their conduct] today, later on they will regret it. Those saying this are people who've already gone through these types of problems. They say that they better do a somersault and start their life anew.
Q: Thus, it is a forum of good advice?
A: It's about persuasion and advice. In my view, indigenous justice builds upon a fundamental pillar which has been very little studied: giving advice and persuasion. And this is the reason why (…) they don't come up with resolutions so easily, as if indigenous justice would find solutions within an hour or so – no. One spends one day, two days, until the problem is solved. Why? Because they try to persuade, to give advice, and to make a person reflect upon their situation. It's not about: "Ah, you committed this mistake, so here is the resolution". No. What they look for is that a person expresses his/her sentiments, and (…) offers apologies of their own free will. But in order to get there, persuasion and, advice are used. Sometimes, in some cases, one could even say pressure – but pressure not understood as punishment. (…) For instance, by saying: "You are making me look bad and feel ashamed before the entire family. I am your father". Thus one is feeling pressured. Or they also say: "All your siblings have overcome this problem. You are the only one who hasn't". Or other things they used to say: "If you don't sort out your domestic affairs, you won't return to my house" – parents use to say this. And: "I won't give you any inheritance". In cases of infidelity with another woman, they say: "You have your rights. You can go with your lover. But in my house the rights will correspond to your children and your wife – not to you".

(Interview 1–23.11.2011)

The *cabildo* (the next superior instance of indigenous justice) was hardly ever called upon to resolve cases of violence, among other reasons because violence was conceived of as a family issue, because the neutrality of *cabildo* members was put into question in cases where they were relatives or friends of parties to a conflict, or because husbands intimidated women so that they would not denounce violence to external institutions. In the rare cases where the *cabildo* did process a case of domestic violence, the procedure tended to involve a conversation that ended in the aggressor pledging to change his conduct – a resolution that did not effectively prevent a recurrence of violence in the future.[102]

Only in extremely severe cases of violence would indigenous women turn to state legal operators in the town of Otavalo, even though they were usually not clear about the norms, procedures and consequences this step might involve. Obstacles indigenous women faced when accessing these state institutions referred to the impossibility to communicate in their own language Kichwa, to the need to give their testimonies over and over again and in an unfamiliar environment, to the lengthiness of procedures and the obligation to return to the town several times, forcing them to leave their children and their household tasks unattended. Women were not convinced that a monetary fine or the imprisonment of their partners was the adequate answer to their grievances. Moreover, measures designed to protect victims of violence from acts of vengeance of the perpetrator could not be implemented in the community, as no nearby police station was available.[103]

Diffusion of new legal concepts

In response to the advocacy of a group of women based in the town of Otavalo and a female municipal councillor, the first Office of Family Guidance and Judicial Consultation (*Oficina de Orientación Familiar y Asesoría Jurídica*) opened its doors in 1997 and was accredited as a Women's and Family Office one year later. In addition to a lawyer, a secretary, and a promoter, several professionals (psychologists, doctors) offered their services on a voluntary basis in order to support the service of the institution. Supported by the recently created NGO Centre for Education and Action of Otavaleña Women (*Centro de Educación y Acción de Mujeres Otavaleñas*, CEAMOS), this institution organised public events and training in educative centres in the town of Otavalo so as to sensitise the population of the matter of domestic violence and circulate information about Law 103. But as representatives of the Women's and Family Office realised, their videos, publications and informative materials, produced in the Spanish language and focused on mestizo–urban contexts, remained incomprehensible to rural–indigenous audiences; gradually, therefore, they developed alternative information sheets with which they hoped to reach out to the indigenous population. Still, given the limited capacities in staff and financial resources vis-à-vis a densely populated canton with more than 80 indigenous communities, many of them – including La Rinconada – had never seen these representatives arrive in their community until the early 2000s.[104]

From the perspective of FICI, the way the State dealt with the matter of domestic violence was unilaterally focused on women, but did not sufficiently take the entire family background into account. As a matter of principle, FICI was opposed to the idea of creating institutions exclusively concerned with the interests of men *or* women, which is why – in contrast to its own umbrella organisation CONAIE – FICI had never incorporated a commission on women within its internal structure. According to its representatives, women should instead become involved in all issues pertaining to the collective interests of indigenous peoples, and in so doing, exercise their right to participation just as their male counterparts did. The fact that a woman (Carmen Yamberla) had long headed the organisation served to reinforce this position. Consequently, if FICI representatives visited the community of La Rinconada – which did not occur very often – their actions tended to focus on local concerns or consciousness-raising about the collective rights of indigenous peoples.[105]

As La Rinconada had thus far remained outside of the scope of external institutions, and because its young residents displayed very low educational levels, an NGO entirely constituted by indigenous persons originating in the canton Otavalo and the neighbouring canton Cotacachi named Corcima (*Corporación de Comunidades Indígenas Maquipurashun*) approached the community council in 2001 in order to evaluate the possibility of collaborating with the community in the realm of the education and wellbeing of children. It was the first time that ideas on rights of specific groups – children and adolescents – diffused into the community. With the consent of the community assembly, the NGO promoted the establishment of a pre-school centre and extended the coverage and facilities of the existing elementary school. Corcima provided scholarships for children and adolescents from poor families, thereby enabling their longer school attendance and preventing them from becoming a financial burden for their family. The performance of scholarship receivers was constantly monitored by the NGO; by this means, potential weaknesses or personal problems could be attended in a timely fashion. The scholarships had a particularly strong effect on girls, whose school attendance in years gradually increased until reaching a fairly gender-balanced school attendance by the time of the author's fieldwork (October-December 2011). The project was complemented by a series of didactic and recreational activities for children and adolescents, but also conversations with the parents (mostly mothers) on issues such as education, health, nutrition, reproduction or the rights of children and adolescents.[106]

In summary, in La Rinconada, no explicit *change initiative* had been staged by commoners until the early 2000s – for the reasons explained above. Instead, the representatives of the NGO Corcima who had recently started to cooperate with the community in the realm of education would soon become sensitised to the issue of family violence and develop activities directed at the promotion of gradual change.

Which factors facilitated or obstructed the initiation of legal change efforts in La Rinconada?

Interpretive frame providing justification for change-orientated action

While conducting activities with children and adolescents in the community, Corcima employees became aware of the violence that these students endured within their broader family context. They engaged the mothers of their scholarship receivers in careful dialogue in order to understand the underlying problems that traversed family life. During these talks, they learned that violence was not only exerted against children, but that most mothers themselves were subject to acts of violence. They also found out that a growing number of women were abandoned by their husbands without receiving alimony for their children. Further, ever more female adolescents became pregnant prematurely and preferred to raise their children on their own, arguing that the maintenance of a relationship with the (equally young) fathers would most probably result in constant arguments and violence. Despite the prevalence and severity of these problems, the NGO was informed that the *cabildo* neither paid much attention nor offered effective mechanisms to respond to these problems. Against this background, the NGO came to the conclusion that in order to achieve their objectives in the implementation of children's and adolescents' rights in the community, they needed to broaden their focus towards the wellbeing of entire families and to the strengthening of the community council's capacities to address family conflicts.[107]

Political opportunities at the starting point of the legal change efforts

Around 2003, the NGO turned to the authorities of La Rinconada to present the proposal to broaden their scope of activities in the community. Its representatives explained that they would like to implement projects designed to enhance the self-esteem of women and help them create options to enhance the family income by promoting some productive activities within the community. They also wished to engage young and adult commoners to reflect on non-violent forms of communication and living together. Lastly, they also proposed to strengthen the *cabildo's* authority and its capacity to resolve conflicts in the community, among other things, by providing guidance on the rights that they enjoyed as community council, and by developing strategies to respond to the challenges with which their administration of justice was confronted. When assessing Corcima's proposal, authorities found that the cooperation between the community and the NGO until this moment of time had been very beneficial for many families of La Rinconada, who were relieved that their children were now guaranteed a longer education. Corcima helped to extend and improve the educational institutions of the community. Its representatives were themselves residents of the area, they spoke Kichwa and were familiarised with the local context. They were respectful of local authorities' decisions, and, at the same time, willingly provided good advice about the cases with which the community authorities and ordinary residents approached them over the time. Based on these positive antecedents, the *cabildo* signalled its consent in expanding the cooperation, not least, because it expected to enhance its own legitimacy by improving its capacities to respond to conflicts occurring within its territory.[108]

Availability of resources at the starting point of the initiative

Corcima was constituted by a small team of highly motivated and skilled indigenous professionals who were familiarised with indigenous values and practices, and who had gained recognition for their work in around 20 communities in the cantons of Otavalo and Cotacachi. In order to carry out their activities in these locations, Corcima had successfully applied for financial funding from the international NGO World Vision. World Vision had initiated its programme in Ecuador in the late 1970s and ever since engaged in the promotion of social equity and development of marginalised societal sectors, such as indigenous and Afro-Ecuadorian children, adolescents, their families and communities (Visión Mundial Ecuador 2008; 2011). Given that advances of children and adolescents in these realms could neither be achieved nor meaningfully measured within a limited time period, cooperation with local partners like Corcima usually stretched over a longer project cycle, allowing these organisations to establish medium-term work plans and – provided that project phases were evaluated positively – a relatively stable resource basis.[109]

Which factors have influenced the *change initiative* throughout the subsequent stages of its evolution?

Target of change, strategy and tactics

The main objective of Corcima's engagement in La Rinconada was to achieve an improvement in the living conditions and the wellbeing of children, adolescents and families in the community. The promotion of more balanced gender relations and a culture of non-violence, but also the strengthening of the *cabildo's* administration of community affairs and justice, constituted vital strategies for achieving this objective. Accordingly, the Corcima team designed very creative lines of action for children, adolescents and adults. As far as violence is concerned, Corcima set out to organise spaces of dialogue for women in order to promote discussion about their problems and inform them about their rights. In these spaces, topics such as reproduction and methods of family planning, but also the matter of domestic violence came to the fore. Becoming aware of the existence of constitutionally enshrined norms that protected their integrity and freedom from violence, women came to feel that violent conduct within their own families would necessarily have to be reduced. However, their attempts to engage their husbands in dialogue on their rights at home were not very successful; quite the contrary, such attempts sometimes provoked even more aggression. These incidences prompted Corcima not only to shift from exclusively female spaces to activities involving both women *and* men, but also to translate the fundamental ideas behind women's rights into ideas and practices that were closer to local realities. Thus, in conversations with women and men they used instruments such as humour, provocative questions or practical advice, in order to stir debates among participants and promote fresh reflections on prevailing attitudes.[110]

In order to not only talk, but also put alternatives into practice, Corcima proposed that the *cabildos* of the 20 communities covered by its work organise the ancestral celebration of *Inti Raymi* (Andean Celebration of the Sun around solstice in June of each year) – but without alcohol. This idea grew out of women's claims that violence peaked during the month of June, precisely because these celebrations went hand in hand with increased alcohol consumption. Against the doubts expressed by many commoners, who wondered whether people would enjoy themselves in such a 'dry' celebration, Corcima created incentives such as the facilitation of food, music, as well as the organisation of a dancing contest. The first celebration of this kind was more successful than expected and participating communities expressed their wish to repeat this celebration on an annual basis and to rotate the host community. Over the following years, this celebration became more and more popular and attracted up to an estimated 4,000 people in the *Inti Raymi* of 2011. And while it was not possible to convince all visitors to abstain from the consumption of alcohol during this event, a clear majority of visitors did. It must be emphasised, however, that this celebration was held on only one occasion during the year.[111]

Another tactic designed to question widely held understandings of roles and rights of women and men was the realisation of an intercommunal soccer competition among women. In addition to regular soccer games at weekends, intercommunal competitions between male teams had been held for decades in the region, but similar events for women had thus far never been seen in the area. The resistance this *initiative* encountered in its initial phase by some community authorities, commoners and even representatives of the Church, confirmed to Corcima that soccer fields, and the question of recreation in general, were clearly male-dominated spheres. The first women willing to join the soccer team of La Rinconada needed a lot of courage, as they had to convince their partners and families to let them participate in the event, to leave their daily tasks aside, and to play soccer without prior training or experience. The competition was also incentivised by a prize for the winning team. Reactions by kin members of participating soccer players were mixed, for while some families would not even permit women to participate in the competition, others actively supported them by assuming – at least during the games – their responsibilities in the household. The female soccer competition also came to be repeated every year. Critically, it could be added that this experience remained limited to a relatively small group of women, and that their shared activity was confined to a short period of the year. On the other hand, the competition helped raise the self-esteem of the involved women, and a handful of them were also encouraged to engage more actively in the community council or other local groups later on.[112]

In order to foster the *cabildo's* capacity to administer justice in the realm of family conflicts and violence, Corcima raised the authorities' awareness on the responsibilities implied by the assumption of a community office and supported the *cabildo* in updating its internal statute. In doing so, Corcima informed the *cabildo* about the existence of the Quota Law, prescribing a minimum percentage of party lists reserved for female candidates for public offices.[113] They engaged the authorities in a discussion on whether a similar passage in the updated community statute would make sense in the case of La Rinconada, with the result that a minimum of two *cabildo* positions were reserved for female candidates.[114] In addition, Corcima organised several reunions between the council, interested commoners, state legal operators and experts in violence (from the Women and Family Office, the public attorney office and the NGO CEAMOS) in order to stimulate debates on children's and women's rights and the responses that state and indigenous justice systems had at their disposal to confront these problems. Participants learned about the mechanisms provided by the State to investigate and sanction domestic violence and sexual crimes, but also to deal with the recognition of paternity and alimony. Commoners were familiarised with recently introduced DNA tests that enabled all doubts on paternity to be reliably resolved within a short time frame. Legal operators also clarified the criteria by which judges decided about the rights of separated parents in terms of access to their children. With respect to the administration of indigenous justice, the external guests learned how justice was dispensed in the community and used the occasion to express their concerns about the lack of proportionality between violent acts and the sanctions emitted by the *cabildo*, which from their view did not take into account the harm caused to the victim and proved insufficient to prevent the aggressor from recidivism. In the same vein, commoners were encouraged to think about a partial adaptation of state norms on alimony within their own jurisdiction. Instead of the relatively high standard alimony prescribed by state laws (US$70 per child), commoners argued that they had the means to evaluate the financial situation of a family and, based on this evaluation, to establish a monthly amount of money or other goods (clothes, food, school utilities, among others) that could be realistically paid by fathers who lived separated from their families. Last, participants in these talks reflected upon the potential means by which indigenous and state legal authorities could mutually support each other. In this regard, state legal operators suggested that indigenous authorities could inform victims of violence about the possibility to be attended by psychologists in the town of Otavalo. They suggested that cases of violence in which a *cabildo's* intervention proved ineffective be forwarded to state justice operators; a report on the antecedents written by indigenous authorities could serve as a valuable source of information for the further processing of the case. They also offered support in those cases in which DNA tests would remain the only viable means to assess the paternity of a child.[115] All these talks provided subsequent community authorities with relevant information on state procedures in order to deal with problems that were prevalent in the community. They also felt prompted to critically assess and reform their treatment of cases of domestic violence, the neglect of children's rights, the abandoning of families and alimony. At the same time, the asymmetries between formally educated, professional, Spanish-speaking mestizos representing state justice and human rights on the one hand, and ordinary community members on the other, could not be effectively balanced during these talks, and although both sides opened up to the respective other, tensions and incomprehension remained constant features of these spaces of dialogue. Another weakness of this activity could again be seen in the fact that – with the exception of elected authorities – only few ordinary villagers came to take part in these sessions over time.[116]

Lastly, Corcima opened a conflict mediation centre within its office. In so doing, the NGO aimed to establish an additional instance of conflict resolution for people whose conflicts could not be resolved before the *cabildo*, but who were unwilling to resort to state legal operators. The advantages of this institution were seen in the fact that mediators were themselves indigenous residents of the area and thus cognisant of the local context; that these mediators were familiarised with both the indigenous and the state legal systems and hence able to explain the existing options, including their advantages and disadvantages, to the parties in conflict; that a mediation would only take place in cases where all parties voluntarily agreed on it; and that absolute confidentiality could be offered to those involved. With the exception of the issue of violence that could not be submitted to mediation (due to the asymmetry between aggressor and victim), the centre has supported residents from La Rinconada and other communities to resolve other family disputes such as alimony and agreements on the rights and obligations of separated parents.[117]

Political opportunities

Throughout the years of cooperation between Corcima and the community of La Rinconada studied here (2001-2012), the work of this NGO was seen by a majority of commoners as beneficial. Thus, even though specific activities were debated and at times resisted – reactions actually intended by the Corcima team in order to incentivise changes in attitudes and practices – this did not preclude subsequent presidents of La Rinconada from remaining open to Corcima's proposals and consenting to its interventions.

Indirectly, the *change initiative* was supported by FICI throughout this period, as well, by means of their convening of meetings with state legal operators (police, attorneys, judges) in the town of Otavalo to talk about indigenous communities' right to administer justice. These efforts arose from the fact that some *cabildos* of the canton suffered from discrimination by state legal operators who were neither well informed about international and national norms and legislation on this matter nor willing to respect indigenous judicial competence. In some cases, police forces had intervened in legal sessions held by *cabildos* or community assemblies, arguing that these were exclusively responsible for petty crimes. On other occasions, indigenous authorities were accused of unlawful usurpation of legal functions or similar offences. Such occurrences have led to an increased uncertainty on the part of indigenous communities about the actual scope of competencies. In their initial phase, these talks were very difficult and tense, not least due to the prejudices against indigenous justice displayed by the invited state operators. Gradually, however, the atmosphere in this space changed, with the result that, by the end of the 2000s, more operators were willing to coordinate cases with *cabildos.* Indeed, in some occasions, cases were returned to indigenous communities by legal state operators who acknowledged that these fell primarily within a community's jurisdiction.[118]

Not as helpful, by contrast, was FICI's positioning towards indigenous women's obstacles to access justice. Its representatives argued that – at least in the Imbabura Province – women were relatively empowered, overlooking thereby communities such as La Rinconada in which the situation did not fit into their overall picture. In the same vein, FICI stressed that *machismo* was not a problem exclusive to indigenous people;

that violence was most present in rural communities where a relation of subjection of women towards their husbands existed (contradicting thereby their previous argument); and that alcoholism lay at the heart of most violent acts, while shifting the responsibility to eradicate violence and alcoholism onto the State. FICI criticised Law 103 because of the risk that women could abuse the state justice system in order to pressure their husbands, but the organisation has not developed a more constructive approach of its own to deal with violence in rural communities.[119] Hence, in this respect, communities such as La Rinconada were left alone in their efforts to find adequate responses to domestic violence.

Similar to Cotacachi, there were several female municipal councillors elected as candidates of MUPP-NP who, in the legislative periods of 1996-2000 and 2000-2004, formulated municipal ordinances directed towards more gender equality within the canton of Otavalo. Among other things, they achieved the establishment of the abovementioned Women's and Family Office and a Women's and Family Department within the municipal government. The councillors helped to design a cantonal Plan for Equal Opportunities and installed a female leadership school at the beginning of the 2000s. They advocated for the incorporation of a gender perspective in any municipal ordinance and oversaw the improvement of labour conditions and career paths of female public employees. However, in the legislative period of 2005–2009, other new female councillors not connected to their predecessors did not further develop these *initiatives*. In 2009, one of the former councillors was re-elected to the municipal council, but given that she now found herself in the opposition to her former colleague, mayor Mario Conejo (who changed his political vehicle in the 2009 elections; see Fn. 95), her concern for women's issues lacked the political support of earlier periods. Indeed, the municipal Women's and Family Department was even closed during this legislative period. Importantly, in comparison to the municipal government of Cotacachi, the government of Otavalo did not show a particular interest in issues such as access to justice or domestic violence, partly because most municipal government members seemed to be of the opinion that existing institutions sufficed in order to attend these issues, but also because communities such as La Rinconada remained relatively disassociated with the municipal instances of citizen participation. What could be observed, in turn, was a gradual improvement in the cooperation between state legal operators, special institutions and NGOs for women and children and the Hospital San Luis in Otavalo. However, these efforts were the result of the *initiative* of the institutions involved, and not because of special attention on the part of the municipality.[120] Thus, Corcima's efforts in the communities were not backed by related *initiatives* from the municipal level throughout the research period.

Availability and deployment of resources

Throughout the 2000s, Corcima worked with financial support from World Vision. Thus, even though La Rinconada's demand for scholarships and other necessities constantly exceeded the available resources (something common in all communities covered by the NGO), Corcima was able to maintain its team and carry out many of the planned activities throughout the major part of the investigation period. Over the years, trust between Corcima's representatives and the population of La Rinconada grew, not least due to their constant support of children's development, but also because the NGO provided critical advice in a legal process before the state justice system against a hacienda-owner who denied commoners their access to water for irrigation. Importantly, legal know-how and the capacities of local authorities to resolve conflicts of different types have increased over the years, as well. And while the *cabildo* members continued to consult Corcima on dealing with complicated issues, they have likewise gained more self-assuredness in their management of community affairs, including their administration of justice.[121]

What results have the legal change process yielded in La Rinconada by the end of the research period?

Normative and institutional change

By 2011 a considerable number of children and adolescents, and a smaller number of adults had participated in one of the distinct activities offered by the NGO Corcima. Throughout some of these activities, issues such as gender roles, entitlements, violence or access to justice were touched upon; therefore, awareness about the necessity of respectful, dialogue-based, equitable and violence-free relationships among family members was raised among villagers. One of the messages conveyed in some of the talks and activities was that, instead of silencing the issue, violence was an offence that should be communicated towards trustworthy family members or the *cabildo*, in order to convince the aggressors to reconsider their conduct and achieve just solutions for all family members involved.[122]

The community council has committed itself to include at least two women among its office-holders. In this way it guaranteed a minimal presence of women in the council's decision-making processes, including the administration of justice. In comparison to earlier times, the *cabildo* was now willing to process cases of violence according to a relatively clearly defined procedure: it would call upon the parties to the conflict, and, if required, other family members, to appear at a session in which the situation of the family was evaluated. All parties to the conflict would be given the time to speak and express their views and feelings. Aggressors were to be informed of the existence of the right to freedom from violence and confronted with the long-term consequences violence might have on the wellbeing of the family. Aggressors were expected to apologise to the victims; they received advice on how to deal with future conflictive situations in a more adequate manner; and, depending on the severity of the harm caused, they were sanctioned by a number of strokes with a whip or a bath with stinging nettles, all of which was considered to have a curative and purging effect on the aggressor. Lastly, aggressors were also admonished that recidivism would necessarily imply a more severe punishment before the entire community assembly or the forwarding of the case to the state legal authorities.[123]

Enforcement of reformed norms and institutions

Results with regard to women's increased participation in the *cabildo* were mixed, as there was still a lot of distrust of men towards the enhanced involvement of their spouses in communal affairs. Not only did men argue that women would neglect their other responsibilities in the household, the education of the children and the work at the fields if they were elected to community office. They were also confirmed in their jealousy when it became known that, on one occasion, a female and a male *cabildo* member had a romantic affair. Many men still held that community affairs should be dealt with exclusively by more experienced, male community members. Simultaneously, elected female council members also faced severe obstacles to playing an active role in this space. Only a few would raise their voice or make proposals, but many others felt inhibited to speak up as they have never learned how to negotiate and assert themselves in critical situations in the face of resistance or opposing arguments expressed by others. Not least, the timing of *cabildo* sessions (Monday evenings/nights), which rendered women's participation difficult, remained unaltered.[124]

Due to the increased authorities' awareness of the issue of violence, coupled with the reduction of excessive consumption of alcohol during the main festivities in the community, some men abandoned severe forms of physical violence that could be perceived by the public, preferring other, less visible forms of causing harm to their partners.[125] Thus, violence has by no means disappeared, and compared with the situation before the intervention of Corcima, the strategies of women to deal with this situation have become more individualised and varied: a considerable number of women preferred to silently endure violence out of fear of even more force, but also out of shame. Indeed, in such cases, it were the victims' concerned mothers who asked the *cabildo* for intervention. Other women preferred to seek the support of their family members, but would not dare communicate their grievances to external instances. A handful of women did have the courage to denounce violence before the *cabildo*; but in 2011, these amounted to only two women in La Rinconada. While some interventions proved effective in terms of bringing the violence to a halt, in other cases aggressors reoffended against the victim, despite the punishment and admonition of the community authorities. Another group of women preferred to seek the support of the mediation centre of Corcima to tackle their marital problems; and while other issues such as unfulfilled obligations of their male partners towards the family or their children were the focus of these mediation sessions, more often than not the mediators realised in confidential dialogues with those involved that violence formed likewise part of the marital problems. A very small group of women turned to state legal operators, but usually only after a very long period of enduring violence. And lastly, an ever-increasing number of adolescents and young women intentionally decided to raise their children on their own and not engage in a formal relationship with the fathers – not least as a means to protect themselves from violent relationships. In this sense, the number of cases related to paternity recognition and the payment of alimony claims dealt with by the *cabildo* soon came to outnumber the cases related to domestic violence. While some conflicts on alimony were effectively resolved before this instance, some paternity issues were resolved after a successful coordination with state legal instances, which – as previously agreed – indeed facilitated the realisation of a DNA test.[126]

Sustainability of reformed norms and institutions

Without doubt, the most impressive effects of Corcima's work referred to the improvement of schooling of children and adolescents. Most children from La Rinconada attended school for more years than previous generations, and more gender equality in school attendance was likewise observable. As Corcima could not finance all, but only some students per family, there were families who were now willing to take out a loan in order to guarantee a longer education for all of their children. There were even students from La Rinconada entering university for the first time ever during the time of the author's fieldwork. In respect to gender relations, the Corcima team placed many of their hopes in this young generation who had also participated more consistently in its recreational and didactic activities, at an age in which they were most open to learn new attitudes and role models.[127]

A final promising development that might come to fruition in the future could be seen in the circumstance that the freshly elected community council for the year 2012 was determined to take young community members and women more into account, especially by strengthening their self-esteem and their skills to undertake activities and projects, and encouraging them to assume more responsibility in community affairs. In this regard, it was decided to send one of the female *cabildo* members to be trained in organisational issues. She was determined that once she finished the course, she would strive to create a women's group in La Rinconada that would not only serve as a platform for dialogue, but also be dedicated to productive activities.[128] It remained to be seen whether these *initiatives* would partly remedy existing weaknesses in female organisation and leadership in the community.

Notes

1 Data of the 2010 Census generated from the website of Ecuador's National Institute for Statistics and Censuses (INEC): www.ecuadorencifras.gob.ec (last access 10.06.2015).

2 The Ecuadorian territory accounts for 283,561 sq km, in comparison to 1,285,216 sq km in Peru and 1,098,581sq km in Bolivia; see the websites of these countries' respective national statistic institutes: www.ecuadorencifras.gob.ec (Ecuador); www.inei.gob.pe (Peru), www.ine.gob.bo (Bolivia) (last access to all three pages 10.06.2015).

3 This percentage is generated from a question referring to self-identification according to one's culture and customs; personal conversations with Silverio Chisaguano from Comisión Nacional de Estadísticas para Pueblos Indígena, Afroecuatorianos y Montubios (CONEPIA) (National Statistics Commission for Indians, Afro-Ecuadorians, and Montubios), a special entity of INEC (18.10.2011; 09.12.2011); see also Comisión Económica para América Latina y el Caribe (CEPAL) 2014: 90.

4 Montubios are peasants residing in the Ecuadorian coast who first claimed their recognition as a distinctive identity group in the 2000s. Montubios have Indian, African and European roots and differentiate themselves from the mestizo coastal population by their customs, their dialect and their socio-economic marginalisation; see Clark and Becker 2007: 12; Roitman 2008.

5 See Fn 1.

6 See Albó 2009: 118–119; CEPAL 2014: 91–92; Guerrero and Ospina 2003: 118–124; personal conversations with Silverio Chisaguano from CONEPIA (see Fn 3; 18.10.2011; 09.12.2011).

7 Albeit contested, the adoption of this term was chosen by Ecuadorian indigenous peoples themselves; see Lucero 2007: 216–219.

8 The highland Kichwas included the Karanki, Natabuela, Otavalo, Kayambi, Kitukara, Panzaleo, Salasaka, Chibuleo, Puruhá, Waranka, Kañari, Saraguro and the Kisapincha. In the Sierra they accounted for 388,078 persons; and the Amazonian Kichwa accounted for 328,149 persons in the 2010 Census; see www.siise.gob.ec/siiseweb (last access 10.06.2015).

9 See Fn 1.

10 As an alternative to *comunas*, a rising number of indigenous groups opted to found associations and cooperatives, especially from the 1970s onwards, as these implied the completion of far less formal–legal requirements; see Martínez 1998.

11 The *National Indigenous Uprising* was spearheaded by the umbrella organisation CONAIE (coordinating the regional highland organisation ECUARUNARI, the Amazon organisation CONFENIAE and the smaller coastal organisation COICE) and joined by affiliates from the class-based FENOC-I (later renamed in FENOCIN) and the evangelical Christian FEINE; for the

full names of these organisations see the Abbreviations section of this book. The ten-day protest involved road-blocks, the cutting off of transport links, hunger strikes, the occupation of a church and other public spaces and protesters presented a list of demands including the proposal to establish a *plurinational* State meant to allow for differentiated citizenship for the indigenous population so as to complement a mere formal–legal equality with substantial changes in the political, economic and social realms; see Albó 2009: 132–133; Llasag 2012b: 122–125; Pallares 2007: 154; Van Cott 2005: 110–111; Yashar 2005: 144–147.

12 Ecuador ratified ILO C 169 on 15 May 1998; see ILO website: www.ilo.org/dyn/normlex/en/f?p=1000:11300:0::NO:11300:P11300_INSTRUMENT_ID:312314 (last access 10.06.2015).

13 Two draft laws aiming at the delineation of competences of state and indigenous legal systems were elaborated in the aftermath of the 1998 Constitution, but while the first was vetoed by then President Noboa in January 2003, the second was declared unlawful by the legislative branch in the same month; see García 2005: 155–160; Salgado 2002; Simon 2009: 40–42; Trujillo, Grijalva and Endara 2001.

14 The introduction of the principle of gender equality in indigenous justice ranged among the proposals for the constituent process elaborated by CONAIE (Grijalva 2011: 105); indigenous women, spearheaded by the NGO *Red de Mujeres Kichwas de Chimborazo* (Kichwa Women's Network of Chimborazo), effectively advocated for these rights at the constituent assembly in Monte Christi; see Cucurí 2009; Picq 2013.

15 See art. 344, Código Orgánico de la Función Judicial.

16 See art. 65, 66, Ley Orgánica de Garantías Jurisdiccionales y Control Constitucional.

17 See Acosta 2012; Ospina 2011; 2012. One of the main redistributive instruments, the cash transfer programme *Bono de Desarrollo,* had been first incentivised by the World Bank at the end of the 1990s and was paid to mothers of poor families, the elderly and handicapped persons. The Correa administration enhanced the original amount of US$15 in several consecutive steps up from US$30 in 2006 up to US$50 in 2013. The number of this programme's beneficiaries amounted to 1.9 million in 2012. This policy was accompanied by other programmes focusing on safe housing, nutrition and access to credits; see Ministerio de Inclusión Económica y Social (21.01.2013); Ortiz 2011: 225.

18 Indigenous citizens were not consulted on key legislative projects on water and mining in 2009 and 2010, even though they were directly affected by these measures. In peaceful protests against these laws, some indigenous leaders were detained and charged with crimes such as terrorism and sabotage; see Amnesty International 2012.

19 These include the International Covenant on Civil and Political and Rights (ICCPR), the International Covenant on Economic, Social and Cultural Rights (ICESCR), the International Convention on the Elimination of All Forms of Racial Discrimination (ICERD) and the American Convention on Human Rights (ACHR).

20 The corresponding regulation of Law 103 was approved on 18 August 2004 by the Executive Decree 1982.

21 In 2005, only 1.9 per cent of all denounced acts of violence ended with a final sentence. In 2006, the percentage of denounced cases resolved by the judiciary was 2.4 per cent, and in 2007, it rose to 3.1 per cent: see Presidente Constitucional de la República 2007: 11.

22 Between 2007 and 2009, the government spent US$9,011,834 to implement the Plan; see Carrera 2011: 88. For 2010, the State reported to have spent an amount of US$2,720,825; see Organización de los Estados Americanos/ Mecanismo de Seguimiento de la Convención de Belém do Pará 2012: 177.

23 'Patrimonial violence' was defined in this survey as the transformation, misappropriation, destruction, retention or defraudation of objects, personal documents and values, patrimonial rights or economic resources destined to satisfy the necessities of a victim; see INEC 2011a.

24 The remaining 0.2 per cent self-identified as 'others'; data generated from the INEC website: www.ecuadorencifras.gob.ec (last access 10.06.2015).

25 As the parish of San Francisco and another parish, El Sagrario, were categorised as 'urban', the data from these two administrative entities were not disaggregated, but instead subsumed under the data of the town Cotacachi in the national censuses. Given the mestizo majority residing in the urban centre of Cotacachi, their higher educative levels and incomes and their privileged situation in terms of provision with basic services, the fairly distinct socio-economic situation of the predominantly indigenous population residing in these two 'urban' parishes was invisiblised in these accounts. By contrast, data from the rural parishes were disaggregated in the censuses and thus provided a more realistic picture of the respective communities. Fortunately, UNORCAC conducted a survey among its 43 member communities in 2006 (see UNORCAC 2006), thereby allowing for a more concise picture of La Calera.

26 Data generated from the online System of Social Indicators of Ecuador (SIISE): www.siise.gob.ec/siiseweb (last access 10.06.2015).

27 See Interview 26./27.10.2011; UNORCAC 2006: 26–27.

28 See Fn 17; Ortiz 2011: 225–226.

29 Interviews 26./27.10.2011; 1–27.10.2011; 1–28.10.2011; 31.10.2011.

30 Interviews 26./27.10.2011; 1–27.10.2011; 09.11.2011.

31 Upon CONAIE's decision to create its own electoral vehicle – the Pachakutik Plurinational Unity Movement – New Country (MUPP-NP) – in the mid 1990s, the organisation promoted Tituaña's candidacy for mayor in his home canton Cotacachi. Tituaña was not an UNORCAC affiliate and his candidacy was only accepted after negotiations with the UNORCAC leadership who traditionally proposed their own members as candidates for municipal elections. Ultimately, Tituaña's social prestige associated with his university degree in economics from Cuba and his professional experience in the development sector not only convinced UNORCAC members of his viability as candidate, but made him also an attractive candidate for parts of the mestizo electorate. With only 24.1 per cent of the votes, Tituaña won the 1996 elections; given the success of his participative governance model, he was confirmed in office in 2000 (78.03 per cent) and in 2004 (55.49 per cent); see Cameron 2010: 91–95; Lalander 2010: 62–63, 68–71; Van Cott 2008: 141.

32 Interviews 1–27.10.2011; 1–01.11.2011.

33 Manduriacos is a relatively big parish located in the subtropical zone of the Cotacachi canton.

34 Interviews 1–26.10.2011; 1–01.11.2011.

35 Interviews 1–26.10.2011; 04.11.2011.

36 All citations of interviewees were translated into English by the author.

37 The Quota Law constituted one component of an Electoral Law Reform approved by the Ecuadorian Congress in 2000. Starting off from 30 per cent, the quota was meant to be increased by 5 per cent consecutively throughout the following national elections until reaching 50 per cent. One of the

obstacles to achieving this objective was seen in the fact that voters could select individual candidates from political party lists. Still, women's representation in the National Assembly rose from 17.4 per cent in 2000 to 32 per cent in 2009 and 39 per cent in 2013. For the first time in Ecuadorian history, the current National Assembly (2013–2017) has been presided by a female president and two female vice-presidents; see Archenti 2011: 27–29; Secretaria Nacional de Gestión de la Política (15.05.2013).

38 See UNORCAC 2008; Interview 1–27.10.2011.

39 See Ortiz 2011: 107; Interview 26./27.10.2011.

40 See Nájera 2008; Interviews 1–26.10.2011; 26./27.10.2011; 1–27.10.2011; 5–27.10.2011; 03.11.2011; 04.11.2011.

41 Interview 26./27.10.2011.

42 Interviews 1–26.10.2011; 26./27.10.2011; 1–27.10.2011; 03.11.2011.

43 Interviews 1–26.10.2011; 26./27.10.2011; 1–27.10.2011.

44 Interviews 1–26.10.2011; 26./27.10.2011; 2–28.10.2011; 31.10.2011; 03.11.2011.

45 Interviews 1–26.10.2011; 26./27.10.2011;1–27.10.2011; 5–27.11.2011; 03.11.2011; 04.11.2011.

46 This information is based on copies of the digital archives of the CIAWF kindly handed out by its staff to the author during her fieldwork.

47 Parallel to their participation in the struggle for collective rights conducted by the Zapatista National Liberation Army (EZLN) in the 1990s, Tojola'bal, Chol, Tzotzil and Tzeltal women started to demand the democratisation of gender relations within their communities. The *Revolutionary Law of Women* published on 1 January 1994 enlisted ten of their key demands, among them the right to freedom from violence; to choose their partners and not being forced into marriage; to decide on the number of children they wished to have; to participate in community affairs and hold authority positions; to take part in the collective struggle and hold military ranks in the revolutionary armed forces; to education and access to primary attention in health services and nutrition issues; see Speed, Hernández and Stephen 2006. The Law acquired symbolic relevance for many indigenous women in Mexico and elsewhere, as the example from Cotacachi demonstrates.

48 Interviews 1–26.10.2011; 26./27.10.2011; 1–27.10.2011; 5–27.10.2011; 03.11. 2011; 04.11.2011; 16.12.2011.

49 The pre-selected pilot communities were El Batan and Topo Grande in the El Sagrario parish; San Antonio del Punge from the Quiroga parish; Colimbuela from Imantag parish; and La Calera from the San Francisco parish.

50 Interviews 1–26.10.2011; 26./27.10.2011; 5–27.10.2011; 03.11.2011.

51 Interviews 1–27.10.2011; 04.11.2011; 09.11.2011.

52 Interviews 1–26.10.2011; 26./27.10.2011; 1–27.10.2011; 03.11.2011; 04.11. 2011.

53 Interviews 1–26.10.2011; 26./27.10.2011; 1–27.10.2011.

54 Interviews 1–26.10.2011; 26./27.10.2011; 5–27.10.2011; 03.11.2011; 16.12.2011.

55 Interviews 1–26.10.2011; 26./27.10.2011.

56 CONAMU, and later the municipal government, paid only one (minimum) salary for an indigenous promoter; thus, the two women who filled this position divided this salary into two parts while working full time for the CIAWF.

57 Interviews 1–26.10.2011; 5–27.10.2011; 1–01.11.2011; 16.12.2011.

58 Interviews 1–26.10.2011; 26./27.10.2011; 4–27.10.2011; 5–27.10.2011; 03.11. 2011.

59 See Sumak Kawsaipa Katikamachik – Reglamento para la buena convivencia

comunitaria (n.d.) Cotacachi.

60 Interviews 26./27.10.20111–27.10.2011; 03.11.2011; 04.11.2011.

61 Interviews 1–26.10.2011; 26./27.10.2011; 1–27.10.2011; 03.11.2011; 04.11. 2011.

62 Interviews 1–26.10.2011; 26./27.10.20111–27.10.2011.

63 See Minuta de reunion entre UNIFEM y el Proyecto 'Implementación del reglamento para una buena convivencia en las comunidades indígenas de Cotacachi' (18.09.2008); Interviews 2–27.10.2011; 3–27.10.2011; 03.11.2011.

64 See Minuta de reunion entre UNIFEM y el Proyecto 'Implementación del reglamento para una buena convivencia en las comunidades indígenas de Cotacachi' (18.09.2008).

65 Interviews 26.10.2011; 03.11.2011.

66 Interview 04.11.2011.

67 Interviews 1–28.10.2011; 04.11.2011.

68 Interviews 1–26.10.2011; 1–28.10.2011; 03.11.2011; 16.12.2011.

69 In the Cotacachi canton, 77.65 per cent voted in favour of the Constitution in the referendum held on 28 September 2008; see Lalander 2010: 107.

70 Interview 1–26.10.2011.

71 Interviews 1–26.10.2011; 26./27.10.2011; 1–27.10.2011; 04.11.2011.

72 This networks' Spanish name is *Red contra la Violencia Intrafamiliar* (*Red VIF*). It was established about the same time as the CIAWF and was constituted by representatives of all institutions involved in the prevention and legal treatment of violence in Cotacachi; see Nájera 2008, Interview 1–26.10.2011.

73 The establishment of such *Centros de Equidad y Justicia* was promoted by the 2007 National Plan to Eradicate Gender Violence. The objective behind these centres was to unite all institutions involved in the protection of the rights of children, adolescents and women under one roof so as to facilitate their access to the judicial system and accelerate the processing of legal transgressions. Institutions not only included the police, the Women's and Family Commissariat, the public attorney and competent courts, but also psychologists and public workers and a mediation centre; see Distrito Metropolitano Quito (n.d.); La Hora (25.10.2011). This model of a one-stop shop offering integrated legal services has been a common feature of policy innovations in various world regions; see UN Women 2011:57.

74 Interviews 1–26.10.2011; 1–28.10.2011; 2–01.11.2011; 04.11.2011; 19.11.2011.

75 Interviews 1–26.10.2011; 16.12.2011; personal notes taken during conversation with UN WOMEN representative María Andrade (21.10.2011).

76 See Fn 14; Interview 16.12.2011.

77 See *Justicia Nuestra. Mujeres Indígenas Latinoamericanas y el Acceso a la Justicia.* (2009).

78 Interviews with 26./27.10.2011; 03.11.2011.

79 Interview 2–27.10.2011.

80 Interviews 26./27.10.2011; 2–27.10.2011.

81 Interviews 26./27.10.2011; 1–27.10.2011; 31.10.2011.

82 Interviews 26./27.10.2011; 1–27.10.2011.

83 During her fieldwork, the author observed how women from La Calera gave advice on the treatment of violence to the *cabildo* of San Antonio del Punje; Interview 1–25.10.2011.

84 Interviews 26./27.10.2011; 2–27.10.2011; 4–27.10.2011.

85 Interviews 26./27.10.2011; 2–28.10.2011; 31.10.2011.

86 Interviews 26./27.10.2011; 1–27.10.2011; 2–27.10.2011; 3–27.10.2011; 4–27.10.2011.

87 Data from the 2010 Census on the Otavalo canton generated from the INEC website: www.ecuadorencifras.gob.ec (last access 10.06.2015).
88 The remaining 0.1 per cent self-identified as 'others'; data generated from the INEC website; see Fn 88.
89 The proportion of the mestizo residents in all *comunas* of the Otavalo canton did not exceed 2 per cent on average; see Ortiz 2011: 104.
90 Interviews 2–21.11.2011; 3–22.11.2011; 1–23.11.2011; 2–24.11.2011; 26.11. 2011.
91 Interviews 1–18.11.2011; 2–18.11.2011; 3–22.11.2011; 1–23.11.2011; 2–23.11. 2011; 2–24.11.2011; 26.11.2011; 1–29.11.2011.
92 Interviews 17.11.2011; 1–18.11.2011; 3–21.11.2011; 3–22.11.2011.
93 On the Otavalo weaving tradition and its evolution, see, e.g., Kyle 2001; Meisch 1987; Salomon 1981.
94 In the second half of the 2000s, FICI accounted for 160 member communities in four cantons of the Imbabura Province; see El Comercio 09.06.2013; Lalander 2010: 273–281. But given the general weakening of the national indigenous movement over the 2000s, coupled with the institutionalisation of parish juntas as new vehicles for citizen participation in the canton, the increased role of the municipal government in the promotion of local development and the growing social differentiation (and, hence, interests) of its indigenous affiliates, the organisation lost some relevance in its role as broker between indigenous *comunas* and external institutions; see Ortiz 2011: 145.
95 Conejo won the 2000 municipal elections (with 45.9 per cent of the votes) and the 2004 elections (54.4 per cent) on the ticket of the MUPP-NP. His often uneasy relation to FICI and the shift towards a narrower focus on indigenous issues by MUPP-NP, which he deemed unhelpful in a municipal context in which, from his perspective, the interethnic divides should be reduced rather than accentuated, influenced his decision to leave Pachakutik in 2006 and join a local movement named Minga Intercultural, which allied with the government party Alianza País in the 2009 municipal elections, allowing Conejo to win a third time (42.9 per cent); see Lalander 2010: 113; Ortiz 2011: 198.
96 Interviews 1–18.11.2011; 2–18.11.2011; 1–24.11.2011; 2–24.11.2011.
97 Interviews 1–18.11.2011; 2–18.11.2011; 3–22.11.2011; 2–23.11.2011; 1–24.11.2011; 2–24.11.2011; 26.11.2011; 1–29.11.2011.
98 Interview 1–18.11.2011; 2–18.11.2011; 1–23.11.2011; 1–24.11.2011; 1–29.11.2011; personal observations during *cabildo* session (21.11.2011).
99 Interviews 2–18.11.2011; 2–23.11.2011; 1–24.11.2011; 2–24.11.2011; 1–29.11.2011; personal notes taken during conversation with Corcima representative during a visit of different communities (17.11.2011).
100 Interviews 1–18.11.2011; 2–18.11.2011; 3–22.11.2011; 2–24.11.2011; personal notes taken during conversation with Corcima representative during a visit of different communities (17.11.2011) and during conversation with Corcima representative in his office (30.11.2011).
101 Interviews 1–18.11.2011; 2–18.11.2011; 1–23.11.2011; 2–23.11.2011; 2–24.11. 2011.
102 Interviews 2–18.11.2011; 1–23.11.2011.
103 Interviews 14.11.2011; 2–18.11.2011; 1–22.11.2011; 1–23.11.2011; 2–23.11. 2011; 1–24.11.2011; 2–29.11.2011.
104 Interviews 1–22.11.2011; 2–22.11.2011; 1–23.11.2011.
105 Interviews 20.11.2011; 2–22.11.2011; 3–22.11.2011; 1–23.11.2011.
106 Interviews 1–18.11.2011; 2–18.11.2011; 1–24.11.2011; personal notes taken during conversation with Corcima representative in his office (30.11.2011).

107 Interviews 17.11.2011; 1–18.11.2011; 1–23.11.2011; 26.11.2011; personal notes taken during conversation with Corcima representative in his office (30.11.2011).
108 Interviews 2–18.11.2011; 3–18.11.2011; 1–21.11.2011; 2–21.11.2011; 3–22.11.2011; 1–23.11.2011.
109 Personal notes taken during an evaluation session between World Vision and Corcima in Otavalo and during a team meeting of Corcima, both held in November 2011.
110 Interview 1–18.11.2011; personal notes taken during conversation with Corcima representative in his office (30.11.2011).
111 Personal notes taken during conversation with Corcima representative during a visit of different communities (17.11.2011).
112 Interviews 1–18.11.2011; 29.11.2011; personal notes taken during conversation with Corcima representative during a visit of different communities (17.11.2011)
113 See Fn 37.
114 Interviews 17.11.2011; 1–23.11.2011.
115 Interviews 14.11.2011; 17.11.2011; 1–18.11.2011; 3–18.11.2011; 1–22.11.2011; 26.11.2011; 2–29.11.2011.
116 Interviews 17.11.2011; 3–18.11.2011; 3–22.11.2011; 2–24.11.2011.
117 Interviews 1–18.11.2011; 1–23.11.2011.
118 Interviews 20.11.2011; 2–22.11.2011; 2–29.11.2011.
119 Interview 20.11.2011.
120 Interviews 1–22.11.2011; 2–22.11.2011; 2–29.11.2011.
121 Interviews 17.11.2011; 3–18.11.2011; 2–21.11.2011; 3–22.11.2011; 1–23.11.2011.
122 Interviews 1–18.11.2011; 1–23.11.2011; 2–24.11.2011; 26.11.2011.
123 Interviews 17.11.2011; 1–18.11.2011; 3–18.11.2011; 3–22.11.2011; 1–23.11.2011; 26.11.2011.
124 Interviews 2–18.11.2011; 3–22.11.2011; 1–23.11.2011; 2–23.11.2011; 26.11.2011; 1–29.11.2011.
125 Interviews 1–18.11.2011; 1–24.11.2011; 2–24.11.2011; 1–29.11.2011.
126 Interviews 17.11.2011; 1–18.11.2011; 3–18.11.2011; 3–22.11.2011; 1–23.11.2011; 2–23.11.2011; 1–24.11.2011; 2–24.11.2011; 26.11.2011; 1–29.11.2011.
127 Interviews 1–18.11.2011; 3–21.11.2011; 3–22.11.2011; 1–23.11.2011; 24.11.2011; 1–29.11.2011.
128 Interviews 3–22.11.2011; 26.11.2011.

Chapter 4

'As if I was sleeping, and then I woke up!'

Chacabamba and Tungasuca, Peru

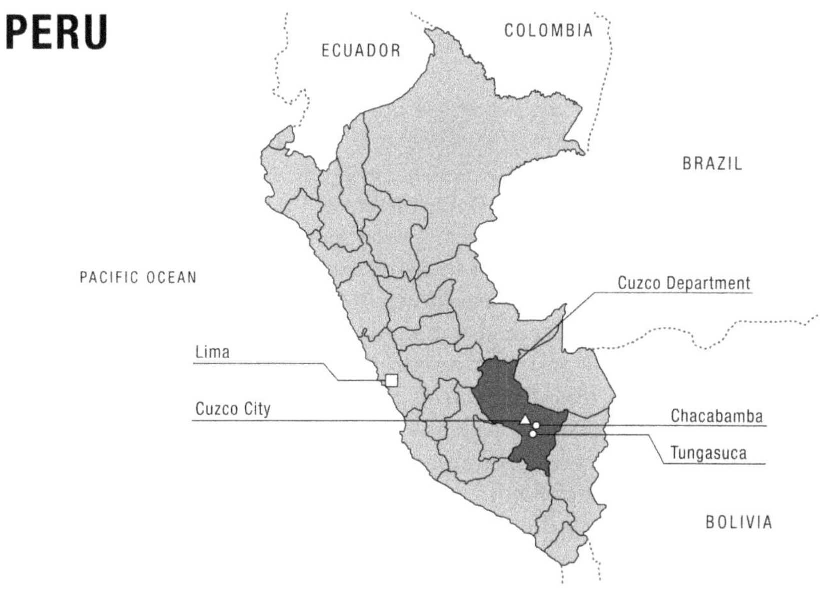

Map 4.1 Peru

In Peru, the search for reliable data on the indigenous peoples is complicated: first, because the range of external and self-denominations (such as *andino, serrano, campesino, cholo, nativo, indígena*) is broad and dynamic (De la Cadena 1998; Lucero and García 2006); second, because the label 'indigenous' continues to be associated with negative markers such as backwardness, servitude and poverty (Degregori 1998: 168; Yashar 2005: 226, Fn 4); and third, because estimations on the proportion of the indigenous population vary considerably between 15.7 per cent according to the 2007 Census of the National Institute of Statistics and Informatics (INEI) in which the mother tongue was used as the only indicator for self-identification,[1] 35–40 per cent according to some analysts (e.g., Yashar 2005: 225–226) or even 47 per cent (Barié 2003: 479; see also Van Cott 2005: 141–142). Adopting the arguably narrow data from the National Census of 2007 and the II Census of Indigenous Communities of the Peruvian Amazon 2007 in order to obtain an idea about the numbers of these peoples, 3,360,331 persons (of a total of 25,810,331 Peruvians above the age of three) were Quechua speakers, constituting thereby the largest group with about 83 per cent of the entire indigenous population. They were followed by 443,248 Aymara speakers, accounting for 11 per cent of the indigenous population. Both groups were concentrated residentially in the Andean highlands (*Sierra*), but also represented a considerable number of residents in urban areas (45.7 per cent of the Quechua and 43 per cent of the Aymara, respectively). This picture is complemented by a (still underestimated) diversity of 51 ethnic groups spanning eleven linguistic families who are dispersed across eleven north-eastern Departments of the Peruvian Amazon. Their total number amounted to 333,975 persons according to the 2007 Census, with the Asháninkas as the largest group (88,703 persons). The Department of Cuzco, where the two communities studied in this chapter are located, ranged among the four departments in which Quechua speakers accounted for more than half of the overall population (51.4 per cent or 566,581 persons).[2]

Indigenous peoples were mentioned for the first time in the 1920 Constitution of Peru, just 100 hundred years after independence, and earlier than in neighbouring states. The Constitution conferred on the State the task of 'protect[ing] the indigenous race' (art. 58), while declaring their lands as imprescriptible (art. 41). Even though indigenous communities were henceforth given the option to voluntarily register in a designated state agency, the expansion of the hacienda system could not be deterred until 1969, when the populist military government of Juan Velasco Alvarado (1968–75) introduced a far-reaching Agrarian Reform based on expropriation of the former landowners and redistribution of these lands to newly created peasant cooperatives. Under this government the term 'indigenous' was abolished from state legal language, and a consequential line between native communities in the Amazon and *campesino* communities in the Sierra was officialised (Barié 2003: 473–487; Hurtado and Du Puit 2006: 226–227; Yashar 2005: 228–229; Yrigoyen 2002: 160–161). The 1970 Special Statute of Campesino Communities (Supreme Decree 37–70–AG) assigned these entities a status of cooperatives, defined the criteria for membership and determined their property and labour regimes. Disregarding traditional indigenous authorities and forms of organisation, a new administrative structure based on a general assembly, an administrative council and a monitoring council (*concejo de vigilancia*) was introduced (Robles 2002: 88–104). In order to get access to state benefits, the communities were obliged to assimilate the new structure and expected to affiliate with state-created agrarian associations. While the new structure facilitated communication with state agencies, it was common to observe communities maintaining some of their previous authority positions or merging former community-based institutions with the newly created entities (Albó 2009: 178–180; Gonzales de Olarte 1994: 187; Yashar 2005: 232–235). In 2002, 886 *campesino* communities were registered in the Department of Cuzco (Diez 2011: 27).

Recognition of legal pluralism

While the Constitution of 1979 remained silent on the issue of indigenous justice, legislation enacted from the second half of the 1980s onwards gradually came to reflect the fact that the state judiciary was not the only institution that exerted jurisdictional functions throughout the Peruvian territory: the 1987 General Law on Campesino Communities (Law 24656) mentioned the existence of 'autochthonous customary law' (art. 1b), whereas its 1991 Regulation Law (Supreme Decree 008–91–TR) ruled that community members could be held accountable for transgressions of the community statute and the law. Deliberations on transgressions were supposed to include the antecedents of the person, eventual recidivism, the circumstances in which the transgression occurred and local customs (*usos y costumbres*). While proposing potential sanctions such as verbal or written admonitions, fines and suspension of communal rights, the Law also allowed for the determination of other sanctions in community statutes. The communal board (*directiva comunal* – a body into which the former administrative and monitoring councils were merged, constituted by the community's elected president, vice-president, secretary, treasurer, fiscal agent and several substitutes) – was in charge of the pronunciation of smaller sanctions, while the more severe ones were supposed to emanate from the general assembly (art. 32–36; 69k Regulation Law). Besides, the community could also opt to create a *ronda campesina* (peasant patrol) as one of its specialised committees (art. 18k Law 24656; art. 73 Supreme Decree 008–91–TR).

As a consequence of the withdrawal of many hacienda-owners in the context of Agrarian Reform and a vacuum of social control that was neither filled by the quasi absent State, nor by some pre-existing indigenous or *campesino* community, *rondas campesinas* or local rotative systems of nocturnal vigilance, first emerged in 1979 in the Department of Cajamarca (Yrigoyen 1993). *Rondas* came to deal with issues such as cattle robbery, debts, inheritance, territorial demarcation, family conflicts and even homicide and, to a certain extent, the applied norms, procedures and sanctions shared similarities to indigenous forms of justice. Due to its effectiveness and social legitimacy, the *ronda* model promptly spread to other regions in Peru. In the context of the extension of the internal armed conflict between the State and guerrilla organisations (*Shining Path*; *Revolutionary Movement Tupac Amaru*) in the second half of the 1980s and a corresponding increase of crimes against civilians perpetrated by insurgents, state security forces and criminal gangs, a growing number of native communities in the Amazon and *campesino* communities in the southern Departments such as Cuzco also opted for the creation of *rondas* as specialised committees within pre-existing community structures (Decoster and Rivera 2009: 44–57; Picolli 2008; Yrigoyen 1993).[3] With Law 24571 (1986), the government of Alan García (1985–1990) aimed to take advantage of this development by incorporating the *rondas* into the State's counterinsurgency efforts. His successor in office, Alberto Fujimori (1990–2000) (who became known for his authoritarian rule, the dismantling of democratic institutions, corruption scandals and severe human rights violations) progressively elaborated on these policies by promoting the conversion of *rondas* and other vigilante groups into armed and trained committees of self-defence (*comités de autodefensa*; Picolli 2008: 29–30, 35; Yashar 2005: 248; Yrigoyen 1993; 2002: 156–166).

Amidst increasing international pressure after Fujimori's 'self-coup' in 1992 with which he suspended the 1979 Constitution and dismantled the legislative and judiciary branches, and in line with the regional shift towards the adoption of multicultural citizenship regimes, the government adopted a new Constitution in 1993 that recognised the right to ethnic and cultural identity (art. 2.19), the legal status and autonomy of *campesino* and native communities (art. 89), indigenous legal authorities, as well as their right to administer justice:

> The authorities of the campesino and native communities, with the support of the rondas campesinas, may exert jurisdictional functions within their territories in accordance with customary law, as long as they do not violate the fundamental rights of the individual. The law establishes the coordination between this special jurisdiction with the Justices of the Peace and other instances of the judicial branch.
>
> (art. 149; author's translation)

Despite the formal recognition of legal pluralism in the 1993 Constitution, the relationship between the State and indigenous peoples remained highly ambivalent throughout the following two decades. On the one hand, Peru ratified ILO C 169, which affirms indigenous peoples' right to administer justice in 1994.[4] The State also responded to the controversy on whether the *rondas* should be regarded as an entity of support to community authorities or rather as a judicial instance in their own right, by implementing Law 27908 on Rondas Campesinas in 2003 in which the *rondas*' own competence to resolve conflicts was clearly affirmed. Furthermore, in 2006, a modification to the Penal Code ruled that state courts should not deal with cases in which indigenous authorities had already intervened (*ne bis in idem* principle; art. 18.3 Penal Code). On the other hand, the Constituent Assembly had missed a historic opportunity to adopt the term 'indigenous peoples' into the Magna Carta, and controversies about those who were entitled to self-identify as 'indigenous' (and those who were not) have ever since complicated the implementation of policies and rights of indigenous peoples in Peru.[5] With respect to legal practice, many incidences became known in which state courts have prosecuted indigenous authorities for exercising their right to administer justice (Ardito 2011: 44; De Belaúnde 2006: 131–132, 136; Schönbohm 2011: 37–99; Yrigoyen 2002: 170). Moreover, the recognition of cultural diversity stood in stark contrast to other norms of the 1993 Constitution and subsequently enacted neoliberal policies, which seriously threatened indigenous peoples by abolishing the inalienability of their lands and by promoting foreign investments in the exploration of natural resources.[6] Consequently, the number of socio-ecological conflicts involving the State, private companies and non-consulted indigenous groups across the country increased.[7] This process culminated in the deadly conflict in Bagua (5 June 2009)[8] – a wake-up-call that paved the way for the adoption of a Law 29785 on the Right to Previous Consultation to Indigenous Peoples (2011) by the government of Ollanta Humala.[9]

By the end of the 2000s, it was especially due to the judiciary that progress in the realm of legal pluralism was achieved: the Supreme Court of Peru confirmed in 2009 a long-standing demand of the *rondas* when it ruled that their faculty to administer justice be recognised independently of whether or not they belong to a *campesino* or native community (Corte Suprema de Justicia 2009). International congresses on intercultural justice were organised throughout 2010 and 2011 in three regions of the country so as to facilitate dialogue on legal pluralism between state, indigenous and *ronda* representatives (Corte Suprema de Justicia; Consejo Ejecutivo del Poder Judicial; Centro de Investigaciones Judiciales del Poder Judicial 2011; Ruiz 2010: 76–77). The National Office of Justice of the Peace and Indigenous Justice (ONAJUP) was assigned the task of supervising all *initiatives* aimed at improving the coordination between all jurisdictions in Peru. In various departments, including Cuzco, schools for intercultural justice were created to foster the training of and articulation between state and non-state judicial authorities (Consejo Ejecutivo del Poder Judicial 2014: 7). Lastly, the Supreme Court submitted a draft proposal for a Law on the Intercultural Coordination of Justice to the legislature in 2011, where it was approved in the Commission of Andean, Amazon, Afro-Peruvian Peoples, the Environment and Ecology by the end of 2013; as is the case with any legislation affecting indigenous peoples, this draft law would have to be subject to a consultation of the affected groups before its final adoption by the legislative branch.[10]

Importantly, this overview on what is commonly denominated 'communal justice' in Peru – particularly in the *Sierra* – would not be complete without the mention of other legal intermediaries. For in contrast to Ecuador and Bolivia where the limits between indigenous and state jurisdictions have been more clear-cut and indigenous organisations' resistance against state intervention in their autonomous spaces of self-regulation has been stronger (IDL 2005: 49–52), in Peru patterns of legal hybridity are more pronounced:

The *justices of the peace*, introduced briefly after Peru's independence, were established based on the idea that the resolution of minor problems and offences at the local level would require the use of common sense and prevalent customs rather than the expertise of a lawyer. Until the Agrarian Reform of 1969, the function of the justice of the peace was typically conferred to hacienda-owners or members of wealthy families. As the exercise of this function was uncontrolled, it lent itself for many kinds of abuses.[11] Especially in the *Sierra*, the justices' negative reputation changed considerably after *campesino* communities were given the right to propose candidates in their own right in the aftermath of the Agrarian Reform.[12] Nowadays, justices of the peace are mostly ordinary community members, they are familiar with local traditions, culture and language, offer immediate resolutions in minor offences, conflicts between relatives, neighbours or commoners, and their services involve minimal costs for involved parties (IDL 2005; Lovatón 2005). While most conflicts are resolved via conciliation, in some issues (e.g., the fixing of alimony payments), the justices' decisions can obtain mandatory status. More than 5,102 justices of the peace existed in Peru in 2005, out of which 73 per cent were located in the Andes. For many rural inhabitants, these judges presented the only state judicial institution they have ever entered into contact with.[13]

The governor (*gobernador*) at the district level and the deputy governor (*teniente gobernador*) at the community level have equally assumed a (not explicitly assigned) role in conflict resolution in some communities. These authorities acted as official representatives of the President of the Republic, were part of the Ministry of the Interior and were answerable to the regional and provincial governments. Their competencies[14] included the support for the compliance with the Constitution and the Laws in their respective jurisdictions, which could imply the forwarding of human rights violations to the competent institutions. (Deputy) governors were often of local origin and elected by the co-commoners of their jurisdiction, hence people sometimes also directed themselves to these governors when seeking redress for different sorts of conflicts (Ardito 2011: 36; IDL 2005: 200).

In some regions, including Cuzco, the aforementioned *committees of self-defence* have not disappeared with the containment of the armed conflict.

Some of these entities continue to form part of the community administration and performing functions of surveillance and crime prevention (IDL 2005: 209).

From 2002 onwards, the State started to promote the creation of citizen security groups (*juntas vecinales de seguridad ciudadana*) that were elected by their respective communities and that were expected to assume functions related to the maintenance of order and crime prevention (SINASEC 2009).

How exactly the co-existence of all these authorities played out depended on the local context and the relationship that actors developed amongst each other. In some locations these agents negotiated an effective division of labour, whereas in other cases such constellations have provoked competition and disunity (Decoster and Rivera 2009: 89; Franco 2007: 112; IDL 2005: 200-201). Not least, community members' decisions on whom to refer to hinged on the trust they had in particular office holders, their effectiveness in conflict resolution, as well as their geographical proximity.[15]

Legislation on violence against indigenous women

Peru signed all relevant international treaties that guarantee the right to equality, equal treatment and non-discrimination, as well as the right to freedom from violence, such as the ICERD (in force in Peru since 1971), ICCPR (1978), ICESCR (1978), ACHR (1978), CEDAW (1982) and the Convention Belém do Pará (1996). The country also developed a national legal and political framework to address violence against women. This includes articles 1 and 2 of the 1993 Constitution which establish, *inter alia*, the respect for human dignity, the right to life, to moral, psychical and physical integrity, to equal treatment before the law and non-discrimination, and to attention by a competent authority. Law 26260 on the Protection against Family Violence, with its first version enacted in December 1993, defined distinct dimensions of family violence (physical, psychological, sexual), determined potential aggressors who could be held legally accountable for violent acts (former or current spouses; former or current partners; family members until the fourth degree of kinship; people residing in the victim's house; persons who procreated a child with the victim) and regulated the intervention by the police, public prosecutors and judges. The Law also enabled legal operators to enact protective measures such as the temporary distancing of the aggressor from the victim's home. In addition, the National Program against Family and Sexual Violence (2002–2007) fostered the already initiated setting up of Emergency Centres for Women (*Centros de Emergencia de la Mujer*, CEMs) in which multiprofessional teams consisting of psychologists, lawyers and social workers were to attend to victims of domestic and sexual violence and support them in the respective legal procedures. The programme involved the construction of women's shelters and activities to spread information about domestic violence. Experts bemoaned the little relevance that violence prevention was assigned in these policies and emphasised the ineffectiveness of many measures: while the establishment of CEMs in larger cities, especially in Lima, spread from 36 of such centres in 2002 to 114 in 2010, many of them were insufficiently supplied with basic services and lacked financial and human resources so as to offer the envisioned services. The basis for action of legal operators was formulated very broadly, thus leaving police officers, doctors, attorneys and judges a considerable scope of discretion in the fulfilment of their roles, the assessment of the severity of the injury,[16] and the determination of sanctions. Most justice operators were not trained in gender-related issues, and many reports bore witness to the persistence of gender stereotypes guiding the operators' actions and rulings. Cases rarely reached the courts, and if they did, victims of violence had to endure long waiting periods until receiving a legal response because of bureaucratic procedures and the case overload of the judiciary. In addition, most of the protection measures were poorly implemented (Boesten 2010: 113–124; DEMUS 2011: 91; Franco and González 2009: 37; Llaja 2012: 313). Accordingly, the high rates of violence in Peru persisted.

The 2012 National Demographic Survey on Family Health (INEI 2012: ch. 12) found that 36.4 per cent Peruvian women have experienced physical and 8.7 per cent sexual forms of violence by their current or last intimate partner. Psychological violence was measured by four distinct dimensions: 66.3 per cent Peruvian women suffered from the exercise of control by their current or last intimate partner;[17] 21.7 per cent experienced humiliating verbal expressions or acts made by their current or last intimate partner in the presence of other persons; 11.3 per cent

Table 4.1 Violence against women in Peru (2012)*

	Psychological violence by current or last intimate partner (in %)	*Physical violence by current or last intimate partner (in %)*	*Sexual violence by current or last intimate partner (in %)*
Nationwide	Exercise of control 66.3 Humiliation 21.7 Menaced with harm 11.3 Other menaces 19.9	36.4	8.7
Cuzco	Exercise of control 74.2 Humiliation 29.3 Menaced with harm 18.9 Other menaces 26.3	49.2	20.0

Source: Adapted from Encuesta Demográfica y de Salud Familiar (2012); see INEI 2012.

* This national survey included 12,842 currently or ever-partnered women between 15 and 49 years.

received threats from their (ex-)partner as to which they themselves or another person close to them would be inflicted harm; and 19.9 per cent were threatened with being abandoned, losing custody of their children or economic support from their (ex-)partner. In Cuzco, the region where the two communities included in the study are situated, violence rates were considerably higher: 49.2 per cent women suffered from physical violence, and one in every five women (20 per cent) experienced sexual violence exerted by their (ex-)partner. In addition, 74.2 per cent experienced situations of control by their intimate partners (or ex-partners), 29.3 per cent reported to having been placed in a humiliating situation, 18.9 per cent were threatened with harm being inflicted to them or someone close to them, and 26.3 per cent were threatened with being abandoned, losing custody of their children or economic support from their (ex-)partner.

Unfortunately, ethnically disaggregated data on gender violence were not provided in official surveys – a critique that was already expressed in 2007 by the UN CEDAW Committee – which stressed that this shortcoming would also impede the State from designing appropriate policies against gender violence (UN Committee on the Elimination of Discrimination against Women 2007: para. 10; see also para. 36, 37). And even though the recent National Plan against Violence towards Women (2009–2015) highlighted the importance of adopting an *intercultural* focus in the struggle against violence, this insight remained declaratory in nature as it was not translated into concrete strategies, actions and indicators. Instead, the Plan focused on three general objectives, namely the implementation of public policies targeting violence against women, the improvement of public services related to violence, and the transformation of permissive attitudes in society towards violence, but without addressing the role of indigenous legal systems and the obstacles indigenous women encounter when seeking justice. The Plan also envisioned the adoption of similar programmes at Department level (DEMUS 2011: 311–312; IDL 2010: 93–97; Ministerio de la Mujer y Desarrollo Social 2009).[18] However, as the case studies of this chapter will show, multiple obstacles have thus far complicated the effective implementation of such a plan in Cuzco.

Chacabamba–Paucartambo Province (2002–2012)

Chacabamba, administratively ascribed to Cuzco's Paucartambo Province and only a few kilometres away from the capital of the district Huancarani (also named Huancarani), is located on the upper side of a mountain slope at the altitude of around 3,800 meters. In contrast to some neighbouring sectors, the community successfully resisted the invasion of hacienda-owners and was proud to become host of one of the Province's first rural elementary schools in the 1950s. In the course of the Agrarian Reform Chacabamba was renamed a *campesino* community and adjusted its

Image 4.1 Banner promoting the *defensoría comunitaria* in Chacabamba

administrative system to the legally prescribed requirements (including a communal board, a general assembly and several specialised committees). Throughout the period of armed violence, which affected the Cuzco Department from the mid 1980s to the first half of the 1990s, the community was fortunately not directly affected by the invasion of insurgents or soldiers, but it followed the example of many communities in the region in creating a nocturnal vigilante group (*comité de vigilancia*), which performed some of the security functions commonly associated with a *ronda campesina.* Once the threat diminished, the group dissolved. With its population growing, public services were broadened in the 1990s to include a secondary school and a public health post; in the mid 2000s, the community was declared a populated centre (*centro poblado*), which implied the provision of more facilities such as a civic centre (in construction in 2012) and the right to elect additional authorities (a mayor – *alcalde,* a deputy – *regidor* and a justice of the peace, the latter of which was not installed until 2012). In earlier times a journey to Cuzco city hinged on the passing by of a truck and took about 5 to 6 hours; but with the construction of a paved road by the end of the 2000s the time for travelling to the Department's capital with a minibus was reduced to an hour.[19]

At the time of fieldwork (January-early March 2012), the population of Chacabamba amounted to an approximate number of 100 families and 40

Image 4.2 Defensoría member (left) and neighbour in Chacabamba

additional ones living in a neighbouring settlement (*anexo*). Virtually all inhabitants of Chacabamba spoke Quechua and self-identified as *campesinos*. Traditionally, most community members were Catholics, but throughout the 2000s, around a third has converted to evangelical Churches.[20] Young women in the Paucartambo Province had three children on average in 2007 due to increased migration and longer education periods. This number compared with six children (who survived) among the eldest generation of women in a fertile age. Malnutrition and low-quality health care services ranged among the causes of a high mortality rate (17 per cent) of children who were born alive. Illiteracy rates declined from 29.2 per cent (1993) to 18.2 per cent (2007) among men and from 61.6 per cent (1993) to 48.2 per cent (2007) among women. Around 40.7 per cent women and 14.8 per cent men above the age of 15 in Paucartambo abandoned elementary school without a qualification. It was not easy to make a living in Chacabamba. In the entire district of Huancarani, 91.6 per cent of the 6,910 inhabitants fell below the poverty line, and 68.6 per cent were regarded as extremely poor in 2007.[21] Traditionally, people had subsisted from some agricultural products (e.g., potatoes, barley, beans) and livestock breeding. With the growth of the population distributable land parcels became ever smaller, which is why parents felt prompted to send their children not only to elementary but also to secondary school (sons *and* daughters alike), while at the same time seeking employment opportunities outside of the community for themselves. Male commoners worked in construction projects or as masons in urban zones, and, to a minor degree, in the transportation sector or in the mines in the Amazon. Those few able to achieve some technical training found jobs in workshops in urban centres. Depending on the concrete occupation, men returned on evenings, weekends or every couple of weeks. Meanwhile, their wives took care of the crops and animals and were responsible for reproductive activities. Some of them occasionally gained money by selling their handicrafts. Younger and unmarried women also sought employment in Cuzco, for instance in hotels or restaurants. Adolescents increasingly migrated to urban centres such as Cuzco to attend schools or to seek work, but they kept returning to the community on weekends, vacations and for traditional festivities such as the carnival.

Why did claims for legal change emerge in Chacabamba?

Shifts in local power relations

Until the beginning of the new century, local governance was clearly demarcated along gender lines. Men dominated public affairs, while women took hold of the family sphere. When men married, they became entitled to become a qualified commoner (*comunero calificado*), to be inscribed as 'head of family' in the community registry, and to be assigned a land parcel. Qualified commoners enjoyed all the rights, but were also expected to comply with all obligations stipulated in the community statute. This included participation 'with voice and vote' in the general assembly (which met regularly once every three months), and in the communal works (*faenas*). Every two years, the qualified commoners gathered in a general assembly to elect the communal board, which was responsible for the administration of community affairs. The board consisted of the president, vice-president, a secretary, fiscal agent, a treasurer and three deputies; office holders could be re-elected as well as revoked from office at any time during their term in case of improper exercise of the office. The participation of women in the general assembly was limited to widows who assumed the rights and the obligations of their deceased husbands, and to women who substituted their husbands in case these could not participate. The absence from assemblies and *faenas* had to be anticipated with a respective notification of the communal board, and despite the substitution of qualified commoners by their wives, the family was obliged to pay a fine. In cases of the repeated absence of a qualified community member across several assembly sessions the substitution by his wife would no longer be accepted and the assembly would agree upon a sanction to remind the commoner of his duties. Exceptions from this regime were made for extraordinary assemblies that were convened in emergencies that required immediate resolution. As a result, there were few women taking part in regular assemblies and they were elected as secretaries or treasurers to the communal board only in exceptional cases – especially if the women were literate.[22]

Alongside the assembly and the board, there also existed specialised committees that were responsible for the management of particular matters, such as irrigation. Beginning in the 1980s, several women's groups, whose establishment was stimulated by the State to locally organise the delivery and distribution of food to the poorest community sectors, became incorporated in this organisational structure: the mothers' club (*club de madres*) received seeds and training in cultivation methods and nutrition; the communal kitchen (*comedor popular*) was supplied with food so as to prepare warm meals for school children and other persons of low income; and the glass-of-milk committee (*vaso de leche*) distributed milk powder, often enriched with oatmeal, quinoa or other nutrients, among families with young children.[23] The fact that all women – independent of marital status, literacy, etc. – were free to becoming engaged in these groups, could be regarded as positive on its own. Group members elected a directory board among themselves and learned how to administer available resources and comply with the functions they were assigned.[24] However, the empowerment of women in realms extending beyond the core objectives of these programmes was neither intended by the State[25] nor did women from Chacabamba take advantage of the new skills acquired by their engagement in these groups so as to mount demands for more participation in other community institutions (such as the board or the assembly). This was a phenomenon observed in some other areas of the Cuzco Department where communities were badly hit by armed violence and had lost a considerable part of their male population, or where husbands' work migration periods extended to prolonged periods and women began to take on more responsibilities in local governance.[26]

Inappropriate resolution of cases of domestic violence by existing institutions

Unless it became highly public and 'excessive' (because of clear markings on women's bodies), domestic violence against women was usually not commented on in Chacabamba. Only in very extreme cases would people talk, express their opposition, and advise the victim to seek help by the first (and often the only) suitable group in this type of conflict: the family, and particularly the parents and godparents of the couple. This kin intervention was based on dialogue and good advice, and its effectiveness depended on the actual authority these family members exerted on the couple and the attitudes of these persons towards violence. Moreover, this private sphere lacked the effect of public ostentation that was present in conflict-resolution sessions of the communal board or the assembly.[27]

If kin intervention proved ineffective, women had few avenues within the community to seek justice, as neither the communal board, nor the general assembly, were understood as spaces where 'domestic' problems should be discussed. These bodies responded instead to controversies over the demarcation of land parcels, delinquency, cattle theft, severe or recurrent disputes between commoners, or incompliance with community duties stipulated in the community statute. If at all, they would refer the parties in conflict to the deputy governor – a state intermediary – who generally offered to mediate in cases of 'minor' problems, such as damage of crops caused by a neighbour's cattle or debts that did not exceed the amount of S/.100 (about US$35 at the moment of writing). The deputy governor was not specifically trained in issues such as violence, thus his acting upon a case was guided by the same standards he applied in other types of conflict. His aim was to find a quick resolution and facilitate reconciliation of the parties in conflict, but the expectation of women that resolution procedures would make the aggressors reflect upon the harm caused to their wives, or an orientation in more respectful forms of relationship, was not met.[28]

The next-proximate institutions that could likewise be called upon were situated in the district capital Huancarani. Here women could turn to a justice of the peace, whose acting upon cases of domestic violence throughout the 1990s had a mixed record at best. Here too there was no profound analysis of the concrete situation of the couple and, based on this, no concise orientation offered about how the violent behaviour of the husband might be changed.[29] Severe cases of violence had to be passed by the justice of the peace to the Huancarani police station. Throughout the 1990s, police officers did neither react promptly nor sensitively to the women's needs. They were impatient, did not dispose of the time to actually hear women's testimonies (the indigenous women preferred to give their testimonies in Quechua, but policemen were not willing to allow them to do so) and were not trained in how to deal with victims of domestic violence. Therefore, they often failed to direct women to a specialised doctor so as to assess the physical harm caused. What is more, by offering an animal or a meal in a restaurant to the involved officer, aggressors could successfully bring investigations to a halt. The mostly male police officers tended to declare women co-responsible or culpable for the violence exerted against them, and cases would often end in an 'extra-judicial agreement' arranged by the officer. Hardly ever did cases of violence pass this stage in the chain of legal intervention offered by the State.[30] A CEM was installed in 1999 in the Department capital Cuzco, but women in Chacabamba were unaware of its existence. Over its 12 years of operation, the rate of indigenous women residing in rural parts of the Department attended by the CEM did not exceed 20 per cent, and upon the author's asking whether the diffusion of information about the centre's services included radio spots in Quechua – radios constitute the most frequently used means of communication among the rural population in the Andes – the representative responded that this idea was actually worth considering.[31]

Diffusion of new legal concepts

In Chacabamba, domestic violence was essentially considered a 'normal' conduct exerted both by parents against their children and by husbands against their wives. Just as children needed to be controlled in their conduct by their parents, adult men translated the scheme to their spouses:

> Women are really taking the worst part, but children as well, because here the father beats the mother, but also the mother beats the children (…). This is why a woman also causes injuries, as she feels that this is the form of punishment by which conduct can be corrected. And deep inside this woman also feels that if she is punished, well, then perhaps she has done something wrong and that is why she receives a justified punishment by her spouse.
>
> (Interview 17.02.2012)

While this violent behaviour might have been related to men's efforts to maintain the authority as 'heads of families', another relevant factor that has a disinhibiting effect on men was the excessive consumption of alcohol. Chacabamba's calendar of Catholic festivities, in addition to weekly meetings of young men whose main objective consisted in getting drunk, offered many occasions on which men got drunk collectively. But alcohol was also consumed during work on the fields or at home. In such situations, any pretext (e.g., jealousy, the raising of an objection), could prompt men to use violence against their spouses.[32]

Until 2001, the idea that violence was a 'normal' conduct remained unchallenged in the community, and there had never been an agent in Chacabamba working on the issue of violence. The medical personnel working in the local health post have refrained from raising women's awareness about this issue, even though they were supposed to attend cases of violence according to a recently adopted General Law 26842 on Health (1997). Therefore, a turning point in Chacabamba was the visit of a UNICEF employee in 2002. She approached the communal board and asked to present the model of the *defensoría comunitaria* (community defence office) to the community. As she explained, such *defensorías* were currently being created in several provinces of the Cuzco Department with the objective of improving the wellbeing of children, women and the family. The community assembly accepted the proposal of UNICEF to host a *defensoría* in their community, for which they were asked to select male and female community members who would receive training in a topic of which they had been largely unaware of: human rights.[33]

One of the origins of the *defensorías* can be traced back to Brazil, where in poor, semi-urban neighbourhoods the institution of legal counsellors were created throughout the second half of the 1980s so as to assist citizens in claiming their constitutionally guaranteed rights before the competent state authorities. By the end of the 1990s, the Ministry of Women in Peru began to promote the establishment of municipal defence offices (*Defensorías Municipales del Niño y del Adolescente*, DEMUNA), with the aim of protecting the rights of children and adolescents. Very soon, DEMUNA employees learned that the focus of their attention needed to be broadened, as the mothers who brought their battered children to these offices turned out to be victims of domestic violence, as well. With the growing demand for the opening of such *defensorías*, UNICEF and a national NGO specialised on legal issues, *Instituto de Defensa Legal* (IDL), signed an agreement in 1999 to establish *defensorías comunitarias* in three Departments in which a considerable part of the population was affected by extreme poverty – Cajamarca, Apurímac and Cuzco. For Cuzco, it was agreed that UNICEF would concentrate on the provinces of Paucartambo and Paruro, while IDL would focus on the province of Canas. The *defensorías* were supposed to attend problems such as domestic violence and other family issues (alimony, visiting rights of divorced parents, birth certificates), thereby filling a gap of access to justice in poor urban sectors and rural communities. Importantly, the *defensorías* were supposed to emanate from locally rooted social organisations. In the city of Cuzco, this included the mother's clubs and *vaso de leche* committees, whereas in rural Cuzco *campesino* federations or *campesino* communities could decide on whether or not such an institution should be established in their jurisdictions. Each participating community was supposed to elect commoners who would hold the office of defenders (*defensores*) for a given period of time. *Defensores* would be trained in the legal issues necessary to facilitate orientation in family problems, as well as in methods to deliver high-quality attention sensitive to the needs of the rural population. They would also accompany the users to the respective *campesino* or state authorities, support them in presenting their complaints, and monitor legal processes so as to ensure that these would not stagnate. UNICEF and IDL agreed that the *defensorías* should have a strong focus on rights, team work and female leadership.[34] But after first experience with exclusively female *defensorías*, these organisations changed their strategy by promoting gender mixed *defensorías* in rural communities:

> Initially it was not foreseen that there were men in the defensorías; however, particularly women from the rural zones, from communities,

> asked that men be trained as defenders, too. And the argument they used in that moment was that them, male defenders, would make themselves more heard by the aggressors, and that by forming mixed teams they themselves [women] would obtain a stronger backing by the community. I believe that there was the idea that spaces exclusively reserved for women would break with the community principle of equilibrium.
>
> (Interview 10./16.01.2012)

Incompatibilities among institutional sets relevant for women's lives

At the end of the 1990s, women in Chacabamba had a low educational level, many of them were monolingual and never had the opportunity to travel outside the community and exchange experiences with other women. The training they received by the abovementioned women's groups did not include issues related to violence or rights. Therefore, it was not until a first group of elected *defensores* participated in 2002 in a UNICEF training on human rights and domestic violence that they began to perceive an incompatibility between the right to freedom of violence on the one hand and the violent conduct tolerated within their families and community on the other hand.

> A: Thus I have already spent six days of training; there I became aware of the rights of women, of children, of adolescents (...)
>
> Q: And was this the first time that you heard about rights?
>
> A: Yes, the first time. Just by then I heard of them. And I also – as I was –. (...). As if I was sleeping, and then I woke up! I opened up my eyes! I, as well, had been abused by my husband, totally abused. And I suffered from violence! Thus I cried when I understood how it is-!
>
> (Interview 01./02.03.2012)

Through the training, the *defensores* arrived at the conclusion that violence was not an adequate means of conflict resolution, but that quite to the contrary, violence could seriously put the wellbeing of children and women at risk. They also came to understand that all humans – men, women, children – were bearers of rights, and that these rights could be invoked before competent authorities. In view that neither the community authorities had been willing to attend 'domestic' problems, nor the most proximate state agencies had thus far facilitated a viable means to attend victims of violence, the contradiction between what they learned and what was offered by the local institutions was felt strongly by the *defensores* and prompted them to lobby for change.[35]

Which factors facilitated or obstructed the initiation of legal change efforts in Chacabamba?

Political opportunities at the starting point of the legal change efforts

In its approach to the community in 2002, UNICEF first established contact with the communal board and asked for permission to present their project in a general assembly. When explaining the characteristics and functions of a *defensoría*, UNICEF could already refer to first encouraging results achieved by *defensorías* that had been installed throughout the previous years in other communities of the Cuzco Department. After the clarification of questions raised by commoners, a clear majority of the assembly voted in favour of the installation of a *defensoría* in their community. Given that at this early stage of the process most people did not have a concrete idea of what exactly the work of the *defensoría* would look like, more general considerations may have motivated the majority vote in Chacabamba. Until that point, the community did not figure prominently on the radar of state and non-state agencies. The fact that an international organisation showed interest in this rather remote place, that it was willing to invest resources and train community members in new thematic issues, and that the community would thereby be incorporated in a larger programme connecting it other places of the Department, was certainly playing a role in the decision-making process. Moreover, UNICEF followed the local protocol of how to approach a community, leaving the decision on whether to establish *defensoría* or not at the discretion of the assembly. The services provided by the *defensoría* would not imply any costs for the users. And those offering services in this newly created institution would not be foreigners, but elected commoners. Indeed, the assembly decided to send a group of three women and three men to the first round of training, among them also the then vice-president of the community. It was clear from the beginning that these individuals would not reserve the knowledge they gained for themselves, but always report on their new insights in the general assembly. Not least, the topic of human rights was one that raised curiosity, as most commoners were not cognisant of what exactly such rights entailed and how far they might benefit from them.[36]

Interpretive frame providing justification for change-orientated action

When returning from their first training by UNICEF, the *defensores* evaluated the situation of the situation as follows: family life was traversed by violence and negligence. The needs of children and adolescents with respect to their health care, alimentation, education and their general wellbeing were not taken into account in many families, and instead of love and protection, parents resorted to violence so as to educate their children. Similarly, women were often suffering from violence exerted by their husbands, with severe consequences for their health and wellbeing. While this violent conduct was long held to be normal and passed from one generation to the next, it could no longer be tolerated from the perspective of the future defenders. During their training they learned that there were international norms and national laws that stated that all human beings, independent from age, gender or other characteristics, were holders of rights. At their core, these rights stipulated that everybody should live a life in dignity, which implied respect and a life free from violence. Thus, even though most community members thought they were acting correctly by recurring to violent means to resolve marital problems and to educate children, the defenders should incentivise commoners to start to think differently.[37]

The establishment of a *defensoría comunitaria* in the community appeared to them as an adequate means for addressing family problems and violence. The *defensoría* would act as an entity where community members could be heard and obtain guidance and, if necessary, be accompanied to the competent authorities. The individuals who received training from UNICEF would share this knowledge with the community in assemblies and workshops and conduct activities to promote non-violent forms of family and communal life.[38] When pondering benefits and risks, the *defensoría* team was aware that it would be dealing with attitudes that were long internalised not only by their co-commoners but also by themselves. To turn away from machismo and authoritarian education methods would undeniably be a very difficult task. Due to the strong asymmetries that existed between state agencies and people from rural communities, the defenders wondered whether they were able to effectively support commoners in claiming their rights before these agencies. And the women in the team were also uncertain of whether they could combine their tasks as defenders with other activities in the household and agriculture without getting into trouble with their husbands. Six days spent outside the home for training had already required negotiation with their spouses. The option to bring small children to the training was therefore highly welcomed by these women. These uncertainties notwithstanding, the benefits of the proposed *defensoría* were clearly defined at that moment. First, solutions to confront violence offered by community and state institutions had hitherto been unsatisfactory at best. Second, the *defensoría* would not compete with the existing authorities in the community, as neither the communal board nor the assembly felt responsible for family affairs and domestic violence. Third, during their initial training UNICEF also assured them that they would receive more training over the coming years, and that a consultant would regularly visit them so as to give advice on particular cases and thus not leave them alone if they did not know how to proceed. Finally, the function of a defender was voluntary and not supposed to be occupied by any member for more than a couple of years; defenders could refrain from this position whenever they deemed they could no longer perform it. And the (re-)election of *defensoría* members should be aligned with the election of all other office holders in the community by the general assembly taking place once every two years.[39]

When the *defensoría* team presented this *initiative* before the general assembly and the women's groups, they received a mixed reception. The strongest resistance came from the elder generation of men who were not willing to change long-held attitudes and who considered that the entire discussion was not of interest for them. However, for other sectors of the community, the problems addressed by the defenders were very convincing. Among them were not only large numbers of women who asked the defenders to organise more frequent conversations with the different women's groups of the community. Of more 'political' weight in the assembly were the voices of the then president of the community and the younger generation of men in general, who ultimately decided to support the *defensoría*. Given that the interpretation of the defenders was not exclusively highlighting problems of women but the wellbeing of children, and that there was no blaming of a particular group (all commoners were supposed to rethink their conduct), the proposal had a particular appeal for young men who were more formally educated than their fathers, who felt a strong desire to improve the living conditions of their families, and for whom their children constituted a crucial element of social mobility. Given their own experiences when seeking work outside the community, they understood that their children would need to be equipped with self-esteem and a good education so as to stand up to the discriminatory context they would encounter when trying to make a living in urban zones. Negligence and violence suffered during childhood would actually lead to the opposite and complicate their later integration in the society and labour market. Also, the discourse of the defenders was welcomed by those families who had converted to the Evangelical Church over the past few years. As the missionaries of this religion strongly advocated the abolition of alcohol consumption because of its devastating consequences for the family, they were also among those endorsing the proposal of the *defensoría*.[40]

Availability of resources at the starting point of the initiative

When starting to advocate for change in the community, the six *defensores* had to accept that some of them, especially the women, had not assumed leadership positions thus far. Not all of them could read and write. They did not know how exactly they could apply in practice what they had learned in the training. Despite these uncertainties, they knew that they would not assume their new role alone, but in a team where they could complement each other. If the workload became heavier, they could divide tasks among them and invite other commoners interested in their work to support them. Of much relevance was the assurance of UNICEF to continue with the training and to counsel the defenders in the resolution of difficult cases. By means of such accompaniment the defenders would also learn how to effectively organise their work, to design plans of activities, and to coordinate cases with other legal authorities.

Another important resource referred to the fact that most *defensores* had themselves lived in violent relationships both as aggressors and as victims of violence. They knew how it felt to be in such a situation and they held that this experience helped them find the right words while attending other persons undergoing similar situations. In the same way, the women in the team felt that it was positive that there were men among the team members, because their presence in challenging situations in which they would have to confront aggressors or authorities was considered helpful so as to achieve effective solutions.

Regarding material resources, *defensores* were informed from the beginning that the engagement in the *defensoría* was considered a voluntary office offered to the community without any costs; therefore, no financial compensation would be paid to them. But UNICEF covered the travel and subsistence expenses while the defenders participated in the trainings held in Cuzco or other cities. The agency also provided them with materials they used to prepare themselves for their work and to circulate among commoners. Finally, the community provided a small room which served as the office of the *defensoría*.[41]

Which factors have influenced the *change initiative* throughout the subsequent stages of its evolution?

Target of change, strategy and tactics

The *change initiative* promoted by UNICEF and IDL in the Cuzco Department aimed at a normative shift towards the non-tolerance of violence in the participating communities (such as Chacabamba), as well as an institutional change insofar as community and state authorities be prompted to respond effectively to cases of violence and other rights violations of hitherto marginalised groups, particularly women and children. The strategy to achieving this goal was threefold. First, defenders should make the problem of violence visible by promoting rights and engaging in activities directed towards the prevention of violence. Second, they should attend and provide information to victims of violence and to parents with problems related to their children and discuss with them the available options by which these problems might be resolved. Third, the *defensores* were expected to accompany these persons through the legal processes they initiated and closely follow the advances so as to ensure that the relevant institutions would actually act upon the claims raised.[42]

The first line of action – the promotion of rights and non-violence – was undertaken by talks held in the general assembly and local women's groups. It was here where defenders shared their new insights with larger sectors of the community, where tensions between traditional practices and alternative understandings of a dignified community life were played out and, thus, where the degree of the acceptance of the *defensoría* as such could be measured. While interventions of the defenders in the general assembly had to be precise and short (due to the usually long agendas of these gatherings), there was more time to talk in the women's groups. Here, women repeatedly expressed the demand to learn more about the rights or women and children, and they also felt more confident to ask questions, raise doubts and talk about their own family problems. In addition, the defenders started to organise talks with teachers, parents and school children on children's rights. Later on, the news of the existence of the *defensoría* in Chacabamba made its way to neighbouring communities. The authorities of those locations asked the *defensoría* team to hold presentations in their assemblies. The defenders willingly accepted these invitations and gave advice about how the community could create an own *defensoría*.[43]

As the condemnation of the excessive consumption of alcohol turned out to be a point of convergence in many discussions, the *defensoría* team started to visit those small shops of the community where they knew that high-percentage beverages were sold on a regular basis. They engaged in conversations with the shopkeepers and tried to convince them that by ending the sale of alcohol they would contribute to a more peaceful atmosphere in families and the entire community. Given that alcohol was an important source of income for local shop owners, this tactic of the *defensoría* required a high degree of insistence and repetitive rounds of conversations with the shopkeepers. After several years of persuasion work, and with the growing reputation of the *defensoría*, high percentage alcohol gradually disappeared from the shelves of many local stores.[44]

After a couple of years of local engagement, and with the support of some allies such as the Ombudsman in Cuzco, the *defensoría* was asked to present their work before state institutions (municipality, police station, justice of the peace, health care personnel, teachers) and the civil society in the district capital Huancarani. For the *defensoría* team, this was the first time that they talked about violence in front of an urban public – reverting thereby the asymmetrical relationship that usually existed between urban–municipal agents and rural *campesinos*. On this occasion, the defenders applied creative methods, such as paintings of persons who suffered from violence and persons who lived in contexts free from violence to underline the message they wished to convey. Indeed, the municipal agents showed an interest in the anti-alcohol campaign conducted in Chacabamba and asked the defenders to help organise a similar action in Huancarani.[45]

Not least, one of the long-serving defenders began to compose songs in Quechua in which she touched upon difficult topics such as violence, but where she also stressed the existence of rights that protected women and children. On various occasions, she used those songs as another means of promoting the culture of non-violence towards the respective public.[46]

With regard to the second line of action – counselling services – the team first organised its work by electing a coordinator among themselves, determining office hours (usually Sundays in the afternoon), and elaborating a plan of activities. From the very first day the *defensoría* opened its doors, there was a considerable amount of people seeking advice. The users obtained all the time they needed to talk about their problems, they could do so in their own mother tongue Quechua and did not have to pay for the services offered. Many women directed themselves to the *defensoría* with the sole aim of speaking with somebody about their marital problems, without desiring that other steps would result from this conversation. There were also many cases where arguments among couples ended in instances of very minor psychic and physical violence. In such cases, the *defensores* were solicited to intervene, engage the couple in a conversation about the problems that had led to the discussion and elaborate with them points of agreement on how they wished to continue their relationship. There were also many reports of severe forms of domestic violence exerted against women, children and adolescents. In such cases the *defensoría* explained to the victims that their fundamental rights had been violated and that they could raise a complaint so as to obtain justice for the harm caused to them. Depending on the age of the victim and the severity of the harm caused, they evaluated with them which authorities were competent to attend their case and clarified which steps the entire legal process would imply. They also assured the victims that they would accompany them throughout the entire process, supporting them in making their voice heard, in the filling out of documents, and in making their testimonies, so as to assure that their problem would be attended with due diligence. The ultimate decision on how to proceed always resided in the users (or their parents), and defenders clarified that they would respect any decision. Some victims did not wish to stage a complaint before the authorities; others withdrew from the process because some extra-judicial agreement was made; and again others decided to engage in and stick with the legal process, because the active support of the *defensoría* members made them feel confident that their situation could be improved through a legal resolution. Interestingly, in almost all cases, victims preferred to denounce violent acts before state entities, and not before the community authorities, for even though local authorities agreed that domestic violence should be reduced, they continued to regard themselves as not competent to rule on this issue. Once the initial obstacles in the coordination with the most proximate state intermediaries and operators (justice of the peace, police, attorney, court, DEMUNA) had been overcome (see also below) and some first cases of violence had been effectively resolved, this path to respond to severe cases of violence became the most viable option for victims of violence in Chacabamba. The effective intervention of the *defensoría* in its first cases resulted in an ever higher demand for their support not only within Chacabamba, but also by commoners from surrounding communities.[47]

The third line of action – the monitoring of cases – refers to the fact that almost all cases attended by the *defensoría* implied a follow-up process. This included regular visits to families where problems had occurred. In doing so, the defenders had the chance to observe the development of the family for a longer period; they made sure that eventual agreements were adhered to; and, in case the situation had not clearly improved, they could also motivate the conflict parties to return to dialogue and think about distinct options of how to proceed. In case victims of violence submitted a complaint before the state legal system, defenders would try to remain informed of the process and remind the respective authorities of their obligations – a task that proved complicated to comply with, particularly if aggressors intended to influence the legal operators' decisions by means of 'gifts' or special 'favours'. Another outstanding feature of Chacabamba's *defensoría* was that they came to understand and comply with their role in a very pro-active way. Once they were more self-confident in their capacities, they felt that their scope of activity would not have to remain limited to their official office hours; nor did defenders always wait until a victim of violence asked them for support. Over the course of time, they developed a particular sensitivity for family life in the community, or, as they themselves would call it: they have deployed their 'antenna' across the entire community. Sometimes, they became aware of particular problems through ordinary conversations with neighbours. On other occasions, they witnessed critical situations by incidentally passing by a neighbour's house and hearing the discussions taking place inside. The *defenders* intervened in such cases whenever they deemed that commoners required protection, or at least somebody advocating for their rights. Commoners, as well, did not wait until the official office hours of the *defensoría* when seeking help. The local school requested the intervention of the defenders in cases where children suffered from mistreatment by their teachers or negligence by their parents. Not least, some of the most severe cases, such as a husband who almost beat his wife to death, or the abuse of a young girl, occurred at night when means of transport and the availability of the competent authorities in Huancarani were particularly difficult, all of which would not detain defenders from intervening and trying to find adequate solutions.[48]

Political opportunities

Ever since the *change initiative* started in 2002, the positions of the community authorities and the deputy governor had been regularly subject to elections and, thus, to change. The *defensoría* team (whose participants were likewise confirmed or substituted in these elections) had to arrange with the newly elected office holders and to seek agreements on how to deal with critical situations in the community. With a majority of these authorities, a relatively constructive relationship could be established. Given the effectiveness of the *defensoría*, the members of subsequent communal boards and the deputy governor maintained the position according to which domestic violence and other problems related to children's rights belonged to the exclusive realm of the *defensoría*. Thus, whenever they took notice of a case pertaining to one of these realms, these authorities would redirect the case to the *defensoría*. In return for that, authorities pledged their assistance in complex cases, and effectively, critical cases such as the aforementioned nocturnal interventions were resolved with the cooperation of all community authorities.[49]

Another aspect which facilitated the *defensoría's* work was the creation of the Departmental Coordinating Group of the Community Defence Offices of Cuzco (CODECC) in 2003, of which the *defensoría* in Chacabamba became a member from the very beginning. CODECC's role was to advocate towards the recognition of the *defensorías* by the justices of the peace, police officers and prosecutors who often rejected the accompaniment of victims of violence by the *defensores*. CODECC produced an accreditation card for all trained defenders that they could use when presenting themselves before the competent authority. The organisation also signed cooperation agreements with the Cuzco-based Human Rights Ombudsman and the Lawyers College and, jointly with these agents, CODECC organised training on domestic violence and the role of *defensorías* for state legal operators. Given the Ombudsman's interest in facilitating access to justice to marginalised citizens, defenders were given the option to denounce before the Ombudsman those operators who did not attend cases of violence according to the statutory provisions; indeed, they soon discovered that merely mentioning this option to the respective operator was sufficient to secure a more effective response on particular cases. In decentralised locations, such as Huancarani, it was also due to the *initiative* of the Ombudsman that joint workshops could be held among defenders and local legal operators, and that the latter gradually became more willing to cooperate with the former. Hence, within a few years, legal operators in Huancarani refrained from questioning the *defenders'* accompaniment of victims of violence in legal processes, and sometimes they even solicited information or the intervention of the *defensoría* of Chacabamba in cases that involved persons from the community.[50]

A problem faced by most rural *defensorías* – the geographic distance to higher level judicial instances – was also diminished by CODECC through the establishment of a network that stretched from the most remote communities to the capitals of the districts and provinces up to the Cuzco city. At each node of this network, one coordinator was elected by the *defensorías* pertaining to its jurisdiction, and these coordinators accompanied those cases that were forwarded from lower level to higher level judicial operators. In this way, victims of violence were at no point of the process left alone, while defenders from rural communities did not have to spend time and money to make repeated journeys to distant cities. One coordinator of the Chacabamba *defensoría* was elected as coordinator for the district of Huancarani, with which she came to hold responsibility over all cases that required an intervention of the institutions in Huancarani. Over the years, the number of *defensorías* in the district grew from four to sixteen; correspondingly, her workload (which remained voluntary and unpaid) increased considerably, as well.[51]

Another important shift in the opportunity window for the further evolution of the *defensoría* in Chacabamba referred to UNICEF's decision to withdraw from the *defensoría* programme in Cuzco in 2006. Its partner NGO IDL decided to assume responsibility for the *defensorías* created by UNICEF. However, the most important mechanisms by which UNICEF had cooperated with the *defensorías* – regular training and visits to the communities – were quickly shifted towards CODECC and, given a gradual modification of priorities of CODECC, their enlargement in terms of member *defensorías* across the Department and a reduction of the available resources, the *defensoría* in Chacabamba became ever more reliant upon its own resources so as to maintain the service offered to the community.[52]

Availability and deployment of resources

With respect to the immaterial resources at the disposal of the *defensoría* in Chacabamba, we can first list its increasing acceptance and recognition by many sectors of the community. The internal sources for this recognition resided in its resolute acting upon cases of violence and advocacy for the rights of children and adolescents, the ever more effective coordination with local and state institutions, and its actions to promote the reduction of alcohol consumption in the community. (This latter line of action occurred together with the equally persistent missionary work of the evangelical church in Chacabamba). The users of the *defensoría* services also learned that they could trust that the information discussed with the defenders was treated confidentially. But there were also external sources of recognition, such as the increasing consultations with the *defensoría* by authorities from other communities of the district; the fact that UNICEF invited representatives from other States to get to know the Chacabamba *defensoría* in 2006;

and that the coordinator of the *defensoría* was invited to present this *initiative* at several congresses in Peru and Bolivia in the second half of the 2000s.[53]

Until the withdrawal of UNICEF, the newly elected and existing *defensoría* members continued to be trained and provided with professional advice on a regular basis. This situation was altered with the handover of the responsibility from UNICEF to IDL. While IDL planned to continue supporting the defensoría programme in Cuzco until 2012, the resources this NGO had at its disposal for this purpose were gradually decreasing. Moreover, in meetings with CODECC it was agreed that, as a means of securing the sustainability of the *defensorías* on a longer term, IDL would gradually pass its competences to CODECC and concentrate more on the technical advice for this organisation. Accordingly, CODECC should be provided with the know-how on fundraising so as to apply for funds from state and non-state agencies. In 2006, IDL successfully supported CODECC in its soliciting funding from the US-based foundation National Endowment for Democracy. This money was used to train CODECC representatives and *defensoría* coordinators in strategies to solicit funds from the recently introduced participatory budgets at municipal level.[54] Another consequence of the agreement made between IDL and CODECC was that the latter would assume the training of defenders. CODECC established its own committee for this task, and it also received support by an external consultant so as to improve its didactic methods. However, the training and visits of CODECC representatives in the communities were provided on a significantly less regular basis, first because the *defensorías* they covered extended from two dozen in the first half of the 2000s to 65 by the end of the 2000s, and second, because the resources they had at their disposal to perform this function were relatively small. All elected CODECC representatives remained voluntaries who were not compensated for the considerable amounts of time they spent to perform their tasks. And while a growing number of training sessions would take place in Cuzco, defenders who wished to participate made the experience that resources sometimes did not even suffice to cover their travel and subsistence costs.[55]

In its role as coordinator of the *defensorías* of the Huancarani district, one *defensoría* member of Chacabamba took advantage of the training in fundraising and succeeded in applying for a share of the participatory budget of the municipality in Huancarani for several subsequent years. These resources partly compensated the reduced support from IDL and CODECC and were used to organise training of the *defensorías* in the Huancarani district, to provide the *defensorías* with some materials, and to cover the costs implied in the accompaniment of particular cases.

However, in Chacabamba, the *defensoría* team would gradually shrink from six to two people by the end of the 2000s. As it was a time-consuming office, most of the original defenders withdrew after several years of office and were then replaced by other commoners, who similarly resigned from this position after a period. Some commoners came to assume that the reason why the two remaining defenders had been willing to engage in the *defensoría* throughout all the years was some sort of financial compensation – even though the *defensoría* team had always denied this. In order to convince these persons, the defenders invited them to join them for a period so as to prove that it was not a financial incentive, but instead a personal motivation to assist persons in emergency situations that was guiding their engagement. Indeed, these additional defenders became witnesses of the general process of resource reduction at the Department level and realised that the participation in the trainings sometimes even involved the spending of some own money. As a result, the two defenders were again left alone and thus could no longer pursue all their activities as originally foreseen, but instead focused their attention of cases. Ultimately, the *defensoría* office had also to be returned to the community because the authorities required this space for other purposes. The defenders moved their equipment and materials to a small room provided by an ex-defender, but were no longer able to use them effectively when attending cases.[56]

What results have the legal change process yielded in Chacabamba by the end of the research period?

Normative and institutional change

Compared with the beginning of the *change initiative* in Chacabamba in 2002, domestic violence was no longer considered as 'normal' by considerable parts of the population in 2012, when the period of investigation ended. Women were aware that they did not have to condone violent acts committed by their partners against them, and they did not wait until violence became excessive in order to seek external assistance. If kin intervention proved ineffective, they turned to the *defensoría* to obtain guidance and advice. The community authorities and the deputy governor likewise took a more critical stance on violence. While they themselves did not deal with the cases, they not only signalled their willingness but actually coordinated cases with and supported the *defensoría* in the management of difficult cases. The young generation who visited school in Chacabamba over the past decade grew up in a context where their right to psychological and physical integrity has been effectively taken care of. The school talks organised by the defenders and the interventions in case children, who were beaten or treated with negligence, made them become aware of the limits between tolerated and non-tolerated spheres of conduct. And even though not all commoners agreed with this new normative context – especially the older male generation – all commoners understood that violent acts would most probably not go unchallenged and entail an intervention informed by respective procedures and sanctions.

Important changes have been achieved with regards to the institutional level, as well. A new institution – the *defensoría* – was established in Chacabamba so as to close the missing link between domestic violence and an effective response by the competent authorities. Due to its sensitivity and cultural closeness to the persons who sought assistance, its relentless promotion of rights and non-violence, its pro-active compliance with its functions and its effectiveness in the search for just solutions for battered women, adolescents and children, the *defensoría* has gained the respect of the community and many external authorities and communities. The work of the *defensoría* also altered the way that local authorities dealt with violence. Both the communal board and the deputy governor no longer turned a blind eye to domestic violence, but instead advised commoners to seek the assistance of the *defensoría*. Not least, the cooperation with the most proximate institutions in the district capital Huancarani (justice of the peace, police) in cases of domestic violence gradually improved upon the persisting efforts of the defenders, the realisation of joint workshops and campaigns and the advocacy towards their work exerted by the *defensoría's* allies.[57]

Enforcement of reformed norms and institutions

Until the end of the investigation period, the *defensoría* promoted non-violence in families and the community, helped victims of violence to navigate through viable options by which violence could be brought to a halt, and closely monitored the developments within families and advances of legal processes at the competent authorities so as to make sure their accompaniment would lead to a palpable result. The *defensoría* also intervened in critical situations in which no family member had even asked the *defensoría* for support. They thereby forcefully signalled to aggressors that violence would not be tolerated as a matter of principle, and that any sort of privacy could not be used as a shield when rights of women, children and adolescents were violated. In addition, their campaigning against the sale of high-percentage alcohol, joined by parallel efforts of the Evangelical Church, whose adherents grew to around of one-third of the community over the 2000s, had the overall effect that alcohol consumption in Chacabamba declined. The previous practice of weekly meetings of young men to becoming drunk was gradually given up; the participants of festivities related to the Catholic calendar of celebrations became fewer and the amount of alcohol consumed on such occasions was reduced. Young families came to prefer to invest the little money they had at their disposal in the education of their children instead of hosting costly community celebrations. As a result of the *change initiative* and the reduction of alcohol consumption, domestic violence decreased considerably throughout the second half of the 2000s. In 2011, there were only a handful cases attended by the *defensoría*. But as the remaining defenders stressed, this positive development does not mean that violence was eradicated: sexual violence particularly continued to be a taboo issue among indigenous women.

The *defensoría* has been well received by the community. Its legitimacy was reconfirmed not only in the regular (re-)elections of the defenders by the general assembly, but also by the considerable numbers of individuals and authorities seeking guidance from this institution over the years. But due to the shortage in training, visits and resources of the respective institutions that accompanied the work of the *defensoría* from Cuzco (first UNICEF, later IDL and CODECC), and the reduction of its local personnel, the *defensoría* could no longer perform all its lines of action (rights promotion, counselling service, monitoring of cases) with the same commitment as during the first years of the research period.[58]

Sustainability of reformed norms and institutions

As of 2012, the Achilles' heel of this *initiative* seemed to be the reduction of the *defensoría* members to only two persons who had performed this function over many years. The team work – originally considered one of the major features of the *defensoría* because it facilitated the distribution of tasks and the evaluation of problems from multiple perspectives – could not be upheld by two people alone. Both defenders expressed that they were tired and wished to withdraw from this position. However their efforts to persuade commoners to assume their roles were hampered, among other reasons, by the fact that defenders sometimes even had to pay a share of the expenses while monitoring cases and travelling to other parts of the Department. The idea that this office could be particularly interesting for representatives of the younger generation was complicated by the circumstance that these individuals spent a considerable amount of time outside the community and thus may not be available if an emergency occurred. Given that the *defensoría* ultimately had no operational office in which to install furniture, work materials and, especially, computers – devices that might be appealing to young people – was also regarded as a complication of the recruitment of new defenders.[59]

These difficulties have been also recognised by IDL and CODECC, and formed part of the future plans of CODECC in 2012, shortly before the IDL withdrew from the programme in Cuzco.[60] Moreover, due to the visibility the *defensorías* had gained over the past decade, the Department for Social Development of Cuzco's regional government recognised the *defensorías*' contribution to the improved access to justice by marginalised citizens. In its Regional Programme against Violence towards Women (2008–2010)[61] the government envisioned, among other things, the creation of decentralised 'modules of legal community services' in rural municipalities and *campesino* communities wherein all local legal operators (e.g. communal board, *rondas campesinas*, justices of the peace and *defensorías*) should be provided an office so as to facilitate the coordination and processing of legal cases. Unfortunately, this project has suffered from many legal and political hurdles ever since its initiation, among them the question of how *campesino* communities could hand out parcels of their communal territory to the government so as to initiate the construction of such modules. With Paucartambo included amongst the pilot Provinces where such modules were supposed to be constructed,[62] it remains to be seen whether the eventual realisation of this programme would motivate more commoners from Chacabamba to engage in the *defensoría* in the near future.

Tungasuca Ccollana – Canas Province (2001–2012)

Tungasuca Ccollana is located at the foot of a lagoon amidst an Andean high plain at the altitude of 3,849 metres. At the time of the fieldwork (January-early March 2012), around 150 Quechua-speaking families lived in Tungasuca. Administratively, the community was ascribed to the Canas Province, which historically was populated by Aymara-speaking people who were incorporated to the Inca Empire. Tungasuca was also the capital of the district Tupac Amaru, named after its most known resident José Gabriel Condorcanqui 'Tupac Amaru II', descendent of the Inca Tupac Amaru and

Image 4.3 Tungasuca Ccollana

cacique of Surimana (his community of origin), Tungasuca and Pampamarca, who staged a revolt against the Spanish colonial forces in November 1780.[63] After his and his partner's (Michaela Bastidas) assassination in 1781, his numerous lands were transferred to *criollos*, and it was not until the Agrarian Reform (1969) that Tungasuca gradually recovered its communal territory from a handful of hacienda-owners by way of lengthy judicial processes. In 1966 Tungasuca registered as a *campesino* community before the state authorities. In common with the other state intermediaries located in Tungasuca (district mayor, justice of the peace, governor, deputy governor), the community authorities were subject to severe threats when *Shining Path* entered the zone in the second half of the 1980s. The small police office located in Tungasuca proved unable to protect the population and completely withdrew from the district. In reaction to that, the community adopted a nocturnal vigilance system organised by a *ronda campesina* in order to at least impede the looting of homes and cattle theft by criminal gangs, which co-occurred with the guerrilla presence in this zone. In the first half of the 1990s, a military camp was temporarily set up in Tungasuca, and the population felt caught in the middle between insurgents and soldiers. The *ronda* was substituted by a committee of self-defence and its members were armed and trained by the military. Several years later, a criminal gang stole most of these arms and – in contrast to surrounding communities – the committee of self-defence was no longer operative once the external threat diminished.[64]

In Tungasuca and other areas of the Canas Province, women were affected by Fujimori's sterilisation policy of the late 1990s,[65] many of whom reported to suffer from lasting health problems. In 2007, the average birth rate in the province stood at 2.8 children, whereas the mortality rate of children who were born alive amounted to was 16.8 per cent. Among the population above the age of 15 in Canas, 29.9 per cent women and 7.3 per cent men did not finish elementary school. In 1993, 48.1 per cent of women and 14.8 per cent of men were illiterate; this rate declined to 32.7 per cent and 8.1 per cent, respectively, in 2007. By this latter date, rates of school enrolment and the period of education of the youngest generation (girls and boys) were higher and longer than those of previous generations, and access to the educative system was facilitated by the existence of a primary and secondary school in Tungasuca.[66]

Until the 1990s, most families merely subsisted from the cultivation of agricultural products (e.g., potatoes, barley, beans, wheat, corn) and their cattle. However, after training carried out by Cuzco-based NGOs that specialised in rural development, investment by the district mayor and the strong desire of the younger generation of commoners to improve the living conditions after the period of political and crime-related violence, productive associations were formed, livestock breeding was qualitatively improved (especially milk cows), the access to regional markets was

Image 4.4 Woman with her children in Tungasuca Ccollana

extended and, by 2011, the community became the seat of a dairy plant. Here, the milk delivered by commoners was made into cheese and then carried to a market in Cuzco. Thus, while some male commoners worked outside of the community (e.g., in the construction sector), many others strived to make a living with productive activities within the community itself.[67] Still, in 2007, 76.1 per cent of the district's population (composed of ten communities and a total of 2,965 inhabitants) fell below the poverty line; 46 per cent of them were regarded as extremely poor. Similarly, many families lacked access to basic services such as sanitation or electricity.[68] Given the underdeveloped infrastructure many commoners used bicycles or walked to get around the district. With the few available means of public transport people from Tungasuca could get to the capital of the Yanaoca province (8 kilometres distance from Tungasuca) or to Combapata, where they could connect to the northbound Department capital Cuzco (a 2.5-hour drive).[69]

Why did claims for legal change emerge in Tungasuca?

Shifts in local power relations

Beginning with the 1980s, several women's groups such as a mothers' club, a popular kitchen and a glass-of-milk committee had been founded in

Tungasuca (see also previous section on Chacabamba). Each of these groups was incorporated as a specialised committee in the general community organisation structure. Just as in the case of Chacabamba, these groups were set up as local entities to implement the national government's social policies to reduce malnutrition and poverty, and the scope of activities of any of these groups did not exceed the ones foreseen by the State. But at the beginning of the 2000s there existed a Secretary of the Peasant Woman of Canas (*Secretaria de la Mujer Campesina de Canas*, SOMUC) in the provincial capital Yanaoca, which operated as an entity of the Provincial Peasant Federation of Canas (*Federación Provincial Campesina de Canas*, FPCC) and held regular meetings with representatives of the community-based women's groups so as to represent their interests at higher levels of the federation.[70] Despite the support of SOMUC, the spaces for political and legal decision-making in Tungasuca remained an uncontested male terrain. One of the root causes of the unequal access to these spheres was the different levels of education men and women have enjoyed, as parents tended to send their sons to school for much longer than their daughters. Also, the different literacy programmes conducted by successive governments did not effectively remedy the resulting illiteracy of many women.[71] Most women lacked access to their own source of income and financially depended upon their husbands. The money earned by men, in turn, was not always shared with their spouses in a way that ensured all costs of the household were covered. As women performed a long list of daily tasks in the household and in the fields, there was hardly ever time left for other activities, such as the engagement in community affairs. And indeed, the involvement of women in the latter was not welcomed as a matter of principle: The participation 'with voice and vote' in regular sessions of the general assembly taking place every three months was open for qualified commoners only (married men as 'heads of family'). Women could replace their husbands, but even so, a fine had to be paid for the absence of the husband. Exceptions from this rule were made for widows and in case an extraordinary assembly had to be convened urgently. Even so, most women hardly ever dared to raise their voice, as men clearly let them know that their contributions were not relevant. In the same vein, virtually all existing positions within the community board and most specialised committees (responsible for cattle-raising, machinery, irrigation, etc.) were occupied by men. Therefore, the only spaces where women's participation was relatively uncontested were the above-mentioned women's groups in which politically relevant matters were never discussed. In such a context where women from a very young age were relegated to a subordinate role in many realms of family and community life, they themselves tended to underestimate their legitimate needs and interests. Their underdeveloped self-esteem made them think that they were inferior, that their opinions would not be of any value in public deliberations and that they were not capable of assuming more responsible positions within the community.[72]

Inappropriate resolution of cases of domestic violence by existing institutions

Domestic violence was very prevalent in Tungasuca, but as this conduct was commonly not considered an offence, and because aggressors often succeeded in intimidating their victims, most women would not seek help until their situation became desperate and unbearable.[73] The first instance a woman would turn to were the parents and godfathers, or eventually also elder siblings of the couple. If the conversations held in this private sphere were not effective, women lacked the option of turning to the communal board or the general assembly, as these authorities only considered themselves competent to treat problems such as delinquency, demarcation between territories, severe disturbances of the communal order and the repetitive non-compliance with community rules stipulated in the community statute.[74] To start judging one of their neighbours because of domestic violence would have implied to judge many others. And no commoner wished to be publically stigmatised for the violent acts committed in his house:

> [S]omething very, very difficult in the Andean culture is that they publicly blame you to be an abuser. Independent from the fact that they already know it, but that they say this in presence of everybody is very hideous, it's a sanction. A public sanction is the worst; that they say of you that you are a stealer, a cattle thief, a violator – this is the worst.
> (Interview 30.01./05.03.2012)

Therefore, it was a convenient option to shift such cases to the Tungasuca-based justice of the peace who would try to steer the conversation towards conciliation between the parties in conflict, a solution that did not necessarily meet the needs of the victims. More severe cases were passed by this authority to the police office in Yanaoca. The police enjoyed a bad reputation among women from Tungasuca, not only because of their retreat during the internal conflict in the 1990s and its considerable degree of corruption, but also because their complaints about violence were not treated with due diligence. When they arrived at the police station with evident signs of physical violence, the officers would sometimes ask the women what they had done to provoke their husbands in such a way, so the blame was reverted to the victims. Sometimes, the reports of the doctors who evaluated the physical injuries were not submitted promptly to the police. In other cases, the police would arrange some extrajudicial agreement between the aggressor and the victim, with the result that the attorney in Yanaoca hardly ever became aware of such cases. But attorneys and judges were equally not trained in the due processing of cases of domestic violence. Thus even at these levels of the judiciary the issue was often minimised or resolved by some form of 'agreement' among the parties involved. As there was no police officer available in Tungasuca, nobody could protect the victim from acts of revenge of the aggressor throughout or after a legal process. Finally, the option of a formal separation was not considered viable by most women. First, because the value of family unity was highly esteemed by the population and, thus, the decision to separate from her husband would involve a lasting stigmatisation of a woman, and second, because most women economically depended on their husbands and knew that they would not be able to sustain themselves (and their children) without their support. Thus, what women were actually seeking was a place where they could talk about their problems and obtain guidance on potential ways to resolve the conflict with their partners.[75]

Diffusion of new legal concepts

Until the early 2000s, the notion that violence against women was to some extent a 'normal' male behaviour remained unchallenged in Tungasuca. The recently established CEM in Cuzco (1999) remained focused on the urban neighbourhoods, and information about this institution had not made its way to remote provinces. Even though some external agents already worked with the community, such as an NGOs specialising in rural development, they had not yet incorporated the matter of gender in their projects. The training the women's groups received from state agencies, in turn, focused on nutrition topics and did not include sensitisation on the rights of women. As in Chacabamba, violence was exerted as a common method to discipline children whom would learn that violence was a viable method to resolve conflicts. In combination with a prevailing *machista* culture, which ascribed men a superior role in many realms of family and community life, men also used force to resolve critical situations by violent means. Such forms of violence ranged from verbal abuse to forced sexual relations, and the consumption of alcohol – which was very common in cultural festivities and daily work on the fields – often preceded disputes and abuse in the couples' homes.[76]

It was not until the NGO IDL approached the community in 2001 to present the regional programme of community defence offices (*defensorías comunitarias*), which were being created by this NGO and UNICEF in several provinces of the Department of Cuzco,[77] that the idea of a right to live free from violence started to circulate in the community. The contact between IDL and Tungasuca was established after the aforementioned SOMUC became aware about this project at a very early stage.

> [T]hese leaders [from the FPCC] understood that women effectively lived in difficult situations of violence, physical and psychological

> aggressions. And these leaders also said: "This is not normal, even though this woman who is violated may regard this as something normal, as if her spouse had a right to mistreat her," but these male and female leaders understood that this should not be like this.
>
> (Interview 13.02.2012)

SOMUC asked IDL to extend their project to the Canas Province, and soon after, the first *defensorías* in Yanaoca and one rural community (Kunturkanki) were created. After positive experiences with these first *defensorías*, IDL contacted other communities of the Province, as well, and the authorities of Tungasuca showed interest and invited the NGO to present its proposal before a general assembly.[78]

Incompatibilities among institutional sets relevant for women's lives

As recently as a first *defensoría* team from Tungasuca was trained by IDL in human rights and domestic violence, these persons became aware that, according to international and national norms, all human beings enjoyed the same rights, independent of their age, sex or other characteristics. Up to this point, their legal horizon did not exceed the community statute in which only 'qualified commoners' were considered as holders of rights and obligations. Thus, the message that women, children and adolescents, as well as all other residents who were not assigned the status of a 'qualified commoner', were rights holders, made a considerable difference in their assessment of the living conditions of all persons in their community. Gradually, the *defensores* began to notice the discrepancy that existed between the violent means by which most of them had been raised and the persistence of domestic violence on the one hand, and norms protecting the psychic and physical integrity of all persons on the other hand. They saw that, until this moment, neither community authorities nor state intermediaries and justice operators responded to acts of violence with due diligence, which is why they became convinced that the creation of a new institution, the *defensoría*, might constitute a necessary option for people who found themselves in a difficult situation characterised by violence.[79]

What factors facilitated or obstructed the initiation of legal change efforts in Tungasuca?

Political opportunities at the starting point of the legal change efforts

The community board of Tungasuca reacted positively to a letter from the IDL by inviting this NGO to the community and showing an interest in the *initiative.* As a first step, the IDL held a workshop for all community authorities and representatives of local groups in which they made them reflect upon the most pressing problems that were present in the community and on the ways these were dealt with. In a second step, the participants were sensitised about the issue of domestic violence and the rights of victims of violence, followed by the proposal to create a *defensoría* that might help to protect the rights of victims and other often neglected rights of children and adolescents. IDL also reported on the initial experiences of other *defensorías* in Canas and proposed that a general assembly deliberated upon the question of whether such an institution might be established in Tungasuca, as well. The communal board indeed placed this matter on the agenda of the next general assembly, where a majority of qualified commoners voted in favour of the *initiative* and selected several community members who would become trained by IDL to exerting the office of a *defender.* The benefits the community hoped to gain from the creation of a *defensoría* were, among others, that such an institution might strengthen the organisational capacities of the community and that local expertise on rights-related issues could be built up. Aspects such as the IDL's willingness to invest resources for the implementation and accompaniment of the *defensoría* and the backing of this *initiative* by the FPCC were likewise relevant for the decision-making process of the assembly. Not least, IDL also made clear from the beginning that the community itself would take all decisions related to the *defensoría,* including the question of whether or not continue with the *initiative.*[80]

Interpretive frame providing justification for change-orientated action

When the initial team of defenders returned from its first training session, the concern that they brought before the general assembly was very similar to the one presented by the defenders in Chacabamba: all human beings, women, adolescents and children included, were equipped with rights. Every person was entitled to protection, respect and a life of dignity. The use of violence, whichever form it may take – emotional, physical or sexual – would go against these rights. The consequences of violence were serious and enduring and affected family and community life alike. A change in people's attitudes and conduct was necessary so as to provide the children of Tungasuca with the opportunity to grow up in a more peaceful context. If parents wished to serve as a model for their children, they would have to abstain from violent acts against their children and against each other. Considering that alcohol often triggered violent acts at home, its consumption had to be urgently reduced, as well.

The defenders also stated that community authorities have thus far not been involved in problems related to domestic violence, whereas intermediaries' and state authorities' responses had not been satisfactory. In order to deal with rights violations of women and children more effectively in the future, the defenders advocated for the installation of the *defensoría* in the community, the same of which would serve as a first point of access to justice, either by helping to resolve small issues with the assistance of the *defensoría* team, or by redirecting and accompanying users to the competent authorities in case severe problems had to be addressed.

While weighing potential risks and benefits of this solution, the defenders were conscious about the difficulties they might encounter when urging their neighbours to change their conduct, as for a majority of the male population violence presented the most convenient means to resolve problems and work off their frustrations. It would likewise be difficult for parents to abstain from education methods that they themselves had inherited from their parents. They also feared the asymmetries existing between them and judicial operators. Most defenders had not attained a high school degree, and state agents often treated *campesinos* in a discriminatory manner. Thus, they were uncertain about whether they could effectively assist victims of violence in case they had turn to the state judicial operators. But they also knew that they could count on IDL, which assured them they would closely accompany them in their work, as well as on other *defensorías* that were already operative in Canas, which signalled their willingness to provide good advice. Not least, they were convinced that the provision of a local, free, confidential service provided by commoners who spoke Quechua would meet the needs of community members who sought for advice in such critical situations.[81]

The response the defenders received from the community was divided. The idea of promoting non-violence within families and the community was enthusiastically welcomed by the women's groups of Tungasuca. Many women had to first become accustomed to the idea that violence exerted by their partners against them was not as 'normal' as them had previously thought. But they hoped that the creation of the *defensoría* could help them to reduce the level of violence in their homes and also assist them in resolving their marital problems more generally. Another group that became convinced of this *change initiative* was the younger generation of male commoners who, following the end of the armed conflict and the gradual recovery of the communal territory, were now highly motivated to promote local development. They wished to provide their children with a brighter future by offering them longer school education and by serving as a model for their children. Domestic violence was clearly running counter to such visions, and they understood that some practices they had seen in their parents' houses required a change. The defenders' advocacy against alcohol consumption also appealed to these young men: if the agricultural productivity of the community was to be improved, commoners would have to abandon the practice of drinking while working at their fields. Not least, they were also interested in normative developments at the national level and were willing to adopt such norms if they proved beneficial for the community. Much less support came from many older and middle-aged men. They held that issues such as the rights of women and children were not relevant, that the persons participating in the trainings of the IDL would do so simply because they felt like it and that prevailing practices should not be altered. Despite these critical voices, a majority voted in favour of the *defensoría* in the assembly.[82]

Availability of resources at the starting point of the initiative

The operation of the *defensoría* was based on team work. The team principle allowed for the pooling of distinct experiences and know-how and the incorporation of various perspectives when attending particular cases. When confronting critical situations with aggressors or submitting a case before state authorities, the fact that defenders appeared as a team also fostered their self-esteem and assertiveness. In case one person was unable to attend on certain dates, there were others who could replace them. From the beginning, the *defensoría* also invited other commoners to observe their work and assist them with smaller tasks. In doing so, the recruitment of new defenders was taken care of. As in Chacabamba, defenders were not supposed to perform their office for a lifetime but for a limited period of time. They could be (re-)elected for a two-year period by the general assembly, and they were free to withdraw from this work if other obligations would not allow them to continue with this office. Incoming defenders should be able to count on the accompaniment of the more experienced defenders so as to guarantee a consistently good service.[83] An instance to which the *defensores* could refer to in case they required support was the Secretary for the *Defensorías Comunitarias* in Canas, which was created by the FPCC, monitored the work of the *defensorías* in Canas, and facilitated coordination among them (Franco 2003: 60).

As far as immaterial resources were concerned, the initial *defensoría* team was aware that its knowledge about dealing with violence-related problems was still very limited. The female team members especially also feared that their time resources would become very strained, as their husbands expected them to comply with their other productive and reproductive tasks just as they had done before assuming this new role as defender. An aspect that reassured the team was the understanding that IDL would accompany their work by regular visits, where not only advice on the treatment of particular cases would be provided, but also where consultants would also pay attention to team building measures as such. At the same time, training in nearby locations such as Yanaoca would be held so as to deepen and refresh their knowledge on violence and rights-related issues. On these occasions, the *defensores* could exchange their experiences with other *defensoría* teams of the province. Of equal importance was the fact that most of the defenders themselves had experienced violence throughout their life course – either as victims or as perpetrators. They held that these experiences made them empathetic towards the problems with which people would turn to the *defensoría*. And they also agreed that the incorporation of men in the *defensoría* was a clear advantage so as to gain acceptance for their *initiative* in the community. With respect to material resources, the defenders were informed that their engagement was considered as voluntary and would thus be unpaid. IDL would provide travel and subsistence expenses for their participation in trainings and support them with informative and promotional material they could use for their work. The community facilitated an office and some basic furniture for the *defensoría*.[84]

Which factors have influenced the *change initiative* throughout the subsequent stages of its evolution?

Target of change, strategy and tactics

In view of the fact that the model of *defensorías comunitarias* in the Cuzco Department was agreed upon and adhered to by UNICEF and IDL, the objective, strategies and tactics with which the *defensoría* in Tungasuca operated were identical to those pursued by the *defensoría* in Chacabamba. The objectives behind this *initiative* were to promote a normative shift towards the non-tolerance of violence and to prompt community and state authorities to respond effectively to cases of violence and to give due attention to rights of children and adolescents. The lines of action in order to achieve these objectives consisted of the promotion of rights, the attention of cases and the close accompaniment and monitoring of cases. With regard to the first line of action, the *defensores* of Tungasuca held talks in the general assembly and the local women's groups so as to inform them about what they have learned during their training and to stress the importance of non-violence. They also coordinated their work with two other *defensorías*, which had been established in the district of Tupac Amaru (located in Surimana and Ccotaña). They divided the district into three zones, and each *defensoría* was responsible for conducting promotional work in its respective zone. For the defenders in Tungasuca this implied an extension of their talks on rights to the communities of Lalla, Rosasani and Cochapata. The Secretary of the Defensorías in Yanaoca backed these rights sensitisation measures by elaborating radio sports called 'the voice of the *defensorías*' and broadcasting them across Canas for several years.[85] Regarding the second line of action, the defenders organised their work by setting up office hours, elaborating a plan of activities, and electing a coordinator from among them. Throughout the first years of operation, commoners approached the *defensoría* with a wide scope of problems, including marital disputes, husbands' abandonment of the family, non-recognition of children of unmarried parents, disputes on child maintenance, domestic violence and sexual abuse. Similar to Chacabamba, in minor cases of violence the *defensoría* team of Tungasuca often intervened directly, whereas more severe cases were expeditiously forwarded to the state authorities in Yanaoca. As commoners from surrounding communities became aware of the existence of the *defensoría*, the defenders soon came to attend cases from these locations, as well. Regarding the third line of action, the *defensores* started to accompany plaintiffs throughout legal processes, advocating for their rights and keeping plaintiffs up to date about the advances made in particular cases.[86]

Political opportunities

From 2001 to 2007, the *defensoría initiative* in Tungasuca was effective and its work gained acceptance by the community and its authorities. While the authorities maintained their position according to which domestic violence did not belong to their scope of competence, they were satisfied to know that such cases were now promptly attended by the *defensoría*. In cases which exceeded the capabilities of the *defensoría*, or where more weight of an authority was required to exert influence on an aggressor, the authorities were willing to support the team, with the result that some complex cases were effectively dealt with on the basis of a cooperation between the *defensoría*, the community president, the deputy governor, the justice of the peace and the local health station.

Police officers and judicial operators in Yanaoca were very dismissive towards the *defensores* in the beginning of the *initiative*: they asked them who they were and what they were doing and denied their presence while processing a case. But given that the FPCC and allied institutions from Cuzco gradually succeeded in advocating for the work of the *defensorías*, the cooperation became ever more fluid over the course of several years. In this regard, CODECC, founded in 2003, played a key role. This representative vehicle, of which Tungasuca's *defensoría* was a member, effectively promoted the work of the *defensorías* in cooperation with the Region's Human Rights Ombudsman, the Lawyers College and the Regional Roundtable Against Violence in Cuzco. The meetings and joint workshops with operators from the state justice system, civil society and political decision-makers gradually allowed for more openness and recognition of the service provided by the *defensorías* not only in Cuzco city, but also in the rural parts of the Department. CODECC also provided trained defenders with an accreditation card that helped defenders to present themselves more assertively before the competent authorities. For the *defensoría* in Tungasuca, these advances implied that the channelling of cases through the state judiciary became ever less hampered by discriminatory attitudes or undue procedures. This positive development was brought to a halt after UNICEF's decision to withdraw from the regional programme in Cuzco in 2006, after which IDL felt prompted to assume the supervision over the *defensorías* created by UNICEF. This change went hand in hand with shortages of human and financial resources, with negative implications for the *defensoría* in Tungasuca.[87]

Availability and deployment of resources

IDL itself had to deal with a reduction of the resources available to continue with the accompaniment of the *defensoría* programme in Cuzco until 2012. Soon after the withdrawal of UNICEF, IDL and CODECC agreed that CODECC would take over the functions of training and consultancy of the *defensorías*, while IDL would focus its support on the organisational development of CODECC. Given that the number of *defensorías* in the Department rose from two dozen to 65 and that human and financial resources for maintaining the training and visits of the *defensorías* were reduced, *defensorías* such as the one in Tungasuca could no longer count on the regular visits and accompaniment of CODECC.[88] The *defensoría* was particularly hit by the fact that a contract with one IDL consultant came to an end. This consultant had established a very close relationship to the team, and it was not least due to his personal *initiative* that the motivation of the defenders was upheld, despite the sometimes difficult and time-consuming work.

> The defensoría comunitaria (…) was very strong around 2005, 2006, 2007. But then it deteriorated. (…) There was a companion. He (…) had to look after the communities, visited them. And I know that they felt strengthened. This companion left – and they forgot everything. (…) It depended on him, you know? I mean, we all knew at which date he would come and organise a workshop: "Let's go there!" We attended cases. And once this companion went away, everything deteriorated. (…) [H]e always helped us to fill out forms, the documents we had to write, to go to the judge – he helped us so much. And after he had gone, everything decayed considerably. (…) Everyone went their own way.
>
> (Interview 1–21.02.2012)

Until the withdrawal of this IDL consultant, around six defenders, some of whom were re-elected by the general assembly, some replacing others, consistently occupied the *defensoría*. From 2006 onwards, this team disintegrated and three new people were elected to replace the former team. However, their work was complicated by the rule upheld by CODECC that the function of a defender could only be performed by people who had received three successive training sessions in which they became familiarised with all the know-how necessary to provide a qualitatively good service to the users. For CODECC it became ever more difficult to conduct such training in the Provinces, thus the organisation asked newly elected defenders to travel to Cuzco city to participate in such trainings. The journey to Cuzco was time-consuming, and only two of the three new *defensoría* members managed to attend all three training sessions. The third person soon withdrew from the *defensoría*, leaving only two male defenders. Their demand that CODECC should more often organise decentralised workshops or visit the community to obtain some guidance on their work could often not be responded to by CODECC. In contrast to the female defender in Chacabamba who seized opportunities to become elected as district coordinator of the *defensorías* and be trained in fund-raising through which she managed to partly counterbalance the reduction of CODECC and IDL resources and presence, the two remaining defenders of Tungasuca worked full time on their fields and thus did not have time to deepen their engagement in the *change initiative*. The reduced communication with CODECC and IDL made them feel they had been forgotten by these organisations; as the *defensoría* was no longer supplied with basic material for their work, the defenders even had to cover the costs for the paper on which they wrote out of their own pockets. In addition, the search for more people to foster the work of the *defensoría* proved difficult because most commoners came to expect some form of financial incentive for their engagement. Unsurprisingly, the defenders' motivation to perform the tasks of the *defensoría* declined, and in the last quarter of the 2000s, they limited their engagement to an *ad hoc* based attention to specific cases. As a result, many commoners no longer perceived the *defensoría* as an operative institution.[89]

While our analysis of the *change initiative* could stop here, it is important to signal that other agents came to partly fill the vacuum created by the *defensoría's* decline: Tungasuca had long been the seat of a justice of the peace. The office holder by the time of the author's fieldwork was a community member who was elected for this office as early as 1994. At a time when the community underwent critical changes – the recovering from armed conflict, the closing of the military camp, the reinstitution of the community organisation and *initiatives* to foster local economic development – this intermediary was present and attempted to provide legal support to all commoners to the best of his knowledge and belief. He grew in this role and the community responded by repeatedly confirming him in office. When the *defensoría* was established in 2001, he was open-minded about this new service and willingly cooperated with this institution. His own formation in legal issues had been very limited until the early 2000s, but this changed considerably once the regional judiciary of Cuzco started to provide local justices of the peace with regular training on human rights and even domestic violence. Thus, when the *defensoría* could no longer maintain its office hours, commoners from Tungasuca and other communities of the district turned to him in order to seek guidance. Having attended the human rights training, his attention to victims of violence became more responsive to the needs of the victims than in earlier periods. Minor instances of violence were resolved by involving the parties in conflict in dialogue and elaborating a protocol of understanding in which agreements and also consequences in case these agreements would be violated were fixed. If the aggressor did not adhere to the agreements, the justice of the peace would remind him about the agreements and enact the sanctions stipulated in the protocol, sometimes with the support of the community authorities. Repetitive or severe cases of violence were forwarded to the state judiciary in Yanaoca. Thus, even though other elements such as teamwork or the close monitoring of the processing of cases before the state authorities were not present here, victims of violence knew they could turn to this authority in order to seek support.[90]

Furthermore, the district governor of Tupac Amaru, whose office was located in the municipality of the district, also came to attend marital disputes and cases that involved domestic violence. Some commoners expressed their doubts about whether the governor was actually trained for this task and whether his normatively regulated competences included the dealing with such cases. According to Decree 004–2007–IN, the governor could register and forward complaints about violations of human rights lodged by the local population towards the competent institutions. But the decree did not stipulate the governor's faculty to provide conciliations of any sort.[91] The task of rights promotion has also been gradually assumed by others during the second half of the 2000s. First, NGOs working in rural development in Tungasuca (*Arariwa, IAA*) have increasingly incorporated a gender focus in the designs of their projects and included the topic of gender equality in their regular talks with the community. Second, the department of social development of the district municipality of Tupac Amaru started to offer training for members of women's groups on issues, such as the management of organisations and leadership, and it conducted campaigns against gender violence on International Women's Day (8 March). Third, the most recent element of the state's social policy to reduce poverty and malnutrition – the programme 'Together' (*Programa Juntos*) – was introduced in the community. This programme required participating families (mostly represented by mothers) to take care of the alimentation, health and education of their children in exchange for the payment of monthly rates of S/.100 (around US$35 at the moment of writing). Registering for this programme would also imply women's regular participation in training, which included the issue of domestic violence. Lastly, the Evangelical Church was conducting its missionary work in the district. Families converting to this religion would typically reduce their alcohol consumption, and, as a result, the number of severe cases of domestic violence among them decreased to some extent, as well.[92]

What results have the legal change process yielded in Tungasuca by the end of the research period?

Normative and institutional change

The institutional setting in Tungasuca was altered by the creation of a *defensoría* in 2001. With the work of the *defensoría*, the tolerance and lenient treatment of violent conduct towards women, adolescents and children diminished temporarily. The understanding according to which violence was not at all 'normal', that it violated fundamental rights of individuals and that it seriously put at risk the development of families and the community, became more and more appealing to many women and the younger generation of the community. This altered normative standpoint towards domestic violence was not only conveyed discursively by raising awareness talks; the new norm was also justiciable: until its gradual disintegration after 2007, this entity attended victims of violence and other problems related to the rights of children and adolescents. This service was welcomed by the community authorities, and many commoners from Tungasuca and surrounding communities turned to the *defensoría* to seek guidance and legal advice. And while the community board and the general assembly maintained their position according to which domestic violence did not fall within their competency, they were happy to channel such problems to this new institution. In cases where their authority was required to exert influence on aggressors, the community authorities were willing to support the *defensoría* in its work.[93]

Enforcement of reformed norms and institutions

From 2001 to 2007, Tungasuca's *defensores* strived to resolve minor marital problems by themselves. More severe cases were forwarded to the state authorities in Yanaoca. Initially, the *defensores* had many difficulties in coordinating with these authorities, not least because of prevailing discriminatory attitudes, corruption and ineffective processing of cases of violence. With the support of allies in Cuzco and in Yanaoca, such obstacles were gradually reduced. Due to a notable shortage in terms of communication, training and accompaniment of IDL and CODECC, and a subsequent decline of the motivation of the remaining defenders, the *defensoría* service deteriorated after 2007. Afterwards, it was the justice of the peace and, to a much lesser degree, the governor of the district, who came to replace the *defensoría* by offering their own forms of conflict resolution to victims of domestic violence. While the attention of the justice of the peace to such cases resembled, to a certain degree, that formerly offered by the *defensoría*, the governor turned to conciliatory schemes based on his own understanding of how such problems might be dealt with. NGOs, the district municipality and the state programme 'Juntos' assumed the *defensoría's* task of norm promotion. To the detriment of victims of violence, the result of this gradual replacement of the *defensoría* by other agents was that authorities, procedures and sanctions became vague, ambiguous and dispersed across uncoordinated agents, each of whom pursuing distinct agendas and interests respectively. And even though the justice of the peace registered a reduction of cases of physical violence towards the end of the research period (2012), commoners expressed the view that cases of (perhaps less visible) forms of violence continued to exist in the community, and that there were still many women who preferred to keep silent and who did not turn to any of the available institutions.[94]

Sustainability of reformed norms and institutions

At the end of the research period, the sustainability of the *defensoría* as an institution seemed highly questionable. The two defenders fulfilled their tasks more on a nominal than on a practical basis, and they admitted to not having attended cases for quite a long time. In the same vein, most of the representatives of the women's groups were not well informed about the service of the *defensoría* or unsure about whether it was still operative. When asked where women could turn to in case they suffered from violence, these women responded that they would rather turn to the justice of the peace or the governor in order to seek redress. Throughout the second half of the 2000s, the influence of the women's organisation SOMUC, which had actually inspired the creation and helped to coordinate the *defensorías* in the Canas Province, diminished, as well. Next to more general leadership problems in the FPCC, local women's interest in this representative entity also declined because of the region-wide institutionalisation of social programmes, such as the aforementioned 'Juntos'. This programme not only absorbed a significant amount of the limited time resources of women from rural communities, but even more importantly, it offered an unequivocal benefit (money) in exchange for women's (obligatory) participation in the reunions and activities it organised. As a consequence, the appeal of engaging in voluntary organisations, such as SOMUC or the *defensorías*, diminished considerably. Indeed, when searching for fresh personnel interested in the work of the *defensoría*, the two defenders from Tungasuca were often confronted with the question as to whether the performance of this function would entail some form of 'compensation'. This mentality not only worked against the principle of voluntariness performed by the *defensoría* team, but actually against all offices of the community organisation, which were likewise exerted on a voluntary basis.[95]

The sustainability of the *defensoría* in the near future would be related to the course of some other developments, as well. First, in 2012, the community board was considering to enhance community-based crime prevention and to strengthen communal responses to any form of legal transgression by pooling available expertise in the community. These discussions revolved around an improved and coordinated action of all existing authorities and included not only the justice of the peace, the governor and deputy governor, the communal board, but also the *defensoría*. If these plans were implemented, the possibility existed that the *defensoría* and its particular competence in the realm of domestic violence might be revalued.[96] Second, CODECC and IDL (the latter of which withdrew from the regional *defensoría* project in the mid of 2012) were aware of the problems *defensorías* in remote districts were facing, and they signalled that such issues would be dealt with when elaborating the strategy for the next mid-term plan of CODECC.[97] Third, the sustainability of *defensorías* in Tungasuca and elsewhere would also depend on the appreciation of the contribution of *defensorías* in facilitating the access of marginalised citizens to justice by the regional government of Cuzco. While its Regional Programme Against Violence towards Women (2008–2010)[98] to improve access to justice for victims of domestic violence in rural communities, which included the creation of decentralised 'modules of legal community services', constituted a first step in the right direction (see also case study Chacabamba), legal and political difficulties to implement this Plan in the pilot communities have thus far hampered practical advances in this regard. And as no community in the Canas Province was included among the selected pilot communities of this programme, the *defensoría* in Tungasuca would certainly need to have a lot of staying power in order to benefit in some way from this process.[99]

Notes

1 The criterion of mother tongue fails to recognise that there is an ever-growing number of indigenous Peruvians migrating to urban areas where parents tend to raise their children with Spanish as a first language; that persons who grow up in a bilingual context may encounter difficulties in answering this question; and that there are many people who may identify with an indigenous culture even though they no longer speak a native language. The population under three years of age is also excluded here; see Albó 2009: 171–172; data of the 2007 National Census generated from the INEI website: www.inei.gob.pe (last access 10.06.2015).

2 The other departments with a considerable proportion of Quechua speakers were Apurímac (70.6 per cent), Huancavelica (64 per cent) and Ayacucho (63 per cent); see data of the 2007 National Census and the II Census of Indigenous Communities of the Peruvian Amazon generated from the INEI website; see Fn. 1.

3 The indigenous population was one of the sectors most affected by the armed conflict in Peru; see Comisión de la Verdad y Reconciliación Nacional 2002.
4 See ILO website: www.ilo.org/dyn/normlex/en/f?p=1000:11300:0::NO:11300:P11300_INSTRUMENT_ID:312314 (last access 10.06.2015).
5 Recent examples for problems implied by the unclear terminology can be seen in the unwillingness of President Ollanta Humala to concede *campesino* communities the status of 'indigenous peoples' and the controversies about a data base of indigenous peoples elaborated by the Peruvian Vice-Ministry for Interculturality; see La República 09.08.2013; Servindi 27.10.2013.
6 See Law 26505 on private investments in the development of economic activities in lands pertaining to the national territory and those of campesino and native communities (1995); Albó 2009: 206–207; Barié 2003: 495; Thorp and Paredes 2010: 175; Yashar 2005: 238.
7 According to the social conflict monitor of the Peruvian Human Rights Ombudsman (*Defensoría del Pueblo*), the number of conflicts increased from 47 in December 2004 (with 5 per cent of the conflicts related to the mining sector) to 223 active and latent conflicts in December 2011 (56.5 per cent of which categorized as socio-ecological conflicts. Cuzco accounted for 12 active socio-ecological conflicts in December 2011; see the Ombudsman's website: www.defensoria.gob.pe/conflictos-sociales/ (last access 10.06.2015).
8 On this day, around 33 people were killed and 200 injured in a conflict between state security forces and indigenous lowland peoples who protested against national legislation threatening their lands; see Amnesty International 2009.
9 Law 29785 (2011) and its Regulatory Law (Supreme Decree 001–2012–MC, 2012) did not meet the expectations of indigenous and *campesino* organisations, among other reasons, because the results of consultations were not legally binding; see Servindi, 03.03.2012; The Guardian 05.06.2012.
10 See Congreso de la República, Comisión de Pueblos Andinos, Amazónicos, Afroperuanos, Ambiente y Ecología 2013; Consejo Ejecutivo del Poder Judicial 2014: 10–11.
11 See Corte Suprema de Justicia de la Republica; Comisión de Trabajo sobre Justicia Indígena y Justicia de Paz 2011: 2; Decoster and Rivera 2009: 42–43; IDL 2005: 41–43; Poole 2009: 604–608; Yashar 2005: 227 Fn 7; Yrigoyen 2002: 159.
12 The recognition of justices of the peace was also fostered by the 1993 Constitution and regulatory Law 28545 (2005), by which the justices' former designation by the judiciary was substituted by popular elections held in their jurisdictions; see Corte Suprema de Justicia de la República; Comisión de Trabajo sobre Justicia Indígena y Justicia de Paz 2011; IDL 2005.
13 See IDL 2005: 53. The Cuzco Department accounted for the third highest number of justices of the peace (364 of a total of 5,102); see Lovatón 2005: 71.
14 On the competences of the governor and deputy governor, see Law 28895 (2006); Supreme Decree 004–2007–IN (2007); Supreme Decree 001–2008–IN (2008); Supreme Decree 006–2008–IN (2008).
15 The jurisdiction of a justice of the peace, for instance, typically extends to several communities, and governors are responsible for an entire district. Their offices may be very close or else remote from particular communities; IDL 2005: 72, 201.
16 In Peru, doctors have to verify the denunciation of the victim by undertaking a physical examination. They decide whether the physical harm is to be classified as a 'minor' or a 'severe' injury. While the former implies the holding of the perpetrator for 24 hours at a police station, the latter, which stipulates the victim was'incapacitated' for more than ten days, allows for the legal prosecution of the accused; see Boesten 2010: 113–114.

17 In this survey, 'exercise of control' referred to situations in which the (ex-) partner becomes jealous or angry; accuses a woman of infidelity; impedes a woman to visit or being visited by friends; insists to being informed on the places the woman goes to; or does not trust her in financial matters; see INEI 2012: 324–327.

18 In 2010, the Peruvian government spent S/.31,169,956 (around US$10.9 million) for its policies to combat violence; in 2011, the amount rose to S/.38,855,023 Peruvian Soles (or US$13.6 million); see Organización de los Estados Americanos/Mecanismo de Seguimiento de la Convención de Belém do Pará 2012: 179.

19 Interviews 1–25.02.2012, 2–25.02.2012; 3–25.02.2012; 1–29.02.2012; 4–29.02.2012; 7–29.02.2012; 01./02.03.2012).

20 Interview 1–25.02.2012. This development was observed in the entire region; in 2007, the Huancarani district registered 56 per cent Catholics and 40 per cent Evangelists; data based on the 2007 Census generated from INEI's website www.inei.gob.pe (last access 10.06.2015).

21 Data based on the 2007 Census generated from INEI's website; see Fn 1, and INEI 2009: 19, 46–47, 52, 72, 80–81.

22 Interviews 1–25.02.2012; 3–29.02.2012; 4–29.02.2012; 5–29.02.2012.

23 These programmes have characterised Peru's social policies from the 1970s onwards. They were first installed in poor urban neighbourhoods, but quickly extended to rural communities, as well; see Boesten 2010: 48–49; Rousseau 2010: 149.

24 Interviews 1–29.02.2012; 2–29.02.2012; 5–29.02.2012.

25 The programs were criticised, among other things, for the affirmation of the role of women as caretakers, for serving as a clientelist tool for politicians and for their sometimes adverse effect on poverty reduction; see Boesten 2010: 3. One of the main state institutions in charge of the food distribution (*Programa Nacional de Asistencia Alimentaria*, PRONAA) was closed due to its inefficient management and food scandals in May 2012, only to be replaced by a new provider 'Qali Warma'; see El Comercio 11.06.2012.

26 Interviews 29.01.2012; 30.01./05.03.2012; 09.02.2012.

27 Interviews 10./16.01.2012; 30.01./05.03.2012; 13.02.2012; 1–25.02.2012; 1–29.02.2012; 4–29.02.2012.

28 Interviews 1–25.02.2012; 1–26.02.2012; 2–26.02.2012; 3–29.02.2012; 7–29.02.2012; 01./02.03.2012.

29 Interviews 1–29.02.2012; 01./02.03.2012.

30 Interviews 29.01.2012; 02.02.2012; 13.02.2012; 1–25.02.2012; 1–29.02.2012; 01./02.03.2012.

31 Interview 31.01.2012.

32 Interviews 09.02.2012; 3–25.02.2012; 1–26.02.2012; 1–29.02.2012; 5–29.02.2012.

33 Interviews 3–25.02.2012; 1–26.02.2012; 01./02.03.2012.

34 Interviews 10./16.01.2012; 29.01.2012; see also CODECC, Franco and Haworth 2005; Franco 2003.

35 Interviews 1–26.02.2012; 01./02.03.2012.

36 Interviews 13.02.2012; 3–25.02.2012; 1–26.02.2012.

37 Interviews 3–25.02.2012; 1–26.02.2012; 7–29.02.2012; 01./02.03.2012.

38 Interviews 1–26.02.2012; 1–29.02.2012; 01./02.03.2012.

39 Aspects such as the constant accompaniment and training of the defenders as well as the idea that the function of a defender should be regularly passed among distinct community members were determined by the two agencies promoting the creation of the *defensorías comunitarias* in the Cuzco

Department; Interviews 10./16.01.2012; 29.01.2012; 3–25.02.2012; 1–26.02.2012; 1–29.02.2012; 01./02.03.2012.

40 Interviews 09.02.2012; 1–25.02.2012; 3–25.02.2012; 1–26.02.2012; 1–29.02.2012; 7–29.02.2012; 01./02.03.2012.

41 Interview 10./16.01.2012; 13.02.2012; 1–26.02.2012; 01./02.03.2012.

42 Interviews 10./16.01.2012; 20.01.2012; 02.02.2012; 13.02.2012; 30.01./05.03.2012.

43 Interviews 1–25.02.2012; 2–25.02.2012; 3–25.02.2012; 1–29.02.2012; 3–29.02.2012; 01./02.03.2012.

44 Interviews 1–26.02.2012; 01./02.03.2012.

45 Interviews 1–25.02.2012; 2–25.02.2012; 3–25.02.2012; 1–26.02.2012; 1–29.02.2012; 3–29.02.2012; 5–29.02.2012; 01./02.03.2012.

46 Interview 01./02.03.2012.

47 Interviews 10./16.01.2010; 13.02.2012; 1–25.02.2012; 1–26.02.2012; 1–29.02.2012; 01./02.03.2012.

48 Interviews 1–25.02.2012; 1–26.02.2012; 1–29.02.2012; 01./02.03.2012.

49 Interviews 1–26.02.2012; 2–26.02.2012; 01./02.03.2012.

50 Interviews 29.01.2012; 02.02.2012; 13.02.2012.

51 Interviews 29.01.2012; 01./02.03.2012.

52 Interviews 29.01.2012; 13.02.2012.

53 Interviews 1–25.02.2012; 3–25.02.2012; 1–26.02.2012; 1–29.02.2012; 5–29.02.2012; 01./02.03.2012.

54 Participatory budgets at the municipal level constituted one important element of Peru's decentralisation policies enacted throughout the 2000s; see General Law 28056 on Participatory Budgeting (2003); McNulty 2013.

55 Interviews 20.01.2012; 29.01.2012; 13.02.2012; 01./02.03.2012.

56 Interviews 29.01.2012; 1–26.02.2012; 01./02.03.2012.

57 Interviews 1–25.02.2012; 2–25.02.2012; 3–25.02.2012; 1–26.02.2012; 2–26.02.2012; 1–29.02.2012; 3–29.02.2012; 5–29.02.2012; 7–29.02.2012; 01./02.03.2012.

58 Interviews 29.01.2012; 1–25.02.2012; 3–25.02.2012; 1–26.02.2012; 3–29.02.2012; 5–29.02.2012; 01./02.03.2012.

59 Interviews 3–25.02.2012; 1–26.02.2012; 1–29.02.2012; 01./02.03.2012.

60 Interviews 29.01.2012; 13.02.2012.

61 See Gobierno Regional Cusco 2008; Gobierno Regional Cusco (n.d.).

62 Interviews 09.02.2012; 17.02.2012.

63 See Chuquimia 2012: 170–171; Decoster and Rivera 2009: 71; Municipalidad Distrital de Tupac Amaru 2011: 4–5; Interview 1–23.02.2012.

64 Interviews 2–18.02.2012; 6–18.02.2012; 4–21.02.2012; 2–23.02.2012; 1–03.03.2012; 2–03.03.2012.

65 Between 1996 and 2000, public health personnel conducted a massive sterilisation campaign of women (most of whom would participate in an uninformed and involuntary manner), especially in the rural Peruvian Sierra; see CLADEM 1999; Defensoría del Pueblo 1999.

66 See INEI 2009: 19, 46–47, 52, 72, 80–81; Municipalidad Distrital de Tupac Amaru 2011: 26–29; Interviews 2–18.02.2012; 1–21.02.2012.

67 See Municipalidad Distrital de Tupac Amaru 2011: 10–14; Interviews 2-18.02.2012; 1-03.03.2012.

68 Data based on the 2007 Census generated from INEI's website www.inei.gob.pe (last access 10.06.2015).

69 See Municipalidad Distrital de Tupac Amaru 2011: 15–16, 22, 51–52, 57–58.

70 Interviews 3–18.02.2012; 4–18.02.2012; 1–21.02.2012; 3–21.02.2012; see also Franco 2003: 31.

71 Interviews 3–18.02.2012; 1–21.02.2012; 3–21.02.2012; 1–23.02.2012; 2–03.03.2012.
72 Interviews 3–18.02.2012; 4–18.02.2012; 1–21.02.2012; 4–21.02.2012; 1–23.02.2012; 2–23.02.2012; see also Franco 2003: 31.
73 Interviews 1–21.02.2012; 4–21.02.2012; 2–03.03.2012.
74 Interviews 2–18.02.2012; 2–21.02.2012; 1–23.02.2012; 2–23.02.2012; 1–03.03.2012.
75 Interviews 31.01.2012; 02.02.2012; 13.02.2012; 17.02.2012; 1–21.02.2012; 4–21.02.2012.
76 Interviews 13.02.2012; 17.02.2012; 3–18.02.2012; 6–18.02.2012; 7–18.02.2012; 1–21.02.2012; 4–21.02.2012.
77 For more information on the regional *defensoría comunitaria* programme, see the case of Chacabamba in the same chapter.
78 See Franco 2003: 28, 31; Interview 1–21.02.2012.
79 Interviews 3–18.02.2012; 3–21.02.2012; 2–03.03.2012; see also Cabrera and Díaz 2005; Franco 2003.
80 See Franco 2003: 39–40; Interviews 13.02.2012; 1–18.02.2012; 1–21.02.2012; personal notes taken during conversation with municipal representative (21.02.2012).
81 Interviews 29.01.2012; 13.02.2012; 1–18.02.2012; 1–21.02.2012.
82 Interviews 1–21.02.2012; 4–21.02.2012; 2–23.02.2012; 1–03.03.2012.
83 Interview 10./16.01.2012; 1–21.02.2012.
84 Interviews 20.01.2012; 29.01.2012; 13.02.2012; 1–18.02.2012; 1–21.02.2012.
85 Interviews 1–18.02.2012; 1–21.02.2012; 2–03.03.2012.
86 Interviews 29.01.2012; 02.02.2012; 1–18.02.2012; 7–18.02.2012; 2–03.03.2012; see also Franco 2003: 42.
87 Interviews 29.01.2012; 02.02.2012; 13.02.2012; 1–18.02.2012; 7–18.02.2012; 2–03.03.2012.
88 Interviews 29.01.2012; 13.02.2012.
89 Interviews 1–18.02.2012; 7–18.02.2012; 1–21.02.2012; 2–21.02.2012; 4–21.02.2012, 1–03.03.2012.
90 Interviews 1–21.02.2012; 4–21.02.2012; 1–23.02.2012.
91 Interviews 4–21.02.2012; 1–23.02.2012; 1–03.03.2012.
92 Interviews 1–18.02.2012; 3–18.02.2012; 3–21.02.2012; 1–21.02.2012; 1–03.03.2012.
93 Interviews 1–18.02.2012; 2–18.02.2012; 7–18.02.2012; 1–21.02.2012; 2–03.03.2012.
94 Interviews 1–18.02.2012; 3–18.02.2012; 6–18.02.2012; 7–18.02.2012; 1–21.02.2012; 4–21.02.2012.
95 Interviews 1–18.02.2012; 2–18.02.2012; 3–18.02.2012; 4–18.02.2012; 5–18.02.2012; 1–21.02.2012; 2–21.02.2012; 1–03.03.2012.
96 Interview 2–18.02.2012.
97 Interviews 20.01.2012; 29.01.2012; 13.02.2012.
98 See Gobierno Regional Cusco 2008; Gobierno Regional Cusco (n.d.).
99 Interviews 09.02.2012; 17.02.2012.

Chapter 5

'Sometimes we as women undervalue ourselves'

Mojocoya and Tarabuco, Bolivia

Map 5.1 Bolivia

A surprising development in respect to the indigenous population has recently occurred in Bolivia, where, according to the controversial Census of 2012, the percentage of surveyed persons above the age of 15 declaring to pertain to an indigenous people dropped from 62 per cent (in 2001) to around 41 per cent, with which the indigenous population appeared to no longer represent a majority in the just refounded Plurinational State of Bolivia.[1] The overall Bolivian population was estimated at 10,027,254 in 2012. Of the (still considerable) 2,806,592 people above the age of 15 self-identifying as indigenous (or Afro-Bolivian), the overall majority was made up of the Quechua (1,281,116) and the Aymara (1,191,352) who mainly resided in the Andean Departments La Paz, Potosí and Oruro and in the inter-Andean valleys stretching across Cochabamba and Chuquisaca. Among the indigenous groups originating in the lowlands, the Chiquitano (87,885) constituted the largest group according to the 2012 Census. The Department of Chuquisaca, where the two municipalities included in the present study were located, accounted for a population of 576,153 in 2012, with 256,664 people (or 44.5 per cent) self-identifying as Quechua.[2]

Structures of indigenous self-governance in the rural Bolivian highlands varied: beginning with the Land Reform of 1953, headed by President Victor Paz Estenssoro, indigenous groups were supposed to assimilate into a national mestizo identity by abandoning the term *indio* in favour of the class-based denomination of *campesino* and by registering in a state-sponsored peasant union organised at the local, provincial, departmental and national levels (National Confederation of Peasant Workers of Bolivia, *Confederación Nacional de Trabajadores Campesinos de Bolivia*, CNTCB). The union model was most strongly embraced in regions where the hacienda system had thoroughly disarticulated traditional forms of indigenous organisation in previous periods (Van Cott 2005: 52–53; Yashar 2005: 155–163). In such cases, the local administration was shifted to the hands of elected union functionaries (e.g., executive secretaries, secretaries of justice, etc.) and the general assembly made up of all community-based union members. Problems that were not resolved at the community level could be shifted towards functionaries at higher levels of the union. In some locations, traditional authorities of colonial and republican origin (such as the *corregidor, agente cantonal, alcalde de campo*) were integrated into the new union structure (CERES 1999; Orellana 2004). In other highland regions that had remained free of large estates or where the State's presence remained weak, the adoption of the union structure seemed less appealing, and it was not uncommon to see how elements of the union (such as its nomenclature) were accommodated within the prevailing governance structure (made up of the smallest unit *orígen; ayllu* compounding several *orígenes*; *marka* composed of several *ayllus*; and *suyu* – representing a nation) while simultaneously maintaining the traditional rotation system of authorities and pre-existing forms to administer justice. Not least, there were also regions such as Northern Potosí where communities maintained their prevailing forms of self-rule (Rivera [1990] 2010: 167–175; Yashar 2005: 160–163). Beginning in the late 1980s, and incentivised by the consciousness-raising activities of the La Paz-based Workshop of Oral Andean History (THOA) and the support of some development cooperation agencies, many communities decided to reject foreign organisational schemes and to reconstitute traditional Andean structures at the local level. This trend was followed by the foundation of *ayllu* federations in the Departments and a representative body at the national level, the National Council of Ayllus and Markas of the Qullasuyu (CONAMAQ) in 1997 (Albó 2009: 55–56; Choque and Mamani 2001; Chuquimia 2012: 188).

Recognition of legal pluralism

After the emergence of Andean intellectual movements (*Kataristas* and *Indigenistas* in the late 1960s and 1970s) and new unionised highland organisations (such as the Unitary Syndical Confederation of Peasant Workers of Bolivia (*Confederación Sindical Única de Trabajadores Campesinos de Bolivia*; CSUTCB)[3] in 1979 and the parallel female organisation National Federation of Campesino Women of Bolivia – Bartolina Sisa (*Federación Nacional de Mujeres Campesinas de Bolivia – Bartolina Sisa*; FNMCB-BS)[4] in 1980), the increasing political participation and mobilisation of indigenous people in the context of austerity policies throughout the 1980s,[5] it was the 650 kilometres long *March for Territory and Dignity* in 1990 from the lowland city Trinidad to the political centre of Bolivia, La Paz, organised by the Confederación de Pueblos Indígenas de Bolivia (Confederation of Indigenous Peoples of Bolivia; CIDOB), which eventually reminded the political elites of the particular problems faced by indigenous groups in this country (Van Cott 2005: 60–61; Yashar 2005: 198–212). Among the immediate steps taken by the government was the ratification of ILO C 169 in 1991,[7] which stipulates the right of indigenous peoples to administer justice, as well as a constitutional reform (1994) with which, for the first time in the Bolivian history, the multiethnic and pluricultural nature of the State was recognised (art. 1). Indigenous peoples were guaranteed social, economic and cultural rights and access to land titles called *Tierras Comunitarias de Origen* (TCOs; art. 171). With respect to indigenous justice, the constitution ruled that indigenous and *campesino* authorities could dispense justice according to their customs and procedures and in conformity with the Constitution and Bolivian laws, but their justice systems were only regarded as an 'alternative form of conflict solution' (art. 171). Also, the constitution envisioned the implementation of a law that should render the legal functions of indigenous peoples 'compatible' with the state jurisdiction (art. 171; see Barié 2003: 148–149).

In the second half of the 1990s, the Ministry of Justice and Human Rights commissioned several scientific institutions to conduct studies on 'community justice' in several indigenous lowland and highland communities (e.g., CERES 1999; Fernández 2000; Molina 1999). These studies provided rich insights into the diversity and complexity of legal orders co-existing with state law on Bolivian territory and were meant to provide the ongoing debate on how to regulate this jurisdictional plurality with basic information. Among the few concrete steps following from these new insights was a reform of the Penal Code in 1999 providing for special measures such as the consultation of experts in indigenous issues in case indigenous citizens were processed for penal offences before the state legal system (art. 391). If a legal transgression occurred in an indigenous territory and was resolved by indigenous authorities, the state judiciary could not revise the case a second time (*ne bis in idem* principle, art. 28). Unfortunately, this norm was neither widely diffused nor taken into account by the majority of legal operators (Orellana 2004: 17). More generally, and similar to Ecuador and Peru, the formal recognition of indigenous peoples' rights occurred against the background of the adoption of neoliberal policies, marked by the privatisation of state-owned firms, the opening of key sectors such as the hydrocarbon industry to foreign capital and the cutting of social services and price subsidies for domestic products. These policies provoked mass mobilisations against the privatisation of water and concessions to transnational corporations interested in exporting natural gas and resulted in the ousting of President Gonzalo Sánchez de Lozada from office in 2003 (Albro 2005; Arze and Kruse 2004; Laurie, Andolina and Radcliffe 2002). It was the first indigenous President Evo Morales – head of the Movement toward Socialism (*Movimiento al Socialismo*; MAS) and of the coca-growers union, elected in 2005, and confirmed in office in 2009 and 2014 – who put an end to the governability crisis by enacting policies to renationalise natural resources, to invest the revenues from extractive industries in social programmes to fight poverty and to re-establish the dignity of indigenous peoples by attempts to ridding the country of its colonial and racist traits (Anría *et al.* 2010; Postero 2010). Morales convened a democratically elected Constituent Assembly (with 55.8 per cent of the delegates self-identifying as indigenous), which worked under extremely difficult conditions until agreeing on a new constitutional text, the same of which was approved in a referendum by 61.43 per cent of the votes and entered in force in February 2009 (Albó 2009: 96–107; Postero 2010; Schilling-Vacaflor 2010). The Magna Carta recognised the *plurinational* composition of Bolivia's citizenry, established the indigenous concept of living well (*vivir bien*) as well as political, economic, *judicial*, cultural and linguistic pluralism as fundamental principles of the State, and guaranteed an extensive package of individual and collective rights to Bolivians. *Indigenous originary campesino nations and peoples*[8] were guaranteed the right to self-determination that entailed their right to autonomy, self-government and the consolidation of their lands, within the unitary state of Bolivia (art. 2). They were entitled to administer their legal systems, exercised by corresponding authorities by means of their own principles, values, norms and procedures, the same of whom should respect the right to life, to defence and all other constitutionally enshrined rights and guarantees (art. 30 II 14, art. 190). While stipulating that the personal competence of indigenous jurisdiction extended to all members of indigenous peoples, and that the territory of an indigenous group circumscribed the territorial competence, the concretisation of the material competences was shifted to a future Law on Jurisdictional Delimitation (art. 191 II; 192 III). In an unprecedented move, indigenous jurisdiction obtained the same hierarchical status as the ordinary justice system (art. 179 II) and was declared a component of the unitary judiciary of the State (art. 179 I). Correspondingly, all state authorities were held to abide by decisions emanating from indigenous legal systems (art. 192 I).

A newly created Vice-Ministry of Indigenous Justice set out to conduct consultations with delegates from indigenous organisations in all Departments throughout 2010 and passed a draft law to the Plurinational Legislative Assembly where, to the disappointment of observers and indigenous organisations, the draft was subject to major changes by parliamentarians who viewed indigenous law with distrust (Albó 2012a: 242–248; El Diario 14.12.2010; Grijalva and Exeni 2012: 723). Article 10 of Law 073 on Jurisdictional Delimitation (*Ley de Deslinde Jurisdiscional*; LJD; 2010) especially presented an exhaustive list of subject matters for which indigenous legal authorities should *not* be responsible, which has engendered criticism.[9] In essence, this article restricted the material competence of indigenous authorities to those legal matters and conflicts, which they traditionally and historically used to address. Considering the highly dynamic nature of indigenous forms of justice and their adaptability to changing living conditions and circumstances over time, the critics could not understand why indigenous legal authorities were now viewed as incapable of finding adequate solutions for more recent or emerging problems within their communities (Albó 2012a; Grijalva and Exeni 2012). Importantly, the LJD clarified that indigenous authorities were only competent in cases where personal, territorial and material jurisdictions concurred (art. 8). Thus, while indigenous legal authorities could rule on conflicts occurring among the constituents of their respective indigenous group and within the confines of their territory (such as a community or TCO), their competence did neither extend to cases in which non-indigenous persons transgressed community norms on their territory, nor could they judge on conflicts among community members occurring outside of their territory (art. 9, 11). With respect to women, the LJD ruled that indigenous and ordinary state jurisdictions should respect women's rights and guarantee their equal access to legal authority positions (art. 5 II). With the exception of rape, which should be exclusively dealt with by the state judiciary (art. 10 II), both indigenous and state legal systems should prohibit and sanction other forms of violence against children, adolescents and women. In addition, all jurisdictions were held to refrain from conciliation to resolve cases of violence (art. 5 IV).[10] With respect to mechanisms of coordination and cooperation among the ordinary and the indigenous jurisdictions, the LJD envisioned the exchange of information among indigenous and ordinary legal operators so as to support one another in the resolution of cases. The cooperation was supposed to be guided by principles such as equity, transparency, solidarity and celerity and should not involve any costs (art. 15, 16). Lastly, the Law also proposed the creation of spaces for dialogue and exchange of experience about the application of human rights and methods of conflict resolution, among other mechanisms that might emerge in the future (Barrera 2012; Grijalva and Exeni 2012: 725–729).

To complete the picture of state-sanctioned legal pluralism in Bolivia, two other aspects should be highlighted: first, the Constitution opened the option for indigenous authorities to ask the Plurinational Constitutional Tribunal (whose seven members, among them at least two indigenous authorities, were now to be elected by the Bolivian citizens)[11] for guidance on the compatibility of their norms with constitutional rights in concrete cases (art. 202 no. 8). Should the Tribunal arrive at the conclusion that a norm applied by indigenous authorities was unconstitutional, it was expected to propose an alternative, culturally sensitive solution for the conflict at hand, the same of which was mandatory for the indigenous authorities.[12] Similar to the Ecuadorian provisions on the same issue, the constitutional control of resolutions emanating from indigenous jurisdictions in Bolivia remained centralised in the Tribunal in the capital Sucre, rendering the access to this revision mechanism for most indigenous people very complicated (Barrera 2012: 378). Second, the 2009 Constitution and the General Law 031 on Autonomy and Decentralization (*Ley Marco de Autonomías y Descentralización*; LMAD; 2009) paved the way for the conversion of pre-existing municipalities (but also TCOs or regions) into autonomous indigenous territories (*Autonomías Indigena Originario Campesinas*; AIOC; art. 291 Constitution of 2009). Once established, such autonomous territories opened indigenous peoples new avenues for self-governance, including the administration of indigenous justice according to own norms and procedures (art. 304 I 8. Constitution of 2009). And while these innovations have been criticised for a number of reasons, among them the limitation of the creation of such entities to pre-existing territorial units in disregard of the current areas of residence and organisation of indigenous groups; the bureaucratic requisites for the conversion into an autonomous indigenous territory; and the extremely reduced public funds provided to the Ministry of Autonomy that was in charge of supporting the conversion processes (Cameron 2013; CEDLA 2010), a majority of citizens of eleven municipalities[13] decided in a referendum held in December 2009 to embark on this process – two of them, Tarabuco and Mojocoya – provide the focus of the present chapter.

Legislation on violence against indigenous women

With respect to international treaties protecting rights to equality and non-discrimination, as well as a freedom from violence, Bolivia ratified the

CERD (1970), the ACHR (1979), the ICCPR and ICESCR (both in 1982), the CEDAW (1989) and the Belém do Pará Convention (1994). In order to comply with the obligations following from the two latter instruments, the 2009 Constitution condemned violence and stipulated the State's responsibility to prevent, eradicate and sanction any violent act occurring in private or public spaces (art. 15). In the previous decade, Bolivia adopted Law 1674 Against Family or Domestic Violence (*Ley Contra la Violencia en la Familia o Doméstica*; 1995), which categorised distinct forms of violence (physical, psychological and sexual) and determined the scope of addressees that could be held accountable for violent acts (spouses, partners, kin members, persons who held the custody of children). The Law envisioned penalties in form of fines and imprisonment of up to four days as well as alternative measures such as therapy or community service. In addition, the Law also foresaw protective measures such as the temporary staying away of the aggressor from the victim's home. The relatively minor sanctions raised the critique of feminist organisations in Bolivia, especially if compared with the long list of measures of preventive character considered by this Law (e.g., awareness-raising on violence among school children, rural communities, public health personnel, legal operators and the media; see Coordinadora de la Mujer 2011: 37). While the Law paved the way for the creation of a specialised entity within the police (Brigades of Family Protection), which could intervene in cases of violence, Supreme Decree 25087 (1998) also promoted the establishment of Offices for Integral Legal Services at the municipal level (*Servicios Legales Integrales Municipales*; SLIMs), which were supposed to support victims of violence with legal, psychological and social services while staging formal denouncements before the ordinary justice system. Notwithstanding these legal provisions, the access to the judiciary for victims of violence has been hampered by bureaucratic procedures, lengthy processes, untrained personnel, the limited presence and underfunding of SLIMs and legal operators in a considerable part of municipalities of the country,[14] but also by social and kin pressures prompting many victims to desist from a formal accusation. Other aspects criticised by women's advocates were the fact that this legislation's main emphasis was to maintain the integrity of the family (instead of focusing on the harm caused to victims) and that it privileged conciliation over the legal prosecution and sanctioning of domestic violence.[15] Interestingly enough, article 16 of Law 1674 took indigenous justice into account, ruling that the 'natural' authorities of indigenous and *campesino* communities could also resolve violence occurring within the family, based on their customary law (*usos y costumbres*), on condition that these customs would not contravene the Constitution and the spirit of this Law. In comparison to Peru and Ecuador where similar laws have not reflected upon indigenous legal authorities' role in addressing violence, the inclusion of this aspect in the respective legislation this early in Bolivia is remarkable. At the same time, we should consider that some indigenous legal authorities have intervened in cases of domestic violence for a long time without any 'official permission' to do so, and that due to lacking diffusion of this Law among indigenous organisations, most of them have remained unaware of this article (CERES 1999; Mendoza 2009: 219–220). Where knowledge on this Law existed, it was not considered helpful, as it did neither concretise the role of indigenous authorities nor the means by which these could coordinate legal action with state legal operators (Ministerio de Justicia, Viceministerio de Género y Asuntos Generacionales 2008: 82). Lastly, it should not go unmentioned that a new Law 348 to Guarantee Women a Life Free from Violence[16] was enacted in 2013; however, as this Law entered into force after the finishing of the research period of the present study (2012), it will not be further analysed here.

With regard to other policies adopted by the Morales government to address violence, the Vice-Ministry of Gender and Generational Issues designed a 'National Plan on Equal Opportunities' (2008),[17] which in its theoretical–conceptual introduction provided a critical analysis of the effects of the neoliberal politics of the past two decades on women. Taking a look back in Bolivian history, it was argued here that unjust gender relations had been present in precolonial times, thereby challenging the view of some indigenous leaders that violence against women was basically rooted in colonialism. Further, it was contended that existing patriarchal structures in the Bolivian society should be abandoned towards more horizontal and reciprocal relations among women and men, especially by means of a fresh conceptualisation of the Andean principle of complementarity. Following from that, the document proposed five fields of action as particularly conducive for changing the situation of women: body, space, time, movements and memory, incorporating thereby elements of a recent theoretical strand of 'communitarian feminism' promoted by the women's group *Mujeres Creando Comunidad* (Women Creating Community; see Paredes 2010; 2012). However, when turning to the concrete strategies, the Plan did not take these fields of action into account, but instead proposed to improve the system of attention to victims of violence, to train the personnel attending to cases of violence and to strengthen the protective measures of the police and the judicial operators, among other things. Unfortunately, the Vice-Ministry fell short of elaborating concrete indicators by which progress in the implementation of these actions could be measured, and just as many other realms of the Bolivian administration, this institution had only few financial resources at its disposal in order to effectively enforce this Plan.[18]

While a new national survey on gender violence was being prepared by the time of writing (see PIEB 24.02.2015), Bolivia's most recent official data on violence dated back to a National Study on Demography and Health conducted in 2008 (INE 2009): Accordingly, 43.5 per cent of women (between 15–49 years) had fallen victim of psychological, physical or sexual

Table 5.1 Violence against women in Bolivia (2008)*

	Psychological violence by current intimate partner during last 12months (in %)	*Physical violence by current intimate partner during last 12 months (in %)*	*Sexual violence by current intimate partner during last 12 months (in %)*
Nationwide	39.7	23.1	6.4
Chuquisaca	39.6	25.2	6.9

Source: Adapted from Encuesta Nacional de Demografía y Salud (ENDES) 2012; see INE 2009.

* This national survey included 11,567 currently or ever-partnered women between 15 and 49 years of age. The data gathered exclusively referred to violent acts occurred throughout the 12 months preceding the survey.

violence exerted by their intimate partner, whereas 8.5 per cent women reported violent acts by non-partners throughout the past year.[19] Violence conducted by intimate partners was predominantly psychological in nature (39.7 per cent), followed by physical (23.1 per cent) and sexual forms of violence (6.4 per cent). Meanwhile, 5.1 per cent of violent acts perpetrated by non-partners were classified as physical and 3.7 per cent as sexual. In the Chuquisaca Department, where the two municipalities incorporated in this book are located, 39.6 per cent women became victim of psychological, 25.2 per cent of physical and 6.9 per cent of sexual forms of violence, the same of which were exerted by the partners of these women. In comparison to that, 4.5 per cent women were affected by non-partner violence in Chuquisaca in the same time period; 3.1 per cent of such violent acts were physical and 1.6 per cent sexual in nature.

Mojocoya – Zudañez Province (2009–2012)

Mojocoya was located in the northern part of the Department Chuquisaca and belonged to the Zudañez Province; about 184 kilometres (or a five-hour bus drive) separated this site from the capital of the Department, Sucre. The municipality's territory has an area of 1,188km^2, and its variation in altitude (1,000–3,000 m.a.s.l.) corresponded to diverse ecological zones and respective climates (Alcaldía Municipal de Mojocoya 2011). Situated in the inter-Andean valley region, this place had been populated by different ethnic groups in pre-Columbian times and was incorporated into the Inca Empire in the fifteenth century. With the arrival of the Spanish colonisers the original capital of this municipality, Villa Mojocoya, was founded by captain Melchor de Rodas in 1584 as part of a strategy to fortify the 'frontier zone' between already colonised areas and the resisting Chiriguano from the eastern lowlands. The fertile plain surrounding Villa Mojocoya rendered this zone conducive for agricultural production, which is the reason for its partitioning among a handful of

Image 5.1 Main plaza of Redención Pampa (Mojocoya)

landowners who exploited the local workforce during the colonial and republican eras.[20] With the creation of a first school in 1936 in a relatively central site of the zone, the local population aspired after a gradual redemption from ignorance and illiteracy, so it was decided to name this site 'Redención Pampa' (redemption plain). In the following decades, ever more people from surrounding communities would build houses in Redención Pampa not only to shorten the distance for their children to the school, but also because this place would evolve into a focal point for commerce and transport. Beginning with the Agrarian Reform 1953, land was redistributed among the local population who from now onwards would identify as *campesinos* and organise in agrarian unions (*sindicatos*) at the community level, grouped together in a sub-central (*subcentralía*) at the level of Mojocoya.[21] After the creation of the autonomous national union CSUTCB (1979) and its departmental affiliate *Federación Sindical Única de Trabajadores Campesinos de Chuquisaca* in 1982 (2006 renamed in *Federación Única de Trabajadores de Pueblos Originarios de Chuquicasa*; FUTPOCH), the Mojocoyan union joined this organisation and evolved to a protagonist agent of the zone. Aiming to improve local economic development, the sub-central began to coordinate its efforts with a local cooperative as well as state agencies and NGOs. As a result, beginning with the 1990s, new methods to retain irrigation water during dry periods were introduced, the cultivation of agricultural products was improved and diversified and options for commercialisation were expanded.[22] With Law 1551 of Popular Participation (1994), Mojocoya was converted into a municipality, implying the adoption of many decentralised competences and the introduction of democratically elected municipal authorities (e.g., mayor, municipal council). Due to its protagonist role in the economic realm, the sub-central soon gained the upper hand over local public affairs; candidates for municipal offices and the municipal oversight committee (*comité de vigilancia*), which monitored the spending of resources of the municipal government, were often recruited among former union leaders.[23]

During the period of fieldwork (mid March–May 2012), the municipality was divided in three administrative zones (north, centre, south) and comprised 30 communities and two populated centres (Villa Mojocoya, Redención Pampa). According to the 2012 Census[24] 8,086 people lived in Mojocoya, indicating a very slow population growth compared with a population of 7,926 in the previous Census of 2001. Around 79.6 per cent (6,421) of the local population self-identified as Quechua in 2012. Illiteracy rates fell from of 21 per cent (2001) to 10.5 per cent (2012) among men and from 45 per cent (2001) to 18.4 per cent (2012) among women, which corresponded with a predominantly young population and improvements

Image 5.2 Interview of the author (right) with the President of Mojocoya's Autonomy Assembly

in the local educative system over the past decade, particularly the construction of primary education centres in many communities and several so-called core centres (*núcleos*), which offered secondary education and accommodation of students from remote communities. A small proportion of the young generation migrated to cities in order to attain a higher level of education. Many families lacked access to basic services and infrastructure such as sanitation, electricity and safe housing. Agriculture and, to a minor degree cattle raising, constituted the most important sources of income, and a growing share of the production was used to supply external markets such as the one in Sucre. Traditional products (wheat, potatoes, corn, barley grown in the plain and the higher zones; beans, peanuts, cane sugar and fruits harvested in the valleys), have been recently complemented by amaranth. After the harvesting period, many men and women tended to increase their family income by temporarily migrating to urban and rural zones of Chuquisaca, Cochabamba and Santa Cruz to work as informal masons, agricultural workers or domestic employees. The municipality hosted a small hospital in Redención Pampa and several decentralised health posts, but serious illnesses had to be treated in Sucre. Two times a day, a bus connected Redención Pampa with Sucre, whereas public intercommunal transport on unsealed land routes was lacking.

Why did claims for legal change emerge in Mojocoya?

Shifts in local power relations

At the outset of the new century, differentiated educational levels and literacy rates among men and women resulted in a relatively low self-esteem of the latter. While agricultural work was shared by both men and women, there was a clear divide between domestic tasks reserved for women and public affairs in the hands of men. The community administration was exerted by the *sindicato*, and in order to become a member therein, commoners were required to come of age, be married, possess a (usually hereditary) land parcel and reside in the community. Union membership was limited to one person per family – typically the husband as the 'head of family' – who, in exchange for regular contributions (financial dues, communal work) had the right to participate in regular assemblies where deliberations and decisions on community affairs took place. If women were present in these assemblies, it was either in representation of their husbands, or because their families explicitly encouraged them to do so, or because some leaders came to gradually open this space for more participation of all community members. Still, communal leadership positions (president, vice-president, secretaries of protocol, relations, economy, conflicts, culture, sports, deputies and others) were typically held by men.[25]

As a response to this, several women decided to form their own organisation (*Organización de Mujeres Campesinas de Mojocoya*) at the municipal level in the first half of the 2000s. They established a small executive committee and encouraged women from the distinct communities to form their own local female groups and to affiliate with the women's organisation. Given the predominant status of the sub-central in Mojocoya, it was strategically decided to not establish this organisation as a separate entity, but instead to integrate it into the general structure of the union. Initially, the organisation's activities referred to classical female spheres such as cooking, weaving, sewing and the taking care of vegetable gardens. But gradually, seizing the opportunities provided by an ever more favourable legal framework for women's participation in political and social organisations at the national level (see also below), representatives of the women's organisation came to assume leadership positions within the *sub-centralía*. At the beginning of the research period (2009), the organisation disposed of a consolidated structure in two-thirds of the communities and served as an effective vehicle to articulate women's interests within the union. Representatives of the women's organisation regularly participated in the reunions of the executive committee of the *sub-centralía*, gave account of their activities and were involved in the decision-making processes of the union. The president of the women's organisation occupied the second most important position within the administrative structure of the *sub-centralía* – just behind the executive of the sub-central himself, and was also a member of the oversight committee that exerted social control over the municipal administration.[26] Also, as subsequent national governments have introduced women's quota and the principles of parity and alternation for municipal elections from the mid 2000s onwards, potential female candidates for the municipal council in Mojocoya came to be recruited from among members of the women's organisation. However, because of their lack of experience and preparation for this public office, the first female municipal councillors faced many difficulties and were not yet able to meet the expectations of the population in the same manner as their male colleagues, who usually had occupied a number of leadership positions within the union structure before becoming eligible for this political office. Regardless of their engagement in organisational or political activities, women were expected to also comply with their other roles in the household, the care of their children, the elder and ill family members and their work in the fields. And even though the women's organisation effectively captured some space for participation at the municipal level, the picture was still mixed in the communities, with some *sindicatos* displaying more openness than others for the participation of women in communal affairs.[27]

Diffusion of new legal concepts

Since the mid 2000s, the leaders of the women's organisation participated in a series of training provided by several NGOs. Plan International, for instance, regularly held talks in the municipality on violence against women and women's rights, thereby sensitising women on a topic that hitherto had neither figured prominently in the agenda of the union nor of the women's organisation in Mojocoya. The Aclo Foundation (*Fundación Aclo*), a Sucre-based NGO, organised a leadership school for representatives from the entire northern region of the Chuquisaca Department, and some female leaders from Mojocoya seized the chance to participate in this school. The curriculum included topics such as democracy, citizen participation, public administration, rural development, among others. Shortly before the referendum on the autonomy was held (December 2009), *Centro Juana de Azurduy*, a Sucre-based NGO specialised in women's rights, held several trainings for municipal leaders. Throughout these trainings, leaders of the women's organisation were familiarised with new normative ideas, ranging from international rights to the 2009 Constitution and national laws. They learned how they could appropriate these instruments so as to analyse concrete problems at the local level, how to formulate proposals based on this analysis and how to exert influence in political decision-making processes. By maintaining their partners informed on their activities and talking to them about the things they have learned, these women also found a way to reduce the jealousy of their husbands who often viewed their absence from home with suspicion.[28]

In terms of concrete legal ideas, women developed a particular interest in the principle of gender equality and the right to political participation based on equal conditions between women and men, because, if taken seriously, these norms could pave the way for the enforcement of many other women's rights, including their equal access to justice and the right to freedom from violence. In a first step, they started to invoke laws prescribing women's quota (such as the reformed Electoral Code of 2004 according to which 30 per cent of the candidate lists for municipal elections should be reserved for women) not only to pressure for the inclusion of female candidates for the elections of the municipal council, but also to claim for more female participation in eligible positions within the sub-central. And while this law did not foresee a sanction in case its provisions were not complied with, this situation changed with the adoption of the 2009 Constitution. Given that new Magna Carta was facilitated by the first indigenous Bolivian President (Evo Morales) who enjoyed a high degree of approval by the local *campesino* population, the Constitution elaborated during his first term was very thoroughly read and enjoyed a high degree of legitimacy by both male and female leaders of Mojocoya.[29] Taking advantage of this circumstance, female leaders could now point more self-assuredly to those constitutional articles that affirmed their right to political participation on the basis of gender equality and the principles of alternation and parity (art. 8, 14, 26, 147, 209, 210, 278 of the 2009 Constitution). Importantly, the communitarian forms of democracy such as the one practised by the union in Mojocoya were likewise supposed to be practised under equal conditions between women and men (art. 11). Lastly, the Transitional Electoral Regime Law (2009)[30], which regulated the departmental and municipal elections to be held in April 2010, equally confirmed these principles. Indeed, the male leadership demonstrated their willingness to follow these new rules, for example, by a corresponding nomination of candidates for the municipal elections of 2010, with the result that two of the five Mojocoyan municipal councillors and three substitutes turned out to be women.[31]

Incompatibilities among institutional sets relevant for women's lives

Given the knowledge women in Mojocoya gained with respect to women's rights by means of previous training, and the long list of rights women were entitled to by the Constitution of 2009, leaders from the women's organisation became ever more aware of the discrepancies that existed between these constitutional rights and the still disadvantaged situation of many Mojocoyan women. The tensions perceived referred to realms such as education (illiteracy and short schooling periods versus the right to access all levels of education), health (missing inclusion of traditional medicine and midwifes and insufficient facilities versus the right to a universal, gratuitous, equitable, intercultural and participative health care), economy (economic dependence from husbands, underestimation of domestic work, lacking access to land titles, credits and technology versus recognition of domestic labour, access to tenancy and inherence of lands and labour rights), political participation (under-representation of women in leadership positions of the *sindicatos* versus right of participation on the basis of equal conditions among women and men), violence (prevalence of domestic violence versus right to a life free from violence) and even leisure time (enormous scope of daily tasks and labours performed by women versus right to an balanced repartition of domestic responsibilities among spouses). Precisely because the 2009 Constitution pointed to so many aspects that remained unfulfilled in their immediate context, and because they understood that this Constitution was highly valued by their male commoners, this document came to be appreciated by leaders from the women's organisation as a valid instrument upon which claims on the improvement of any of these aspects should be raised.[32]

Inappropriate resolution of cases of domestic violence by existing institutions

In terms of domestic violence, women were unsatisfied with both the dealing with such cases within their own legal system and the state legal system. If kin intervention proved ineffective, women could turn to the secretary of conflicts (sometimes also called secretary of justice) of the community who was responsible for resolving small disputes on territorial demarcation, cattle theft and controversies between neighbours and family members. In virtually all communities, this function was occupied by a man. In cases of domestic violence, some secretaries of conflicts tended to hold a conversation between the conflicting parties and finished the session with the formulation of a written resolution (*acta*) in which the aggressor pledged to change his conduct. If the aggressor would not comply with his own pledge, the resolution would also envision some consequences such as the payment of a fine or the realisation of communal works. From the view of women, such sanctions proved toothless and did not really address the harm caused to women. Besides, in many communities, the secretaries of conflicts lacked effective authority so as to oblige the aggressors to adhere to the agreements. By the same token, there were authorities who refrained from intervening in cases of violence, either because they did not know how to duly resolve these cases or because they were akin to one of the parties in conflict. Thus, they preferred to pass such cases towards the next-higher legal instance, the secretary of justice of the sub-central. The person who occupied this office for many years in Mojocoya was a deeply religious man, and his interventions in cases of violence were based on an analysis of the underlying problems of the couple, the giving of advice based on local and religious–moral norms and reconciliation among the parts in conflict. However, he was likewise unable to guarantee that the aggressor complied with the resolutions accorded under his authority. Moreover, women complained that violent acts committed by powerful union leaders or municipal authorities were silenced from the outset, without any intervention by the competent legal authorities.[33]

As far as the state justice system was concerned, a SLIM, a police station and a judge were located in Redención Pampa. The obstacles to access the SLIM were, first, geographic in nature: the SLIM team did not dispose of its own vehicle, and no public and regular transport between the communities and Redención Pampa existed. Second, the SLIM team was composed of only two persons, among them a male lawyer, whereas many women would have preferred to obtain guidance from a female person of confidence first. Third, police officers and SLIM employees either tended to invite the victim and the aggressor to a conversation without establishing any further consequences or follow-up measures, or they would advise couples to separate. But none of these options actually responded to women's understanding of a comprehensive and just solution. Last, many women did not dare to denounce aggressors before the state authorities because they feared acts of vengeance from the aggressors. These obstacles in their access to justice in cases of domestic violence convinced the women's organisation that this matter would have to be included among their list of demands they planned to raise during the process of the conversion of Mojocoya into an indigenous autonomous territory.[34]

Which factors facilitated or obstructed the initiation of legal change efforts in Mojocoya?

Political opportunities at the starting point of the legal change efforts

In Mojocoya, the aspects facilitating the *change initiative* were abounding. A majority of 88.31 per cent of Mojocoyans voted in favour of the conversion into an autonomous territory in the referendum held on 6 December 2009 (Cameron 2013: 181). Indeed, the population had a reason *sui generis* for approving this conversion: over the past decades, the rivalry between the capital of the municipality Villa Mojocoya, which was mainly inhabited by descendents of the former landowner elite, and Redención Pampa with an overwhelmingly peasant population, had increased not only in terms of numbers: in 2001, Mojocoya accounted for 366 inhabitants, whereas Redención Pampa had 1,411 residents (Alcaldía Municipal de Mojocoya 2011: 33). Apart from the municipal building, most other social, economic and public institutions were situated in Redención Pampa, and this site has long outshone Mojocoya in terms of commerce and transport. The rivalry was also reflected in continuous acts of discrimination towards the *campesino* population and conflicts over the use of municipal resources:

> [A]ll the political power was still concentrated in Mojocoya. There was some resentment. There was a lot of discrimination. They didn't want to receive us there [in the municipality]. (...) It was discrimination, because they treated [us] as 'indios', 'campesinos'. "You shouldn't come down here. What do you want here? Go somewhere else".
>
> (Interview 1–22.04.2012)

Ultimately, the dispute over the lending of a municipal tractor for public works, accompanied by physical aggressions, threats, the temporary taking of hostage of the mayor and damage to farm machinery, served as a trigger for an emotional outburst among the *campesino* population. In a municipal-wide union assembly it was held that this situation was no longer tenable and that *campesinos* had long enough suffered from humiliation by a small but still powerful group. Thus, on 4 October 2007, hundreds of *campesinos* marched towards Villa Mojocoya, entered the municipal offices and removed furniture, equipment and documents to Redención Pampa, which, from now on would be regarded by them as the sole legitimate capital of the municipality. As the mayor and three municipal councillors were also representatives of the *campesino* population at that moment, they bowed to the pressure of the masses and agreed to this procedure. Residents of Villa Mojocoya responded with protests and also charged several union leaders before the state judiciary for an act that – if seen from a purely legal perspective – was unlawful. For the *campesino* population, in turn, the removal of the municipal capital represented the liberation from an imposed domination by a minority. After consultations with legal experts and regional allies from the MAS party, they found the conversion of the municipality into an autonomous territory – a process foreseen in the draft of the new constitution – to be the only viable option to sanction the unlawful removal of the capital.[35] Thus, after the adoption of the new Constitution in February 2009, a task force was established among union leaders so as to prepare all necessary documents and collect the signatures required to apply for the initiation of the conversion process. Once their formal request was accepted by the national government, union leaders campaigned among their bases to vote for the autonomy in the referendum – a successful strategy, as the high approval in the referendum showed. And long before the concrete procedures of the conversion were regulated in the respective LMAD (July 2010), municipal and union leaders were already engaged in the planning of the deliberative assembly, which would be in charge of elaborating the future autonomy statue. Importantly, these leaders understood that in order to pass through all difficulties this conversion entailed (including the opposition from Villa Mojocoya), consent and unity among the entire *campesino* population was needed – a circumstance that strengthened the position of women. The women's organisation seized this opportunity by becoming involved in the process of planning from the beginning and by claiming an equal participation of women in all steps of the conversion.[36]

Interpretive frame providing justification for change-orientated action

Next to a political opportunity window widely open for change claims, the *change initiative* also benefitted from a discursive interpretation of the current situation that was shared by both male and female leaders. These leaders held that they found themselves amid a profound process of change, which had started with the taking of office of the first indigenous Bolivian President whose government was approved by a majority of Mojocoyans, followed by the adoption of a Constitution that likewise enjoyed a high degree of legitimacy by the local population, and culminating in a genuine opportunity of local emancipation, which would facilitate Mojocoyans to govern themselves autonomously and according to their own criteria. These leaders wished to be a model for other municipalities in Bolivia, and they knew that this would lead to some long-practised patterns of internal marginalisation being left behind – including the exclusion of women:

> [I]n any sense it is now with the participation of both [women and men]. Nobody shall be excluded, because this is how we will improve [our self-governance]. Until this date we know so many instances in the union–, in the majority it's men who participate. The non-participation of our señoras is just another regress. We have to–, we are obliged to make our señoras participate in order to jointly achieve this change.
> (Interview 5–22.04.2012)[37]

The women's organisation aimed to take advantage of this window of opportunity and advocated for the full participation of women at all stages of the autonomy process and the inclusion of their long list of demands into the statute of the future autonomy. When weighing risks and benefits of this *initiative*, they knew that many obstacles would stand in their way. Given that most events would take place in Redención Pampa, women residing in remote communities would have difficulties participating because of geographic distance and as it was difficult to sustain themselves financially during their absence from home. They also knew that there were still many partners and leaders who would not agree with women's participation and thematic proposals. Women's relative low degree of education and the fact that they did not have the same command of the Spanish language as their male counterparts would also complicate their understanding of the political and legal framework underlying the autonomy process.[38] On top of that, women felt that due to their lacking self-esteem, they sometimes would not dare to assume more responsibility for public affairs. Indeed, on some occasions, women had been offered leadership positions but refused to accept them, raising concerns about the incompatibility with other family tasks, potential conflicts with their husbands or that they felt they could not fulfil these functions effectively. From the perspective of the women's organisation, women tended to undervalue their potentials and thereby missed the chance to contribute to the collective and personal development:

> In my community, for instance, community leaders support women. (…) [T]hey always ask them to attend some event or training – and they don't want to go: "Because I have a lot of work, I have children" – and all that. But it's actually not like this. Men don't marginalise us as

> much as before. In earlier times they were... they didn't esteem us. (...) Sometimes we as women undervalue ourselves.
>
> (Interview 3–22.04.2012)[39]

Due to such doubts, it proved helpful for women that municipal leaders recognised at a very early stage of the conversion process that the pool of young leaders from which office holders of the future autonomy could be recruited was actually very small. Thus, male leaders, as well, started to encourage and even to demand more participation of women in the municipal affairs. Instead of missing a historic opportunity window for the participation in the design of a future autonomy statute, the women's organisation was willing to assume this challenge and motivated more women to do so, as well.[40] Their *initiative* obtained positive resonance from many local female groups affiliated with the women's organisation, and from the more open-minded leaders of the union and municipal institutions. However, given that this *initiative* implied that women would more forcefully than ever become part of spaces of decision-making hitherto dominated by men, there was still a not negligible group of male leaders who viewed this *initiative* with suspicion, but who felt inhibited to overtly exert resistance because of the clear affirmation of women's rights to participation stipulated in the new Constitution – the same of which they strongly defended because of other rights secured for them.[41]

Availability of resources at the starting point of the initiative

The change promoters disposed of a well-established vehicle for mobilising – the women's organisation. This vehicle facilitated an effective means to convoke women in case consensus-building among their members on important issues was required. And although the conversion into an indigenous autonomy was an unprecedented process nation-wide and thus no previous experience had been collected from which women could have derived some lessons, female leaders from the organisation felt that they should trust in the leadership skills gained during the past years to raise their claims throughout the conversion process. However, they understood that many women from the communities lacked such skills and that they would have difficulties to raise their voices in public deliberations and defend their standpoints before broader audiences. In this regard, it was particularly helpful for them to know that the conversion process would be accompanied by consultants from the departmental Ministry of Autonomy and the NGOs *Fundación Tierra* and *Proagro*, the latter of which would also delegate an expert in gender issues to Mojocoya. These agents signalled to the women from the beginning that they would assist them in legal and methodological know-how, materials and logistics, so as to secure the realisation of their right to participation during all stages of the process.[42]

Which factors have influenced the *change initiative* throughout the subsequent stages of its evolution?

Target of change, strategy and tactics

Given that the autonomy statute of Mojocoya would constitute the basic fundament of the future autonomy, the concern of the women's organisation was to avoid that the rights guaranteed for women in the new Constitution of 2009 would become lost over the course of the conversion process. Thus, their goal was to safeguard that these rights, including their freedom from violence, would be reflected in the new autonomy statute of Mojocoya. The strategy to achieve this goal consisted in the active participation of women along all stages of the conversion process, from the planning stage up to the closing referendum in which residents were asked on their approval of the statute.[43] A first tactic was to advocate in the planning committee for the inclusion of women in the election of members of the deliberative assembly, which was charged with the task of designing the future statute. Given that this committee was composed of some like-minded male leaders, a fairly participatory composition of the assembly members was indeed negotiated. Accordingly, each of the 30 communities would send two representatives to the assembly – one woman and one man. Also, all other local institutions (e.g., municipality, union, women's organisation, SLIM, civic committee, churches, educative and health centres, agricultural and transport associations) were invited to delegate two or more representatives to the assembly, with the overall result that 34 (32 per cent) of the 106 assembly members were female. In comparison to other deliberative assemblies (such as the one of Tarabuco, see below), this percentage was a remarkable result.[44] Driven by the strong desire to advance with the conversion as fast as possible, the constitutive session of the assembly took place five months before the actual referendum on the autonomy (4-5 July 2009). Here, the assembly members elected an executive committee from among themselves, in which one woman was elected as the vice-president of the assembly and two others, among them the current head of the women's organisation, held offices as secretary of protocol and economy secretary. In this session, the assembly also agreed upon its general proceedings: the assembly should convene in ordinary and extraordinary sessions, accompanied by work sessions of seven commissions focusing on specific matters. Among these commissions, one was charged with the task to deliberate on the judicial system of the future autonomy. The change promoters achieved that female delegates would be present in each commission, and it proved helpful for women and men alike that they themselves could decide in which commission they wished to participate, as this procedure facilitated peoples' association with the topic they were most familiar with.[45]

Within the commission on the judicial system, six of the 15 members were female. Over the course of more than one year, the debates in this commission revolved around the strengths and weaknesses of the current judicial system based on kin intervention, communal secretaries of justice and communal presidents, communal assemblies and the secretary of justice at the sub-central level. In order to strengthen the own jurisdictional authority, commission members proposed to amplify the superior legal instance at the sub-central level both in terms of personnel and the period in which these authorities would exert this function. Commission members discussed about the characteristics a legal authority should possess in order to be eligible for this position (e.g., whether this person should show an exemplary conduct, be married or not, possess a certain level of experience) and addressed the problem that no woman has ever occupied this position in Mojocoya. They also listed all material issues pertaining to the responsibility of their legal authorities and attempted to determine the respective procedures and sanctions corresponding to each of these issues. In this regard, they held that some legal transgressions required more severe sanctions in order to actually become exemplary or deter transgressors from the repetition of these acts. They also noticed how difficult it was to put all these elements of a traditionally oral practice on paper. However, the constructive deliberations were abruptly brought to a halt with the implementation of the LJD in December 2010. While the committee members hoped that this law would provide them with some useful indications for their own work, their expectations were frustrated by the legal text. Given that the Law was very restrictive on the material competence of indigenous authorities (see introduction of this chapter), they not only felt that it rendered the constitutionally established principle of equal hierarchy between state and indigenous justice meaningless, but they even feared that their written concretisations on offences, procedures and sanctions of the Mojocoyan judicial system might not withstand the revision of the Plurinational Constitutional Tribunal, which would examine the draft of the autonomy statute after its approval by the deliberative assembly and a specialised state agency *Servicio Intercultural de Fortalecimiento Democrático* (SIFDE).[46] Consequently, the commission members agreed to remove many already formulated passages and to limit their draft text to some general aspects of their legal system. At the same time, they expressed that the deliberations held in this committee should be borne in mind and inspire a later regulatory law on their legal system once the autonomy was established.[47]

During the first sessions of the assembly and the committees, the women's organisation realised that many of the anticipated obstacles of an effective participation of women (inability to assist due to geographic, financial, gender-related obstacles) were indeed retaining many female assembly members to participate and defend their standpoints. Therefore, taking advantage of a socialisation phase of the assembly deliberations in the communities in 2011, the organisation approached the accompanying state and non-state institutions with the proposal to organise decentralised women's meetings in the three administrative zones of the municipality. These institutions responded positively to this request, offering their support in terms of material and logistic resources and technical know-how. In order to not enter into potential conflicts with the male leaders involved in the process, the idea on these women's meetings was accorded with the executive committee of the assembly as well as the sub-central. As these meetings were designed as one element of a broader socialisation strategy that, next to women, would also include reunions with communities, the youth and elderly, no objections were raised against this proposal. Indeed, many women of different ages followed the convocation of the women's organisation. As these meetings were particularly reserved for women, and because deliberations were held in Quechua, these spaces facilitated a fruitful exchange of views, experiences and ideas. In the first instance, female assembly members reported on the current state of affairs in the assembly. Afterwards, participants would divide into small working groups on specific thematic matters such as rights, education, health and productive development. In several groups, domestic violence and access to justice became a much debated issue. Women shared personal experiences about violence committed within their families and neighbourhood and complained about their frustrated efforts to seek redress for the injustice before state and own justice systems. They complained that secretaries of justice would sometimes resolve cases of rape by material compensations (e.g., by the passing of an animal to the victim's family). They understood that what actually was negotiated here was their dignity, and raised the question why they had tacitly acquiesced to these practices for such a long time. Women also reflected upon the need for more severe sanctions for violent acts within their own justice system and expressed the opinion according to which aggressors should not be eligible for public offices of the future autonomy. Overall, participants of these three events elaborated proposals in a broad range of thematic areas, thereby demonstrating that their concerns not only referred to the fulfilment of their individual rights, but also to the integral development of the entire population. As for domestic violence, women demanded the implementation of their right to freedom from violence, the equal treatment of women and men before their legal system and sanctions that would correspond the severity of a legal transgression; women also claimed their participation, on equal footing with men, as authorities in the administration of justice. The female assembly members present in these meetings felt strengthened by the dialogue with other women and committed themselves to advocating for the incorporation of these proposals in the draft statute. When returning to the autonomy assembly, some of them raised their voice more self-assuredly than before, with the result that some male delegates reckoned that the assembly deliberations would have benefitted even more from such women's meetings if these would have taken place at an earlier stage of the process.[48]

Political opportunities

Even though the two national laws of relevance for autonomy process – LMAD, July 2010, and LJD, December 2010 – were criticised for many other reasons (see introduction of this chapter), their respective provisions on women actually strengthened the *change initiative* in Mojocoya. The former affirmed, among other things, that women's rights should be guaranteed in the conformation, policies and exercise of public functions within the future autonomous territories (art. 5.11; 62.11. LMAD). Meanwhile, the latter favoured women's interests by stressing that all jurisdictions should respect, promote and guarantee the equality between women and men; that women should have equal access legal authority roles of their jurisdictions; and that violence should be prohibited and sanctioned by all jurisdictions (art. 4. h), 5. II, IV LJD).

Among the positive aspects at the municipal level was the circumstance that the two most influential local institutions – the sub-central and the municipal authorities – maintained a supportive stance in terms of the conversion process. Especially for the municipal authorities elected in April 2010, this was not at all self-evident if considering that their regular five-year term would have to come to an end in the moment the indigenous autonomy statute was approved by the population (art. 55 I. 2. LMAD). In some other municipalities, which likewise initiated a conversion to an autonomous territory, the clinging of municipal authorities to their positions was precisely one of the reasons why the process was seriously jeopardised (Albó 2012b: 73–77, 265–267; Cameron 2011; 2012; 2013). In Mojocoya the mayor and several councillors participated as delegates in the deliberative assembly – among them also one former representative of the women's organisation, who thus endorsed the *change initiative.* In addition, in deliberations on the participation of women in the future autonomous regime, it was precisely the composition of the current municipal council (based on the principles of alternation and parity) that was often referred to as a model.[49]

Lastly, a lengthy and vigorous debate on the norms and procedures of the future autonomous territory turned out to be supportive for the women's cause. As stipulated in the Constitution and the LMAD, the future regime of the autonomous indigenous territories was held to be based upon local norms and customs. This prompted union leaders to propose that the electoral norms and procedures for leadership positions at the *sindicato* and sub-central level should be transposed one-to-one to the elections of the future autonomy authorities. This would have implied that only those who permanently resided in Mojocoya, who were union affiliates, and who have had served in different community positions, would have been eligible for an office. In addition, the requirement of having passed the military service was also listed in the draft proposal of the statute. This proposal excluded most women from becoming eligible for future authority positions, but also those not affiliated with the *sindicato*, others who did not permanently reside in Mojocoya, and the young male generation above the age of 18. These young men attended school for longer periods than previous generations and sometimes moved to other places for temporary work or studies, which prevented them from starting a family and affiliate with the union, and actively engage in community affairs at an early stage of their lives. Throughout the debates it became evident that the actual pool of people from among that future authorities would be recruited did not at all coincide with those inhabitants of Mojocoya above the age of 18 who, according to the Constitution, did enjoy full rights of active and passive political participation. Next to legal concerns, many people also argued that this electoral scheme would prevent all educated, talented or motivated persons from contributing their skills to the overall development of the future autonomy. Given that these norms and procedures have constituted the prevalent scheme to access leadership positions in the sub-central and even in the municipal government for decades, and that some leaders feared that their time and efforts invested in a leadership career were no longer esteemed, the debate on this matter was highly contested. With the pressure of young and female leaders, but also due to the legal advice of the NGO consultants accompanying these deliberations, a majority of the assembly finally accepted these arguments. They removed from the draft proposal the requisites of union affiliation and of a longer leadership career within the union, limited the requirement of residence in Mojocoya to a period of two years and clarified that the requisite of military service only referred to men. Another requisite according to which eligible candidates should have a clean record, in turn, accommodated the claim of women that antecedents of domestic violence or rape should prevent aggressors from applying for public offices. Overall, this debate was transcendental for the entire deliberation process on the future autonomy, not only because women's demands for equal participation came to be echoed by other groups in Mojocoya, but also, because many assembly members became sensitised on the discriminatory features of the existing system of self-governance.[50]

Availability and deployment of resources

The resources provided by the national government to the competent Ministry of Autonomy supervising and supporting the indigenous autonomy processes in all eleven municipalities were very scarce (Cameron 2013). The departmental ministry of autonomy of Chuquisaca therefore proposed the formation of an inter-institutional platform in which this ministry and other interested agents such as Fundación Tierra and Proagro would pool their resources in order to cover the most urgent expenses for required logistics and materials. More often than not, these resources proved insufficient in order to fully cover the transport, accommodation and subsistence of the assembly members during the sessions held in Redención Pampa. The municipality of Mojocoya also assumed some costs, for instance, by reserving the few vehicles available for the transport of those assembly members who lived in the remote parts of the municipality; still, many others had to walk to participate in the sessions. Assembly members, all of whom voluntarily invested two to three labour days for each of the 17 sessions that took place between July 2009 and February 2012, also expressed their discontent because of the very late arrival of their official accreditation cards – the only palpable item that actually verified their status and engagement in the autonomy process. Their patience was also stretched because major laws such as the LMAD and the LJD were enacted long after the assembly had been constituted; rendering thereby some thoughtfully elaborated draft passages of the statute meaningless. They also waited until the second half of 2011 for a state-contracted agency that was supposed to assist the assembly in converting their draft statute in a 'legally legible' document. Precisely because the conversion process came to stretch over several years, commoners began to raise doubts on the advantages of this apparently complicated conversion process during community-based consultations.[51]

These difficulties notwithstanding, the women's *initiative* benefitted from the committed engagement of several NGO consultants who assisted them in the planning, realisation and written systematisation of the results of the decentralised women's meetings, and who accompanied the deliberations of the autonomy assembly with legal expertise and considerate impulses.[52] Additionally, the Ministry of Autonomy organised national meetings for women from the eleven municipalities that found themselves in the conversion process in Cochabamba (December 2010), Yotala (August 2011) and Oruro (March 2012).[53] Several women from the Mojocoyan deliberative assembly were able to attend some of these meetings. These spaces proved relevant for the exchange about the challenges of women with respect to their participation in the conversion process. Among other things, they discussed how principles such as equality, complementarity and (especially in case of Aymara women) duality could be incorporated into the autonomy statutes. Mojocoyan women became aware that they were not alone in their struggle to reduce power imbalances among women and men, and the exchange of views generated in these spaces inspired them in their continuation of their own *initiative* in Mojocoya.[54]

Which results has the legal change process yielded in Mojocoya by the end of the research period?

Normative and institutional change

In the final draft of the statute, the section referring to the future Mojocoyan jurisdiction (art. 36–45) established that justice was to be administered in conformity to the pertinent norms of the Constitution of 2009 and the LJD. The draft statute thereby affirmed, among other things, that domestic violence was justiciable within the future judicial system. Women and men should enjoy an equal access to justice. The first two communal instances of conflict resolution – the secretary of justice, sometimes assisted by the community president, and the general assembly of the community – were maintained. Cases that could not be duly resolved at the community level, in turn, should be passed to a newly created Justice Council at the municipal level, which should act as the highest legal authority of the Mojocoyan jurisdiction. The council was to comprise five persons, among them the secretary of justice of the sub-central and four members from different administrative zones of the municipality, the same of which should be elected according to the principle of gender equity. And while the concrete procedure of how men and women could administer justice at the community level was not stipulated in the draft, the involved assembly members expressed that this option was covered by the general right to equal representation of women and men as stipulated in article 16 of the statute. Among the ideas of how this could be put into practice, one option was that women and men would perform the office of the secretary of justice at community level in an alternate manner. Overall, women's demands in respect of a normative change (justiciability of violence and equal treatment of women and men before their own justice system) and institutional change (access of women to judicial authority positions) were fully considered in the draft proposal of the autonomy statute.[55]

Enforcement of reformed norms and institutions

The final draft statute was intensively debated by the deliberative assembly in October–November 2011, followed by a phase of last corrections, and its final approval in February 2012. Mojocoya was among the first municipalities that finished its draft autonomy statute, but had to wait until November 2014 to receive the Plurinational Constitutional Tribunal's confirmation of the statute's full compatibility with constitutional norms (ANA 12.11.2014). At the time of writing, Mojocoyans are still waiting for the scheduling of a referendum on the autonomy statute. And even though the lengthy and bureaucratic process might result in a lower approval rate than in the first referendum on the initiation of the conversion process, the probability that a majority of Mojocoyans will ultimately vote in favour of the autonomy is fairly high – considering the reason *sui generis* that motivated the population to initiate the process. One of the first tasks of the new authorities after the conversion will consist of the formulation of several fundamental laws, among them a law on the own legal system.[56] Women will have to closely monitor this process and, if necessary, remind the future authorities on the internal debates and agreements made in the respective commission of the deliberative assembly in order to safeguard that the advances made in terms of their improved access to justice be maintained and concretised within this new law.

Sustainability of reformed norms and institutions

The enforcement of the normative and institutional changes proposed by women in Mojocoya is awaited at the time of writing. Moreover, local leaders stressed that the conversion into an indigenous autonomous territory had to be seen as part of a larger decolonising process in which many features that have characterised local governance and community life thus far (including gender relations) would have to come under close scrutiny.[57] Not only would this process require a lot of staying power and continued awareness-raising at the community and the municipal level. Leaders themselves expressed uncertainty as to whether women *and* men would be able to effectively fulfil the political and legal functions as foreseen in the new system of self-governance. In order to render the change process more sustainable, leaders initiated the setting up of a leadership school in Mojocoya in 2012 in which five persons elected from each community (two women, two men and one former assembly member), as well as representatives from the union, the women's organisation and the municipality were invited to participate. The curriculum of this school was envisioned to entail historic, political, economic, social and legal issues, but also the aspect of gender relations. Lessons were learned from the autonomy assembly process, one being that the course was planned to take place in three decentralised educative centres in order to address the problem of geographic accessibility. Several institutions had already signalled their support by providing materials and expertise for the school. For women, this school presented an important opportunity to deepen their knowledge and leadership skills so as to being able to contribute more effectively to the development of municipality in the future.[58]

An important side effect of the deliberations of women on their difficulties to access justice during the conversion process was the municipality's decision to enlarge the SLIM team by a Quechua-speaking social communicator. His task was not to wait in his office until battered women would come seeking advice, but instead to regularly lend a municipal vehicle and visit the communities and hold talks on domestic violence in general assemblies and schools. His visits were not limited to preventive measures, as he also used these occasions to directly intervene in cases of violence if the conflicting parties asked him to do so. Thus, even though this institution still lacked many resources, such as more female employees and an own vehicle to respond more effectively to cases of emergency, the first important steps towards the opening of this municipal institution for women's claims had been undertaken.[59]

Tarabuco – Yamparáez Province (2009–2012)

Tarabuco is situated in the northern part of Chuquisaca and is ascribed to the Yamparáez Province. Its main town (Tarabuco) is located 62 kilometres (or a 1.5-hour bus drive) from the Department capital Sucre. Until the adoption of the 2009 Constitution, Tarabuco was divided into two cantons (Tarabuco, Pajcha). Its area is over 999 km² and varied in altitude from 2,000 to 5,000 m.a.s.l. (Gobierno Municipal de Tarabuco 2008). Archaeological findings associated with the Mojocoya culture (ninth to eleventh centuries) and the Yamapra culture (ninth to fourteenth centuries) suggest that this area was inhabited by various ethnic groups until its incorporation into the Inca Empire in the fifteenth century.[60] The village of Tarabuco, in

Image 5.3 Tarabuco town

turn, was founded in 1578 with the subsequent colonisation by Spanish forces. The Spanish and *criollo* elites established several haciendas in the zone, but the penetration of the zone was not exhaustive, thus leaving the local population with the option of maintaining some land and scope of autonomy. In the context of the independence struggles, Tarabuqueños supported the couple Manuel Ascensio Padilla and Juana Azurduy in their 'Battle of Yumbate' (1816) against the Spanish forces. Still, the newly gained independence carried not much relief for the local population, as they would face new tributes and an increased acquisition of their lands by hacienda-owners, particularly between 1880 and 1930. Therefore, the Agrarian Reform of 1953 was welcomed by a majority of the population, even though the titling process started late and stretched over a lengthy period. As in Mojocoya, the population or Tarabuco adopted the agrarian union system as its basic organisation structure. Tarabuco's 73 communities were organised as *sindicatos*, grouped in nine sub-centrals (*sub-centralías*) and one central (*centralía*) at the level of Tarabuco, the same of which affiliated with the corresponding departmental federation and the national agrarian union (now FUTPOCH and CSUTCB, respectively). After the adoption of the Law of Popular Participation (1994), some union leaders seized the opportunity to engage in political affairs in the newly introduced municipal council, but it was not until 2005 that union members, elected as MAS candidates, gained the position of the mayor and the majority of the municipal council (Albó 2012b: 205–214, 228).

Based on year-long reflections about their identity and interests, and influenced by the example of the nearby *ayllu* Quila Quila (Oropeza Province), seven *campesino* communities decided to reconstitute themselves as traditional *orígenes* (communities) united in one *ayllu* in the early 2000s. All these communities were located in the south-western part of the municipality and concentrated within two sub-centrals (Pisili, Puka Puka, Angola, Kollpa Pampa and Jatun Rumi in the sub-central Pisili; Thola Mayu and Misk'a Mayu in the San José de Paredón sub-central). The Tarabuco *ayllu* affiliated with the recently established national organisation CONAMAQ and gradually changed its internal governance system from the former union structure to that of a traditional *ayllu*. The *ayllu* leaders' intention was to overcome foreign organisational schemes, an imposed *campesino* identity and political partisanship, while gaining more autonomy by adopting autochthonous, historically grounded forms self-rule and identity. In the longer term, they aspired to convince more Tarabuqueños to follow their example in order to build a more extended and solid governance structure (*marka* Tarabuco) as part of the Yampara nation. Tarabuco's *campesino* union, which still represented the majority of the local population, dismissed this *initiative* as an unnecessary step back to a remote past and criticised it as divisive and politically motivated.[61]

Photo 5.4 Session of the Autonomy Assembly in Tarabuco (20 April 2012)

Overall, 16,944 persons inhabited the municipality in 2012, which hinted at a notable population decline compared with the 2001 Census (19,554).[62] Most residents lived in the rural *campesino* communities and *orígenes* (13,967 or 82.4 per cent), whereas the urban zone around Tarabuco town accounted for 2,977 (17.6 per cent) residents who were organised into five neighbourhood committees (*juntas vecinales*). Many of the latter worked in the services sector (commerce, transport, gastronomy) but did not considerably distinguish themselves from the remaining population with respect to their origin.[63] Around 66.8 per cent (11,323) of the population self-identified as Quechua and 16.6 per cent (2,819) as Yampara in the 2012 Census (even though the latter category was not officially recognised in the Constitution and the Census). One of the reasons for the demographic decline might be seen in the prevalence of poverty and extreme poverty that, back in 2001, had affected 92.5 per cent and 60.2 per cent of the population, respectively. The availability of many basic services such as clean water, sewage, energy, health care and educational institutions was unsatisfactory. Around 26.7 per cent women and 17.2 per cent men acknowledged being illiterate in the 2012 Census. With the gradual expansion of educative services from elementary to secondary schools, the provision of boarding schools, the contracting of more teachers and the provision of nutritious breakfasts, the municipal authorities have attempted to increase school attendance over the past years. For most Tarabuqueños, agriculture (potatoes, wheat, barley, corn and, to a lesser degree, beans, peas, some vegetables and fruits) and livestock breeding constituted the main sources of subsistence. But due to a predominantly mountainous relief, soil erosion, an unequal distribution of rainfalls along the year and scarce availability of irrigation technologies, about 90 per cent of lands could only be used for dry farming, with correspondingly limited crop yields. Therefore, many young men and women used to (temporarily) migrate to Sucre, other Departments, or other countries such as Argentina, to earn money as agricultural workers, domestic employees, construction workers or small traders.[64] Of particular cultural relevance for this place was the production of traditional textiles; next to its renowned dancing festivity (*Pujllay*) in March of each year, the dominical market, where the precious textiles were regularly presented and sold, have converted Tarabuco into a major ethno-tourist attraction over the past decades.[65]

Why did claims for legal change emerge in Tarabuco?

Shifts in local power relations

In comparison to Mojocoya, power disparities between women and men in Tarabuco were more accentuated. Not only did women possess less access to education, land and economic resources, they were also relegated in the participation in public affairs. In the communities organised as *sindicatos*, the overall majority of affiliates to the organisation were married men in possession of a land parcel. These members were supposed to participate in regular community assemblies (usually once a month) and to assume positions within the communal executive committee (consisting of the general secretary and secretaries of protocols, relations, economy, conflicts, etc.). Having proved their leadership skills at the community level, commoners became eligible for positions within their corresponding sub-central or even the union central at the municipality level. Until recently, participation of women in such spheres was extremely rare, and it was not uncommon to see women who had replaced their absent husbands in communal assemblies refusing to express their opinions on certain issues, arguing that they could not take a stance until their husbands had been consulted. There were also occasions in which not enough male candidates were present in electoral assemblies for all vacant positions to be filled. When women expressed their will to fill these vacancies, their husbands would sometimes appear on the next official event in order to assume the function of their wives in their own right.[66] Only recently, influenced by the 2009 Constitution and electoral reforms, and followed by an increased inclusion of women in the national and departmental unions, syndical leaders in Tarabuco realised that their resistance against women's participation was no longer politically tenable. An office especially designed for women (*cartera femenina*) was created within the community-based executive committees. Still, only a handful of women have been able to seize this opportunity and to assert themselves in this position, and many male commoners regarded this position as a purely 'fill-out office' (*cartera de relleno*), pointing to the little relevance that it conveyed in comparison to other positions within the communal governance structure. Union leaders also blocked the creation of a women's syndical organisation that would affiliate with the corresponding departmental and National Confederation of Campesino Indigenous Originary Women of Bolivia – Bartolina Sisa (CNMCIOB-BS) with the argument that such a strategy would put the unity of the union at risk, but they were willing to open more space for women's participation *within* their syndical structure, with the result that several positions at the *sub-centralía* and even two offices at the *centralía* level were occupied by women during the time of the author's fieldwork (mid March-May 2012). Most of these women had higher school degrees and were young, unmarried or did not yet have children – all facilitative aspects for their involvement in their new public roles.[67]

As for the *ayllu* organisation that – theoretically – was based upon dual performance of all leadership positions, the situation was not very different from that in the union. The elections of authorities (which responded to a rotation scheme both within an *orígen* and at the *ayllu* level) focused primarily on eligible men (usually married, with an exemplary conduct), whereas women were supposed to accompany their elected husbands in the fulfilment of their office. No case in which this regime would have been turned the other way round in the sense that a female candidate stood in the focus and her husband was supposed to accompany her was reported for Tarabuco – a problem shared with many women of other *ayllu* organisations in Bolivia.[68] Women had difficulties assuming the responsibilities implied by their function not only because of a lack of self-esteem, knowledge, experience and leadership skills, but also because no accommodation had been made to assist them in carrying out their other household tasks (education of children, cooking, washing, cleaning) and work in the fields. Thus, their accompaniment of their husbands in public spaces was often symbolic in nature, and male leaders recognised that a more gender-balanced management of community affairs posed a great challenge for the still-young *ayllu* organisation.[69]

Organised female groups that existed in some communities belonging to the *ayllu* or union organisation were composed of mothers of school children and health monitoring groups, which took care of regular health controls of children below the age of five. Such groups were neither political in nature, nor were they expected to extend their outreach over the borders of the own communities.[70] In the urban centre of Tarabuco, by contrast, there were many women who earned some money by preparing meals (e.g., for schools, public events) and who formed their own organisation (*organización sindical de vivanderas*) in the second half of the 2000s.[71] In the same period, the first female candidates were elected for the office of municipal councillor in Tarabuco, taking advantage of the newly introduced women's quotas and principles of parity and alternation in public elections.[72] As in Mojocoya, the assumption of office was not free from obstacles – not only because these women felt unprepared and had to learn on a day-by-day basis how to best tackle their challenging tasks, but also because they sometimes felt marginalised by their male colleagues.[73] To sum up, at the end of the 2000s, next to one urban female organisation there were a handful of women from the rural communities who recently came to engage in organisational and public affairs. They lived dispersed over distinct communities and had no shared platform at their disposal that would have facilitated a cross-community and cross-organisational communication.

Diffusion of new legal concepts

The influx of normative ideas and possibilities to exchange views among women about their grievances and interests was very limited in Tarabuco until the end of the 2000s. The handful of women who participated in higher-level leadership positions of the union had gained some knowledge on national norms and the 2009 Constitution while participating in different events and meetings related to their office.[74] Due to their genuine interest in the reconstitution of autochthonous forms of autonomy and self-governance, leaders from the *ayllu* organisation invested more time and resources in educating themselves and their children on political, economic, social and cultural aspects of their own history. Not only have some families facilitated their children a longer school education or even university studies in Sucre, they also travelled to events and training offered by CONAMAQ or non-governmental foundations in order to exchange experiences and establish contacts with leaders from other regions. Even though women often did not participate in such events, they benefitted from the local practice (based on the principle of reciprocity) to share insights gained from these experiences in reunions and conversations at home. Thus, on average, their knowledge about cultural and historical topics was more grounded than that of women from *campesino* communities.[75] Women organised in the urban *vivanderas* association were also interested in enhancing their knowledge on rights, particularly because they wished to increase the pressure for better labour conditions for women. However, there were few possibilities to acquire such knowledge, as most governmental and non-governmental institutions present in the municipality throughout the 2000s have conducted projects related to basic infrastructure, agriculture, health and education, without adopting a particular rights-based or gender focus within their activities.[76] If at all, it was the municipal agency SLIM and the defence office for children and adolescents (*Defensoría de la Niñez y Adolescencia*; DNA) – which tried to sensitise the general population, teachers, school children and parents about violence by means of talks and the training of communal promoters of rights and non-violence. However, the agencies' scope of activities was not only limited because of a very small budget and a tiny team consisting of one lawyer and one social worker responsible for both SLIM and DNA services, but also because some communal authorities resisted the realisation of activities within their communal territory, arguing that these operators were unduly favouring women in their attendance of cases of violence.[77] Lastly, at the end of the 2000s, the Sucre-based women's NGO *Centro Juana Azurduy* established first contacts with the municipality to analyse the situation of women and their interests. According to this NGO, most women's notion on rights was vague, but their curiosity to learn more about these topics was evident.[78]

Inappropriate resolution of cases of domestic violence by existing institutions

After signing an agreement with the municipality of Tarabuco on different activities (improvement of the attention of victims of violence, political participation of women, dignified work and cross-communal communication), Centro Juana Azurduy contracted additional personnel for the SLIM office in Tarabuco and conducted a study on the resolution of cases of violence (Centro Juana Azurduy 2011), so as to understand how the attention of violence by community-based indigenous authorities and the state legal operators in the municipality could be improved. According to this study, women and men in both *ayllu* and *campesino* communities acknowledged that violence in its psychological, physical and sexual forms existed, but that most women preferred to talk about this issue in the third person rather than talking about their personal experience. Due to feelings of shame, fear or culpability, but also because of their economic dependence from their husbands' income, women tended to endure the violence perpetrated by their partners for long periods of time. Typically, they would only direct themselves to family members (e.g., parents, godparents) and ask them to intervene in this situation. Only if violence did not stop or was aggravated after kin intervention, women sometimes considered to turn to the secretaries of conflicts or to the highest communal authority such as the executive secretary or *kuraka*, respectively. While authorities would not refuse to process cases of domestic violence, they usually regarded this transgression as a minor one compared with acts such as rape, abortion or murder, which were commonly understood to seriously affect the equilibrium of the community. The procedure adopted in cases of violence was typically based on dialogue and the attempt to reconcile the parties in conflict. The process ended with the signing of a protocol in which agreements among the couple were fixed, as well as the setting up of a fine that corresponded to the severity of the violence. Women complained that such sanctions were not exemplary so as to deter aggressors from recidivism; that the fines actually affected women (and children) as well; and that, in some cases, these sanctions were not complied with. They also stressed the impossibility of an impartial processing in case the accused and the legal authority were kin members. In cases of infidelity, women often received more severe sanctions in comparison to male adulterers. In other occasions, both aggressors *and* victims were sanctioned for the occurrence of violence. Besides, there were also singular cases reported in which women's access to local authorities was denied, for example, because the majority of the community assumed the woman to be culpable of the violence exerted against her from the outset, or because the woman's antecedents (e.g., having been unfaithful to her husband; incompliance with her responsibilities as a mother) would bar her from the right to seek justice before local authorities as a matter of principle.[79] If cases were repetitive or severe (rape) communal authorities sometimes opted to write a report and forward the case to the SLIM. In this regard, women's access was hampered by the distance and lacking means of transport to Tarabuco town. They also complained that they were often immediately expected to stage a formal denunciation at the SLIM, without having the option to first convoke the aggressor for a conversation in which the couple would have had the chance to reflect upon the underlying reasons for the violence occurred. And they criticised the corruptibility of state justice operators in Tarabuco – a circumstance due to which cases of violence sometimes resulted in complete impunity. Moreover, women were concerned that the forwarding of cases to the state justice system usually implied that their own legal authorities would deem themselves no longer responsible for the further proceedings of the case. Without their support, and given that no other authorities (e.g., police) were present in the communities, there was nobody left who could protect women from potential acts of vengeance of the aggressors, who would guarantee that aggressors complied with agreements or protective measures dictated by the state justice system, or who could simply monitor how the situation developed over a longer period of time.[80] As for women residing in Tarabuco town, the situation was somewhat different. The neighbourhood committees administrating the urban zones of Tarabuco town had no experience of conflict resolution, so female residents had to directly turn to the state justice operators. However, even though some women did take advantage of the circumstance that all agents involved in the processing of cases of domestic violence (SLIM, police, a small hospital, a fiscal agent, two judges and even a prison) were situated in their immediate neighbourhood, other women preferred to keep silent on violence exerted by their partners out of fear of acts of vengeance and economic disadvantages for them and their children.[81]

Incompatibilities among institutional sets relevant for women's lives

Until the end of the 2000s, there were only few women who gradually became aware of existing incompatibilities between the locally practised norms and alternative normative sets referring to women's rights. Women from the *ayllu* organisation, for instance, came to understand that the *cosmovisión* of autochthonous governance of their organisation actually provided for the exercise of gender parity for any leadership position, including the function to administer justice. And even though they themselves often felt unprepared to effectively assume the co-responsibility implied by the authority position exerted by their husbands, the latter have likewise not been very supportive in terms of a more shared distribution of tasks within the household, which would have provided women with more time for the fulfilment of their role as authority. In the same vein, those women, who had already occupied first leadership positions in the union or the municipality and who were aware of their rights enshrined in the 2009 Constitution, were confronted with the fact that their participation and proposals were only respected as long as they did not interfere with the interests of their male colleagues, and that women's problems usually did not enjoy a priority in the agenda discussed in these spheres. Apart from a few women, a considerable part of the female population of Tarabuco has not yet been familiarised with normative and institutional sets different from the ones prevailing in their communities. In addition, institutions regulating their lives were relatively 'coherent' insofar as they relegated women to a secondary role in many realms of daily life, stretching from education, to the little estimation of their reproductive labour, their access to land and their participation in legal and political affairs. Hence, it was not before Centro Juana Azurduy initiated promoting a *change initiative* in 2010 that more women in Tarabuco would become sensitised on alternative legal concepts and feel encouraged to formulate claims on this basis.[82]

Which factors facilitated or obstructed the initiation of legal change efforts in Tarabuco?

Political opportunities at the starting point of the legal change efforts

In Tarabuco, the approval for the conversion process to an autonomous indigenous territory was even higher than in Mojocoya: 90.8 per cent voted in favour of this process in the referendum held on 6 December 2009 (Cameron 2013: 181). Both the MAS-dominated municipal government and the agrarian union in Tarabuco strongly backed the idea of converting the municipality into an autonomy, and *centralía* leaders were engaged in 'passing this political line' top-down to the *subcentralía* and *sindicato*-levels while holding communal assemblies and collecting signatures to prepare the formal request to initiate the conversion into an autonomy – even though for most people it remained essentially unclear what the autonomy process would actually imply. The *ayllu* organisation, which aspired after the reconstitution of a traditional regime of self-rule, held that the conversion into an autonomous territory was worth an attempt, even though, from their perspective, the establishment of this autonomous territory along the rather artificially drawn and ahistorical municipal borders seemed questionable. And as the approval of 86.5 per cent of the residents of Tarabuco town demonstrates, their (initial and not well informed) interest in adopting this new regime did not differ significantly from the rural population.[83]

Due to this strong endorsement, the municipal government, which – supported by the *centralía* and the departmental Ministry of Autonomy of Chuquisaca – was occupied with complying with the formal requirements to initiate the conversion process throughout 2009, was not at all antipathetic to the Centro Juana Azurduy's proposal to collaborate with the municipality along the conversion process with a specific focus on women and in realms such as political participation, services for victims of violence and dignified work. The NGO offered to enlist gender experts to oversee future proceedings at the autonomous assembly and advocated for the inclusion of women in the assembly. But while signing a three-year agreement (starting from 2010) with this NGO, the municipal government stressed that its concrete activities would have to be agreed with the three organisations present in the municipality. As for the urban centre of Tarabuco, the *vivanderas* welcomed the *initiative* of the NGO and signalled their interest in the planned activities. The positioning of the *ayllu* organisation towards the *initiative* was more nuanced, particularly because of the NGO's focus on the strengthening of women's capacities. As a male *ayllu* leader emphasised, the division between women and men (in terms of interests, needs, rights, etc.) was an artificial one, which had been inculcated in the society by colonising forces. This argument notwithstanding, *ayllu* leaders acknowledged that there were still considerable discrepancies in terms of political participation and leadership skills between women and men, thereby signalling their openness for the activities of the Centro Juana Azurduy.[84] The position of the *centralía* leaders was rather adverse towards the proposal of this NGO. Politically, union leaders had doubts as to how far the NGO endorsed the political line of the MAS government. Concerning the *change initative*, union leaders admitted that the participation of women was lacking within the union, but they shifted the responsibility for this circumstance to the limited education and self-esteem of women, and only few would overtly recognise that many men were not willing to cede their traditionally dominated decision-making spaces to women. Even more accentuated than *ayllu* leaders, *centralía* leaders criticised the planning of activities exclusively reserved for women, contending that many men, as well, lacked information on the autonomy process and that the principle of gender equality should be understood as to involve both genders instead of only one. In view of these objections, the NGO agreed to co-organise a socialisation campaign in the communities on autonomous indigenous territories at the beginning of its project phase in 2010. This campaign would be conducted in cooperation with other institutions in all ten *sub-centralías* and be open for participation of all residents.[85]

Interpretive frame providing justification for change-orientated action

The interpretation of the current moment conveyed by the Centro Juana Azurduy was that, for the first time in Bolivian history, indigenous peoples' full right to self-determination and to govern themselves according to their own norms and procedures had been recognised by the Constitution of 2009. The Magna Carta was based on a series of principles, such as respect and equality, dignity and complementarity, equity in the distribution of wealth, without which the living well (*vivir bien*) could not be established. The Constitution also overcame many discriminatory features of the Bolivian society by affirming full rights to all citizens of the nation, including indigenous peoples, but also women, children, adolescents, the elderly and handicapped persons. The political participation of *all* these groups in the ongoing construction of the new, decolonising state and the future autonomies was seen as a key right, for only with the inclusion of the views and interests of all persons could a just society gradually be constructed. The NGO also referred to the historical role of Tarabuqueños in the independence struggles of the region, which was not followed by a corresponding recognition as equal citizens in the Bolivian republic. For most parts of the nineteenth and twentieth centuries, the Bolivian state remained monocultural and centralist in nature, and it was not until the very recent political shifts that formerly marginalised sectors became respected as political subjects on their own right. The right to self-determination of indigenous peoples offered the possibility to alter prevalent power relations and transform the society to one in which social justice would prevail. The construction of indigenous autonomies was an important element of this transformation, and in order to guarantee that no new colonising patterns would overshadow the process, all persons, women included, should be given the opportunity to participate in the design of the future autonomy on equal conditions.[86]

While this outline resonated with those women who started to participate in the activities of the Centro Juana Azurduy in Tarabuco, in reality, other agents coined the dominating discourse on the issue of autonomy in Tarabuco, most importantly by the *centralía* and the *ayllu* organisation. The latter argued that the opportunity of the conversion process should be used to engage in a thorough process of decolonisation of prevalent structures and mentalities, which were products of external and illegitimate impositions that remained ignorant of local cultures and traditional forms of governance. *Ayllu* leaders found that all commoners should first obtain a real chance to inform themselves on the ongoing debate that hitherto had been mainly led at the leadership level, and to engage in reflections on what autonomy and self-governance could or should actually imply. They stressed the incoherence between current municipal borders and the Yampara nation and its historic extension and held that the future autonomy structure would necessarily have to adopt ancestral modes of self-rule. Well aware of their minority position in terms of the actual population grouped in their organisation, *ayllu* leaders strategically played the 'authenticity card' (Cameron 2013: 190) by stating that the autonomy was a factor that could not be resolved by simple majority votes and advocating in favour of a participation of all three existent organisations (*ayllus*, union, neighbourhood committees) in the conversion process on an equal footing. Union leaders, in turn, derived their identity not as much from pre-colonial times, but rather from the 1952 Revolution in which their grandparents and parents gained their right to vote and access to land titles. What they hoped to achieve by the conversion was an enhanced capacity to improve local economic development, followed by progress in other realms such as education or health services. Union leaders were not particularly interested in the dissolution or restructuring of existing organisational and governance structures, as it was not least due to these structures that they had gained access to resources and political power over the past decades. As an answer to the *ayllu'* position, the *centralía* played the 'majority card', arguing that it would be simply undemocratic and unfair to neglect that a great majority of Tarabuqueños were registered as union members. Accordingly, this majority situation should be duly reflected in the future deliberative assembly and autonomy structure as such. Vis-à-vis these two major opponents, the neighbourhood committees had not developed such a strong ideological position and thus played a secondary role in shaping the discourse on the autonomy. Their interests focused on their political, economic and social status quo. Leaders from this sector hoped to be able to continue pursuing their economic activities (commerce, transportation, other services) or to work as professionals employed in local educational and health institutions in the future autonomy without major shifts in the prevailing governance scheme – by which their position was rather close to the union position. But they were also aware of the fact that, in numbers, they only accounted for a minority of the population of Tarabuco. In this sense, they shared the *ayllu*' interests in so far as they did not want to be overrun by a dominant majority vote of the *centralía* throughout the decision-making processes of the autonomy assembly.[87]

As these discursive lines demonstrate, the three organisations of Tarabuco developed quite divergent visions on what the conversion process should imply, each of which imbued with political interests in respect to their influence within the deliberative assembly and the future autonomy (Cameron 2013: 189–190). Given the relative strength of these male-dominated organisations, which was not counterbalanced by empowered and organised women, there was no room left for the inclusion of women's visions and interests in the conversion process.

Availability of resources at the starting point of the initiative

In Tarabuco, women did not possess an own organisational vehicle comparable to the women's organisation in Mojocoya, which could have facilitated the communication among women across communities and across the prevailing organisations. Additionally, there were only a handful of women who already disposed of some knowledge on political, cultural and normative issues and who had gained leadership skills and the courage to speak up in the public. Many women felt unprepared due to a low level of education and limited mastering of the Spanish language. Next to the manifold tasks in the household, the geographical distances from remote communities to Tarabuco would likewise pose an obstacle for the participation of women in the autonomy assembly. Therefore, women interested in the autonomy process felt relieved to count on the presence of the Centro Juana Azurduy in the municipality, the same of which would convert to their most important ally and provider of legal, strategic and methodological knowhow. Besides, consultants contracted by the NGO would participate in the sessions of the deliberative assembly and thus be able to support and lend weight to the arguments of female participants. The funds this NGO disposed of for its activities in Tarabuco were limited, however, so that the actual number of women who in some way would benefit from their activities would remain small, as well.[88]

More generally, representatives and consultants would accompany the autonomy process in Tarabuco from state agencies (especially the departmental Ministry of Autonomy) and various Sucre and Potosi-based NGOs (next to Centro Juana de Azurduy, *Fundación Tierra, Proagro, Kawsay, Sumactiva*). In comparison to the strategic and legal advice these agents provided, the financial and material resources for the realisation of assembly sessions in Tarabuco were insufficient – similar to Mojocoya. Hence, parts of the expenses for transport, alimentation and accommodation of the assembly members were expected to be organised with the help of the *centralía* and the *ayllu* organisation.[89]

Which factors have influenced the *change initiative* throughout the subsequent stages of its evolution?

Target of change, strategy and tactics

The main objective of the Centro Juana Azurduy was to support women from Tarabuco in their participation in the deliberations and decision-making processes of the autonomous assembly. The basic strategy to achieve this goal was the generation of spaces where women would gain knowledge about their rights, where they could reflect upon issues relevant for them with respect to the future autonomy, and where they would develop ideas on how to best articulate and defend their interests within the deliberative assembly. Among the lines of action adopted so as to pursue this strategy was the NGO's support for the socialisation of details on the autonomy process for a mixed population at the sub-central level, together with other governmental and non-governmental institutions. Second, they set up a leadership school for women, with a curriculum focussing on the Bolivian history from the pre-colony to the *plurinational* State. The course involved a year-long circle of various two-day training sessions held in Quechua, and aimed at making women aware of their history, their current living conditions and that they as women were active subjects of their own development. Women who completed the leadership school were expected to become more involved in communal or municipal affairs, for instance, by claiming and assuming a position in their communal executive committees. Due to very limited resources, the NGO could only extend its work to four of the ten sub-centrals (Pisili, San José Paredón, Cororo, Morado K'asa) and Tarabuco town. Given the distance and lacking means of transport, only women from the most proximate communities of a respective sub-central usually attended a course. Still, along the three cycles stretching over the years 2010, 2011 and 2012, on average 25 women attended a training session of the school, among them 11 elected assembly members. Interestingly, while the *ayllu* organisation eventually accepted that the school focused on the training of female leaders, the union regularly delegated at least one male representative to the courses in order to remain informed on the contents discussed in there. But while this may be regarded as a measure of control, there were indeed many female participants who argued that the presence of men would actually be very important in order to render them more open-minded to the reflections and lessons learned in these spaces.[90]

A third activity related to the *initiative* was the elaboration of the above-mentioned study on the resolution of gender violence by indigenous and state legal authorities in Tarabuco (Centro Juana Azurduy 2011). The study outlined how indigenous legal authorities in various *orígenes* and *campesino* communities had dealt with several recently occurred cases (related to rape, domestic violence, abuse of women and children, recognition of children, aliments, adultery). The information collected in interviews with parties of conflict, authorities and ordinary commoners, served afterwards to improve the coordination of the SLIM with community-based legal authorities in the attention of cases of violence, but also constituted a fundament for later debates and proposals on violence and indigenous jurisdiction in the context of the formulation of the autonomy statute of Tarabuco.[91]

From March 2011, the NGO also organised several women's meetings in four sub-centrals and Tarabuco town so as to collect proposals for the future autonomy statute. During these meetings, women would first discuss matters such as violence, health, education, economic issues, tourism and then articulate ideas on how the situation in each realm might be improved – a step that also implied that women would return to their communities and consult with other women on their views and suggestions on the respective issues. With respect to domestic violence, many elder women considered violence to be a 'normal' conduct among couples that simply had to be accepted. Some of the younger women who already had gained knowledge on their rights countered that violent conduct could no longer be tolerated, and that women were now entitled to live free from violence. Hence, the latter demanded that domestic violence be condemned within the autonomy statute, and that future leadership offices be occupied by persons without antecedents in domestic violence. As for their access to justice, the insufficient procedures and sanctioning of domestic violence and rape as well as the gender-differentiated sanctioning for the same legal transgression ranged among the most frequently problematised aspects. Some participants stressed the need of women's participation in the administration of justice, arguing that women would feel more confident to denounce violence and speak about intimate details before female authorities. Overall, just as in Mojocoya, the deliberations during these women's meetings were intense and encompassed a wide scope of topics, all of which, as they hoped, would be duly taken account of within the draft of the autonomy statute. Problematic, in turn, was once again the limited and uneven participation of women in these spaces. Limited financial resources allowed the Centro Juana Azurduy to organise these meetings in some, but not all sub-centrals of the municipality. Female assembly members, who would have been the most pertinent persons to defend the proposal in later debates of the deliberative assembly, were not necessarily invited to these meetings. Besides, some union leaders appeared to not having duly informed the respective female population on the invitations to these meetings. And given the rising conflicts between the union and the *ayllu* organisation, the NGO saw itself forced to organise separate meetings for women pertaining to the urban centre, the *ayllu* organisation and the union, by which the cross-communal communication and consensus-building of the female population was hampered even more.[92] Regardless of these difficulties, women decided that a former female member of the executive committee of the *centralía* should present the systematised women's proposal (Centro Juana Azurduy 2012) in a session of the deliberative assembly in April 2012. However, precisely because of the above-mentioned shortcomings, the *initiative* faced the reproach of union leaders to be a product mainly elaborated by *ayllu* women. Some female assembly members who had not been invited to the elaboration of the proposal also took a critical stance and did not off-handedly appropriate the document as their own. Thus, the woman who was supposed to present the proposal in the deliberative assembly and hand out a copy of the document to each head of commission had difficulties to set her presentation on the session's agenda and waited patiently until getting only a few minutes time for her discourse, which – needless to say – did not receive the attention it deserved.[93]

Political opportunities

The longer the conversion process evolved, the more accentuated became ideological divergences on the autonomy between the union and the *ayllu* organisation, up to the point that leaders, assembly members and the general population came to call the conversion process as such into question. The deliberative assembly, commissioned with the elaboration of the draft statute, was reconstituted several times throughout 2009 to 2011, each time with a size and composition that varied from the previous one. The assembly was inaugurated as early as 21 July 2009 – before the very referendum on the issue was held. This first assembly consisted of 31 members, 20 of whom represented the union, while the *ayllu* organisation and the neighbourhood committees delegated two representatives, respectively. Although *ayllu* leaders were discontent with their minority status in this assembly, they decided to wait until the promulgation of the announced LMAD to see how this issue would be legally addressed. The remaining seven members of the assembly were representatives from the municipal government and other local institutions (Albó 2012b: 241–242). The female participation in this assembly was reduced to only three women (or 9.7 per cent). The assembly was presided by the former executive secretary of the *centralía*, while the highest *ayllu* representative of that time formed part of the executive committee of the assembly. After the referendum on 6 December 2009, the preparations for the next municipal elections to be held on 4 April 2010 brought the incipient work of the assembly to a halt, mainly because many assembly members became involved in the electoral campaign. The assembly president (Gregorio Ignacio) was nominated by the MAS party as candidate for the municipal mayor – to the great displeasure of another union leader and then municipal council member for the MAS party (Adrián Valeriano), who himself had hoped to be nominated for this position and whom changed the political party (*Movimiento Sin Miedo*, Movement without Fear; MSM) to participate as an opposing candidate in the elections. The fact that the MAS candidate ultimately won these municipal elections resulted in the need to reconstitute the assembly (Albó 2012b: 245–248). The rivalry between the two opponent candidates also led to political divisions among union members who just until recently had stood united behind the MAS. The election of two additional MSM candidates as municipal councillors – among them one *ayllu* representative – added to the contentious nature of this legislative period. Moreover, from a relative early point of his term, the former head of the assembly and now mayor seemed to have lost interest in supporting the autonomy process, especially if weighing his personal benefits from a still unclear outcome of the autonomy process against the perspective of maintaining his office as mayor for an entire five-year term. As a reaction to the political controversies and shrinking support of the autonomy process, the presence of representatives from the municipality was no longer welcomed by parts of the newly constituted deliberative assembly; and in case municipal representatives still attended a session, their arguments were sometimes rejected as political intromission.[94]

Soon after the second deliberative assembly resumed the debate on the future autonomy, the LMAD was enacted on 19 July 2010 and ruled that the final draft statute for an autonomous indigenous territory required the approval of two-thirds of all members of the deliberative assembly (art. 53). As the current composition of the assembly allowed for a convenient two-thirds majority of representatives from the union alone, both the *ayllu* organisation and the *juntas vecinales* staged protests and refused to continue to participate in the deliberation process on the basis of the current assembly composition. Even with reiterated attempts by the then Minister of Autonomy Carlos Romero, the departmental Ministry of Autonomy and NGOs to mediate the conflict, the deliberative process was paralysed for about one year. Ultimately, and under pressures from many fronts, a new assembly that approximately reflected the 2001 Census, was constituted in June 2011. From the total of now 95 assembly members, 66 represented the union, 15 the neighbourhood committees and 14 the *ayllu* organisation. This time, the number of women from all three organisations increased to 23 (24.2 per cent) – a result only achieved by the insistent lobbying of some consultants who reminded leaders on the right to participation of women stipulated in the 2009 Constitution and the LMAD.[95] The assembly accorded to organise its work in general sessions and six commissions, with one of them concerned with the indigenous judicial system. In contrast to the assembly of Mojocoya, representatives could not decide on their own in which commission they could best contribute with their knowledge. Instead, the organisation leaders themselves decided whom to delegate to each commission, assuring that at least one or two experimented leaders able to fiercely defend their interests were present in any of these units. As observers noted, most women were only delegated 'fill-out positions' that had remained vacant after the relevant positions were already distributed. Regardless, there were two important exceptions from this rule: first, there was one female president of a commission (on territorial organisation and self-governance structure) who was an outstanding female leader from the *juntas vecinales* and member of the *vivanderas*. Second, a female union leader was elected as member of the executive committee of the deliberative assembly. And while these two women, joined by several others, were able to actively engage in the deliberations, the same held not true for the majority of the female representatives. Particularly women from remote communities not only had problems in terms of delegating their tasks in the household and convincing their husbands of the importance of their participation, but they also often lacked the financial means to travel to Tarabuco and cover their expenses while attending the two- to three-day assembly sessions. Some other women (and their families) depended on their daily income from work in Tarabuco town, and these likewise had difficulties to change their work against the (uncompensated) engagement in the deliberations. In this sense, around ten to 15 women participated on average throughout an assembly session (and sometimes even fewer).[96]

As could have been expected, a considerable part of the debates within the reconstituted deliberative assembly continued to be traversed by controversies and power struggles among *ayllu* and *centralía* leaders. During the first sessions, representatives argued about the very name of the deliberative assembly, with *ayllu* leaders advocating for the inclusion of the term '*originario*', and *centralía* leaders preferring the term '*campesino*'. In the end, the assembly was simply termed *Deliberative Autonomy Assembly of Tarabuco*.[97] Lengthy discussions also revolved around the future governance structure (which should be composed of a maximum executive authority, potentially exercised by a representative from any of the three organisations according to a rotation scheme, and a legislative council made up of seven representatives from the three organisations) and the respective electoral regime. To make things even more complicated, representatives of the former canton Pajcha (constituting one of the ten sub-centrals with ten *campesino* communities) came to insist on a guarantee for their own representation in the future legislative council, as they were not willing to give up the special status they had enjoyed with the former and no longer valid administrative category of 'canton'. Indirectly, the controversies were also affected by the rising nation-wide tensions provoked by the *Territorio Indígena y Parque Nacional Isiboro-Sécure* (TIPNIS) march in August-October 2011,[98] which resulted in the alienation of CONAMAQ from the Morales government (which CSUTCB continued supporting). Asked about their own standpoint on the controversies, female representatives indicated that, while comprehending the positions of their respective organisations, they would have preferred to seek for points of convergence and the construction of a vision from which all inhabitants would potentially benefit, instead of setting up ever higher barricades that have ultimately resulted in a very tense atmosphere in the commissions and the deliberative assembly.[99]

With respect to the deliberations of the commission of indigenous judicial system, the adoption of the LJD (December 2010) was disappointing for the members of this commission. Just as their colleagues in Mojocoya, union and *ayllu* representatives felt that the Law would unduly restrict their own legal practices. The members analysed how justice was exerted by the secretaries of justice in the *campesino* communities and legal authorities in the *orígenes*, and affirmed that the members of the *juntas vecinales* usually directly turned to the state justice operators located in Tarabuco. As a matter of principle, the commission held that the existing legal institutions of the union and the *ayllu* organisation (family, community authorities, supra-community authorities) should be maintained. But the commission also came to analyse a case that had occurred several years ago and in which legal authorities had exceeded their scope of competences (by assassinating a legal transgressor). The representatives consented to the point that all sanctions would have to respect the right to life, and that a fair chance to review resolutions of legal authorities should be granted in the future autonomy. Therefore, they proposed the creation of a judicial council located in Tarabuco that would be composed of representatives from the three organisations and hold the material competence over severe offences, problems cutting across community borders and issues that had not been resolved satisfactorily by community-based legal instances. Having listened to female commission members on the difficulties of women to denouncing violent acts before male legal authorities, the commission also stressed the necessity to include women in the administration of indigenous justice – a very positive step with which representatives hoped to improve women's access to justice.[100]

Availability and deployment of resources

The technical assistance of various state and non-state actors accompanying the conversion process in Tarabuco did not go hand in hand with sufficient financial resources. The departmental Ministry of Autonomy supervised a considerable number of autonomy processes across Chuquisaca but did not obtain the necessary means for an effective monitoring of all these processes by the national government. Therefore, and just as in Mojocoya, an interinstitutional support platform among the Ministry and the NGOs collaborating with Tarabuco was agreed upon so as to share responsibilities and distribute costs among all actors involved. However, the more the process dragged on and the higher the tensions between the local organisations, the more disagreements between these supporting institutions came to the fore, as well. While the Ministry pushed towards the continuation of the process in order to being able to present its effective work to the public, non-state actors stressed that it was ultimately up to the Tarabuqueños themselves to decide whether, how and at which pace they wished to continue the process.[101]

The NGO that focused its activities on the female population, Centro Juana Azurduy, had likewise not enough resources at its disposal to involve a larger part of the population of the municipality in its activities. The reiterative interruptions of the deliberative assembly complicated the streamlining of its activities with the conversion process. Moreover, its work was sometimes viewed with suspicion (especially by the union) and its focus on women instead of both genders was not always appreciated. Thus, what this NGO hoped to achieve was to support those women who attended its leadership school and meetings to gain knowledge and courage so as to more actively participate and raise their voice in the communal and municipal spaces of decision-making. In doing so, the NGO hoped that these women would motivate and become a model for others. Several female assembly members also took part in the meetings organised by the Ministry of Autonomy for women from all eleven municipalities, which found themselves in the process of conversion to an autonomous indigenous territory (see also case study Mojocoya), and in a meeting of the national coordinating body of these eleven municipalities (*Coordinadora Nacional de las Autonomías Indígena Originario Campesinas*; National Coordinating Office of the Indigenous Originary Campesino Autonomies; CONAIOC) in La Paz in March 2012. As some women did not have a good command of the Spanish language (which was used in these meetings as a common ground for discussions among all participants), they encountered difficulties to really follow the conversations and to return home with new impulses.[102]

Which results has the legal change process yielded in Tarabuco by the end of the research period?

Normative and institutional change

As of the time of writing, it was difficult to estimate to what extent the existing legal and institutional framework to treat domestic violence would become altered in the near future in Tarabuco. Throughout 2012, neither *centralía* nor *ayllu* leaders had signalled their willingness to cede from their respective standpoints. Struggles over the main features of the self-governance system and the composition and elections of the main authorities of the future autonomy continued to dominate all deliberations on the conversion process. Hence, all other issues that were equally supposed to be incorporated in the draft statute (including the own judicial system, economic development, health, education) mostly remained out of the scope of attention. Many assembly members felt tired of the lengthy sessions, which did not allow for progress and the completion of the deliberations. Assembly members from the union especially stood out in terms of their increasing absence from the assembly sessions, prompting union leaders to raise the fines among their members for any unattended day. Representatives from the *juntas vecinales* and the *ayllu*, by contrast, understood that their presence was the only way to guarantee that they were not being overrun by a majority vote of the *centralía* representatives. These representatives even used the non-attendance of the *centralía* members to their advantage, for in the absence of sufficient *centralía* members in the respective commission, decisions on each draft passage of the statute (requiring two-thirds of the votes of the *present* assembly members) came to more and more hinge on the positioning of these two groups. In conversations with local communities, leaders became aware that not only the assembly members but also a considerable part of the general population started questioning the conversion process as a whole. Many commoners expressed their regret for having voted for the conversion into an autonomous indigenous territory without having understood what this process would actually imply. They were concerned that the deliberation process had disunited the population and deepened conflicts among existing organisations.[103]

In mid 2012, some NGOs and assembly members organised meetings in each sub-central, the *ayllu* organisation and the *juntas vecinales*, so as to inform about the current debates and proposals on the future autonomy among the general population. Women who had participated in the elaboration of their own proposals accompanied these events to raise attention about their ideas as well. With the active advocacy of the Centro Juana Azurduy, many proposals of women were ultimately incorporated in a first draft statute that was approved in a session of the deliberative assembly of the 25 August 2012. As for domestic violence, this draft included the affirmation of the LJD. The right to a life free from violence, the obligation of indigenous legal authorities to process and sanction cases of domestic violence, the option to forward cases of domestic violence to the state legal system if these could not be resolved by indigenous authorities and the immediate processing of cases of rape by state legal operators, were stipulated in the draft. In the same vein, the text emphasised the principle of equal treatment of women and men before the indigenous justice systems and women's participation in the administration of indigenous justice. The latter should become reflected in a gender-balanced composition of a new judicial council in Tarabuco, which should comprise a total of six members stemming from the three organisations present in the municipality.[104]

Enforcement of reformed norms and institutions

If the sole incorporation of these demands of women in the draft text has to be regarded as a success on its own, the same cannot be affirmed for the general process of agreeing on a draft statute on 25 August 2012. First, the draft included contradictory passages and left many questions unaddressed that, as consultants argued, would leave Tarabuqueños themselves with many doubts, not to speak of the Plurinational Constitutional Tribunal, which was supposed to review the draft after its final approval. Second, given the absence of a considerable number of *centralía* representatives during the August session, *ayllu* leaders included many of their long-held demands in the text, for instance, by speaking of the autonomous territory as *Marka Tarabuco*, pointing to an ancestral governance model that union leaders have consistently refused to accept. Third, the legal requirement to approve the final draft statute with two-thirds of the *total* number of assembly members was not complied with, as only 56 of a total of 95 assembly members attended and approved the draft text on 25 August. Because of the disagreements about the draft's content and procedural issues, the conversion process was again paralysed for months. Based on the intervention of the departmental Ministry of Autonomy, leaders from all three organisations ultimately decided to submit the draft text as it was to the Constitutional Court and to wait for its revision. In July 2014, the assembly convened again in order to revise the long list of observations made by the Tribunal, but given the absence of many assembly members, the assembly had to be reconstituted a fourth time before continuing with its deliberations.[105] The further developments of this process were difficult to predict as of the moment of writing.

Sustainability of reformed norms and institutions

Even though the context of the conversion into an autonomous territory was not facilitative for the inclusion of women and their interests, there was a group of women that, due to the activities conducted by Centro Juana Azurduy, came to understand more about their rights than they had known before. These women first assumed leadership positions in their communities or dared to express their opinion within the deliberative assembly, overcoming thereby their fears and experiencing the difficulties, but also possibilities the engagement in public affairs entailed. However, as NGO consultants acknowledged, the path from becoming aware of a right to appropriating it according to one's own realities, and to staging claims on its basis, is a long one. Unfortunately, for women in Tarabuco this path would be particularly challenging, not only because they continued to lack their own, cross-communal and cross-organisational platform from which they could built consensus and plan future actions to make their voices heard, but also because the agreement between the Centro Juana Azurduy and the municipality formally concluded at the end of 2012. While some sporadic activities related to the leadership school were still planned for the following year, a more sustainable accompaniment and consulting of women by this NGO was no longer guaranteed.[106]

Notes

1 See INE 2013: 31. Some analysts explained the significant reduction of the indigenous population in Bolivia by the way the question about self-identification was formulated in the 2012 Census, but also by the sustained migration to urban areas and foreign countries, which may go hand in hand with a shift in one's own sense of belonging; see EJU 11.08.2013; El País Edición Internacional 06.08.2013; Tamburini 15.10.2013.

2 See INE 2013: 5, 31; and the Redatam+SP Database: http://200.105.134.133/binbol/RpWebEngine.exe/Portal?&BASE=CPV2012COM (last access 10.06.2015).

3 Confederación Sindical Única de Trabajadores Campesinos de Bolivia; Unitary Syndical Confederation of Peasant Workers of Bolivia.

4 Federación Nacional de Mujeres Campesinas de Bolivia – Bartolina Sisa; National Federation of Campesino Women of Bolivia – Bartolina Sisa. In 2008, the organisation adjusted its name to the new generic term for indigenous peoples accorded in the Constituent Assembly: Confederación Nacional de Mujeres Campesinas Indígenas Originarias de Bolivia – Bartolina Sisa; CNMCIOB-BS.

5 For details on these developments, see Albó 2009: 39–59; Van Cott 2005: 53–67.

6 Confederación de Pueblos Indígenas de Bolivia; Confederation of Indigenous Peoples of Bolivia.

7 See ILO website: www.ilo.org/dyn/normlex/en/f?p=NORMLEXPUB:11300:0::NO::P11300_INSTRUMENT_ID:312314 (last access 10.06.2015).

8 This generic term adopted in the 2009 Constitution can be regarded as a 'salomonic solution' (Albó and Romero 2009: 4) agreed upon by the Constituent Assembly representatives so as to accommodate the various forms of self-identification existing among the Bolivian indigenous population.

9 This list included penal issues (such as violation of the corporal integrity of children and adolescents, rape, assassination and homicide), civil and labour issues, issues pertaining to realms such as social security, taxes, public administration, mining, hydrocarbons, forestry, informatics and agriculture. The only legal matter in that indigenous legal authorities maintained their material competence according to article 10 of the LJD was the adjudication of conflicts about the internal distribution of registered communal lands.

10 Conciliation presupposes that all parties involved participate in the process on an equal footing – a state of affairs that is rare between aggressors and their victims; see Coordinadora de la Mujer 2011: 37, 52; Ministerio de Justicia, Viceministerio de Género y Asuntos Generacionales 2008: 80.

11 See art. 197–199 Bolivian Constitution of 2009 and Law 027 on the Plurinational Constitutional Tribunal (2010).

12 See art. 12, 32, 137–140 of the Law 027 on the Plurinational Constitutional Tribunal.

13 These municipalities were Villa Mojocoya, Tarabuco and Huacaya in Chuquisaca; Totora, Salinas de Garci Mendoza, Chipaya and Pampa Aullagas in Oruro; Jesús de Machaca and Charazani in La Paz; Chayanta in Potosí; and Charagua in Santa Cruz; see Cameron 2013: 181.

14 By 2012, around 155 of the 327 municipalities in Bolivia counted with the presence of a SLIM, but 37 per cent of these services were merged with the Legal Defense Offices of Children and Adolescents (*Defensorías de la Niñez y Adolescencia*); see Organización de los Estados Americanos/Mecanismo de Seguimiento de la Convención Belém do Pará 2012: 7.

15 See Arauco, Mamani and Rojas 2007; Calla 2005; Capítulo Boliviano de Derechos Humanos, Democracia y Desarrollo 2005; Coordinadora de la Mujer 2011: 37; 50–53; Organización de Estados Americanos, Comisión Interamericana de Derechos Humanos 2007.

16 See Ley Integral No. 348 para Garantizar a las Mujeres Una Vida Libre de Violencia.

17 See Ministerio de Justicia, Viceministerio de Género y Asuntos Generacionales 2008.

18 See Ministerio de Justicia, Viceministerio de Género y Asuntos Generacionales 2008: 103–108. The Spanish development cooperation agency Agencia Española de Cooperación Internacional para el Desarrollo (AECID) has funded policies addressing gender violence with €200,000 in 2010; see Organización de los Estados Americanos/Mecanismo de Seguimiento de la Convención de Belém do Pará 2012: 176.

19 As this survey referred exclusively to acts of violence committed throughout the year preceding the data collection, the respective percentages cannot be easily compared with the data provided by the above-mentioned Ecuadorian and Peruvian national surveys. Unfortunately, ethnically disaggregated data on the issue of gender violence have not been provided by the Bolivian Institute of Statistics INE; see INE 2009; and the comprehensive presentation of the results of this survey at INE's website: www.ine.gob.bo/indicadoresddhh/viole1.asp (last access 10.06.2015).

20 See Albó 2012b: 191, referring to studies conducted by John Murra 1972 and Thierry Sagines 1985. See also Cordero 2011; Proyecto Estatuto Autonómico Indígena Originario Campesino de Mojocoya 2012; Interviews 1–18.04.2012; 1–22.04.2012.

21 See Proyecto Estatuto Autonómico Indígena Originario Campesino de Mojocoya 2012; Interviews 1–18.04.2012; 5–22.04.2012.

22 See Alcaldía Municipal de Mojocoya 2011: 94; Interviews 1–22.04.2012; 3–26.04.2012.

23 Interviews 1–18.04.2012; 5–22.04.2012; 1–26.04.2012.

24 Data generated from the website of INE (www.ine.gob.bo) and the Redatam+SP Database http://datos.ine.gob.bo/binbol/RpWebEngine.exe/Portal?&BASE=CPV2012COM (last access to both websites 10.06.2015).

25 Interviews 1–18.04.2012; 1–22.04.2012; 3–22.04.2012; 4–22.04.2012; 1–27.04.2012.

26 Interviews 1–13.04.2012; 2–13.04.2012; 1–22.04.2012; 2–22.04.2012; 3–22.04.2012; 1–26.04.2012; 4–26.04.2012; 1–27.04.2012.

27 Interviews 2–13.04.2012; 17.04.2012; 1–22.04.2012; 5–22.04.2012; 3–26.04.2012; 4–26.04.2012; Organización de Mujeres Campesinas de Mojocoya 2011.

28 Interviews 17.04.2012; 3–22.04.2012; 25.04.2012; 4–26.04.2012.

29 During my fieldwork, I was impressed by the high number of indigenous and *campesino* leaders who had always a pocket edition of the 2009 Constitution at their disposal while deliberating in meetings or assemblies – a certainly unprecedented phenomenon in Bolivian history. See Organización de Mujeres Campesinas de Mojocoya 2011; Interviews 2–13.04.2012; 17.04.2012; 1–22.04.2012; 2–22.04.2012; 3–22.04.2012, 4–26.04.2012; 1–07.05.2012.

30 See Ley Electoral Transitorio No. 4021 (14.04.2009).

31 Based on agreements negotiated in the sub-central, all office holders of the municipal council elected in 2010 should gradually pass their offices to their substitutes after two years in office so as to facilitate all elected candidates the opportunity to gain leadership experience and thereby prepare for new tasks once the future autonomous territory would be established. Thus, during the time of my fieldwork, three women and two men who were actually the substitutes of the previous office holders constituted the municipal council. As women holding these offices still felt insufficiently prepared to fulfil this role effectively, some of the former office holders provided advice so as to support them in complying with their new role. Interviews 1–22.04.2012; 2–26.04.2012; 3–26.04.2012; 4–26.04.2012; 5–26.04.2012.

32 Interviews 2–22.04.2012; 4–26.04.2012; Organización de Mujeres Campesinas de Mojocoya 2011.

33 Interviews 12.04.2012; 2–13.04.2012; 2–22.04.2012; 1–26.04.2012; 4–26.04.2012, 1–27.04.2012.

34 Interviews 2–22.04.2012; 1–08.05.2012.

35 See Cameron 2013: 188; Cordero 2011; Interviews 17.04.2012; 1–18.04.2012; 1–22.04.2012; 5–22.04.2012; 1–26.04.2012; 2–26.04.2012; 3–26.04.2012; 5–26.04.2012.

36 Interviews with 1–22.04.2012; 2–22.04.2012; 2–26.04.2012.

37 See also Interviews 4–22.04.2012; 2–26.04.2012.

38 Interviews 2–22.04.2012; 2–26.04.2012; 1–27.04.2012.

39 See also Interviews 1–13.04.2012; 17.04.2012; 2–22.04.2012; 4–26.04.2012; 30.04.2012; 03.05.2012.

40 Interviews 2–22.04.2012; 2–26.04.2012.

41 Interviews 1–22.04.2012; 1–27.02.2012.

42 Interviews 12.04.2012; 1–13.04.2012; 2–13.04.2012; 3–22.04.2012; 2–26.04.2012; 4–26.02.2012; 1–27.04.2012.

43 See Organización de Mujeres Campesinas de Mojocoya 2011; Interviews 2–13.04.2012; 2–22.04.2012; 1–27.04.2012; 03.05.2012.

44 See Alvarado 2011: 8; Interviews 1–18.04.2012; 1–22.04.2012; 1–27.04.2012.

45 See Acta de Información y Conformación de la Asamblea Constituyente del Municipio de Mojocoya 04.07.2009; Primera Acta de Elección y Posesión de la Asamblea Constituyente Autonómica Originario Campesina de Mojocoya 05.07.2009; Interview 12.04.2012.

46 The Intercultural Service for the Strengthening of Democracy (SIFDE) was a specialised agency of the Plurinational Electoral Office in Bolivia which examined whether all procedures related to the conversion process have been complied with according to the norms and procedures of the respective municipality; see art. 91–93 Law on the Electoral Regime 2010, art. 51, 53.5. Law on Autonomy and Decentralization.

47 Interviews 12.04.2012; 1–26.04.2012; 30.04.2012.

48 See Organización de Mujeres Campesinas de Mojocoya 2011; Interviews 12.04.2012; 2–13.04.2012; 1–22.04.2012; 1–27.04.2012; 03.05.2012.

49 Interviews 12.04.2012; 1–22.04.2012; 2–22.04.2012; 4–22.04.2012; 5–22.04.2012; 3–26.04.2012; 4–26.04.2012; 5–26.04.2012.

50 See art. 22 Proyecto Estatuto Autonómico Indígena Originario Campesino de Mojocoya 2012; Interviews 2–13.04.2012; 1–18.04.2012; 1–22.04.2012; 4–22.04.2012; 2–26.04.2012; 5–26.04.2012; see also Cameron 2013: 191.

51 See Cordero 2011; Interviews 12.04.2012; 1–13.04.2012; 1–18.04.2012; 1–22.04.2012; 4–22.04.2012; 2–26.04.2012; 4–26.04.2012; 1–27.04.2012.

52 See Organización de Mujeres Campesinas de Mojocoya 2011; Interviews 1–18.04.2012; 1–27.04.2012; 03.05.2012.

53 See Alvarado 2011; Ministerio de Autonomías, Viceministerio de Autonomías Indígena Originaria Campesinas y Organización Territorial, Dirección General de Autonomías Indígena Originaria Campesinas (n.d.); personal observations during the III. National Women's Meeting in Oruro (30.–31.03.2012).

54 See Ministerio de Autonomías, Viceministerio de Autonomías Indígena Originaria Campesinas y Organización Territorial, Dirección General de Autonomías Indígena Originaria Campesinas (n.d.).

55 See Proyecto de Estatuto Autonómico Indígena Originario Campesino de Mojocoya 2012; Interviews 2–22.04.2012; 4–26.04.2012; 30.04.2012.

56 Interview 1–18.04.2012.

57 Interviews 5–22.04.2012; 2–26.04.2012.

58 Interviews 2–22.04.2012; 3–22.04.2012; 2–26.04.2012.

59 Interviews 4–26.04.2012; 1–08.05.2012.

60 See Albó 2012b: 205–206, referring to Barragán 1994.

61 See Albó 2012b: 229–238; Arciénaga 2012; Cameron 2012: 13–14; 2013: 189–190; Interview 2–18.04.2012.

62 Data of the 2001 and 2012 Censuses generated from the website of INE www.ine.gob.bo and the Redatam+SP Database http://datos.ine.gob.bo/binbol/RpWebEngine.exe/Portal?&BASE=CPV2012COM (last access 10.06. 2015). See also Albó 2012b: 197–198; Gobierno Municipal de Tarabuco 2008.

63 The percentage of urban residents of Tarabuco increased, if compared with the 2,442 (12.5 per cent) people registered in the 2001 Census. But this number needs to be taken with caution, as there were not few people possessing a double residence in a rural community and Tarabuco town; see Albó 2012b: 193–198; 240.

64 See Albó 2012b: 200, 203; Gobierno Municipal de Tarabuco 2008: 34–47, 70–74, 83–104; Interviews 25.04.2012; 01.05.2012; 2–02.05.2012.

65 Unfortunately, it was not Tarabuqueños, but rather intermediaries, transporters, tourist agencies and other residents from Sucre who captured the largest share of the tourism profits; see Albó 2012b: 220–225; Gobierno Municipal de Tarabuco 2008: 69; 191–193.

66 Interviews 1–13.04.2012; 17.04.2012; 25.04.2012; 1–23.04.2012.

67 Interviews 2–13.04.2012; 1–23.04.2012, 2–23.04.2012; 24.04.2012; 25.04.2012; 2–27.04.2012; 2–02.05.2012; 2–07.05.2012; 2–08.05.2012.

68 See Choque 2012; Choque and Mendizabal 2010; Interview 03.04.2012.

69 Interviews 12.04.2012; 2–18.04.2012; 1–23.04.2012; 25.04.2012; 04.05.2012.

70 See Gobierno Municipal de Tarabuco 2008: 200; Interviews 25.04.2012; 01.05.2012; 2–02.05.2012.

71 Interviews 2–23.04.2012; 25.04.2012; 1–02.05.2012; 04.05.2012.

72 These principles imply that a male candidate must be followed by a female candidate and vice versa in an electoral list, and that a female candidate must have a male substitute in case she lays down her office and vice versa.

73 Interviews 2–13.04.2012; 2–23.04.2012; 2–02.05.2012.

74 Interviews 1–23.04.2012; 2–02.05.2012.

75 See Arciénega 2012: 65–68; Interviews 12.04.2012; 2–18.04.2012; 25.04.2012; 2–02.05.2012.
76 See Gobierno Municipal de Tarabuco 2008: 106; 202; Interviews 25.04.2012; 1–02.05.2012.
77 See Gobierno Municipal de Tarabuco 2008: 135–139; Interviews 2–23.04. 2012; 04.05.2012.
78 Interviews 2–23.04.2012; 25.04.2012.
79 See Centro Juana Azurduy 2011: 85–91, 99, 105–108, 112, 138–139; Interviews 2–18.04.2012; 25.04.2012; 04.05.2012; 2–08.05.2012.
80 See Centro Juana Azurduy 2011: 97, 101–102, 105; Interviews 2–23.04.2012; 2– 02.05.2012; 04.05.2012.
81 Interviews 12.04.2012; 01.05.2012; 1–01.05.2012; 2–02.05.2012.
82 Interviews 17.04.2012; 2–23.04.2012; 25.04.2012.
83 See also Albó 2012b: 243; Arciénaga 2012: 26–28; 65–67; Interviews 2–18.04.2012; 1–23.04.2012.
84 Interviews 2–18.04.2012; 2–23.04.2012; 2–02.05.2012; 04.05.2012; 2–08.05.2012.
85 Interviews 1–23.04.2012; 2–23.04.2012; 25.04.2012; 2–02.05.2012; 2–08.05.2012.
86 See Centro Juana Azurduy 2012: 3–8; Interviews 25.04.2012; 2–08.05.2012.
87 Arciénaga 2012: 28–29, 38–39; Cameron 2012: 13–14; Cameron 2013: 189–190; Interviews 2–18.04.2012; 1–23.04.2012; 2–27.04.2012.
88 Interviews 1–13.04.2012; 2–13.04.2012; 17.04.2012; 2–23.04.2012, 25.04.2012; 01.05.2012; 04.05.2012; 2–08.05.2012.
89 See Alvarado 2011; Interviews 12.04.2012; 1–13.04.2012; 1–23.04.2012; 25.04.2012; personal observations during a session of Commission 2 – Territorial Structure and Self–Governance (14.04.2012) and a session of the deliberative assembly of Tarabuco (20.04.2012).
90 Interviews 2–23.04.2012; 25.04.2012; 04.05.2012; 2–08.05.2012.
91 Interviews 2–23.04.2012; 25.04.2012; 04.05.2012.
92 Interviews 2–23.04.2012; 25.04.2012; 2–08.05.2012; 01.05.2012; 1–02.05.2012; 2–02.05.2012; 2–08.05.2012.
93 Interviews 12.04.2012; 01.05.2012; 1–02.05.2012; 03.05.2012; personal observations during a session of the deliberative assembly of Tarabuco (20.04.2012).
94 Interviews 12.04.2012; 1–13.04.2012; 2–18.04.2012; 1–23.04.2012; 2–02.05.2012.
95 See Alvarado 2011; Cameron 2012: 13; 2013: 189; Reglamento Interno de Debates y Funcionamiento de la Asamblea Autonómica Deliberativa de Tarabuco 2011: 4; Interviews 12.04.2012; 1–13.04.2012; 2–13.04.2012; 17.04.2012; 2–18.04.2012; 2–23.04.2012.
96 See Alvarado 2011; Interviews 12.04.2012; 1–13.04.2012; 2–23.04.2012; 01.05.2012; 1–02.05.2012; own observations during a session of the deliberative assembly (20.04.2012).
97 See Cameron 2012: 13; 2013: 189; Reglamento Interno de Debates y Funcionamiento de la Asamblea Autonómica Deliberativa de Tarabuco 2011.
98 In a 65-day march indigenous citizens walked from Trinidad (Beni Department) to La Paz in order to protest against a highway construction that would cut across their protected territory (*Territorio Indígena y Parque Nacional Isiboro–Sécure*, TIPNIS) and to demand, among other things, their right to prior consultation; see El Diario 17.09.2011; Fundación Tierra 2012; Interviews 1–13.04.2012; 2–23.04.2012.
99 Interviews 01.05.2012; 1–02.05.2012.
100 Interviews 12.04.2012; 24.04.2012.

101 Alvarado 2011; Cameron 2011; 2013: 183; Interviews 12.04.2012; 1–13.04.2012; 1–23.04.2012; 2–23.04.2012.
102 See Ministerio de Autonomías, Viceministerio de Autonomías Indígena Originaria Campesinas y Organización Territorial, Dirección General de Autonomías Indígena Originaria Campesinas (n.d.); Interviews 1–13.04.2012; 2–23.04.2012; 25.04.2012; 01.05.2012, 2–08.05.2012.
103 Interviews 12.04.2012; 17.04.2012; 2–18.04.2012; 1–23.04.2012; 2–27.04.2012.
104 See Anteproyecto del Estatuto Autonómico Indígena Originario Tarabuco (25.08.2012), art. 10, 14, 49–54.
105 See Acta de Octava Sesión Ordinaria de la Asamblea Autonómica Deliberativa dc Tarabuco (25.08.2012); ANA 21.07.2014; Anteproyecto del Estatuto Autonómico Indígena Originario Tarabuco (25.08.2012); Interview 2–27.04.2012; notes taken during conversation with a representative of the departmental Autonomy Ministry in Sucre (24.10.2012).
106 Interviews 2–23.04.2012; 25.04.2012; 04.05.2012; e-mail communication with NGO consultant Tarabuco (25.03.2013).

Chapter 6

Comparative analysis of case studies

Reasons for the emergence of claims for legal and institutional change

With regard to the first research question of the present study, the assumption based on available theory was that claims for change of indigenous community norms and institutions dealing with domestic violence were more likely to emerge if:

- shifts in local power relations from which change-minded groups benefit have occurred; and
- local institutions lost their taken-for-grantedness because:
  (a) new legal models or ideas diffused into the community;
  (b) violence could not be satisfactorily addressed by existing community norms and institutions; or
  (c) community norms addressing violence entered into conflict with other community-based, national or international norms or institutions.

Looking at *La Calera* (*Ecuador*), considerable power shifts preceded the *change initiative* by means of a comparatively high number of literate women who started participating in decision-making spaces at community (community council) and municipal level in Cotacachi (women's panel of the AUCC) and who disposed of a consolidated women's organisation (CWC). While the incompatibility between institutional sets and the unsatisfactory resolution of cases of domestic violence by existing authorities was clearly perceived by these female leaders, it was only following the diffusion of new legal ideas (*Revolutionary Law of Women* from Chiapas, Mexico) by an external agent (UNIFEM representative) that women felt incentivised to develop their own change strategy.

By contrast, in *La Rinconada* (*Ecuador*) no significant power shifts preceded the *change initiative* as women's school attendance and literacy were low; only few women had ever played an active role in communal decision-making; no organisational platform from which joint activities would have been undertaken was available; and women remained disconnected from participative spaces which existed at the cantonal level in Otavalo. Only following the diffusion of new legal ideas circulated by the NGO Corcima (rights of children, adolescents, women) have more local agents become sensitised to the incompatibility between local, national and international institutional sets and the inappropriateness of the way domestic violence was dealt with by local authorities.

As for *Chacabamba* (*Peru*), no significant power shifts preceded the *change initiative.* Women's participation in the community board and the assembly was confined to exceptional cases (literate women, widows or women replacing their absent husbands). Women were also unable to transfer the capabilities they acquired through the administration of existing social programmes concerned with the preparation and distribution of food for the most needy (*club de madres, comedor popular, vaso de leche*) towards other spheres such as the administration of community affairs. It was not until UNICEF's engagement with the community that new legal ideas (rights of children, adolescents and women) came to circulate in the community and that commoners became sensitised to the incompatibility between distinct institutional sets and to the inappropriateness of the way domestic violence was dealt with locally.

Similarly, a lack of power shifts preceding the *change initiative* could be observed in *Tungasuca* (*Peru*), where women's illiteracy rates were relatively high, and where the scope of women's participation in state-incentivised programs (*club de madres, comedor popular, vaso de leche*) did not exceed the ones foreseen by the programmes. The communal board remained a male-dominated sphere, and women participated in the general assembly only in emergencies or to replace their absent husbands. Only following the diffusion of new legal ideas circulated by the NGO IDL (rights of children, adolescents and women) more local agents became aware of the incompatibility between local, national and international institutional sets and of the inappropriateness of the way violence was addressed by local authorities.

With respect to *Mojocoya* (*Bolivia*), considerable power shifts preceded the *change initiative* through the consolidation of a women's organisation and women's enhanced participation in the executive committee of the agrarian union and the administration of the municipality. These female leaders became sensitised to incompatibilities between institutional sets and the unsatisfactory resolution of cases of domestic violence by existing authorities after the engagement of several NGOs (Plan International, Fundación Aclo, Centro Juana Azurduy) and diffusion of new legal ideas (life free of violence; right to political participation; women's rights according to international norms and the 2009 Constitution) by means of training and leadership schools for women.

In *Tarabuco* (*Bolivia*), by contrast, no significant power shifts could be observed at the outset of the *change initiative*, given that only a handful of women have recently started to participate in political affairs at community and municipal level, and that no organisation crossing community and organisational boundaries existed. The incompatibility between institutional sets and the unsatisfactory resolution of cases of domestic violence by existing authorities was perceived only after the NGO Centro Juana Azurduy started to work with and to diffuse new legal ideas (gender equality; women's rights) among women.

Overall, the comparative analysis of the six cases confirmed the relevance of the diffusion of legal ideas and models, and, to some extent, the importance of preceding power shifts from which change-minded agents benefit, in order for change claims to occur at a given setting. Meanwhile the two other variables (inappropriateness of existing norms or institutions to resolve cases of domestic violence; incompatibility between norms or institutions addressing domestic violence and other institutions) required refinement in order to become relevant variables for the study of legal change:

> The probability of the emergence of claims for change of community norms and institutions increases considerably when hitherto unknown legal ideas diffuse into a location. In order to capture the interest of a local population, such legal ideas need to point to the core of existing local grievances, prompt local agents to analyse the local legal status quo and weigh it against the prospects conveyed by the alternative legal norms and institutions, and suggest locally viable pathways to address existing problems.
>
> Power shifts from which change-minded groups benefit cannot account alone for the emergence of claims for legal change. Nevertheless, where these precede a *change initiative* they play a supportive role as they provide change agents with:
>
> - skills to perceive, evaluate and articulate given problems and negotiate potential solutions with powerful agents;
> - experience in dealing with community affairs and the planning and management of projects; and
> - confidence in their capabilities, which encourages them to assume new challenges.
>
> To stage change claims on the grounds that pressing issues (such as domestic violence) are not dealt with in a satisfactory manner by local and state authorities requires a phase of awareness-raising preceding the formulation of such claims. Moreover, becoming aware of such grievances does not automatically lead to the emergence of claims for

legal change: such claims also require the existence of alternatives to which a given status quo can be compared.

In the same vein, it is not so much the mere existence of incompatibilities between the way domestic violence is dealt with by local norms and institutions on the one hand, and other (community-based or external) institutional sets on the other hand, but rather when (a) these tensions are perceived by local agents or (b) when some institutional sets relevant for women's lives indeed are altered and thus enter in contradiction with local institutions dealing with violence, that this variable becomes a relevant factor for facilitating claims for change. If such incompatibilities between distinct institutions or norms are perceived, these alone do not account for the emergence of claims for change (which require a preceding discussion of alternatives), but rather help raising local agents' sense of urgency to take action.

Variables facilitating or obstructing the initiation of legal and institutional change efforts

Regarding the second research question, the theory-based assumption was that change-minded agents were more likely to engage in legal and institutional change efforts related to domestic violence if:

- shifts in political opportunities opened avenues for change-orientated actors to promote their claims;
- change agents succeeded in establishing a shared and resonating interpretive frame for the targeted change; and
- change agents disposed of an organisational platform and a minimum of material and non-material resources, which enabled them to initiate change-orientated action.

At the starting point of the *change initiative* in *La Calera* (*Ecuador*) change agents faced a moderately open opportunity window, considering that the *initiative* was approved by community authorities and women from La Calera. However, concerns expressed by the CWC were not accommodated and the approval of UNORCAC was not sought at this early stage of the process. The same was true for the interpretive frame, which was convincing for some, but not all involved agents. Women had both leadership skills and their own organisational platform at disposal, but the external resources provided first by a NGO and soon after by UNIFEM would only suffice to start the *initiative* in five out of 43 communities.

The initial opportunity window in *La Rinconada* (*Ecuador*) was fairly open, as the community council agreed with Corcima's proposal to conduct activities directed towards normative and institutional change in the community. The same was true for Corcima's interpretive frame justifying their *initiative*, which resonated with the community council and some sectors of the community. Aspects such as the NGO's close relationship with local authorities due to its effective support in other issues and its scholarship programme for children, and the fact that community authorities would themselves become strengthened in their administration of justice, played an important role in this regard. The NGO's activities were funded by World Vision, but no local women's organisation existed with which the NGO could have discussed and coordinated its activities.

In *Chacabamba* (*Peru*) political opportunities were fairly open for the initiation of the *change initiative*, not least as the community had hitherto not figured on the radar of development agencies, because UNICEF respected local decision-making processes, and as the cooperation was associated with the passing of new knowledge to the community and the creation of a new service (*defensoría comunitaria*) managed by elected commoners. The interpretive frame presented by the first elected defenders to the community resonated particularly with female and young male commoners. UNICEF promised to provide specific resources over a prolonged time period; with the *defensoría* team, a small organisational vehicle existed from which activities could be carried out.

Similarly, in *Tungasuca* (*Peru*), local authorities approved the *change initiative* proposed by IDL, among other reasons, because they expected that the existence of a *defensoría comunitaria* would strengthen the community organisation and that community members could gain new capacities in rights-related issues. The backing of this *initiative* by the provincial *campesino* federation, and the fact that the community as such would take all decisions related to the *defensoría*, were likewise relevant for the decision-making process. The interpretive frame presented by the first *defensores* was particularly appealing for women and those authorities and young men who were interested in improving the community's development and providing their children with better prospects for the future. IDL promised to closely accompany the *defensoría's* work with technical advice and training over a prolonged time period; with the *defensoría* team the community had a small organisational vehicle at its disposal from which activities could be carried out.

Regarding *Mojocoya* (*Bolivia*), the window of opportunity was clearly open following the strongly endorsed but unlawful removal of the seat of the municipality from Villa Mojocoya to Redención Pampa and the subsequent understanding that this decision could only be officially sanctioned by the conversion of the municipality into an autonomous indigenous territory. Given the inevitable difficulties that would be encountered along the path of the conversion, Mojocoyan leaders required the highest possible unity of the majority of the *campesino* population. Women were able to seize this moment to negotiate with male leaders about matters of particular concern to them. The *initiative's* objectives fitted in seamlessly with the general interpretive frame constructed by the local authorities in the context of the conversion process (women's participation as an integral and necessary part of a profound process of change). Women disposed of leadership skills and their own organisation, and state and non-state agents promised to provide them with other resources necessary to carry out their *change initiative.*

The *change initiative* in *Tarabuco* (*Bolivia*), proposed by NGO Centro Juana Azurduy, was approved by the municipal authorities, but the *ayllu* organisation, and even more so the agrarian union, expressed their reservations about a project almost exclusively focused on the female population, which is why the NGO did not enjoy a complete backing for its *initiative* from the outset. The dominant interpretive frames of the conversion into an autonomous territory elaborated by the *ayllu* organisation and the agrarian union did not take women's interests into account. Centro Juana Azurduy disposed of limited funds from the beginning, and no local, cross-community organisation existed with which the NGO could have coordinated its activities.

Overall, the comparative analysis of the six cases confirmed the relevance of all three variables posited by available literature:

> A combination of:
>
> - at least moderately open political opportunities;
> - a meaningful interpretive frame offering a concrete and viable solution for the described problem, and resonating with key sectors of the locality – not only the aggrieved, but particularly influential leaders or groups; and
> - a minimum of human, material, and immaterial resources (leadership skills and experiences, networks, organisational vehicles, facilities), including prospects for a future provision thereof,
>
> are required so as to encourage agents to becoming engaged in a *change initiative.*

Variables influencing legal and institutional change processes throughout their further evolution

With regard to the third research question, the theoretically informed assumption was that collective efforts towards normative and institutional change evolved in dynamic and highly contingent ways. The concrete direction, scope and efficacy of proposed reforms were expected to be influenced by:

- actors' goals, strategies and tactics and later adjustments thereof;
- shifts in political opportunities; and

- change agents' disposability and use of material and immaterial resources.

The goal of the *change initiative* in which *La Calera* (*Ecuador*) took part was the elaboration of a legal document (*Law of good living together*) condemning distinct forms of violence and outlining respective procedures and sanctions to be applied by community authorities. In order to pursue this goal, strategies such as women's workshops in five pilot communities; the systematisation of an agreed draft Law; the seeking for the Law's approval by the CWC and UNORCAC; reunions with *cabildos* to incorporate the Law into the internal statutes; the training of promoters of the Law; and the promotion of the *initiative* vía radio spots in Kichwa, were applied. Political opportunities worsened because of a conflict with UNORCAC (change agents had mistakenly assumed that they had obtained an approval for their *initiative* at an UNORCAC Congress) and the election of a new mayor that deprived the Centre for Integral Attention of Women and the Family of its former personnel; the *initiative* was paralysed for 1.5 years, but was resumed after advocacy by allies and a change of strategies. Until the stalemate, the *initiative* received funding from UNIFEM; after the *initiative's* resumption, some funding was again made temporarily available by external supporters.

In *La Rinconada* (*Ecuador*) the goal of Corcima's *initiative* was broad and entailed the improvement of the wellbeing of the entire family, which is why not all of their activities focused on the problem of domestic violence. Awareness-raising among exclusively female groups provoked more violence against their participants. Corcima also aimed to strengthen the capacities of community authorities to administer justice and invited them and state legal operators to exchange information on existing mechanisms to resolve family conflicts, including domestic violence. Unfortunately, few ordinary villagers have participated in these sessions. Other lines of action implied only a short-term engagement of the local population (celebration of *Inti Raymi* without alcohol; female soccer competition). Still, political opportunities remained open for Corcima's engagement, and the NGO continued to receive funding from World Vision. But there was no local women's organisation at hand to which the *initiative* could have been gradually handed over.

As for *Chacabamba* (*Peru*), the *change initiative* clearly targeted the problem of domestic violence: the objective was to establish a specialised service provided by trained community members in order to attend victims of violence and to help them access justice through the *defensoría*. The *defensoría's* strategies involved the promotion of rights and non-violence (talks with community groups; campaigns against the selling of alcohol; training of representatives from state institutions; songs), the attention of victims of violence and their families (listening to the victim; evaluation of the situation at hand; providing advice; presenting available options to denounce acts of violence and explaining steps of the corresponding legal process; coordination with competent community and state authorities) and the monitoring of cases (regular visits of victims; asking for regular updates on the processing of cases). Political opportunities shifted with the withdrawal of the *initiative's* main supporter (UNICEF), which was partly counterbalanced by a *defender's* enhanced engagement in the regional *defensoría* network. Resources were reduced as well when UNICEF withdrew; for some years, the *defensoría* coordinator successfully applied for funds available from the participatory budget process at a municipal level. The members of the *defensoría* team decreased towards the end of the research period.

The objectives of the *change initiative* in *Tungasuca* (*Peru*) were identical to the ones pursued in Chacabamba: the promotion of a normative shift towards non-tolerance of violence and the creation of a specialised community service (*defensoría comunitaria*) to effectively respond to cases of violence. Among the *defensoría's* strategies was the promotion of rights, the attention to victims of violence and guidance in a broad range of family issues (marital disputes, recognition of children, alimony, abandonment, sexual abuse) and the close accompaniment and monitoring of cases, which had been forwarded to state authorities. These lines of action were carried out effectively until 2006, but political opportunities shifted with the reduction of the close accompaniment and frequent trainings of the *defensoría* team by IDL. The *defensoría* team disintegrated and the few volunteers who were willing to replace them lost their motivation due to limited communication with the regional *defensoría* network and reduced their caseload to a barely visible minimum.

The main objective of change agents in *Mojocoya* (*Bolivia*) was to ensure the comprehensive package of women's rights guaranteed in the 2009 Bolivian Constitution, including their freedom from violence, would be reflected in the future autonomy statute of Mojocoya. Therefore, the strategy focused on women's effective participation in the entire conversion process from the planning stage, the sessions of the autonomy assembly, up to the closing referendum on the autonomy statute. Also, decentralised women's meetings were organised to remedy some of the obstacles women had to fully participate in the deliberations of the autonomy assembly. In these meetings a sensitive dialogue on women's grievances could take place, and a proposal addressing violence and women's access to justice (and many other issues of concern) was formulated and presented to the autonomy assembly. Political opportunities continued to be open: first, because all relevant local authorities endorsed the conversion process; second, because the recently adopted Law on Autonomy and Decentralization and the Law on Jurisdictional Delimitation affirmed women's insistence on more gender equality within the future autonomy and in the administration of justice;

and third, because a lengthy and decisive debate on discriminating features of the local governance system was helpful for sensitising assembly members on those groups whose rights would have been neglected in the draft autonomy statute. Resources provided by external supporters, in turn, were not always enough to facilitate the participation of women in the assembly sessions.

Turning to *Tarabuco* (*Bolivia*), the goal of Centro Juana Azurduy was to support women's participation in the deliberations and decision-making processes on the conversion of the municipality into an indigenous autonomous territory. Therefore, the NGO's intention was to generate spaces where women would gain knowledge about their own history and rights and reflect upon matters relevant for them with respect to the future autonomy. Strategies involved a leadership school for women, a study on the resolution of cases of gender violence by indigenous legal authorities, the strengthening of the local SLIM office and the organisation of several women's meetings in which women would discuss and elaborate their own proposal for the autonomy statute. But political opportunities worsened due to increased disagreements between the agrarian union and the *ayllu* organisation on the very fundaments of a future autonomous territory; the fact that the deliberative assembly was paralyzed and reconstituted several times – each time with a distinct composition of representatives; and because the NGO's activities were not supported by all involved agents. Due to the NGO's reduced resources, only a small number of women were able to participate in its activities.

Overall, the comparative analysis of the six cases confirmed existing research and, at the same time, allowed for the refinement of some prevailing propositions:

> Collective efforts towards legal and institutional change evolve in highly dynamic and contingent ways. The direction and concrete shape normative and institutional change efforts in the realm of domestic violence acquire, and their prospects to gradually become accepted by larger sections of a local population, depend on the interplay between:
>
> - change agents' clearly defined and realistic goals, and strategies and lines of action offering both intimate spaces for women's reflections and mixed spaces of deliberation among women and men, as well as sufficient flexibility to being adapted to unexpected or new circumstances (including eventual adjustments of initial interpretative frames);
> - a lasting open political opportunity window; and
> - the continued availability and deployment of resources, the same of which have to correspond in kind and amount with the goal, strategies and tactics envisioned by change agents.

Preliminary results of legal and institutional change efforts at the end of the research period

The available literature suggested that processes of intended legal and institutional change would take a considerable time to materialise, and that ambivalent results, setbacks or stalemate could as likely occur as some kind of 'success'. Considering the relatively short time frames within which the here-analysed *change initiatives* have evolved, and the equally short period in which the author was able to accompany these *initiatives* during her fieldwork, the assessment of the consequences of the *change initiatives* concentrated on:

- the question whether some changed norm or institution was indeed agreed upon at the end of the research period (2012);
- if reformed norms or institutions were in place, the degree to which these were actually enforced and applied; and
- whether there were indicators in the broader environment pointing to a higher or lower sustainability of the achieved changes.

By the end of the research period, more women than previously were willing to denounce acts of violence before community authorities and participated as authorities in the administration of justice in *La Calera* (*Ecuador*). When processing cases of violence, the community authorities applied some elements of the *Law for good living together*, and it was not uncommon to see the authorities requesting the assistance of women who were familiarised with the Law so as agree upon the possible procedural steps to take. At the municipal level, the *Law for good living together* was submitted to revision by all 43 highland communities, a process by which the major objections of UNORCAC and CWC leaders were addressed. The resulting draft municipal ordinance condemning violence and shifting responsibility to legally prosecute and sanction violence to indigenous and state legal authorities was approved in a first debate by the municipal council in the end of 2013 and awaited its final approval by the time of writing. Among the further challenges of this *initiative* was the continued sensitisation of larger parts of the population on the possible mechanisms to address violence and the need of a stronger appropriation of this *initiative* among CWC and UNORCAC leadership.

In *La Rinconada* (*Ecuador*) the community council was now more willing and better trained to attend cases of violence, and it committed itself to include a minimum of two women among its office-holders. But many elected female authorities lacked self-esteem to speak up in debates with men, and the council's late regular office hours continued to pose access barriers to women. Despite this authority's willingness to attend to cases of domestic violence, not many women asked for its intervention. Some kept silent about the violence they endured at home; others turned to their family members to seek help; a handful of women asked the community council for intervention; others sought advice in a mediation centre established by Corcima; and a few turned to state legal operators. In addition, a growing number of adolescents and young women decided to have children alone without a formal relationship with the respective father – a decision that could be interpreted as a means to avoid entering into potentially conflictive and violent conjugal relations. The recently elected community president expressed his willingness to enhance young people's participation in community affairs and offered support for the potential creation of a women's group in the near future.

As for *Chacabamba* (*Peru*), violence was no longer considered 'normal', most commoners were aware of the services offered by the *defensoría*, and if kin intervention proved ineffective, they regularly turned to the *defensoría* to obtain guidance and support. Coordination of cases of violence between the *defensoría* and community authorities or state legal operators of the district has likewise become institutionalised over the years. Despite the success of this *change initiative*, concerns remained as to the little interest of other commoners to replace long-serving *defensoría* volunteers, which was directly related to the shortage of resources provided by external supporters. It remained to be seen whether CODECC or the departmental government of Cuzco would find the means to strengthen the *defensoría* network in the years to come.

Regarding *Tungasuca* (*Peru*), the remaining defenders felt abandoned by its regional allies and the *defensoría* lost visibility in the community. Other intermediaries and state authorities partly substituted some of the *defensoría's* functions (rights promotion, conflict intervention), and options for battered women – whose number remained high – became more diffuse and dispersed among uncoordinated agents. Towards the end of the research period, the community council planned to strengthen communal responses to legal transgressions through improved coordination among local authorities, including the *defensoría* – a plan that might help revitalise this institution in the near future. It also remained to be seen whether CODECC or the departmental government of Cuzco would find the means to strengthen the *defensoría* network in the years to come.

Women in *Mojocoya* (*Bolivia*) successfully incorporated their demands in respect of a life free from violence and an improved participation of women in the administration of justice (together with many other demands) in the draft autonomy statute that was approved by the deliberative assembly and that passed a revision by the Plurinational Constitutional Tribunal. The prospects for the approval of the final statute in a closing referendum by the general population were very high, and so was the later implementation of the statute, considering, for instance, the plans for a leadership school for Mojocoyan women and men. Not least, the women's organisation, which so forcefully struggled for the inclusion of women's rights in the statute, would doubtlessly continue its efforts in order to see these rights implemented in concrete policies of the future autonomy.

Through the engaged advocacy work of the Centro Juana Azurduy, many elements of the women's proposal ultimately found their way into *Tarabuco's* (*Bolivia*) draft autonomy statute in 2012. The draft included the obligation of indigenous legal authorities to legally prosecute and sanction cases of domestic violence; the option for indigenous authorities to forward cases of domestic violence to the state legal system; and the creation of a new higher instance for indigenous justice. However, the final approval of this draft in the deliberative assembly was questioned as it did not meet formal–legal requirements and was internally incoherent. The prospects for a final approval of the autonomy statute in a closing referendum and its later implementation were highly uncertain if considering that the influential organisations did not settle their disagreements and that the general population came to question the conversion process as a whole. Centro Juana Azurduy would soon finish its engagement in Tarabuco, whereas women continued lacking a cross-communal organisation from which they could jointly struggle for the implementation of their demands.

At least two additional aspects come to the fore while analysing the change processes: first, this research has shown the relevance of external agents (e.g., development agencies, human rights institutions, NGOs) for the diffusion of ideas and the support of local agents with technical advice, political–legal and methodological know-how and logistical and financial resources. They can connect local agents with others and facilitate platforms for exchange of experiences. And they may engage in advocacy work that enhances the visibility and effectiveness of local *initiatives*. Still, particularly when thinking about criteria that increase the local acceptance, effectiveness and sustainability of change efforts in any locality, it makes a difference whether these are planned and carried out by an external agent or by a locally rooted group. In two of the three 'more effective' cases studied here, La Calera and Mojocoya, the very drivers of the reform proposals were local organisations and institutions, which – while in need of external support, know-how and resources – would remain engaged on occasions when external agents decided to close their respective project cycles in the locality. Conversely, in two of the three 'less effective' cases, La Rinconada and Tarabuco, the respective change efforts were designed and conducted by NGOs, and no partner such as a local women's organisation with which activities could have been consented, jointly planned and carried out was available. Only by means of such a vehicle would women have enjoyed an opportunity to define their interests and priorities on their own, to assume responsibility and to take on the challenge to struggle for shifts in realms of relevance for them.

A second aspect refers to the leadership qualities present in individuals who fought for legal change in their respective localities. Without any doubt, this factor likewise helps to distinguish the 'more effective' cases from the 'less effective' ones. In La Calera and Mojocoya, organised women had acquired leaderships before staging claims for legal change, the same of which provided them with self-esteem and courage to stage claims and sustain their *initiatives* throughout the entire process. Also, what distinguished the *defensoría* teams in Chacabamba and Tungasuca was, first, the former's pro-active understanding of their role, as this team did not wait for victims of violence to seek its advice during its office hours, but instead had the courage to intervene in violent situations in private homes at the moment of their occurrence. Second, the teams also reacted quite differently to the reduction in accompaniment and resources from external agencies. While defenders in Tungasuca lost their motivation to continue their engagement after the withdrawal of IDL, thereby triggering a disintegration of the *defensoría* that could not be reversed by the few volunteers who tried to replace their predecessors, the *defensoría* coordinator of Chacabamba seized the chance to appropriate her role in a more profound manner by accepting a responsible position within the regional *defensoría* network and by participating in training on fundraising, which enabled her to partly compensate for the shortage in resources from UNICEF.

> Achieving changes to indigenous norms and institutions in the realm of gender violence requires time, considering that any legal order reflects long-held attitudes and practices in a given location. Legal change processes do not stop at the moment when an oral or written agreement on a normative and institutional change is secured. Rather, such changes have to become accepted and practised as a 'new common sense' by leaders and significant sectors of the population in order to provide victims of violence with a sufficient degree of certainty that any violent act will be prosecuted and punished and that the aggressors, and not the victims who denounce violence, will be exposed to social ostracism. Preliminary results of a *change initiative* are thus best assessed if they not only focus on specific agreements about normative and institutional change, but if they also consider whether and how these changes are being enforced and invoked. The prospects for the local acceptance, effectiveness and sustainability of a legal change process increase to the extent that the main driver of change efforts is a locally rooted organisation pooling leadership skills of local agents, or alternatively, if local agents are able to appropriate change efforts and are given the opportunity to increase their leadership skills over the course of its evolution.

Chapter 7

Conclusions and implications

International and regional treaties, as well as national legislation to prevent and eliminate violence notwithstanding, violence against women continues to affect a considerable part of the world's female population. Where statistics provide ethnically disaggregated data, the disproportional affectedness of indigenous women by violence compared with non-indigenous women becomes visible. Indigenous women are often exposed to multiple, mutually reinforcing axes of discrimination that include their cultural, social, economic and political status both vis-à-vis indigenous men in their communities and the non-indigenous population in their respective countries, thereby rendering their chances to live a life free from violence all the more difficult. In order to confront domestic violence, the access to a legal forum at which women can denounce aggressions and claim justice for the harm caused to them seems of utmost importance. However, in many countries all available judicial systems have failed indigenous women in this regard: denouncing rights violations before state legal operators is extremely difficult for indigenous women residing in rural and semi-rural areas, in part because of their limited understanding of the state judiciary, geographic, linguistic, financial barriers, culturally inappropriate, lengthy and bureaucratic procedures, but also the racial, class and gender stereotypes held by many legal operators. Simultaneously, the capacity of indigenous legal systems to address domestic violence has been questioned, as well, among other reasons, because of the tendency of indigenous authorities to reproduce prevailing gendered hierarchies in their administration of justice by excluding women from judicial authority positions, by failing to recognise violence as crime, by shifting victims co-responsibility for the harm caused to them or by adopting inadequate resolutions, which tend to prioritise the wellbeing of the family over that of women. As a consequence, women's attempts to seek redress for the violation of their rights face inaccessible legal authorities on all sides and have often ended in outright impunity. In recent years, the issues of multicultural citizenship, legal pluralism and women's difficulties to access justice have not only concerned social scientists, but also raised the interest of the UN, international development agencies and NGOs, and prompted indigenous organisations and leaders to position themselves against the background of the criticism raised of their legal practices. This study aims to contribute to this global field of inquiry and concern and offers valuable insights for all the above-mentioned agents. It focuses on the qualitative comparison of six thus far underexplored *change initiatives* in the Andean Region (Ecuador, Peru, Bolivia) where indigenous legal institutions have recently been constitutionally recognised, where national policies addressing domestic violence closely resembled one another and where the respective local contexts were relatively similar, and it inquires into the reasons why some of the selected indigenous localities have more effectively than others initiated reforms of their legal norms and institutions in order to improve women's legal standing in the realm of domestic violence. The theoretical approach to analyse processes of intended legal change brings together three research strands within the social sciences, namely legal anthropology, social movement theory and new institutionalism. By combining the propositions of all three approaches and comprehensively adapting them to indigenous local contexts of the Andean highlands, an innovative conceptual framework is proposed in order to address the research question standing in focus of this book. Methodologically this study makes a case for a systematic comparison of three cases where the change efforts yielded more concrete and effective results than the other three cases, at least within the time frame of the research. While the findings of the study are discussed at length in chapter 6 of this book, we can resume them by stating that the variation in the effectiveness of legal change efforts can be explained by the interplay of several factors that influence change processes throughout distinct phases of their evolution, namely the diffusion of new legal ideas or concepts into a site of interest; change agents' ability to construct a meaningful frame for action resonating with major local agents; the definition of realistic goals, strategies and lines of action focusing on the problem at hand; an at least moderately open political opportunity window for the change efforts; and the availability of human, material and immaterial resources, community-based organisations and supportive external allies.

This study confirms many of the hypothesised variables that were elaborated by the three literature strands reviewed in the realm of legal and institutional change – at the same time it provides a more precise understanding of the specific effect of single variables or their respective combination. Social movement scholars have repeatedly expressed their awareness of the fact that theory development has concentrated on movements operating at the national level in democratic regimes of North America and Europe, and that only few analyses have convincingly achieved to conceptualise agency and structure as mutually constitutive forces (e.g., Morris and Staggenborg [2004] 2007: 171; Tarrow 2005:

23–24). The present study addresses these factors by shedding light on relatively small movements located in the Global South, which operate at the sub-national level and in political systems characterised by the intersection of indigenous and state laws and institutions. Moreover, due to a profound involvement with anthropological literature that has developed its own ways to deal with the subject of agency and structure (see chapter 2), the study assesses how and to what extent agents were able to critically evaluate their situation and pursue their interests and thereby influence their lived realities against the background of considerable structural constraints. As far as new institutionalism is concerned, this study has shown that institutionalist analyses do not have to remain confined to settings at the national or international level, but that local indigenous 'polities' may equally constitute interesting sites for the inquiry of processes of institutional continuity and reform. In order to become applicable for indigenous regimes of self-governance, some variables had to be adjusted or refined. For instance, the variable 'power shifts' for women residing in Andean highland communities could not simply refer to the achievement of greater representation in community councils; rather, it proved helpful to include aspects such as increased schooling and literacy of women and their engagement in local organisations as indicators of this variable. Similarly, the variable 'incompatibilities between distinct institutional sets' had to be defined more precisely than outlined by institutionalists, for it was not so much the existence of such tensions, but rather the perception thereof by local agents that rendered them a relevant factor for facilitating claims for change. Given their thematic closeness to the subject matter of this book, legal anthropologists' studies on major aspects shaping processes of change and their cautiousness when it comes to assessing the concrete results of such processes, have proved highly useful in order to understand the here-studied cases. One of the aspects found to be in need of more scholarly attention is the concept of leadership skills in indigenous settings. This factor appeared to play an important role in all three 'more effective' cases, but its conceptualisation and 'measurement' seemed far from straightforward. Due to their immersion in such local sites of interest and their qualitative research tools, anthropologists are certainly best equipped to shed more light into this variable.[1]

States that signed CEDAW and regional treaties (such as the Belem do Pará Convention in Latin America) should more assertively assume the responsibility to fully comply with these legal documents so as to guarantee all women a life free from violence. In order to assess the prevalence of violence among the indigenous population and to design more specific and effective public policies, governments need to include ethnic and gender identity as standardised variables in their national and sub-national surveys. In consultation with indigenous peoples, governments should improve existing legal institutions addressing gender violence by adopting culturally appropriate and geographically accessible services, which should rely on agreements and a close cooperation with community-based authorities and women's groups. Latin American governments in particular should realise that indigenous women's wellbeing is inextricably linked with the full implementation of the collective rights of indigenous peoples – another obligation to which these States have committed themselves by signing ILO C169 and approving UNDRIP. Regarding indigenous peoples' right to apply their own law, governments should (re)formulate comprehensive legislation – again in consultation of indigenous peoples – to provide all legal operators with more legal certainty about their respective jurisdictions and competences. Such laws should devise mechanisms for interlegal dispute resolution and cooperation of indigenous and state legal authorities in specific cases, as well as decentralised and sufficiently funded spaces for dialogue in which mutual respect and openness to learn from the other's knowledge and experience prevails. Further, the matter of legal pluralism should be incorporated in law school curricula, and the state judiciary should be opened for indigenous representation, the consultation of experts on indigenous legal systems and intercultural jurisprudence.

This study shows how development practitioners, NGOs and legal advocacy groups can play a constructive role in local change processes by transferring legal ideas, providing local agents with know-how and resources, facilitating the exchange of experiences among otherwise unconnected local groups or by engaging in advocacy work to enhance the visibility and effectiveness of local reforms. With regard to resources, what seems to matter most is not so much the fact that these are abundant, but rather, that they correspond in kind and amount to the goals, strategies and activities envisioned to carrying out a planned *initiative.* From the very beginning, external supporters should take into account that changes in critical areas, such as gender violence, require time to becoming socially accepted and practised and that their own project cycles do often not correspond with these long-term processes. External agents should therefore take stock of local realities, prevailing gender relations and the degree of empowerment of women in a given locality. Especially in case of short-term project cycles and a low disposability of resources, external agents might be best advised to concentrate their activities in the strengthening of women's self-organisation, leadership skills and capacities to critically evaluate local grievances and to negotiate with influential community agents, instead of proposing far-reaching reforms that may risk exhausting the horizons of all agents involved. In order to increase the prospects for the effectiveness and sustainability of change efforts, their engagement in indigenous localities should allow for the highest possible degree of participation and appropriation of the proposed reforms by local agents who should be able to influence the contents, degree and pace of change.

As demonstrated in this book, the concrete goals, strategies, and lines of action designed by change agents to reduce the social acceptability of domestic violence and to improve women's access to justice were diverse and creative. The strategies referred to the incorporation of women's demands in a future autonomy statute; the designing of a cantonal-wide legal document to combat gender violence; the promotion of gender equality in family and community life and the strengthening of a community council's capabilities to respond to family conflicts; and the institutionalisation of a specialised office (*defensoría comunitaria*) to attend cases of violence. Tactics applied in single cases to promote legal change included the elaboration of radio spots and songs in native languages; anti-alcohol campaigns; female soccer competitions; dialogue forums between indigenous and state legal authorities; the creation of municipal legal councils competent to revise community-based resolutions; and workshops for women where they would learn to speak about their life-long experiences with violence. This rich repertoire displayed in the case studies hopefully may inspire indigenous women and men and their organisations in their own reflections on family violence and the designing of strategies and actions to effectively address this matter through their local legal institutions. No doubt, the specificity and complexity of any locality implies that change proposals have to be embedded in local aspirations, cultural frames and circumstances. When addressing such change proposals, indigenous leaders and authorities should be mindful of the fact that the legitimacy of their legal systems throughout history has more than anything else relied on their adaptability to changing social, economic and political contexts, as well as their ability to effectively mediate pressing internal conflicts and problems. This legitimacy may suffer if the demand to adequately deal with a problem, which affects a considerable number of families, and, thus, the wellbeing of their communities as a whole, is ignored.

Note

1 The role of leadership in social movement literature was likewise found to lack sufficient theorisation. A valuable attempt to summarise the insights on leadership provided by this school of thought was made by Morris and Staggenborg [2004] 2007.

Bibliography

Acosta, A. (2012) Extractivismo y derechos de la naturaleza. In: Santos, B. de and Grijalva, A. (eds). *Justicia indígena, plurinacionalidad e interculturalidad en Ecuador.* Quito: Abya Yala; Fundación Rosa Luxemburg.

Acta de Información y Conformación de la Asamblea Constituyente del Municipio de Mojocoya (04.07.2009). Mojocoya. Unpublished.

Acta de Octava Sesión Ordinaria de la Asamblea Autonómica Deliberativa de Tarabuco (25.08.2012). Tarabuco. Unpublished.

Albó, X. (2012a) Justicia indígena en la Bolivia plurinacional. In: Santos, B. de and Exeni, J. (eds). *Justicia indígena, plurinacionalidad e interculturalidad en Bolivia.* Quito: Abya Yala; Fundación Rosa Luxemburg.

Albó, X. (2012b) *Tres municipios andinos camino a la autonomía indígena; Jesús de Machaca, Chayanta, Tarabuco.* La Paz: CIPCA.

Albó, X. (2009) *Movimientos y poder indígena en Bolivia, Ecuador y Perú.* La Paz: CIPCA.

Albó, X., and Romero. C (2009) *Autonomías indígenas en la realidad Boliviana y su nueva Constitución.* La Paz: Vicepresidencia del Estado Plurinacional de Bolivia.

Albro, R. (2005) The Indigenous in the Plural in Bolivian Oppositional Politics. *Bulletin of Latin American Research* 24(4), 433–453.

Alcaldía Municipal de Mojocoya (2011) *Plan de Desarrollo Municipal. Ajuste del Plan de Desarrollo Municipal Autónomo, Gestión 2011 a 2015.* Villa Mojocoya: Alcaldía Municipal de Mojocoya.

Alvarado, A. (2011) *Memoria Anual 2011 Autonomía Indígena Originario Campesina, Dirección Departamental de Autonomías Chuquisaca.* Sucre: Dirección Departamental de Autonomías Chuquisaca.

Alvarez, S., Dagnino, E. and Escobar. A. (eds) (1998) *Cultures of Politics, Politics of Cultures: Re-visioning Latin American Social Movements.* Boulder, Oxford: Westview Press.

Amenta, E. and Caren, N. ([2004] 2007) The Legislative, Organizational, and Beneficiary Consequences of State-Oriented Challengers. In: Snow, D., Soule, S. and Kriesi, H. (eds). *The Blackwell Companion to Social Movements.* Oxford: Blackwell Publishing.

Amnesty International (2014) *Violence Against Indigenous Women and Girls in Canada: A Summary of Amnesty International's Concerns and Call to Action.* Ottawa: Amnesty International.

Amnesty International (2012) *'So that no one can demand anything'. Criminalizing the Right to Protest in Ecuador.* London: Amnesty International.

Amnesty International (2009) *Peru: Bagua, Six Months On. "Just because we think and speak differently, they are doing injustice to us"*. London: Amnesty International.

Amry, R. (2007) Defensa cultural y pueblos indígenas: propuesta para la actualización del debate. In: Pontífica Universidad Católica del Perú/Universidad de Friburgo, Suiza (eds). *Derecho penal y pluralidad cultural. Anuario de Derecho Penal 2006*. Lima: Fondo Editorial.

Anaya, J. (2005) Indigenous Peoples' Participatory Rights in Relation to Decisions about Natural Resource Extraction: The more fundamental issue of what rights indigenous peoples have in lands and resources. *Arizona Journal of International & Comparative Law* 22(1), 7–17.

An-Na'im, A. (2002) *Islamic Family Law in a Changing World: A Global Resource Book*. London: Zed Press.

An-Na'im, A. (ed.) (1992) *Human Rights in Cross-Cultural Perspectives: A Quest for Consensus*. Philadelphia, PA: University of Pennsylvania Press.

An-Na'im, A. (1990) Problems of Universal Cultural Legitimacy for Human Rights. In: Abdullahi A. and Deng, F. (eds). *Human Rights in Africa: Cross-Cultural Perspectives*. Washington, D.C.: The Brookings Institution.

Anría, S., Cameron, M., Goenaga, A., Toranzo, C. and Zuazo, M. (2010) Bolivia: democracia en construcción. In: Cameron, M. and Luna, J. (eds). *Democracia en la región andina*. Lima: IEP.

Anteproyecto del Estatuto Autonómico Indígena Originario Tarabuco (25.08.2012). Tarabuco. Unpublished.

Aranda, M. (2011) La coordinación entre sistemas de justicia en Colombia, Ecuador y Perú. In: Cóndor, E. (coord.). *Los Derechos Individuales y Derechos Colectivos en la Construcción del Pluralismo Jurídico en América Latina*. La Paz: Fundación Konrad Adenauer.

Arauco, E., Mamani, R. and Rojas, J. (2007) *Violencia contra la mujer en la pareja: respuestas de la salud pública en El Alto, Bolivia*. Serie Mujer y Desarrollo No. 84. Santiago de Chile: CEPAL.

Archenti, N. (2011) *La paridad política en América Latina y el Caribe. Percepciones y opiniones de los líderes de la región*. Serie Mujer y Desarrollo No. 108. Santiago de Chile: CEPAL.

Arciénaga, L. (2012) *La Libre Auto-Determinación Autonómica, Indígena, Originaria, Campesina. Estudio de Caso: Municipio de Tarabuco – Chuquisaca – Bolivia*. Master Thesis. Graduate Institute of International and Development Studies Geneva, Switzerland.

Ardito, W. (2011) Retos que el pluralismo jurídico plantea al poder judicial en el Perú. In: Corte Suprema de Justicia de la República, Consejo Ejecutivo del Poder Judicial, Centro de Investigaciones Judiciales del Poder Judicial (eds). *Congresos internacionales sobre justicia intercultural en pueblos indígenas, comunidades andinas y rondas campesinas "Construyendo un País con Justicia Social"*. Lima: Fondo Editorial del Poder Judicial.

Ardito, W., and La Rosa, J. (2004) *Violencia Familiar en la Región Andina: Análisis Comparado de la Legislación*. Lima: IDL.

Ariza, R. (2010) *Coordinación entre sistemas jurídicos y administración de justicia indígena en Colombia*. San José: IIDH.

Arze, C., and Kruse, T. (2004) The Consequences of Neoliberal Reform. *NACLA Report on the Americas* 38(3), 23–28.

Assies, W. (2001) La oficialización de lo no oficial: ¿(re)encuentro de dos mundos? *Alteridades* 11(21), 83–96.

Assies, W., van der Haar, G. and Hoekma, A. (eds) (2000) *The Challenge of Diversity: Indigenous Peoples and Reform of the State in Latin America.* Amsterdam: Thela Thesis.

Barié, C. (2003) *Pueblos Indígenas y derechos constitutionales en América Latina: un panorama.* 2nd updated and extended Ed. La Paz: Comisión Nacional para el Desarrollo de los Pueblos Indígenas; Gobierno de la República de México; Abya Yala; Banco Mundial.

Barragán, R., Soliz, C., Derpic, J. And Barragán P. (2005) La violación como prisma de las relaciones sociales y el entramado estata en el ámbito jurídico. Ethnografía y hermenéutica de la justicia. In: Calla, P. (ed.). *Rompiendo Silencios: Una aproximación a la violencia sexual y al maltrato infantil en Bolivia.* La Paz: Coordinadora de la Mujer.

Barragán, R. (1994) *¿Indios de arco y flecha? Entre la historia y la arqueología de las poblaciones del norte de Chuquisaca (Siglos XV–XVI).* Sucre: ASUR.

Barrera, A. (2012) Turning Legal Pluralism into State-Sanctioned Law: Assessing the Implications of the New Constitutions and Laws in Bolivia and Ecuador. In: Nolte, D. and Schilling-Vacaflor, A. (2012) *New Constitutionalism in Latin America: Promises and Practices.* Farnham: Ashgate.

Bazurco, M., and Exeni, J. (2012) Bolivia: Justicia indígena en tiempos de plurinacionalidad, in: Santos, B. de and Exeni, J. (eds). *Justicia indígena, plurinacionalidad e interculturalidad en Bolivia.* Quito: Abya Yala; Fundación Rosa Luxemburg.

Bebbington, A. (2009) The New Extraction: Rewriting the Political Ecology of the Andes? *NACLA Report on the Americas* 42(5), 12–24.

Beijing Declaration and Platform for Action (1995) UN Fourth World Conference on Women, Huairou, Beijing, China.

Beijing Declaration of Indigenous Women (1995) UN Fourth World Conference on Women, Huairou, Beijing, China.

Bell, S. (2011) Do We Really Need a New 'Constructivist Institutionalism' to Explain Institutional Change? *British Journal of Political Science* 41(4), 883–906.

Benda-Beckmann, F.von, Benda-Beckmann, K. von and Griffiths, A. (eds) (2009) *The Power of Law in a Transnational World: Anthropological Enquiries.* New York; Oxford: Berghahn Books.

Benda-Beckmann, F. Von, and Benda-Beckmann. K. von (2006) The Dynamics of Change and Continuity in Plural Legal Orders. *Journal of Legal Pluralism and Unofficial Law* 53–54, 1–42.

Benda-Beckmann, F. von, Benda-Beckmann, K. von and Griffiths, A. (eds) (2005) *Mobile People, Mobile Law: Expanding Legal Relations in a Contracting World.* Aldershot: Ashgate.

Benda-Beckmann, F. von (2002) Who's afraid of Legal Pluralism? *Journal of Legal Pluralism and Unofficial Law* 47, 37–83.

Benda-Beckmann, F. von and Benda-Beckmann, K. von (1985) Transformation and change in Manangkabau. In: Thomas, L. and Benda-Beckmann, F. von (eds). *Change and Continuity in Minangkabau.* Athens, OH: Ohio University Center for International Studies.

Benda-Beckmann, K.von (1981) Forum shopping and shopping forums: dispute processing in a Minangkabau village. *Journal of Legal Pluralism* 19, 117–159.

Benford, R., and Snow, D. (2000) Framing Processes and Social Movements: An Overview and Assessment. *Annual Review of Sociology* 26, 611–639.

Benford, R. (1997) An Insider's Critique of the Social Movement Framing Perspective. *Sociological Inquiry* 67, 409–430.

Benford, R. (1993) Frame disputes within the nuclear disarmament movement. *Social Forces* 71, 677–701.

Benford, R. (1987) *Framing Activity, Meaning, and Social Movement Participation: The Nuclear Disarmament Movement.* Ph.D. Thesis. Austin, TX: University of Texas.

Blackwell, M., Hernández, R., Herrera, J., Macleod, M., Ramirez, R., Sieder, R., Sierra, M. and Speed, S. (2009) Cruces de fronteras, identidades indígenas, género y justicia en las Américas. *Desacatos* 31, 13–34.

Blackwell, M. (2006) Weaving in the Spaces: Indigenous Women's Organizing and the Politics of Scale in Mexico. In: Speed, S., Hernández, R. and Stephen, L. (eds). *Dissident Women: Gender and Cultural Politics in Chiapas.* Austin, TX: University of Texas Press.

Blumer, H. (1951) The Field of Collective Behavior. In: McClung, A. (ed.). *Principles of Sociology.* New York: Barnes & Noble.

Blyth, M., Hodgson, G., Lewis, O. and Steinmo, S. (2011) Introduction to the Special Issue on the Evolution of Institutions. *Journal of Institutional Economics* 7(3), 299–315.

Blyth, M. (2002) *Great Transformations: Economic Ideas and Institutional Change in the Twentieth Century.* New York: Cambridge University Press.

Boesten, J. (2010) *Intersecting Inequalities: Women and Social Policy in Peru, 1990–2000.* University Park, PA: Pennsylvania State University Press.

Bohannan, P. (1957) *Justice and judgment among the Tiv.* London: Oxford University Press.

Bott, S., Guedes, A., Goodwin, M. and Adams, J. (2012) *Violence against Women in Latin America and the Caribbean: A comparative analysis of population-based data from 12 countries.* Washington, D.C.: Pan American Health Organization.

Bourdon, N. (2013) Coercive Harmony?: Realizing Women's Rights Through Alternative Dispute Resolution in Dar es Salaam's Legal Aid Clinics. In: Derman, B., Hellum, A. and Sandvik, K. (eds). *Worlds of Human Rights: The Ambiguities of Rights Claiming in Africa.* Leiden: Brill.

Brandt, H-J., and Franco, R. (2007) *Normas, valores y procedimientos en la justicia comunitaria: estudio cualitativo en comunidades indígenas y campesinas de Ecuador y Perú.* Serie: Justicia Comunitaria en los Andes: Perú y Ecuador, Vol. 2. Lima: IDL.

Brandt, H.-J., and Franco, R. (2006) *El tratamiento de conflictos: un estudio de actas en 133 comunidades indígenas y campesinas en Ecuador y Perú.* Serie: Justicia Comunitaria en los Andes: Perú y Ecuador, Vol. 1. Lima: IDL.

Buechler, S. ([2004] 2007) The Strange Career of Strain and Breakdown Theories of Collective Action. In: Snow, D., Soule, S. and Kriesi, H. (eds). *The Blackwell Companion to Social Movements.* Oxford: Blackwell Publishing.

Buechler, S. (1995) New Social Movement Theories. *The Sociological Quarterly* 36(3), 441–464.

Burchardt, H.-J. (2012a) Lateinamerikas soziale Bewegungen zu Beginn des XXI. Jahrhundert: eine Einführung. In: Burchardt, H.-J. and Öhlschläger, R. (eds). *Soziale Bewegungen und Demokratie in Lateinamerika: Ein ambivalentes Verhältnis.* Baden-Baden: Nomos.

Burchardt, H.-J. (2012b) Wie sozial ist Bewegung? Kritische Betrachtungen zu Politik und Demokratie jenseits der Institutionen. In: Burchardt, H.-J. and Öhlschläger, R. (eds). *Soziale Bewegungen und Demokratie in Lateinamerika: Ein ambivalentes Verhältnis.* Baden-Baden: Nomos.

Cabrera, Z., and Díaz, J. (2005) *Defensorías comunitarias: Una experiencia de liderazgo social sostenible.* Lima: IDL.

Calla, P. (ed.) (2005) *Rompiendo Silencios: Una aproximación a la violencia sexual y al maltrato infantil en Bolivia.* La Paz: Coordinadora de la Mujer.

Camarasa i Casals, M. (2009) *Proposal of new indicators to measure the effects of gender violence.* Barcelona: SURT.

Cameron, J. (2013) Bolivia's Contentious Politics of 'Normas y Procedimientos Propios'. *Latin American and Caribbean Ethnic Studies* 8(2), 179–201.

Cameron, J. (2012) Identidades Conflictuadas: Conflictos internos en las autonomías indígena originaria campesinas en Bolivia. In: *Seminario Interdisciplinario "Clase y Etnicidad en los Andes"*, Instituto para el Estudio de las Américas, Londres, UK, 27 February 2012.

Cameron, J. (2011) *La Autonomía Indígena Originaria Campesina en Bolivia ¿Crónica de una muerte anunciada?* Observatorio de Territorios Indígenas – Fundación Tierra. Online: www.territorios.ftierra.org/index.php?option=com_content&view=article&id=114:rair&catid=36:territorio&Itemid=30 (last access 10.06.2015).

Cameron, J. (2010) *Struggles for Local Democracy in the Andes.* Boulder, London: First Forum Press.

Campbell, J. (2010) Institutional Reproduction and Change. In: Morgan, G., Campbell, J., Crouch, C., Pedersen, O. and Whitley, R. (eds). *Oxford Handbook of Comparative Institutional Analysis.* New York: Oxford University Press.

Campbell, J. (2005) Where do we stand? Common Mechanisms in Organizations and Social Movements. In: Davis, G., McAdam, D., Scott, R. and Zald, M. (eds). *Social Movements and Organization Theory.* New York: Cambridge University Press.

Campbell, J. (2004) *Institutional Change and Globalization.* Princeton, NJ: Princeton University Press.

Campbell, J. (1998) Institutional analysis and the role of ideas in political economy. *Theory and Society* 27, 377–409.

Capítulo Boliviano de Derechos Humanos, Democracia y Desarrollo (2005) *Estado de situación de los derechos económicos, sociales y culturales en Bolivia el año 2005. Informe de la sociedad civil al PIDESC de las Naciones Unidas.* La Paz.

Capoccia, G., and Kelemen, D. (2007) The Study of Critical Junctures: Theory, Narrative, and Counterfactual in Historical Institutionalism. *World Politics* 59, 341–369.

Carrera, C. (2011) *Análisis del Plan Nacional de Erradicación de la Violencia de Género hacia la Niñez, Adolescencia y Mujer con Enfoque en Violencia Física, Psicológica, Sexual y Discriminación hacia la Mujer.* Disertación de Grado. Pontífica Universidad Católica del Ecuador, Facultad de Comunicación, Lingüistica y Literatura, Quito.

Carstensen, M. (2011a) Paradigm Man vs. the Bricoleur: Bricolage as an Alternative Vision of Agency in Ideational Change. *European Political Science Review* 3(1), 147–167.

Carstensen, M. (2011b) Ideas are Not as Stable as Political Scientists Want Them to Be: A Theory of Incremental Ideational Change. *Political Studies* 59(3), 596–615.

Castells, M. (1977) *The Urban Question.* Cambridge, MA: MIT Press.

Centers for Disease Control and Prevention (2008) Adverse health conditions and health risk behaviors associated with intimate partner violence United States, 2005. *Morbidity and Mortality Weekly Report* 57(05), 113–117.

Centro Juana Azurduy (2012) *Propuesta de las mujeres para una autonomía con equidad social y de género en Tarabuco.* Sucre. Unpublished.

Centro Juana Azurduy (2011) *Formas de resolución de la violencia contra la mujer en la jurisdicción indígena originaria campesina de Tarabuco.* Sucre. Unpublished.

CEPAL (2014) *Los pueblos indígenas en América Latina. Avances en el último decenio y retos pendientes para la garantía de sus derechos.* Santiago de Chile: CEPAL.

CEPAL (2013) *Mujeres indígenas en América Latina: dinámicas demográficas y sociales en el marco de los derechos humanos.* Santiago de Chile: CEPAL.

CEPAL (2007) *Panorama social de América Latina 2006.* Santiago de Chile: CEPAL.

CERES – Centro de Estudios de la Realidad Económica Social (1999) *Los Quechuas de Tapacarí.* La Paz: Ministerio de Justicia y Derechos Humanos; Banco Mundial.

Chanock, M. (1985) *Law, Custom, and Social Order: The Colonial Experience in Malawi and Zambia.* Cambridge: Cambridge University Press.

Charters, C., and Stavenhagen, R. (eds) (2010) *El Desafío de la Declaración: Historia y Futuro de la Declaración de la ONU sobre Pueblos Indígenas.* Copenhagen: IGWIA.

Chenaut, V. (2007) *Género y justicia en la antropología jurídica en México.* Working Paper No. 15–2007, Centro de Estudios Interdisciplinarios Etnolingüístisticos y Antropológico Sociales.

Chenaut, V. (2004) Prácticas jurídicas e interlegalidad entre los totonacas en el distrito judicial de Papantla. In: Sierra, M. (ed.). *Haciendo justicia. Interlegalidad, derecho y género en regiones indígenas.* México, D.F.: CIESAS.

Chopra, T., and Isser, D. (2012) Women's Access to Justice, Legal Pluralism and Fragile States. In: Albrecht, P., Kyed, H., Isser, D. and Harper, E. (eds). *Perspectives on Involving Non-State and Customary Actors in Justice and Security Reform.* Rome: IDLO; DIIS.

Choque, M. (2012) *Chacha Warmi en procesos de Autonomía Indígena Originaria Campesina.* Consultoría realizada para Fundación Tierra. La Paz. Unpublished.

Choque, M., and Mendizabal M. (2010) Descolonizando el género a través de la profundización de la condición sullka y mayt'ata. *T'inkazos* 28, 81–97.

Choque, M., and Mamani, M. (2001) Reconstitución del ayllu y derechos de los pueblos indígenas: el movimiento indio en los Andes de Bolivia. *Journal of Latin American Anthropology* 6(1), 202–224.

Chuquimia, R. (2012) Historia, Colonia y derecho de los pueblos indígenas. In: Santos, B. de and Exeni, J. (eds). *Justicia indígena, plurinacionalidad e interculturalidad en Bolivia.* Quito: Abya Yala; Fundación Rosa Luxemburg.

CLADEM – Comité de América Latina y El Caribe para de Defensa de los Derechos de la Mujer (1999). *Nada personal. Reporte de derechos humanos sobre la aplicación de la anticoncepción quirúrgica en el Perú, 1996–1998.* Lima: CLADEM.

Clark, K., and Becker, M. (2007) Indigenous Peoples and State Formation in Modern Ecuador. In: Clark, K. and Becker, M. (eds). *Highland Indians and the State in Modern Ecuador.* Pittsburgh, PA: University of Pittsburgh Press.

Clavero, B. (2000) De los ecos a las voces, de las leyes indigenistas a los derecho indígenas. *Alteridades* 10(19), 21–39.

Clemens, E., and Cook, J. (1999) Politics and Institutionalism: Explaining Durability and Change. *Annual Review of Sociology* 25, 441–466.

CODECC, Franco, R. and Haworth, E. (2005) *Hablan las defensoras comunitarias: Una justicia distinta para las mujeres*. Lima: IDL.

Collier, D. (2011) Understanding Process Tracing. *Political Science and Politics* 4, 823–830.

Collier, D. (1991) The Comparative Method: Two Decades of Change. In: Rustow, D. and Erickson, K. (eds). *Comparative Political Dynamics: Global research perspectives*. New York: HarperCollins Publishers.

Collier, R., and Collier, D. (1991) *Shaping the Political Arena*. Princeton, NJ: Princeton University Press.

Comaroff, J. and Roberts, S. (1981) *Rules and Processes: The Cultural Logic of Dispute in an African Context*. Chicago and London: University of Chicago Press.

Comisión de la Verdad y Reconciliación Nacional (2002) *Informe Final de la Comisión de la Verdad y Reconciliación Nacional*. Lima: CVRN.

CONAMU (2005) *Plan de Igualdad de Oportunidades de las Mujeres Ecuatorianas*. Quito: CONAMU.

Cóndor, E. (coord.) (2009) *Estado de la relación entre justicia indígena y justicia estatal en los países andinos: estudio de casos en Colombia, Perú, Ecuador y Bolivia*. Lima: CAJ.

Cook, R. (ed.) (1994) *Human Rights of Women: National and International Perspectives*. Philadelphia, PA: University of Pennsylvania Press.

Coordinadora de la Mujer (2011) *Informe Bolivia 2010. Derechos Humanos de las Mujeres y Justicia de Género*. La Paz: Coordinadora de la Mujer; Articulación Regional Feminista.

Cordero, E. (2011) *Municipio de Mojocoya, Provincia Zudañez, Departamento de Chuquisaca: Hacía la autodeterminación ideológica, política, territorial y sociocultural*. Sucre. Unpublished.

Corradi, G. (2010) Human Rights Promotion in Post Conflict Sierra Leone: Coming to Grips with Plurality in Customary Justice. *Journal of Legal Pluralism and Unofficial Law* 60, 73–103.

Cortell, A., and Peterson, S. (2002) Agents, Structures, and Domestic Institutional Change. In: Cortell, A. and Peterson, S. (eds). *Altered States: International Relations, Domestic Politics, and Institutional Change*. Lanham, MD: Lexington Books.

Cotula, L., and Cissé, S. (2006) Changes in 'Customary' Resource Tenure Systems in the Inner Niger Delta, Mali. *Journal of Legal Pluralism and Unofficial Law* 52, 1–29.

Cowan, J., Dembour, M.-B. and Wilson, R. (2001) Introduction. In: Cowan, J., Dembour, M.-B. and Wilson, R. (eds). *Culture and Rights: Anthropological Perspectives*. Cambridge: Cambridge University Press.

Cox, D., Young, M. and Bairnsfather-Scott, A. (2009) No Justice without Healing. Australian Aboriginal People and Family Violence. *The Australian Feminist Law Journal* 30, 151–161.

Crenshaw, K. (1991) Mapping the Margins: Intersectionality, Identity Politics, and Violence against Women of Color. *Stanford Law Review* 43(6), 1241–1299.

Cress, D., and Snow, D. (1996) Mobilization at the Margins: Resources, Benefactors, and the Viability of Homeless Social Movement Organizations. *American Sociological Review* 61(6), 1089–1109.

Crouch, C. (2007) How to 'do' post-determinist institutional analysis. *Socio-Economic Review* 5, 527–537.

Cucuri, C. (2009) El acceso de las mujeres indígenas a la justicia en la Nueva Constitución del Ecuador. In: Lang, M. and Kucia, A. (eds). *Mujeres indígenas y justicia ancestral.* Quito: UNIFEM.

DANIDA – International Development Cooperation, Ministry of Foreign Affairs of Denmark (2010) *How to Note on Justice Sector Reform.* Copenhagen: Ministry of Foreign Affairs.

Davies, J. (1962) Towards a Theory of Revolution. *American Sociological Review* 27, 5–19.

Davis, G., McAdam, D., Scott, W., and Zald, M. (eds) (2005) *Social Movements and Organization Theory.* New York: Cambridge University Press.

De Belaúnde, J. (2006) *La Reforma del Sistema de Justicia, ¿en camino correcto? Breve balance de su situación actual y de los retos pendientes.* Lima: Fundación Konrad Adenauer; Instituto Peruano de Economía Social de Mercado.

Decoster, J.-J., and Rivera, E. (2009) Estado de relacionamiento en Perú. In: Cóndor, E. (coord.). *Estado de la relación entre justicia indígena y justicia estatal en los países andinos: estudio de casos en Colombia, Perú, Ecuador y Bolivia.* Lima: CAJ.

Deere, C., and León, M. (2002) *Género, propiedad y empoderamiento: tierra, Estado y mercado en América Latina.* 2nd Ed. Bogotá: Tercer Mundo Editores.

Defensoría del Pueblo (1999) *La aplicación de la anticoncepción quirúrgica y los derechos reproductivos II.* Informe Defensoría No. 27. Lima: Defensoría del Pueblo.

Degregori, C. (1998) Movimientos étnicos, democracia y nación en Perú y Bolivia. In: Dary, C. (ed.). *La construcción de la nación y la representación ciudadana en México, Guatemala, Perú, Ecuador y Bolivia.* Guatemala: FLACSO.

De la Cadena, M. (1998) Silent Racism and Intellectual Superiority in Peru. *Bulletin of Latin American Research* 17(2), 143–164.

DEMUS – Estudio para la Defensa de los Derecho de la Mujer (2011) *Los derechos humanos de las mujeres en el Perú 2010.* Lima: DEMUS.

Deveaux, M. (2000) *Cultural Pluralism and Dilemmas of Justice.* Ithaca, NY: Cornell University Press.

Diez, A. (2011) Inversiones privadas y derechos comunales. *Tiempo de Opinion* 2(4), 22–31. Online: www.esan.edu.pe/publicaciones/revista-tiempo-de-opinion/2011/tiempo-de-opinion/ (last access 10.06.2015).

DiMaggio, P. (1997) Culture and Cognition. *Annual Review of Sociology* 23, 263–287.

DiMaggio, P., and Powell, W. (eds) (1991) *The New Institutionalism in Organizational Analysis.* Chicago IL: University of Chicago Press.

Distrito Metropolitano Quito (n.d.) *CEJ Centros de Equidad y Justicia. Juzgados de la Niñez y Adolescencia. Juzgados de Contravenciones. El Quito que queremos es libre de violencia.* Quito.

Domingo, P., and Sieder, R. (eds) (2001) *Promoting the Rule of Law: Perspectives on Latin America.* London: Institute of Latin American Studies.

Earl, J. ([2004] 2007) The Cultural Consequences of Social Movements. In: Snow, D., Soule, S. and Kriesi, H. (eds). *The Blackwell Companion to Social Movements.* Oxford: Blackwell Publishing.

Eckert, J. (2009) Rechtsaneignung: Paradoxien von Pluralisierung und Entpluralisierung in rechtspluralen Räumen. In: Kötter, M. and Schuppert, G. (eds). *Normative Pluralität ordnen. Rechtsbegriffe, Normenkollisionen und Rule of Law in Kontexten dies- und jenseits des Staates.* Baden-Baden: Nomos.

ECMIA, and Chirapaq (2013) *Violence and Indigenous Women. Document presented to the CSW57.* Lima: Continental Network of Indigenous Women of the Americas; Chirapaq.

Edwards, B., and McCarthy, J. ([2004] 2007) Resources and Social Movement Mobilization. In: Snow, D., Soule, S. and Kriesi, H. (eds). *The Blackwell Companion to Social Movements.* Oxford: Blackwell Publishing.

Eisinger, P. (1973) The Conditions of Protest Behavior in American Cities. *American Political Science Review* 81, 11–28.

Elster, J. (2000) Rational Choice History: A Case of Excessive Ambition. *American Political Science Review* 94(3), 685–695.

Elster, J. (1998) Emotions and Economic Theory. *Journal of Economic Literature* 36(1), 47–74.

Emerson, R., Fretz, R., and Shaw, L. (2011) *Writing Ethnographic Fieldnotes.* 2nd Ed. Chicago; London: University of Chicago Press.

Erdmann, G., Elischer, S. and Stroh, A. (2011) *Can Historical Institutionalism be Applied to Political Regime Development in Africa?* GIGA Working Paper No. 166. Hamburg: GIGA Institute.

Ernst, M. (2007) Los delitos sexuales en el Ecuador. Un análisis desde la experiencia. *Revista Aportes Andinos,* 18.

Escobar, A., and Alvarez, S. (eds) (1992) *The Making of Social Movements in Latin America: Identity, Strategy, and Democracy.* Boulder; San Francisco; Oxford: Westview Press.

Estremadoyro, J. (2001) Domestic Violence in Andean Communities of Peru. *Law, Social Justice and Global Development* [Electronic Law Journal], 1, np. Online: www2.warwick.ac.uk/fac/soc/law/elj/lgd/2001_1/estremadoyro/ (last access 10.06.2015).

Faundez, J. (2010) Democratization Through Law: Perspectives from Latin America. *Democratization* 12(5), 749–765.

Faundez, J. (2003) *Non-State Justice Systems in Latin America Case Studies: Peru and Colombia.* Paper prepared for the DFID Workshop on 'Working with Non State Justice Systems', 6–7 March 2003. Online: www.gsdrc.org/go/display/document/legacyid/1340 (last access 10.06.2015).

Fernández, M. (2000) *La ley del ayllu. Práctica de jach'a justicia y jisk'a justicia (justicia mayor y justicia menor) en comunidades aymaras.* La Paz: PIEB.

FIMI (2006) *Mairin Iwanka Raya. Mujeres indígenas confrontan la violencia. Informe complementario al estudio sobre violencia contra las mujeres del secretario general de las Naciones Unidas.* New York: FIMI.

Finnemore, M., and Sikkink, K. (1998) International Norm Dynamics and Political Change. *International Organization* 52(4), 887–917.

Fitzpatrick, P. (1984) Traditionalism and Traditional Law. *Journal of African Law* 28(1–2), 20–27.

Fligstein, N. (2001) Social Skills and the Theory of Fields. *Sociological Theory* 19, 105–125.

Fligstein, N. (1990) *The Transformation of Corporate Control.* Cambridge, MA: Harvard University Press.

Foweraker, J. (1995) *Theorizing Social Movements. Critical Studies of Latin America.* London: Pluto Press.

Franco, R., and González, M. (2009) *Las mujeres en la justicia comunitaria: víctimas, sujetos y actores*. Serie Justicia Comunitaria en los Andes: Perú y Ecuador, Vol. 3. Lima: IDL.

Franco, R. (2007) Miradas cruzadas: el acceso de las mujeres a la justicia desde el género y la cultura. In: IDL (ed.). *Acceso a la justicia en el mundo rural*. Lima: IDL.

Franco, R. (2003) *Defensorías: Una respuesta comunitaria a la violencia familiar. Documento de sistematización del Proyecto "Defensorías Comunitarias: Una propuesta innovadora para la vigilancia de los derechos de la mujer". Julio 2001–junio 2002*. Lima: IDL.

Frey, S., Dietz, T. and Kalof, L. (1992) Characteristics of Successful American Protest Groups: Another Look at Gamson's Strategy of Social Protest. *American Journal of Sociology* 98(2), 368–387.

Fundación Tierra (2012) *Marcha indígena por el TIPNIS: La lucha en defensa de los territorios*. La Paz: Fundación Tierra.

Galanter, M. (1981) Justice in many rooms: courts, private ordering, and indigenous law. *Journal of Legal Pluralism* 19, 1–47.

Gamson, W. ([2004] 2007) Bystanders, Public Opinion, and the Media. In: Snow, D., Soule, S. and Kriesi, H. (eds). *The Blackwell Companion to Social Movements*. Oxford: Blackwell Publishing.

Gamson, W., and Meyer, D. (1996) Framing Political Opportunity. In: McAdam, D., McCarthy, J. and Zald, M. (eds). *Comparative Perspectives on Social Movements: Political Opportunities, Mobilizing Structures, and Cultural Framings*. Cambridge: Cambridge University Press.

Gamson, W., and Wolfsfeld, G. (1993) Movements and Media as Interacting Systems. *Annals of the American Academy of Political and Social Science* 528, 114–125.

Gamson, W. (1992) *Talking Politics*. New York: Cambridge University Press.

Gamson, W. (1990) *The Strategy of Social Protest*. 2nd Ed. Belmont, CA: Wadsworth.

Gamson, W. (1975) *The Strategy of Social Protest*. Homewood, IL: Dorsey.

García, F. (2011) La justicia indígena como espacio de protección de los derechos individuales y los derechos colectivos de los pueblos indígenas. In: Cóndor, E. (coord.): *Los Derechos Individuales y Derechos Colectivos en la Construcción del Pluralismo Jurídico en América Latina*. La Paz: Fundación Konrad Adenauer.

García, F. (2005) El estado del arte del derecho indígena en Ecuador. *Revista IIDH* 41 (Edición especial sobre derecho indígena), 151–170.

García-Moreno, C., Jansen, H., Ellsberg, M., Heise, L., and Watts, C. (2005) *WHO Multi-country Study on Women's Health and Domestic Violence against Women: Initial results in prevalence, health outcomes and women's responses*. Geneva: WHO.

Garret G., and Weingast, B. (1993) Ideas, Interests, and Institutions. In: Goldstein, J. and Keohane, R. (eds). *Ideas and Foreign Policy: Beliefs, Institutions and Political Change*. Ithaca, NY: Cornell University Press.

George, A., and Bennett, A. (2005) *Case Studies and Theory Development in the Social Sciences*. Cambridge, MA: MIT Press.

George, A., and McKeown T. (1985) Case Studies and Theories of Organizational Decision Making. In: Coulam, R. and Smith, R. (eds). *Advances in Information Processing in Organizations*. Vol. 2. Greenwich, CT.: JAI Press.

Geschwender, J. (1968) Explorations in the Theory of Social Movements and Revolutions. *Social Forces* 47, 127-135.

GIZ – Deutsche Gesellschaft für Internationale Zusammenarbeit (2014) *Con más de cinco sentidos: Prevención y lucha contra la violencia hacia mujeres indígenas y afroamericanas y mujeres en zonas rurales*. Bonn: GIZ.

Gluckmann, M. (1965) *The ideas in Barotse jurisprudence.* New Haven, CT: Yale University Press.
Gluckmann, M. (1955) *The judicial process among the Barotse of Northern Rhodesia.* Manchester: Manchester University Press.
Gobierno Municipal de Santa Ana de Cotacachi (2013) *Sumario de Resoluciones 2013.* Cotacachi: Gobierno Municipal de Santa Ana de Cotacachi.
Gobierno Municipal de Santa Ana de Cotacachi (2011) *Plan de Desarrollo y de Ordenamiento Territorial del Cantón Cotacachi.* Cotacachi: Gobierno Municipal de Santa Ana de Cotacachi.
Gobierno Municipal de Tarabuco (2008) *Plan de Desarrollo Municipal. Diagnostico Municipal Tarabuco – Bolivia 2008–2012.* Tarabuco: Gobierno Municipal de Tarabuco.
Gobierno Regional Cusco (2008) *Programa Regional Contra la Violencia Hacia las Mujeres – Allin Kawsay – Cusco.* Cusco: Gobierno Regional de Cusco.
Gobierno Regional Cusco (n.d.) *Mejorar la atención de los servicios comunitarios de justicia a las mujeres campesinas víctimas de violencia familiar en ámbitos rurales priorizados de la región Cusco.* Cusco: Gobierno Regional Cusco – Gerencia Regional de Desarrollo Social.
Goldstein, D. (2012) *Outlawed: Between Security and Rights in a Bolivian City.* Durham, London: Duke University Press.
Goldstein, D. (2005) Flexible Justice: Neoliberal Violence and 'Self-Help' Security in Bolivia. *Critique of Anthropology* 25(4), 389–411.
Gonzales de Olarte, E. (1994) *En las fronteras del Mercado: Economía política del campesinado en el Perú.* Lima: IEP.
Goodale, M., and Merry, S. (2007) *The Practice of Human Rights: Tracking Law Between the Global and the Local.* Cambridge: Cambridge University Press.
Goodale, M. (2002) Legal Anthropology in an Era of Globalization: The Arrival of Western Human Rights Discourse to Rural Bolivia. In: Starr, J. and Goodale, M. (eds). *Practicing Ethnography in Law: New Dialogues, Enduring Methods.* New York: Palgrave Macmillan, 50–72.
Goodwin, J., and Jasper, J. (1999) Caught in a Winding, Snarling Vine: The Structural Bias of Political Process Theory. *Sociological Forum* 14(1), 27–54.
Griffiths, J. (1986) What is Legal Pluralism? *Journal of Legal Pluralism and Unofficial Law* 24, 1–55.
Grijalva, A., and Exeni, J. (2012) Coordinación entre justicias, ese desafío. In: Santos, B. de and Exeni, J. (eds) *Justicia indígena, plurinacionalidad e interculturalidad en Bolivia.* Quito: Abya Yala; Fundación Rosa Luxemburg.
Grijalva, A. (2011) *Constitucionalismo en Ecuador.* Pensamiento Jurídico Contemporáneo 5. Quito: Corte Constitucional para el Período de Transición.
Guerrero, F., and Ospina, P. (2003) *El poder de la comunidad: movimiento indígena y ajuste estructural en los Andes ecuatorianos.* Quito; Buenos Aires: IEE; CAMAREN; ASDI; CLACSO.
Guigni, M. ([2004] 2007) Personal and Biographical Consequences. In: Snow, D., Soule, S. and Kriesi, H. (eds). *The Blackwell Companion to Social Movements.* Oxford: Blackwell Publishing.
Guigni, M. (1998) Was it Worth it? The Outcomes and Consequences of Social Movements. *Annual Review of Sociology* 24, 371–393.
Gurr, T. (1970) *Why Men Rebel.* Princeton, NJ: Princeton University Press.

Habermas, J. (1981) New Social Movements. *Telos* 49, 33–37.

Hall, G., and Patrinos, H. (eds) (2006) *Indigenous Peoples, Poverty and Human Development in Latin America: 1994–2004*. New York: Palgrave McMillan.

Hall, P., and Taylor, R. (1996) Political Science and the Three New Institutionalisms. *Political Studies* 44(5), 936–957.

Harper, E. (2011) *Customary Justice: From Program Design to Impact Evaluation*. Rome: IDLO.

Harty, S. (2005) Theorizing Institutional Change. In: Lecours, A. (ed.). *New Institutionalism: Theory and Analysis*. Toronto: University of Toronto Press.

Hay, C., and Wincott, D. (1998) Structure, Agency and Historical Institutionalism. *Political Studies* 46(5), 951–957.

Hellum, A. (2013) Gender, Human Rights and Legal Pluralities: Experiences from Southern and Eastern Africa. In: Sieder, R. and McNeish, J.-A. (eds). *Gender Justice and Legal Pluralities: Latin American and African Perspectives*. Oxon; New York: Routledge.

Hellum, A., Derman, W., Feltoe, G., Sithole, E., Steward, J., and Tsanga A. (2013) Rights Claiming and Rights Making in Zimbabwe: A Study of Three Human Rights NGOs. In: Andreassen, B. and Crawford, G. (eds). *Human Rights, Power and Civic Action: Comparative Analyses of Struggles for Rights in Developing Societies*. Oxon; New York: Routledge.

Helmke, G. and Levitsky, S. (2006) Introduction. In: Helmke, G. and Levitsky, S. (eds). *Informal Institutions and Democracy. Lessons from Latin America*. Baltimore, MD: Johns Hopkins University Press.

Hernández, A. and Canessa, A. (2012) Identidades indígenas y relaciones de género en Mesoamérica y la Región Andina. In: Hernández, A. and Canessa, A. (eds). *Género, complementariedades y exclusiones en Mesoamérica y los Andes*. Lima: Abya-Yala; IGWIA.

Hernández, A. (2008) Feminismos poscoloniales: reflexiones desde el sur del Río Bravo. In: Suárez, L. and Hernández, A. (eds). *Descolonizando el Feminismo. Teorías y prácticas desde los márgenes*. Madrid: Ediciones Cátedra, Universitat de Valencia.

Hernández, A. (2002) Indigenous Law and Identity Politics in Mexico: Indigenous Men's and Women's Struggles for a Multicultural Nation. *PoLAR* 25(1), 90–109.

Hooker, M. (1975) *Legal Pluralism: An Introduction to Colonial and Neo-Colonial Laws*. Oxford: Clarendon Press.

Huarcacho, F. (2011) *Detrás del cristal con que se mira: Mujeres del Altiplano, órdenes normativos e interlegalidad*. La Paz: Coordinadora de la Mujer.

Hueber, S. (2009) Dinámicas post-constitucionales: cambios en la administración de justicia indígena en Ecuador después de la reforma constitucional de 1998. *Nueva Antropología* XXII(71), 73–91.

Hurtado, J., and du Puit, J. (2006) Derecho Penal y Diferencias Culturales: Perspectiva General con respecto a la situación en el Perú. In: Pontífica Universidad Católica del Perú; Universidad de Friburgo, Suiza (eds). *Derecho penal y pluralidad cultural. Anuario de Derecho Penal 2006*. Lima: Fondo Editorial.

ICHRP – International Council on Human Rights Policy (2009) *When Legal Worlds Overlap: Human Rights, State and Non-State Law*. Versoix: ICHRP.

IDL (2010) *Balance de la justicia 2009-2010. ¿Cómo estuvo la justicia en el Perú?* Lima: IDL.

IDL (2005) *La justicia de paz en los Andes*. Lima: IDL.

IDLO – International Development Law Organization (2013) *Accessing Justice: Models, Strategies and Best Practices on Women's Empowerment.* Rome: IDLO.
Immergut, E. (1998) The Theoretical Core of the New Institutionalism. *Politics and Society* 26(1), 5–34.
INE (2013) *Bolivia: Características de Población y Vivienda. Censo Nacional de Población y Vivienda 2012.* La Paz: INE.
INE (2009) *Encuesta Nacional de Demográfía y Salud 2008.* La Paz: Ministerio de Salud y Deportes; INE.
INEC (2011a) *Encuesta Nacional de Relaciones Familiares y Violencia de Género contra las Mujeres.* Quito: INEC.
INEC (2011b) *Primera Encuesta Nacional de Relaciones Familiares y Violencia de Género contra las Mujeres – Imbabura.* Quito: INEC.
INEI (2012) *Perú: Encuesta Demográfica y de Salud Familiar – ENDES 2012 Nacional y Departamental.* Lima: INEI.
INEI (2009) *Perfil Sociodemográfico del Departamento de Cusco.* Cusco: INEI.
Inksater, K. (2010) Indigenous Justice Systems in Latin America. *Journal of Legal Pluralism and Unofficial Law* 60, 105–142.
Iturralde, D. (1990) Movimiento indio, costumbre jurídica y usos de la ley. In: Stavenhagen, R. and Iturralde, D. (eds). *Entre la ley y la costumbre: El derecho consuetudinario indígena en América Latina.* México, DF; San José: Instituto Indigenísta Interamericano; Instituto Interamericano de Derechos Humanos.
Jasper, J. (1997) *The Art of Moral Protest: Culture, Biography, and Creativity in Social Movements.* Chicago, IL: University of Chicago Press.
Jelin, E. (ed.) (1990) Women and Social Change in Latin America. London; Geneva: Zed Books; UNRISD.
Jenkins, C. (1983) Resource Mobilization Theory and the Study of Social Movement. *Annual Review of Sociology* 9, 527–553.
Jepperson, R. (1991) Institutions, Institutional Effects, and Institutionalism. In: Powell, W. and DiMaggio, P. (eds). *The New Institutionalism in Organizational Analysis.* Chicago, IL: University of Chicago Press.
Johnson, H., Ollus, N. and Nevala, S. (2008) *Violence Against Women. An International Perspective.* New York: Springer.
Justicia Nuestra. Mujeres Indígenas Latinoamericanas y el Acceso a la Justicia. (2009). [DVD] Ecuador: La Mirona – ALER; UNIFEM.
Kent, A. (2007) Custody, Maintenance, and Succession: The Internalization of Women's and Children's Rights under Customary Law in Africa. *Michigan Journal of International Law* 28, 507–538.
Khadiagala, L. (2001) The Failure of Popular Justice in Uganda: Local Councils and Women's Property Rights. *Development and Change* 32(1), 55–76.
King, G., Keohane, R. and Verba, S. (1994) *Designing Social Inquiry. Scientific Inference in Qualitative Research.* Princeton, NJ: Princeton University Press.
Kishor, S., and Johnson, K. (2004) *Profiling Domestic Violence. A Multi-Country Study.* Calverton, MD: ORC Macro.
Koopmans, R. ([2004] 2007) Protest in Time and Space: The Evolution of Waves of Contention. In: Snow, D., Soule, S. and Kriesi, H. (eds). *The Blackwell Companion to Social Movements.* Oxford: Blackwell Publishing.
Koopmans, R. (1999) Political. Opportunity. Structure. Some Splitting to Balance the Lumping. *Sociological Forum* 14(1), 93–105.

Krasner, S. (1984) Approaches to the State: Alternative Conceptions and Historical Dynamics. *Comparative Politics* 16(2), 223–246.

Kriesi, H. ([2004] (2007) Political Context and Opportunity. In: Snow, D., Soule, S. and Kriesi, H. (eds). *The Blackwell Companion to Social Movements.* Oxford: Blackwell Publishing.

Kuppe, R. (2009) Legal Pluralism – Basic Concepts and Debates. In: Austrian Association for the Middle East Hammer-Purgstall (ed.). *Family, Law and Religion. Debates in the Muslim World and Europe and their Implications for Co-operation and Dialogue.* Vienna: Österreichische Entwicklungszusammenarbeit.

Kyed, H. (2011) Introduction to the Special Issue: Legal Pluralism and International Development Interventions. *Journal of Legal Pluralism* 63, 1–23.

Kyle, D. (2001) La diaspora del comercio otavaleño: Capital social y empresa transnacional. *Ecuador Debate* 54, 85–110.

Kymlicka, W. (1995) *Multicultural Citizenship: A Liberal Theory of Minority Rights.* Oxford: Oxford University Press.

Lalander, R. (2010) *Retorno de los Runakuna: Cotacachi y Otavalo.* Quito: Abya Yala.

Lang, M., and Kucia, A. (eds) (2009) *Mujeres indígenas y justicia ancestral.* Quito: UNIFEM.

LAPOP – Latin American Public Opinion Project (2012) The *Political Culture of Democracy in the Americas, 2012: Towards Equality of Opportunity.* Nashville, TN: Vanderbilt University.

Lauth, H.-J. (2000) Informal Institutions and Democracy. *Democratization* 7(4), 21–50.

Laurie, N., Andolina, R. and Radcliffe, S. (2002) The Excluded 'Indigenous'? The Implications of Multi-Ethnic Politics for Water Reform in Bolivia. In: Sieder, R. (ed.). *Multiculturalism in Latin America: Indigenous Rights, Diversity and Democracy.* Houndmills; Basingstoke; New York: Palgrave Macmillan.

Levitt, P., and Merry, S. (2009) Vernacularization on the ground: local uses of women's rights in Peru, China, India, and the United States. *Global Networks* 9(4), 441–461.

Lewis, O., and Steinmo, S. (2012) How Institutions Evolve: Evolutionary Theory and Institutional Change. *Polity* 44(3), 314–339.

Lieberman, R. (2002) Ideas, Institutions, and Political Order: Explaining Political Change. *American Political Science Review* 96(4), 697–712.

Lijphart, A. (1975) The Comparable-Cases Strategy in Comparable Research. *Comparative Political Studies* 8, 158–177.

Lijphart, A. (1971) Comparative Politics and the Comparative Method. *American Political Science Review* 65, 682–693.

Llaja, J. (2012) La violencia contra las mujeres en el Perú. In: Alméras, D. and Coral, M. (coord.). *Si no se cuenta, no cuenta. Información sobre la violencia contra las mujeres.* Santiago de Chile: CEPAL.

Llasag, R. (2012a) Justicia indígena ¿delito o construcción de la plurinacionalidad?: La Cocha. In: Santos, B. de and Grijalva, A. (eds). *Justicia indígena, plurinacionalidad e interculturalidad en Ecuador.* Quito: Abya Yala; Fundación Rosa Luxemburg.

Llasag, R. (2012b) Movimiento indígena del Ecuador a partir del siglo XX: visibilizando el resurgir, sus avances y retrocesos. In: Santos, B. de and Grijalva, A. (eds). *Justicia indígena, plurinacionalidad e interculturalidad en Ecuador.* Quito: Abya Yala; Fundación Rosa Luxemburg.

Lovatón, D. (2005) Justicia de paz en los Andes. *Ideele* 169, 69–79.

Lowndes, V. (2002) Institutionalism. In: Marsh, D. and Stoker, G. (eds). *Theory and Methods in Political Science.* 2nd Ed. Houndmills; New York: Palgrave Macmillan.

Lucero, J. (2007) Barricades and Articulations: Comparing Ecuadorian and Bolivian Indigenous Politics. In: Clark, K. and Becker, M. (eds). *Highland Indians and the State in Modern Ecuador.* Pittsburgh, PA: University of Pittsburgh Press.

Lucero, J., and García, M. (2006) Reflexiones sobre la autenticidad indígena, los movimientos sociales y el trabajo de campo en el Perú contemporáneo. Online: www.voltairenet.org/article144504.html (last access 10.06.2015).

Mahoney, J., and Thelen, K. (2010) A Theory of Gradual Institutional Change. In: Mahoney, J. and Thelen, K. (eds). *Explaining Institutional Change: Ambiguity, Agency and Power.* Cambridge: Cambridge University Press.

Mahoney, J. (2000) Path Dependence in Historical Sociology. *Theory and Society* 29, 507–548.

March, J., and Olsen, J. (1989) *Rediscovering Institutions: The Organizational Basis of Politics.* New York: Free Press.

March, J., and Olsen, J. (1984) The New Institutionalism: Organizational Factors in Political Life. *American Political Science Review* 78(3), 734–749.

Martínez, L. (1998) Comunidades y Tierra en Ecuador. *Ecuador Debate* 45, 173–188.

McAdam, D., Tarrow, S. and Tilly, C. (2001) *Dynamics of Contention.* Cambridge: Cambridge University Press.

McAdam, D., McCarthy, J. and Zald, M. (1996) Introduction: Opportunities, mobilizing structures, and framing processes – toward a synthetic, comparative perspective on social movements. In: McAdam, D., McCarthy, J. and Zald, M. (eds). *Comparative Perspectives on Social Movements: Political Opportunities, Mobilizing Structures, and Cultural Framings.* Cambridge: Cambridge University Press.

McAdam, D. (1996) Conceptual Origins, Current Problems, Future Directions. In: McAdam, D., McCarthy, J. and Zald, M. (eds). *Comparative Perspectives on Social Movements: Political Opportunities, Mobilizing Structures, and Cultural Framings.* Cambridge: Cambridge University Press.

McAdam, D. (1982) *Political Process and the Development of Black Insurgency, 1930–1970.* Chicago, IL: The University of Chicago Press.

McCarthy, J. (1996) Constraints and opportunities in adopting, adapting, and inventing. In: McAdam, D., McCarthy, J. and Zald, M. (eds). *Comparative Perspectives on Social Movements: Political Opportunities, Mobilizing Structures, and Cultural Framings.* Cambridge: Cambridge University Press.

McCarthy, J., and Zald, M. (1977) Resource Mobilization and Social Movements. *American Journal of Sociology* 82, 1212–1241.

McCarthy, J., and Zald, M. (1973) *The Trend of Social Movements in America: Professionalization and Resources Mobilization.* Morristown, NJ: General Learning.

McNulty, S. (2013) Participatory Democracy? Exploring Peru's Efforts to Engage Civil Society in Local Governance. *Latin American Politics and Society* 55(3), 69–92.

Meisch, L. (1998) The Reconquest of Otavalo Ecuador: Indigenous Economic Gains and New Power Relations. In: Barry, I. (ed.). *Research in Economic Anthropology.* Stamford, CT: JAI Press.

Meisch, L. (1987) *Otavalo: Weaving, Costume and the Market.* Quito: Imprenta Mariscal.

Melucci, A. (1985) The Symbolic Challenge of Contemporary Movements. *Social Research* 54, 789–816.

Mendoza, M. (2009) Estado de Relacionamiento en Bolivia. In: Cóndor, E. (coord.): *Estado de la relación entre justicia indígena y justicia estatal en los países andinos: estudio de casos en Colombia, Perú, Ecuador y Bolivia.* Lima: CAJ.

Merry, S. (2006a) *Human Rights and Gender Violence: Translating International Law into Local Justice.* Chicago, IL: University of Chicago Press.

Merry, S. (2006b) Transnational Human Rights and Local Activism: Mapping the Middle. *American Anthropologist* 108(1), 38–51.

Merry, S. (2003) Rights Talk and the Experience of Law: Implementing Women's Human Rights to Protection from Violence. *Human Rights Quarterly* 25, 343–381.

Merry, S. (2001) Changing rights, changing culture. In: Cowan, J., Dembour, M.-B. and Wilson, R. (eds). *Culture and Rights: Anthropological Perspectives.* Cambridge: Cambridge University Press.

Merry, S. (1997) Global Human Rights and Local Social Movements in Legally Plural World. *Canadian Journal of Law and Society* 12, 27–271.

Merry, S. (1992) Anthropology, Law, and Transnational Processes. *Annual Review of Anthropology* 21, 357–379.

Merry, S. (1991) Review Essay: Law and Colonialism. *Law and Society Review* 25(4), 889–922.

Merry, S. (1988) Legal Pluralism. *Law and Society Review* 22, 869–96.

Meuser, M., and Nagel, U. (2009) Das Experteninterview – konzeptionelle Grundlagen und methodische Anlage. In: Pickel, S. *et al.* (eds). *Methoden der vergleichenden Politik- und Sozialwissenschaft: Neue Entwicklungen und Anwendungen.* Wiesbaden: VS Verlag für Sozialwissenschaften.

Meyer, D. (2004) Protest and Political Opportunities. *Annual Review of Sociology* 30, 125–145.

Meyer, J., and Rowan, B. (1977) Institutionalized organizations: formal structure as myth and ceremony. *American Journal of Sociology* 83, 340–363.

Ministerio de Autonomías, Viceministerio de Autonomías Indígena Originaria Campesinas y Organización Territorial, Dirección General de Autonomías Indígena Originaria Campesinas (n.d.) *Resumen II Encuentro Nacional de Mujeres de los Municipios en Conversión a las AIOC.* Sucre, 24 y 25 de agosto 2011. Unpublished.

Ministerio de Justicia, Viceministerio de Igualdad de Oportunidades (2008) *Plan Nacional para la igualdad de oportunidades "Mujeres construyendo la Nueva Bolivia para Vivir Bien".* La Paz: Ministerio de Justicia.

Ministerio de la Mujer y Desarrollo Social (2009) *Plan Nacional Contra la Violencia Hacia la Mujer 2009–2015.* Lima: Ministerio de la Mujer y Desarrollo Social.

Minuta de reunión entre UNIFEM y el Proyecto "Implementación del reglamento para una buena convivencia en las comunidades indígenas de Cotacachi" (18.09.2008). Unpublished.

Molina, R. (1999) *El derecho consuetudinario en Bolivia. Una propuesta de ley de reconcocimiento de la justicia comunitaria.* Justicia Comunitaria no. 9. La Paz: Ministerio de Justicia y Derechos Humanos.

Moore, S. (2001) Certainties Undone: Fifty Turbulent Years of Legal Anthropology, 1949–1999. *Journal of the Royal Anthropological Institute* 7, 95–116.

Moore, S. (1973) Law and Social Change: The Semi-Autonomous Social Field as an Appropriate Subject of Study. *Law and Society Review* 7(1), 719–746.

Morris, A., and Staggenborg, S. ([2004] 2007) Leadership in Social Movement. In: Snow, D., Soule, S. and Kriesi, H. (eds). *The Blackwell Companion to Social Movements.* Oxford: Blackwell Publishing.

Morrison, A., Ellsberg, M. and Bott, S. (2007) Addressing Gender-Based Violence: A Critical Review of Interventions. *The World Bank Research Observer* 22(1), 25–51.

Motta, S. (2009) Old Tools and New Movements in Latin America: Political Science as Gatekeeper or Intellectual Illuminator? *Latin American Politics and Society* 51(1), 31–56.

Municipalidad Distrital de Tupac Amaru (2011) *Plan de Desarrollo Concertado al 2018.* Distrito Tupac Amaru: Municipalidad Distrital de Tupac Amaru.

Municipio de Otavalo (2002) *Plan de Vida Otavalo.* Otavalo: Municipio de Otavalo.

Murra, J. (1972) El control vertical de un máximo de pisos ecológicos en las sociedades andinas. Re-edited in: Murra, J. (2002) *El mundo andino. Población, medio ambiente y economía.* Lima: IEP; Pontífica Universidad Católica del Perú.

Nájera, M. (2008) *Creación de una estrategia educomunicativa para la Coordinadora de Mujeres Urbanas del cantón Cotacachi.* Tesis Universidad Politécnica Salesiana, Quito, Ecuador.

North, D. (2005) *Understanding the Process of Economic Change.* Princeton, NJ: Princeton University Press.

North, D. (1991) Institutions. *Journal of Economic Perspectives* 5, 97–112.

North, D. (1990) *Institutions, Institutional Change and Economic Performance.* Cambridge: Cambridge University Press.

Nostas, M., and Sanabria, C. (2009) *Detrás del cristal con que se mira: Órdenes normativos e interlegalidad. Mujeres Quechuas, Aymaras, Sirionó, Trinitarias, Chimane, Chiquitanas y Ayoreas.* La Paz: Coordinadora de la Mujer.

Nyamu-Musembi, C. (2003) *Review of Experience in Engaging with 'non-state' justice systems in East Africa.* Commissioned by Governance Division of the UK Department for International Development. Sussex: Institute for Development Studies. Online: http://gsdrc.ids.ac.uk/docs/open/DS37.pdf (last access 10.06.2015).

O'Donnell, G. (1999) Polyarchies and the (Un)Rule of Law in Latin America". In: Méndez, J., O'Donnell, G. and Pinheiro, P. (eds). *(Un) Rule of Law and the Underprivileged in Latin America.* Notre Dame, IN: University of Notre Dame Press.

OECD – Organization for Economic Co-operation and Development (2007) *Enhancing the Delivery of Justice and Security.* Paris: OECD.

Offe, K. (1985) New Social Movements: Challenging the Boundaries of Institutional Politics. *Social Research* 54, 817–868.

Okin, S. (1999) Is Multiculturalism Bad for Women? In: Cohen, J. and Howard, M. (eds). *Is Multiculturalism Bad for Women?* Princeton, NJ: Princeton University Press.

Olsen, J. (2009) Change and Continuity: An Institutional Approach to Institutions of Democratic Government. *European Political Science Review* 1(1), 3–32.

Ordenanza Sustitutiva para el Sumak Ally Kawsay (2012). Cantón Santa Ana de Cotacachi. Unpublished.

Orellana, R. (2005) Derecho indígena-campesino: producto y proceso de reinvenciones interlegales. In: Ardilla, E. *et al.* (eds). *Memorias II Conferencia Internacional de Justicia Comunitaria "Construir Democracia Hoy".* Bogotá: Red de Justicia Comunitaria y Tratamiento de Conflicto.

Orellana, R. (2004) *Interlegalidad y Campos Jurídicos: Discurso y derecho en la configuración de ordenes semiautónomos en comunidades quechuas de Bolivia.* Dissertation. University of Amsterdam, WOTRO Netherland Foundation for the Advancement of Tropical Research.

Organización de Estados Americanos, Comisión Interamericana de Derechos Humanos (2007) *Acceso a la Justicia e Inclusión Social. El camino hacia el fortalecimiento de la democracia en Bolivia.* Washington D.C.: OEA.

Organización de los Estados Americanos/Mecanismo de Seguimiento de la Convención de Belém do Pará (2012) *Segundo Informe Hemisférico sobre la Implementación de la Convención de Belém do Pará.* Washington, D.C.: MESECVI.

Organización de Mujeres Campesinas de Mojocoya (2011) *Sistematización de propuestas de las mujeres para el estatuto autonómico indígena originario campesino de Mojocoya.* Sucre: Proagro, Fundación Tierra. Unpublished.

Ortiz, S. (2011) *¿Comuneros Kichwas o ciudadanos ecuatorianos? La ciudadanía y los derechos de los indígenas de Otavalo y Cotacachi, 1990–2009.* Tesis para obtener el título de doctor en ciencias sociales con mención en estudios políticos. FLACSO, Quito, Ecuador.

Ospina, P. (2012) Promesas temporales. Cambio del régimen de acumulación en Ecuador, propuestas y realizaciones de la revolución ciudadana. In: López, L. *et al.* (eds). *¿Otros Mundos Posibles? Crisis, Gobiernos progresistas, alternativas de sociedad.* Medellín: Fundación Rosa Luxemburg; Universidad Nacional de Colombia, Sede Medellín, Facultad de Ciencias Humanas y Económicas.

Ospina, P. (2011) Corporativismo, Estado y revolución ciudadana. El Ecuador de Rafael Correa. In: Büschges, C., Kaltmeier, O. and Thies, S. (eds). *Culturas políticas en la región andina.* Madrid: Iberoamericana Vervuert.

Pallares, A. (2007) Contesting Membership: Citizenship, Pluriculturalism(s), and the Contemporary Indigenous Movement. In: Clark, K. and Becker, M. (eds). *Highland Indians and the State in Modern Ecuador.* Pittsburgh, PA: University of Pittsburgh Press.

Paredes, J. (2012) La opresión que se recicla. In: Coordinadora de la Mujer (ed.). *Mujeres en diálogo: Avanzando hacia la despatriarcalización.* La Paz: Coordinadora de la Mujer.

Paredes, J. (2010) *Hilando Fino Desde el Feminismo Comunitario.* La Paz: Comunidad Mujeres Creando Comunidad.

Peters, G. (1999) *Institutional Theory in Political Science: The 'New Institutionalism'.* London: Pinter.

Pequeño, A. (2009a)Vivir violencia, cruzar los límites. Prácticas y discursos en torno a la violencia contra mujeres en comunidades indígenas de Ecuador. In: Pequeño, A. (ed.). *Participación y políticas de mujeres indígenas en América Latina.* Quito: FLACSO – Sede Ecuador; Ministerio de Cultura del Ecuador.

Pequeño, A. (2009b) Violencia de género y mecanismos de resolución comunitaria en comunidades indígenas de la sierra ecuatoriana. In: Lang, M. and Kucia, A. (eds). *Mujeres indígenas y justicia ancestral.* Quito: UNIFEM.

Phillips, A. (2001) *Multiculturalism, Universalism and the Claims of Democracy.* Democracy, Governance and Human Rights Programme Paper No. 7. Geneva: United Nations Research Institute for Social Development.

Picolli, E. (2008) El pluralismo jurídico y político en Perú: el caso de las Rondas Campesinas de Cajamarca. *ICONOS Revista de Ciencias Sociales* 31, 27–41.

Picq, M. (2013) Indigenous Worlding: Kichwa women pluralizing sovereignty. In: Tickner, A. and Blaney, D. (eds). *Claiming the International.* London; New York: Routledge.

Picq, M. (2012) Between the Dock and a Hard Place: Hazards and Opportunities of Legal Pluralism for Indigenous Women in Ecuador. *Latin American Politics and Society* 54(2), 1–33.

Pierson, P. (2004) *Politics in Time: History, Institutions, and Social Analysis.* Princeton, NJ: Princeton University.

Pierson, P. (2000) Increasing Returns, Path Dependence, and the Study of Politics. *American Political Science Review* 94(2), 251–67.

Poole, D. (2009) Justicia y comunidad en los márgenes del Estado peruano. In: Sandoval, P. (ed.). *Repensando la subalternidad. Miradas críticas desde/sobre América Latina.* Lima: IEP.

Popitz, H. ([1980] 2006) *Soziale Normen.* Frankfurt a.M.: Suhrkamp.

Postero, N. (2010) The Struggle to Create a Radical Democracy in Bolivia. *Latin American Research Review* 45, 59–78.

Poveda, C. (2009) Reflexiones básicas e ideas iniciales sobre el Proyecto de Ley de Coordinación y Cooperación entre el Sistema Jurídico Ordinario e Indígena. In: Espinosa, C. and Caicedo, D. (eds). *Derechos Ancestrales. Justicia en Contextos Plurinacionales.* Serie Justicia y Derechos Humanos, Neoconstitucionalismo y Sociedad. Quito: Ministerio de Justicia y Derechos Humanos.

Presidente Constitucional de la República (2007) *Decreto Presidencial N° 620. Plan Nacional de Erradicación de la Violencia de Género hacia Niñez, Adolescencia y Mujeres.* Quito: Presidente Constitucional de la República.

Primera Acta de Elección y Posesión de la Asamblea Constituyente Autonómica Originario Campesina de Mojocoya (05.07.2009). Mojocoya. Unpublished.

Proyecto Estatuto Autonómico Indígena Originario Campesino de Mojocoya (2012). Mojocoya. Unpublished.

Przeworski, A., and Teune, H. (1970) *The logic of comparative social inquiry.* New York: John Wiley.

Radcliffe, S. (2014) *Mujeres indígenas y afroecuatorianas, compartiendo preocupaciones y agendas.* Quito: GIZ; Oxfam.

Ragin, C. (2000) *Fuzzy-set social science.* Chicago, IL: University of Chicago Press.

Ragin, C. (1987) *The Comparative Method: Moving Beyond Qualitative and Quantitative Strategies.* Berkeley, CA: University of California Press.

Reglamento Interno de Debates y Funcionamiento de la Asamblea Autonómica Deliberativa de Tarabuco (2011). Tarabuco. Unpublished.

Reutenbach, C. (2010) Deep Legal Pluralism in South Africa: Judicial Accommodation of Non-State Law. *Journal of Legal Pluralism and Unofficial Law* 60, 143–177.

Richards, P. (2005) The Politics of Gender, Human Rights, and Being Indigenous in Chile. *Gender and Society* 19(2), 199–220.

Riker W. (1995) The experience of creating institutions: the framing of the United States Constitution. In: Knight, J. and Sened, I. (eds). *Explaining Social Institutions.* Ann Arbor, MI: University of Michigan Press.

Rivera, S. ([1993] 2010) Violencias encubiertas en Bolivia. In: Rivera, S. (ed.). *Violencias (re)encubiertas en Bolivia.* Santander: Otroamerica.

Rivera, S. ([1990] 2010) Democracia liberal y democracia del ayllu: El caso del

Norte de Potosí, Bolivia. In: Rivera, S. (ed.). *Violencias (re)encubiertas en Bolivia.* Santander: Otroamerica.

Roberts, S. (1998) Against legal pluralism: some reflections on the contemporary enlargement of the legal domain. *Journal of Legal Pluralism* 42, 95–106.

Roberts, S. (1979) *Order and Dispute: an Introduction to Legal Anthropology.* Harmondsworth: Penguin Books.

Robles, R. (2002) *Legislación perunana sobre comunidades campesinas.* Lima: Fondo Editorial de la Facultad de Ciencias Sociales, UNMSM.

Rodríguez, C. (2010) Ethnicity.gov: Global Governance, Indigenous Peoples and the Right to Prior Consultation in Social Minefields. *Indiana Journal of Global Legal Studies* 18(1), 263–305.

Roitman, K. (2008) *Hybridity, Mestizaje, and Montubios in Ecuador.* QEH Working Paper 165. Queen Elizabeth House, University of Oxford.

Ross, L. (1977) The intuitive psychologist and his shortcomings: Distortions in the attribution process. In: Berkowitz, L. (ed.). *Advances in experimental social psychology.* Vol. 10. New York: Academic Press.

Rousseau, S. (2010) Populism from Above, Populism from Below: Gender Politics Under Alberto Fujimori and Evo Morales. In: Kampwirth, K. (ed.). *Gender and Populism in Latin America.* University Park, PA: Pennsylvania State University Press.

Rueschemeyer, D. (2009) *Usable Theory: Analytical Tools for Social and Political Research.* Princeton, NJ: Princeton University Press.

Ruiz, J. (2010) Algunos comentarios al Acuerdo Plenario de la Corte Suprema sobre Rondas Campesinas. In: La Rosa, J. and Ruiz, J. (eds). *La facultad jurisdiccional de las rondas campesinas. Comentarios al Acuerdo Plenario de la Corte Suprema que reconoce facultades jurisdiccionales a las rondas campesinas.* Lima: IDL.

Sagines, T. (1985) De la descendencia a la resistencia: Las etnias en los valles de Larecaja. In: IEFA and CERES (eds). *Los Andes orientales: historia de un olvido.* La Paz: IEFA; CERES.

Salgado, J. (2012) El reto de la igualdad: género y justicia indígena, in: Santos, B. de and Grijalva, A. (eds). *Justicia indígena, plurinacionalidad e interculturalidad en Ecuador.* Quito: Abya Yala; Fundación Rosa Luxemburg.

Salgado, J. (ed.) (2002) *Justicia Indígena: Aportes para un debate.* Quito: AbyaYala.

Salgado, R. (2000) La Ley 103 Contra la Violencia a la Mujer y la Familia y la administración de la justicia. In: Herrera, G. (coord.): *Las fisuras del patriarcado: Reflexiones sobre Feminismo y Derecho.* Quito: FLACSO – Sede Ecuador.

Salomon, F. (1981) Weavers of Otavalo. In: Whitten, N. (ed.). *Cultural Transformations and Ethnicity in Modern Ecuador.* Urbana, IL: University of Illinois Press.

Sánchez, E., and Jaramillo, I. (2009) La jurisdicción especial indígena. In: Espinosa, C. and Caicedo, D. (eds). *Derechos Ancestrales: Justicia en Contextos Plurinacionales.* Serie Justicia y Derechos Humanos, Neoconstitucionalismo y Sociedad. Quito: Ministerio de Justicia y Derechos Humanos.

Sánchez, E. (2004) *Justicia y pueblos indígenas de Colombia: La tutela como medio para la construcción de entendimiento intercultural.* 2nd Ed. Bogotá: UNIJUS; Universidad Nacional de Colombia.

Sánchez, M. (coord.) (2005) *La doble mirada: voces e historias de mujeres indígenas latinoamericanas.* Mexico D.F.: UNIFEM; Instituto de Liderazgo de Simone de Beauvoir.

Santos, B. de (2012) Cuando los excluidos tienen Derecho: justicia indígena, plurinacionalidad e interulturalidad. In: Santos, B. de and Exeni, J. (eds). *Justicia indígena, plurinacionalidad e interculturalidad en Bolivia*. Quito: Abya Yala; Fundación Rosa Luxemburg.

Santos, B. de (2010) *Refundación del Estado en América Latina: Perspectivas desde una epistemología del Sur*. Lima: Instituto Internacional de Derecho y Sociedad; Programa Democracia y Transformación Global.

Santos, B. de, and Rodríguez, C. (eds) (2005) *Law and Globalization from Below: Towards a Cosmopolitan Legality*. New York: Cambridge University Press.

Santos, B. de (1987) Law: A Map of Misreading. Toward a Postmodern Conception of Law. *Journal of Law and Society* 14(3), 279–302.

Sartori, P., and Shahar, I. (2012) Legal Pluralism in Muslim-Majority Colonies: Mapping the Terrain. *Journal of the Economic and Social History of the Orient* 55, 637–663.

Sartori, G. (1991) Comparing and Miscomparing. *Journal of Theoretical Politics* 3(3), 243–257.

Schickler, E. (2001) *Disjointed Pluralism: Institutional Innovation and the Development of the U.S. Congress*. Princeton, NJ: Princeton University Press.

Schilling-Vacaflor, A. (2013) Prior Consultations in Plurinational Bolivia: Democracy, Rights and Real Life Experiences. *Latin American and Caribbean Ethnic Studies* 8(2), 202–222.

Schilling-Vacaflor, A., and Kuppe. R (2012) Plurinational Constitutionalism: A New Era of Indigenous-State Relations? In: Nolte, D. and Schilling-Vacaflor, A. (eds). *New Constitutionalism in Latin America: Promises and Practices*. Farnham: Ashgate.

Schilling-Vacaflor, A. (2010) *Recht als umkämpftes Terrain. Die neue Verfassung und indigene Völker in Bolivien*. Reihe Studien zu Lateinamerika, 7. Baden-Baden: Nomos-Verlag.

Schmidt, V. (2010) Taking Ideas and Discourse Seriously: Explaining Change Through Discursive Institutionalism as the Fourth "New Institutionalism". *European Political Science Review* 2, 1–25.

Schmidt, V. (2008) Discursive Institutionalism: The Explanatory Power of Ideas and Discourse. *Annual Review of Political Science* 11, 303–326.

Schneiberg, M., and Lounsbury, M. (2008) Social Movements and Institutional Analysis. In: Greenwood, R., Oliver, C., Sahlin-Andersson, K. and Suddaby, R. (eds). *The Handbook of Organizational Institutionalism*. London: Sage Publications.

Schneiberg, M., and Clemens, E. (2006) The Typical Tools for the Job: Research Strategies for Institutional Analysis. *Sociological Theory* 24(3), 195–227.

Schneiberg, M. (2005) Combining New Institutionalisms: Explaining Institutional Change in American Property Insurance. *Sociological Forum* 20(1), 93–137.

Schönbohm, H. (2011) El pluralismo jurídico – una comparación a nivel de América Latina. In: Cóndor, E. (coord.). *Los Derechos Individuales y Derechos Colectivos en la Construcción del Pluralismo Jurídico en América Latina*. La Paz: Fundación Konrad Adenauer.

Scott, R. (2001) *Institutions and Organizations*. 2nd Ed. Thousand Oaks, CA: Sage.

Scott, R., Meyer, J. and Boli, J. (1994) *Institutional Environments and Organizations*. Thousand Oaks, CA: Sage.

Shepsle, K. (2001) A Comment on Institutional Change. *Journal of Theoretical Politics* 13(3), 321–325.

Shepsle, K. (1989) Studying Institutions: Some Lessons from the Rational Choice Approach. *Journal of Theoretical Politics* 1, 131–147.

Shachar, A. (2001) *Multicultural Jurisdictions: Cultural Differences and Women's Rights.* Cambridge: Cambridge University Press.

Sieder, R. (2013) Sexual violence and gendered subjectivities: indigenous women's search for justice in Guatemala. In: Sieder, R. and McNeish, J.-A. (eds). *Gender Justice and Legal Pluralities: Latin American and African Perspectives.* Oxon, New York: Routledge.

Sieder, R., and McNeish, J.-A. (eds) (2013) *Gender Justice and Legal Pluralities: Latin American and African Perspectives.* Oxon, New York: Routledge.

Sieder, R., and Sierra, M. (2010) *Indigenous Women's Access to Justice in Latin America.* CMI Working paper 2010:2. Bergen: CMI.

Sieder, R., and Macleod, M. (2009) Género, derecho y cosmovisión maya en Guatemala. *Desacatos* 31, 51–70.

Sieder, R. (ed.) (2002) *Multiculturalism in Latin America: Indigenous Rights, Diversity and Democracy.* Bakingstoke; Hampshire; New York: Palgrave Macmillan.

Sierra, M. (2013) Indigenous women fight for justice: gender rights and legal pluralism in Mexico. In: Sieder, R. and McNeish, J.-A. (eds). *Gender Justice and Legal Pluralities: Latin American and African Perspectives.* Oxon; New York: Routledge.

Sierra, M. (2008) Mujeres indígenas, justicia y derechos: los retos de una justicia intercultural. *ICONOS Revista de Ciencias Sociales* 12(2), 15–26.

Sierra, M. (ed.) (2004) *Haciendo Justicia: Interlegalidad, derecho y género en regiones indígenas.* México D.F.: CIESAS.

Sierra, M. (1997) Esencialismo y autonomía: paradojas de las reivindicaciones indígenas. *Alteridades* 7(14), 131–143.

Simon, M. (2013) *The Challenge of Legal Pluralism: Local Dispute Settlement and the Indian-State Relationship in Ecuador.* Doctoral Dissertation. University of Utrecht.

Simon, M. (2012) Legal pluralism and the continuing quest for legal certainty in Ecuador: A case study from the Andean Highlands. *Oñati Socio-legal Series* [Online] 2(7), 57–84. Online: http://ssrn.com/abstract=2009450 (last access 10.06.2015).

Simon, M. (2009) *Legal pluralism and interlegality in Ecuador: The La Cocha murder case.* Cuadernos del CEDLA No. 24. Amsterdam: CEDLA.

SINASEC – Sistema Nacional de Seguridad Ciudadana (2009) *Seguridad Ciudadana compromiso de todos "Sólo faltas tú".* Lima: SINASEC.

Skolnick, J. (1969) *The Politics of Protest.* New York: Ballantine.

Smelser, N. (1962) *Theory of Collective Behavior.* New York: Free Press.

Snow, D., Soule, S. and Kriesi, H. ([2004] 2007) Mapping the Terrain. In: Snow, D., Soule, S. and Kriesi, H. (eds). *The Blackwell Companion to Social Movements.* Oxford: Blackwell Publishing.

Snow, D., and Benford, R. (1988) Ideology, Frame Resonance, and Participant Mobilization. *International Social Movement Research* 1, 197–217.

Speed, S., Blackwell, M., Hernández, R., Sieder, R., Sierra, M., Ramirez, R., Macleod, M. and Herrera J. (2009) Remapping Gender, Justice, and Rights in the Indigenous Americas: Toward a Comparative Analysis and Collaborative Methodology. *Journal of Latin American and Caribbean Anthropology* 14(2), 300–331.

Speed, S. (2008) *Rights in Rebellion: Indigenous Struggle and Human Rights in Chiapas.* Stanford, CA: Stanford University Press.

Speed, S., Hernández, A. and Stephen, L. (eds) (2006) *Dissident Women: Gender and Cultural Politics in Chiapas.* Austin, TX: University of Texas Press.

Spiertz, J. (1991) The Transformation of Traditional Law: A Tale of People's Participation in Irrigation Management on Bali. *Landscape and Urban Planning* 20, 189–196.

Spinner-Halev, J. (1994) *The Boundaries of Citizenship: Race, Ethnicity and Nationality in the Liberal State.* Baltimore, MD: Johns Hopkins University Press.

Starr, J., and Collier, J. (1989) *History and Power in the Study of Law: New Directions in Legal Anthropology.* Ithaca, London: Cornell University Press.

Starr, J., and Collier, J. (1987) Historical Studies of Legal Change. *Current Anthropology* 28(3), 367–372.

Stavenhagen, R. (2006) *Report of the Special Rapporteur on the situation of human rights and fundamental freedoms of indigenous people.* UN Economic and Social Council. Commission on Human Rights. Sixty-second session. 16 February 2006. UN Doc. E/CN.4/2006/78.

Stavenhagen, R. (1990) Derecho consuetudinario indígena en América Latina. In: Stavenhagen, R. and Iturralde, D. (eds). *Entre la ley y la costumbre: El derecho consuetudinario indígena en América Latina.* México, DF; San José: Instituto Indigenísta Interamericano; Instituto Interamericano de Derechos Humanos.

Steinmo, S. (2008) Historical Institutionalism. In: Porta, Donatella della and Keating, M. (eds). *Approaches and Methodologies in the Social Sciences: A Pluralist Perspective.* Cambridge: Cambridge University Press.

Steinmo, S., Thelen, K. and Longstreth, F. (eds) (1992) *Structuring Politics: Historical Institutionalism in Comparative Analysis.* Cambridge: Cambridge University Press.

Stephen, L. (2006) Indigenous Women's Activism in Oaxaca and Chiapas. In: Speed, S., Hernández, A. and Stephen, L. (eds). Dissident *Women: Gender and Cultural Politics in Chiapas.* Austin, TX: University of Texas Press.

Streek, W. (2009) *Institutions in History: Bringing Capitalism Back In.* MPIfG Discussion Paper 09/8. MPIfG: Köln.

Streeck, W., and Thelen, K. (2005) *Beyond Continuity: Institutional Change in Advanced Political Economies.* Oxford: Oxford University Press.

Ströbele-Gregor, J. (2004) Das Schweigen brechen: Indigene Frauen und häusliche Gewalt – Wandlungsprozesse im Bewusstsein über Menschenrechte in indigenen Gemeinschaften. In: Eckert, J (ed.). *Anthropologie der Konflikte. Georg Elwerts konflikttheoretische Thesen in der Diskussion.* Bielefeld: Transkript Verlag.

Subramanian, N. (2008) Legal Change and Gender Inequality: Changes on Muslim Family Law in India. *Law and Social Inquiry* 33(3), 631–672.

Sumak Kawsaipa Katikamachik – Reglamento para la buena convivencia comunitaria (n.d.). Cotacachi. Unpublished.

Swidler, A. (1986) Culture in Action: Symbols and Strategies. *American Sociological Review* 51(2), 273–286.

Tansey, O. (2009) Process Tracing and Elite Interviewing: A Case for Nonprobability Sampling. In: Pickel, S. *et al.* (eds). *Methoden der vergleichenden Politik- und Sozialwissenschaft: Neue Entwicklungen und Anwendungen.* Wiesbaden: VS Verlag für Sozialwissenschaften.

Tarrow, S. (2005) The *New Transnational Activism*. New York: Cambridge University Press.
Tarrow, S. (1998) *Power in Movement: Social Movements and Contentious Politics*. 2nd Ed. Cambridge: Cambridge University Press.
Tarrow, S. (1996) States and Opportunities: The Political Structuring of Social Movement. In: McAdam, D., McCarthy, J. and Zald, M. (eds). *Comparative Perspectives on Social Movement: Political Opportunities, Mobilizing Structures, and Cultural Framings*. Cambridge: Cambridge University Press.
Taylor, C. (1994) *Multiculturalism: Examining the Politics of Recognition*. Princeton, NJ: Princeton University Press.
Thelen, K. (2003) How Institutions Evolve. Insights from Comparative Historical Analysis. In: Mahoney, J. and Rueschemeyer, D. (eds). *Comparative Historical Analysis in the Social Sciences*. Cambridge: Cambridge University Press, 208–240.
Thelen, K. (1999) Historical Institutionalism in Comparative Politics. *Annual Review of Political Science* 2, 369–404.
The World Factbook (2013–14). Washington, DC: Central Intelligence Agency. Online: www.cia.gov/library/publications/resources/the-world-factbook/index.html (last access 10.06.2015).
The World Justice Project (2014) *Rule of Law Index 2014*. Washington, D.C.: The World Justice Project.
THOA ([1984] 1988) *El indio Santos Marka Tula, cacique principal de los ayllus de Qallapa y apoderado general de las comunidades originarias de la República*. La Paz: Ediciones del THOA.
Thorp, R., and Paredes, M. (2010) *Ethnicity and the Persistence of Inequality. The Case of Peru*. Houndmills, Basingstoke: Palgrave Macmillan.
Tilly, C., and Tarrow, S. (2007) *Contentious Politics*. Boulder, CO: Paradigm Publishers.
Tilly, C. (2006a) Afterword: Political Ethnography as Art and Science. *Qualitative Sociology* 29, 409–412.
Tilly, C. (2006b) *Regimes and Repertoires*. Chicago, IL: University of Chicago Press.
Tilly, C. (2001) Mechanisms in Political Processes. *Annual Review of Political Science* 4, 21–41.
Tilly, C. (1978) *From Mobilization to Revolution*. Reading: Addison-Wesley.
Touraine, A. (1977) *The Self-Production of Society*. Chicago, IL: University of Chicago Press.
Trujillo, J., Grijalva, A. and Endara X. (eds) (2001) *Justicia indígena en el Ecuador*. Quito: Universidad Andina Simón Bolívar.
Tsai, K. (2006) Adaptive Informal Institutions and Endogenous Institutional Change in China. *World Politics* 59(1), 116–41.
Tschalaer, M. (2010) Women Entering the Legal Landscape: Negotiating Legal Gender Reforms in a 'Tribal' Women's Forum in South Rajasthan, India. *Journal of Legal Pluralism and Unofficial Law* 60, 41–72.
Ubink, J., and McInerney, T. (2011) *Customary Justice: Perspectives on Legal Empowerment*. Rome: IDLO.
UK Department for International Development (2004) *Non-state Justice and Security Systems*. DFIF Briefing May 2004. Online: www.gsdrc.org/docs/open/ssaj101.pdf (last access: 10.06.2015).

UN (2006) *Ending Violence against Women: From Words to Action. In-depth study on all forms of violence against women. Report of the Secretary-General.* New York: United Nations General Assembly.

UN Committee on the Elimination of Discrimination against Women (2007) *Concluding Comments, Peru,* 2 February 2007, UN Doc. CEDAW/C/PER/CO/6.

UN DESA – United Nations Department of Economic and Social Affairs (2009) *State of the World's Indigenous Peoples.* ST/ESA/328. New York: United Nations.

UNDP, UN WOMEN and UNICEF (2012) *Informal Justice Systems: Charting a Course for Human Rights-Based Engagement.* New York: United Nations.

UNICEF, UNICEF, UNFPA, ILO and OSRSG/VAC (2013) *Breaking the Silence on Violence against Indigenous Girls, Adolescents and Young Women. A call to action based on an overview of existing evidence from Africa, Asia Pacific and Latin America.* New York: United Nations.

UN Office of the Special Adviser on Gender Issues and Advancement of Women and the Secretariat of the United Nations Permanent Forum on Indigenous Issues (2010) *Gender and Indigenous Issues.* Briefing Notes 1–6. New York: United Nations.

UNORCAC (2008) *"Shuk Yuyaylla, Shuk Shunkulla, Shuk Makilla" – "Un solo pensamiento, un solo corazón y una sola mano". Propuesta política y plan estratégico UNORCAC 2008–2010.* Otavalo: UNORCAC.

UNORCAC (2006) *Censo de Condiciones de Vida de las comunidades filiales a la UNORCAC.* Cotacachi. Unpublished.

UN Security Council (2004) *The rule of law and transitional justice in conflict and post-conflict societies. Report of the Secretary-General.* August 2004. UN Doc No. S/2004/616.

UN WOMEN (2011) *Progress of the World's Women 2011–2012: In Pursuit of Justice.* New York: United Nations.

Uriona, P. (2010) Mujeres indígenas, órdenes normativos e interlegalidad. *T'inkazos,* 28, 53–63.

USAID – United States Agency for International Development (2007) *Land Tenure and Property Rights. Volume I: Framework.* Washington, D.C.: USAID.

USAID – United States Agency for International Development (2005) *Afghanistan Rule of Law Project. Field Study of Informal and Customary Justice in Afghanistan and Recommendations on Improving Access to Justice and Relations Between Formal Courts and Informal Bodies.* Washington, D.C: USAID.

Van Cott, D. (2008) *Radical Democracy in the Andes.* New York: Cambridge University Press.

Van Cott, D. (2006) Dispensing Justice at the Margins of Formality: The Informal Rule of Law in Latin America. In: Helmke, G. and Levitsky, S. (eds). *Informal Institutions and Democracy: Lessons from Latin America.* Baltimore, MD: Johns Hopkins University Press.

Van Cott, D. (2005) *From Movements to Parties in Latin America: The Evolution of Ethnic Politics.* New York: Cambridge University Press.

Van Cott, D. (2002) Constitutional Reform in the Andes: Redefining Indigenous-State Relations. In: Sieder, R. (ed.). Multiculturalism in Latin America: Indigenous Rights, Diversity and Democracy. Houndmills; Basingstoke; New York: Palgrave Macmillan.

Van Cott, D. (2000a) *The Friendly Liquidation of the Past: The Politics of Diversity in Latin America*. Pittsburgh, PA: University of Pittsburgh Press.

Van Cott, D. (2000b) A Political Analysis of Legal Pluralism in Bolivia and Colombia. *Journal of Latin American Studies* 32(1), 207–234.

Van Vleet, K. (2002) The Intimacies of Power: Rethinking Violence and Affinity in the Bolivian Andes. *American Ethnologist* 29(3), 567–601.

Villa, R. (2012) Las mujeres nahuas y su experiencia del Juzgado de Cuetzalan, Puebla. In: Hernández, A. and Canessa, A. (eds). *Género, complementariedades y exclusiones en Mesoamérica y los Andes*. Lima: Abya-Yala, IGWIA.

Vintimilla, J. (2012) *Ley Orgánica de Cooperación y Coordinación entre la Justicia Indígena y la Jurisdicción Ordinaria Ecuatoriana: ¿Un mandato constitucional necesario o una norma que limita a los sistemas de justicia indígena?* Serie Justicia Comunitaria en los Andes: Perú y Ecuador Vol. 6. Quito: IDL; PRIF-HSFK; GIZ; CIDES.

Weingast, B. (2005) Persuasion, Preference Change, and Critical Junctures: The Microfoundations of a Macroscopic Concept. In: Katznelson, I. and Weingast, B. (eds). *Preferences and Situations: Points of Intersection between Historical and Rational Choice Institutionalisms*. New York: Russell Sage Foundation.

Whitehead, A., and Tsikata, D. (2003) Policy Discourses on Women's Land Rights in Sub-Saharan Africa: The Implications of the Re-turn to the Customary. *Journal of Agrarian Change* 3(1–2), 67–112.

Whittier, N. ([2004] 2007) The Consequences of Social Movements for Each Other. In: David, D., Soule, S. and Kriesi, H. (eds). *The Blackwell Companion to Social Movements*. Malden: Blackwell Publishing.

WHO (2013) *Global and Regional Estimates of Violence against Women: Prevalence and Health Effects of Intimate Partner Violence and Non-Partner Sexual Violence*. Geneva: WHO Press.

Wiktorowicz, Q. (ed.) (2004) *Islamic Activism. A Social Movement Theory Approach*. Bloomington, IN: Indiana University Press.

Williams, R. ([2004] 2007) The Cultural Contexts of Collective Action: Constraints, Opportunities, and the Symbolic Life of Social Movements. In: David, D., Soule, S. and Kriesi, H. (eds). *The Blackwell Companion to Social Movements*. Malden: Blackwell Publishing.

Williams, R., and Benford, R. (2000) Two Faces of Collective Action Frames: A Theoretical Consideration. *Research in Social Movements, Conflicts, and Change* 20, 127–151.

Williamson, O. (1993) Transaction Cost Economics and Organization Theory. *Industrial and Corporate Change* 2, 107–156.

Wilson, R., and Mitchell, J. (eds) (2003) *Human Rights in Global Perspective: Anthropological Perspectives on Rights, Claims and Entitlements*. London; New York: Routledge.

Wojkowska, E. (2006) *Doing Justice: How informal justice systems can contribute*. Oslo UNDP; Oslo Governance Center.

Woodman, G., Wanitzek, U. and Sippel, H. (eds). (2004) *Local Land Law and Globalization. A Comparative Study of Peri-urban Areas in Benin, Ghana and Tanzania*. Münster: Lit Verlag.

World Bank (2011) *World Development Report 2012: Gender Equality and Development*. Washington, D.C: World Bank.

Yashar, D. (2005) *Contesting Citizenship in Latin America: The Rise of Indigenous Movements and the Post-Liberal Challenge*. New York: Cambridge University Press.

Yilmaz, I. (2005) *Muslim Laws, Politics and Society in Modern Nation States: Dynamic Legal Pluralisms in England, Turkey, and Pakistan.* Aldershot: Ashgate.

Young, I. (1990) *Justice and the Politics of Difference.* Princeton, NJ: Princeton University Press.

Yrigoyen, R. (2011) El horizonte del constitucionalismo pluralista: del multiculturalismo a la descolonización. In: Rodríguez, C. (coord.). *El derecho en América Latina: Un mapa para el pensamiento jurídico del siglo XXI.* Buenos Aires: Siglo Veintiuno Editores.

Yrigoyen, R. (2006) Hitos del Reconocimiento del pluralismo jurídico y el derecho indígena en las políticas indigenistas y el constitucionalismo andino. In: Berraondo, M. (coord.). *Pueblos indígenas y derechos humanos.* Bilbao: Universidad de Deusto.

Yrigoyen, R. (2002) Peru: Pluralist Constitution, Monist Judiciary – A Post-Reform Assessment. In: Sieder, R. (ed.). *Multiculturalism in Latin America: Indigenous Rights, Diversity and Democracy.* Houndmills; Basingstoke; New York: Palgrave Macmillan.

Yrigoyen, R. (1993) *Las Rondas Campesinas de Cajamarca – Perú.* Tesis para optar el título profesional de Abogado. Pontífica Universidad Católica del Perú, Facultad de Derecho, Lima, Perú.

Yüksel, S. (2010) How to integrate Universal Human Rights into Customary and Religious Systems? *Journal of Legal Pluralism and Unofficial Law* 60, 5–40.

Zabala, M. (2011) *Detrás del cristal con que se mira: Mujeres de Cochabamba, órdenes normativos e interlegalidad.* La Paz: Coordinadora de la Mujer.

Zald, M., and McCarthy, J. (1987) Resource Mobilization and Social Movements: A Partial Theory. In: Zald, M. and McCarthy, J. (eds). *Social Movements in an Organizational Society.* Collected Essays. New Brunswick and Oxford: Transaction Books.

International Legal Documents

Inter-American Convention on the Prevention, Punishment and Eradication of Violence against Women "Convention Belém do Pará" (1994)

International Labour Organization Convention No. 169 on Indigenous and Tribal Peoples (1989)

UN Convention on the Elimination of All Forms of Discrimination Against Women (1979)

UN Declaration on the Elimination of Violence against Women (1993)

United Nations Declaration on the Rights of Indigenous Peoples (2007)

Legal documents Ecuador

1998 Constitution

2008 Constitution

1937 Law of Organization and Regime of Comunas/Ley de Organización y Régimen de Comunas

1995 Law 103 on Violence against Women and the Family/Ley Contra la Violencia a la Mujer y la Familia

2000 Electoral Law Reform/Reformas a la Ley de Elecciones
2004 Executive Decree 1982 General Regulation of Law on Violence against Women and the Family/Reglamento General a la Ley Contra la Violencia a la Mujer y la Familia
2009 Law on the Judicial Branch/Código Orgánico de la Función Judicial
2009 Law on Jurisdictional Guarantees and Constitutional Control/Ley Orgánica de Garantías Jurisdiccionales y Control Constitucional

Legal documents Peru

1920 Constitution
1979 Constitution
1993 Constitution
1970 Supreme Decree 37–70–AG Special Statute of Campesino Communities/Estatuto Especial de Comunidades Campesinas
1986 Law 24571 Recognition of the Pacifist, Democratic, and Autonomous Rondas Campesinas/Reconocen a las Rondas Campesinas, Pacíficas, Democraticas, y Autónomas
1987 General Law 24656 on Campesino Communities/Ley General de Comunidades Campesinas
1991 Supreme Decree 008–91–TR Regulation of the General Law on Campesino Communities/Reglamento de la Ley General de Comunidades Campesinas
1993 Law 26260 on the Protection against Family Violence/Ley de Protección frente a la Violencia Familiar
1995 Law 26505 on Private Investments in the Development of Economic Activities in Lands Pertaining to the National Territory and those of Campesino and Native Communities/referida a la inversion privada en el desarrollo de actividades económicas en tierras del territorio nacional y de las comunidades campesinas y nativas
1997 General Law 26842 on Health/Ley General de Salud
2003 Law 27908 on Rondas Campesinas/Ley de Rondas Campesinas
2003 General Law 28056 on Participatory Budgeting/Ley Marco del Presupuesto Participativo
2005 Law 28545 Regulating the Election of the Justices of the Peace/Ley que Regula la Elección de los Jueces de Paz
2006 Law 28895 Abolishing the Prefecturas and SubPrefecturas/Ley que Suprime las Prefecturas y Subprefecturas
2007 Supreme Decree 004–2007–IN Modifications in the Regulation of the Organization and Competences of the Ministry of Internal Affairs/Modifican el Reglamento de Organización y Funciones del Ministerio del Interior
2008 Supreme Decree 001–2008–IN Modifications in the Regulation of the Organization and Competences of Political Authorities/Modifican el Reglamento de Organización y Funciones de las Autoridades Políticas
2008 Supreme Decree 006–2008–IN Modifications in the Regulation of the Organization and Competences of Political Authorities/Modifican el Reglamento de Organización y Funciones de las Autoridades Políticas

2009 Corte Suprema de Justicia: Acuerdo Plenario Nº 1–2009/CJ–116.
2011 Corte Suprema de Justicia de la Republica, Comisión de Trabajo sobre Justicia Indígena y Justicia e Paz: Proyecto de Ley de Coordinación Intercultural de la Justicia. Lima: Corte Suprema de Justicia.
2011 Law 29785 on the Right to Previous Consultation to Indigenous Peoples/ Ley del Derecho a la Consulta Previa a los Pueblos Indígenas u Originarios
2012 Supreme Decree 001–2012–MC Regulation of Law 29785/Reglamento de la Ley N°29785
2013 Congreso de la República, Comisión de Pueblos Andinos, Amazónicos, Afroperuanos, Ambiente y Ecología: Dictamen 01–2013–2014/CPAAAECR.
2014 Consejo Ejecutivo del Poder Judicial: Protocolo de Coordinación entre Sistemas de Justicia. República del Perú, Poder Judicial.

Legal documents Bolivia

1994 Constitutional Reform
2004 Constitutional Reform
2009 Constitution
1994 Law 1551 of Popular Participation/Ley de la Participación Popular
1995 Law 1674 Against Intra-Familiar or Domestic Violence/Ley Contra la Violencia en la Familia o Doméstica
1998 Supreme Decree 25087 Against Domestic Violence/Decreto Supremo Contra la Violencia Doméstica
2007 Law 3760 Presidential Decree ascribing the 46 articles of the United Nations Declaration on the Rights of Indigenous Peoples the Status of a Bolivian law/Decreto que eleva a rango de Ley de la República los 46 artículos de la Declaración de las Naciones Unidas sobre los Derechos Humanos de los Pueblos Indígenas
2009 Law 031 on Autonomy and Decentralization "Andrés Ibañez"/Ley Marco de Autonomías y Decentralización "Andrés Ibañez"
2009 Transitional Electoral Law 4021/Régimen Electoral Transitorio
2010 Law 026 on the Electoral Regime/Ley del Regimen Electoral
2010 Law 073 on Jurisdictional Delimitation/Ley de Deslinde Jurisdiccional
2010 Law 027 on the Plurinational Constitutional Tribunal/Ley del Tribunal Constitucional Plurinacional
2013 Law 348 to Guarantee Women a Life Free from Violence/Ley Integral para Garantizar a las Mujeres una Vida Libre de Violencia

Media articles and press releases

Ecuador chapter

El Comercio (09.06.2013): 160 comunidades resolvieron en una asamblea 'reforzar' la justicia indígena. Online: www.elcomercio.com/seguridad/JusticiaIndigena-comunidades-Otavalo-Imbabura-reforzar-FICI-Conaie-ConsejoJudicatura_0_934706532.html (last access 07.11.2013).
El Universo (01.08.2014): Fallo de Corte Constitucional preocupa a dirigencia

indígena. Online: www.eluniverso.com/noticias/2014/08/01/nota/3301976/fallo-cc-preocupa-dirigencia-indigena (last access 10.06.2015).
El Vistazo (26.05.2010): Correa: Justicia indígena es una monstruosidad. Online: www.vistazo.com/webpages/pais/?id=10127 (last access 07.11.2013).
La Hora (25.10.2011): Entidades unifican esfuerzos a favor de la seguridad familiar. Online: www.lahora.com.ec/index.php/noticias/show/1101225930/-1/Entidades_unen_esfuerzos_a_favor_de_la_seguridad_familiar.html#.UoIYvRAUnK0 (last access 07.11.2013).
Ministerio de Inclusión Económica y Social (21.01.2013): Un total de 1376514 personas que reciben el bono de desarrollo humano y pen–siones asistenciales han actualizados sus datos. Online: www.inclusion.gob.ec/un-total-de-1-376-513-personas-que-reciben-el-bono-de-desarrollo-humano-y-pensiones-asistenciales-han-actualizados-sus-datos/ (last access 07.11.2013).
Secretaria Nacional de Gestión de la Política (15.05.2013): Asamblea Nacional renovada será liderada por mujeres en Ecuador. Online: www.politica.gob.ec/asamblea-nacional-renovada-sera-liderada-por-mujeres-en-ecuador/ (last access 10.06.2015).

Peru chapter

El Comercio (11.06.2012): Nada que parchar. Online: http://elcomercio.pe/actualidad/1426806/noticia-editorial-nada-que-parchar (last access 10.06.2015).
La República (09.08.2013): Consulta previa entrampada al no reconocerse a pueblos andinos. Online: www.larepublica.pe/09-08-2013/consulta-previa-entrampada-al-no-reconocerse-a-pueblos-andinos (last access 10.06.2015).
Servindi (27.10.2013): Base de datos sobre pueblos indígenas es referencial. Se incrementará "poco a poco". Online: http://servindi.org/actualidad/95452 (last access 07.11.2013).
Servindi (03.03.2012): Perú: Publican Reglamento de la Ley de Consulta Previa. Online: http://servindi.org/actualidad/62330 (last access 07.11.2013).
The Guardian (05.06.2012): Peru's indigenous people: from García to Humala their battle goes on. Online: www.guardian.co.uk/global-development/poverty-matters/2012/jun/05/peru-indigenous-people-garcia-humala (last access 10.06.2015).

Bolivia chapter

ANA (12.11.2014): Mojocoya celebra la compatibiliad de su Estatuto Indígena con al CPE. Online: www.ananoticias.com/autonomia-indigena/item/1416-mojocoya-celebra-la-compatibilidad-de-su-estatuto-indigena-con-la-cpe (last access 10.06.2015).
ANA (21.07.2014): Tarabuco recompone su Asamblea Autonómica para viabilizar las observaciones al estatuto. Online: www.ananoticias.com/autonomia-indigena/item/1237-tarabuco-recompone-su-asamblea-autonomica-para-viabilizar-las-observaciones-al-estatuto (last access 10.06.2015).
EJU (11.08.2013): Censo: menos indígenas es un mensaje político. Online:

http://eju.tv/2013/08/censo-menos-indgenas-es-un-mensaje-poltico/ (last access 10.06.2015).
El Diario (17.09.2011): MAS dividido políticamente a pueblos indígenas, originarios, campesinos. Online: www.eldiario.net/noticias/2011/2011_09/nt110917/2_01plt.php (last access 10.06.2015).
El Diario (14.12.2010): Advierten caos jurídico con aprobación de Ley de Deslinde. Online: www.eldiario.net/noticias/2010/2010_12/nt101214/2_03plt.php (last access 10.06.2015).
El País Edición Internacional (06.08.2013): Bolivia es más mestiza que indígena. Online: http://internacional.elpais.com/internacional/2013/08/06/actualidad/1375814823_694555.html (last access 10.06.2015).
PIEB (24.02.2015): INE aplica prueba piloto de encuesta sobre violencia contra las mujeres. Online: www.pieb.com.bo/sipieb_nota.php?idn=9510 (last access 10.06.2015).
Tamburini, L. (15.10.2013): Bolivia Censo 2013: Algunas claves para entender la variable indígena. Online: http://red.pucp.edu.pe/ridei/politica/bolivia-censo-2012-algunas-claves-para-entender-la-variable-indigena/ (last access 10.06.2015).

List of Interviews

La Calera

Interview 1-25.10.2011
Interview 2-25.10.2011
Interview 1-26.10.2011
Interview 26./27.10.2011
Interview 1-27.10.2011
Interview 2-27.10.2011
Interview 3-27.10.2011
Interview 4-27.10.2011
Interview 5-27.10.2011
Interview 1-28.10.2011
Interview 2-28.10.2011
Interview 31.10.2011
Interview 1-01.11.2011
Interview 2-01.11.2011
Interview 03.11.2011
Interview 04.11.2011
Interview 09.11.2011
Interview 19.11.2011
Interview 16.12.2011

San Francisco de la Rinconada

Interview 14.11.2011
Interview 17.11.2011

Interview 1-18.11.2011
Interview 2-18.11.2011
Interview 3-18.11.2011
Interview 20.11.2011
Interview 1-21.11.2011
Interview 2-21.11.2011
Interview 3-21.11.2011
Interview 1-22.11.2011
Interview 2-22.11.2011
Interview 3-22.11.2011
Interview 1-23.11.2011
Interview 2-23.11.2011
Interview 1-24.11.2011
Interview 2-24.11.2011
Interview 26.11.2011
Interview 1-29.11.2011
Interview 2-29.11.2011

Chacabamba

Interview 10./16.01.2012*
Interview 20.01.2012*
Interview 29.01.2012*
Interview 30.01./05.03.2012*
Interview 31.01.2012*
Interview 02.02.2012*
Interview 09.02.2012*
Interview 13.02.2012*
Interview 17.02.2012*
Interview 1-25.02.2012
Interview 2-25.02.2012
Interview 3-25.02.2012
Interview 1-26.02.2012
Interview 2-26.02.2012
Interview 1-29.02.2012
Interview 2-29.02.2012
Interview 3-29.02.2012
Interview 4-29.02.2012
Interview 5-29.02.2012
Interview 6-29.02.2012
Interview 7-29.02.2012
Interview 01./02.03.2012

* Information provided in this interview was relevant for both Peruvian case studies.

Tungasuca Ccollana

Interview 10./16.01.2012*
Interview 20.01.2012*
Interview 29.01.2012*
Interview 30.01./05.03.2012*
Interview 31.01.2012*
Interview 02.02.2012*
Interview 09.02.2012*
Interview 13.02.2012*
Interview 17.02.2012*
Interview 1-18.02.2012
Interview 2-18.02.2012
Interview 3-18.02.2012
Interview 4-18.02.2012
Interview 5-18.02.2012
Interview 6-18.02.2012
Interview 7-18.02.2012
Interview 1-21.02.2012
Interview 2-21.02.2012
Interview 3-21.02.2012
Interview 4-21.02.2012
Interview 1-23.02.2012
Interview 2-23.02.2012
Interview 1-03.03.2012
Interview 2-03.03.2012

* Information provided in this interview was relevant for both Peruvian case studies.

Mojocoya

Interview 03.04.2012*
Interview 12.04.2012*
Interview 1-13.04.2012*
Interview 2-13.04.2012*
Interview 17.04.2012*
Interview 1-18.04.2012
Interview 1-22.04.2012
Interview 2-22.04.2012
Interview 3-22.04.2012
Interview 4-22.04.2012
Interview 5-22.04.2012
Interview 25.04.2012*
Interview 1-26.04.2012
Interview 2-26.04.2012
Interview 3-26.04.2012
Interview 4-26.04.2012

Interview 5-26.04.2012
Interview 1-27.04.2012
Interview 30.04.2012
Interview 03.05.2012*
Interview 1-07.05.2012*
Interview 2-07.05.2012*
Interview 1-08.05.2012

* Information provided in this interview was relevant for both Bolivian case studies.

Tarabuco

Interview 03.04.2012*
Interview 12.04.2012*
Interview 1-13.04.2012*
Interview 2-13.04.2012*
Interview 17.04.2012*
Interview 2-18.04.2012
Interview 1-23.04.2012
Interview 2-23.04.2012
Interview 24.04.2012
Interview 25.04.2012*
Interview 2-27.04.2012
Interview 01.05.2012
Interview 1-02.05.2012
Interview 2-02.05.2012
Interview 03.05.2012*
Interview 04.05.2012
Interview 1-07.05.2012*
Interview 2-07.05.2012*
Interview 2-08.05.2012

* Information provided in this interview was relevant for both Bolivian case studies.

Index

For Product Safety Concerns and Information please contact our EU representative GPSR@taylorandfrancis.com
Taylor & Francis Verlag GmbH, Kaufingerstraße 24, 80331 München, Germany

www.ingramcontent.com/pod-product-compliance
Ingram Content Group UK Ltd.
Pitfield, Milton Keynes, MK11 3LW, UK
UKHW020016200926
475702UK00014B/1908
* 9 7 8 1 1 3 8 0 9 2 8 1 5 *